# The Supernatural in Fiction

Edited by

**Leo P. Kelley**

McGRAW-HILL BOOK COMPANY

New York   St. Louis   San Francisco
Dallas   Atlanta

ACKNOWLEDGMENTS

We are indebted to the following for permission to reprint copy-
righted material:
George Allen & Unwin Ltd. for permission to reprint an excerpt
from *Fifteen Greek Plays (Medea)* edited by Gilbert Murray.
Jerome Bixby for permission to reprint "Share Alike" by Jerome
Bixby and Joe E. Dean. Copyright 1951. Originally published
by Galaxy Publications, Inc. And for "It's A Good Life" by
Jerome Bixby. Copyright 1952. Originally published by Bal-
lentine Books, Inc.
Collins-Knowlton-Wing, Inc. for permission to reprint "Running
Wolf" by Algernon Blackwood. Copyright © 1949 by Al-
gernon Blackwood.
Harold R. Daniels for permission to reprint "The Haunted Wood-
shed" by Harold R. Daniels. Copyright 1967. Originally
published in *Ellery Queen's Mystery Magazine.*
Gordon Dickson for permission to reprint "The Amulet" by
Gordon Dickson. Copyright 1959. Originally published by
Mercury Press, Inc.
Doubleday & Company, Inc., for permission to reprint "Flies,"
copyright 1953 by Fantasy House, Inc. from *Nightfall and
Other Stories* by Isaac Asimov. Reprinted by permission of
Doubleday & Company, Inc. And for permission to reprint
an excerpt from *The Tempest* taken from *The Complete
Works of William Shakespeare*, The Cambridge Edition Text,
as edited by William Aldiss Wright. Published by The
Blakiston Company, copyright 1936 by Doubleday Doran &
Co., Inc.
Forrest Hartmann for permission to reprint "The Lonesome
Place" by August Derleth. Copyright 1947. Originally pub-
lished by All-Fiction Field, Inc. And for "The Outsider" by
H. P. Lovecraft. Copyright 1926. Originally published by
Popular Fiction Company,
Leo P. Kelley for permission to reprint "The Dark Door" by
Leo P. Kelley. Copyright 1970 by Fantasy Publishing Co., Inc.
Harold Matson Company, Inc. for permission to reprint "Home-
coming" by Ray Bradbury. Copyright 1946 by Street & Smith
Publications, Inc. Reprinted by permission of *Mademoiselle*
and Harold Matson Co., Inc. And for permission to reprint
"Hey, Look At Me!" by Jack Finney. Copyright 1962 by
Jack Finney. Originally published in *Playboy* Magazine. Re-
printed by permission of Harold Matson Company, Inc.

**Library of Congress Cataloging in Publication Data**

Kelley, Leo P        comp.
    The supernatural in fiction.

    (Patterns in literary art)
    1.  Ghost stories, English.   2.  Ghost stories,
American.  I.  Title.
PZ1.K277Su  [PR1309.G5]      823'.0872      73–3177
ISBN 0–07–033497–8

*Editorial Development*, Ron Osler; *Editing and Styling*, Linda Epstein; *Design*, Cathy Gallagher;
*Production*, Peter Guilmette.

# Contents

From ghoulies and ghosties
And long-leggéd beasties
And things that go bump in the night,
Good Lord, deliver us!

*Old Scotch Invocation*

# INTRODUCTION

Throughout man's history on earth, he has had experiences which he has been unable to explain as the result of known natural forces—that is to say, supernatural experiences. Supernatural beings have haunted him. Supernatural events have terrified and horrified him. Ghosts, demons, witches, werewolves, vampires, and sorcerers have walked beside him as he made his uneasy way through the world. Because his life was so intimately linked to the supernatural, his literature inevitably came to reflect this fact.

Man's fear of the hostile world in which he found himself was the father of the supernatural tale. Man's imagination was its mother.

Primitive man feared the dark just as children today still frequently fear it. His imagination populated its shadows with dread apparitions. He feared death and this fear was soon transmuted into a fear of the dead themselves who, he believed, did not really die but survived in ghostly fashion and could—and often did—cause harm to the living. From this belief arose the primitive custom of piling heavy stones upon graves to prevent the dead from returning. In some cases, a stake was driven through the chest of the corpse to pin it firmly to the earth. This last example reminds us of one of the aspects of the vampire legend. Driving a wooden stake through the chest of a vampire, the legend tells us, is the only way to make sure that the "undead" will not return to prey upon the living.

Today we place stone or marble monuments upon the graves of our dead. We do it to mark the grave, of course, but perhaps there is an echo of the ancient fear of the dead in this aspect of our behavior. Perhaps our custom of placing heavy monuments on modern graves relates to the much earlier custom of piling stones upon graves to keep their tenants safely in place.

The student of literature can find stories of the supernatural in all cultures from the early Chinese and the Egyptian to the relatively advanced ones of Greece and Rome. In the Middle Ages, people believed in the existence of werewolves and vampires and so stories were told about their deeds and dooms. With the coming of the Renaissance, although people still took such manifestations of the supernatural as ghosts for granted, they were also a more sophisticated people. They therefore demanded more of authors who wrote stories about supernatural beings and incidents.

No longer were readers content with the simple tale of an encounter with supernatural forces which was little more than an unadorned account of events. During the Renaissance, authors began to employ the storytelling techniques that would be more fully developed by writers working at the end of the nineteenth and the beginning of the twentieth century. These Renaissance writers had to refine their art—they had to create an eerie atmosphere, develop belief in the events depicted in their stories on the part of an increasingly enlightened and sceptical reader, create credible characters, build suspense, and present a dramatic conclusion to their tales.

At the turn of the last century, the supernatural story burst into vivid bloom. During the years immediately preceding the death of the nineteenth century and the birth of the twentieth, the works of masters in the craft of the supernatural story appeared. There were the Victorians— Dickens, Hardy, Henry James, and Conrad. Then came such great artists as Arthur Machen, Algernon Blackwood, Walter de la Mare, Edgar Allan Poe, and F. Marion Crawford, to name a few.

However, following this flowering of the supernatural story, there came a period when it withered. Of course, there were occasional ventures into the literary realm of the supernatural—Stephen Vincent Benet's *The Devil and Daniel Webster,* for example—but these were the exception rather than the rule.

Nevertheless, people today have as great an interest in the well-told tale of the supernatural as did those who sat around prehistoric campfires or in the Globe Theater at performances of *Macbeth* or *Hamlet.* One has only to recall the relatively recent success of Ira Levin's story, *Rosemary's Baby,* to realize that the reader's appetite for this fare still exists although it seems destined not to be sated.

The stories in this book reflect man's interest in such issues as survival after death (ghosts), good and evil (gods and devils), superhuman powers (spells and sorcery), the inexplicable (things), and what can only be called supernatural people (witches, werewolves and vampires). In short, the literature in this book reflects some of man's deepest desires and drives. In presenting supernatural events and characters, it succeeds in revealing some of the frequently hidden places in the human mind and heart.

The book is divided into five chapters, each of which deals with a particular aspect of supernatural manifestations. The stories within each chapter range widely in style and treatment. Thus, the student is given an opportunity to compare the ways different writers from different periods of time write about similar events. He is able to see clearly that even within a particular genre of literature—in this case, the supernatural —there is room for diverse treatments of similar material and for various points of view concerning it on the part of its creators.

To assist the student on his excursion into the worlds of the supernatural presented in these stories, general introductions to each chapter have been included as well as short introductions to each individual story. At the end of each story, he will find a number of discussion questions designed to help him fully understand the story itself, the techniques of fiction in general and supernatural fiction in particular, and the relationship of this branch of literature to life.

In these tales of the supernatural, authors address themselves to questions which have puzzled and provoked men everywhere regardless of their cultural or national backgrounds or the period of history in which they lived.

Are the dead really dead?

Can I or anyone else be bewitched?

Are things and people always just what they seem?

These are but a few of the questions raised by the authors included in this book. The answers to them and to other questions equally mystifying are to be found in the stories that follow. Whether or not a reader accepts the answers given by the authors is, of course, not the important point. It is far more important for him to perceive the ways in which skilled writers come to grips with the questions themselves. Such perceptions will give him an understanding of literary techniques and story structure. They will also give a broader view of the world in which he lives—and shares with the supernatural.

Literature of all kinds has always attempted to show mankind his own image and behavior. Literature of the supernatural seeks to do no less. The fact that it is a specialized genre of fiction in no way negates or diminishes either its artfulness nor its value as both entertainer and instructor.

The ghosts of literary giants people these pages. Their stories, we sincerely hope, will hold students spellbound. We hope too that these fine stories will haunt them in the years to come.

# Witches, Werewolves, and Vampires— The Terrible Tribe

# CHAPTER ONE

The legends surrounding such supernatural beings as witches, were-wolves, and vampires are numerous and include many curious details.

Vampires, for example, are believed to be incapable of crossing running water; their reflections do not appear in mirrors; they must return to their coffins before sunrise; their coffins must be lined with earth taken from their graves; and they fear the primary symbol of Christianity—the cross or crucifix.

A werewolf is supposedly a person who assumes the shape of a wolf and becomes a beastly marauder, usually under the light of a full moon. He can be killed only by a silver bullet.

Witches are said to be the servants of Satan who ride broomsticks to the Sabbat, which is the congregation of a coven usually numbering thirteen. There they meet their fiendish lord and master and receive favors and evil powers from him in return for their allegiance and loyalty. Witches have varied powers; they can cause cows to lose their calves, brew deadly potions, and work numerous other evils.

As incredible as many of these legends are, stories of supernatural beings continue to interest us. Perhaps this is so because our lives are relatively well-ordered and the technology that constantly surrounds us tends to sterilize our imaginations. In the literary arena inhabited by witches, werewolves, and vampires, we can, however, for a brief time, enter a world that is quite different from the one we know in our everyday lives. We drop our skepticism and reject reason, if only temporarily, in order to enjoy the excitement and pleasure aroused by a well-written tale about such creatures.

Writers of the supernatural story make conscious attempts to terrify and horrify their readers. Some of them also attempt to weave a moral into their fictional tapestry. The stories in this chapter are from different periods of time and from different cultures. They present differing attitudes toward human beings and the supernatural. These attitudes reflect the moral climate of the time in which the stories were written and also the relative levels of education and sophistication of the audiences for whom the stories were intended.

Part of the enjoyment in reading these stories lies in analyzing the author's point of view toward the people and events he portrays and in deciding whether or not he succeeds in creating a "willing suspension of disbelief" in the reader. In those stories you find most appealing in this chapter, you will want to examine precisely how the author succeeded in drawing you into his story and holding your attention within the fantastic framework he has built with words.

Those members of "the terrible tribe" to be found in the following stories offer you an excellent opportunity to study and enjoy good supernatural literature.

So help me She who of all Gods hath been
The best to me, of all my chosen queen
And helpmate, Hecate, who dwells apart,
The flame of flame, in my fire's inmost heart:
For all their strength, they shall not stab my soul
And laugh thereafter!   Dark and full of dole
Their bridal feast shall be, most dark the day
They joined their hands, and hunted me away.

*from* Medea *by Euripides*

# INTRODUCTION: Share Alike

One of the ways in which authors induce readers to suspend their disbelief concerning supernatural happenings is to place such happenings in the midst of the commonplace and the everyday. Although the shipwreck in the following story is not a common occurrence, it is at least a situation about which we have some knowledge. Therefore, the reader finds himself on relatively familiar ground. However, that familiar ground shifts and shakes as the story progresses, and we recognize a contemporary incarnation of one of the most dreaded members of the terrible tribe!

# Share Alike
## Jerome Bixby and Joe E. Dean

They spread-eagled themselves in the lifeboat, bracing hands and feet against the gunwales.

Above them, the pitted and barnacled stern of the S. S. *Luciano,* two days out of Palermo and now headed for hell, reared up hugely into the overcast of oily black smoke that boiled from ports and superstructure. Craig had time to note that the screws were still slowly turning, and that a woman was screaming from the crazily-tilted afterdeck. Then the smoke intervened—a dark pall that lowered about the lifeboat as the wind shifted, blotting out the sky, the ship.

Fire met water. One roared; the other hissed. Gouts of blazing gasoline flared through the smoke like flame demons dancing on the waves.

Groaning, shuddering, complaining with extreme bitterness, the ship plunged.

Sky and smoke became a sickening whirl, as the lifeboat tore into the churning water in a suicidal effort to follow the parent ship to the bottom. Spray flew; waves loomed, broke, fell away; the lifeboat shipped water. Craig cursed aloud, making rage a substitute for terror. Facing him, Hofmanstahal grinned sourly.

The small boat righted itself. It was still in violent motion, lurching aimlessly across a sea jagged with whitecaps; but Craig knew that the crisis was past. He lifted his face into the cold wind, pulling himself up from the water-slopping bottom of the boat until his chin rested on the gunwale.

4

A wide patch of brownish foam and oil-scum spread slowly from the vortex of exploding bubbles that rose from the vanished ship.

The sea quieted. A gull swooped down and lit on an orange crate that had bobbed to the surface.

"Well," said Craig. "Well. That's that."

Hofmanstahal peeled off his shirt, wrung it out over the side. The hair that matted his thick chest and peeped from his armpits had a golden sheen that was highlighted by the sun. A small cut was under his left eye, a streak of oil across his forehead.

"You were of the crew?" he asked.

"Yes."

"But not an A. B. You are too spindly for that."

"I was navigator."

Hofmanstahal chuckled, a deep sound that told of large lungs. "Do you think you can navigate us out of this, my friend?"

"I won't have to. We're in a well-travelled shipping lane. We'll be picked up soon enough."

"How soon might that be?"

"I don't know. I don't even know if we got an SOS out; it all happened so fast." Craig sighed, rolled over so that he sat with his back curved against the side of the boat. "I doubt if we did, though. The tanks right under the radio shack were the first to go. I wonder who got careless with a cigarette."

"M'm. So we'll eventually be picked up. And in the meantime, do we starve?"

Craig got up tiredly. "You underestimate the Merchant Marine." He sloshed to the stern of the lifeboat, threw open the food locker. They saw kegs of water, tins of biscuits and salt meat, canned juices, a first-aid kit.

"More than enough," Craig said. He turned, searched the surrounding swells. "I wonder if any others survived . . ."

Hofmanstahal shook his head. "I have been looking too. No others. All were sucked down with the ship."

Craig kept looking. Smoke, heaving stained water, débris, a few dying gasoline-flames—that was all.

Hofmanstahal said, "At least we shall be well fed. Did you have any close friends aboard?"

"No." Craig sat down, pushed wet hair back from his forehead, let his hands fall to his lap. "And you?"

"Me? No one. I have outlived all my friends. I content myself with being a man of the crowd. A select group of *bon vivants* for drinking and conversation . . . it is enough."

Sitting with a seat between them, as if each somehow wanted to be alone, the men exchanged backgrounds. By his own account, Hofman-stahal was an adventurer. No locality could hold him for long, and he seldom revisited a place he already knew. He had been secretary to a former Resident in Malaya, and concerned himself with gems in Borneo, with teak in China; a few of his paintings had been displayed in the *Galerie des Arts* in Paris. He had been en route to Damascus to examine some old manuscripts which he believed might contain references to one of his ancestors.

"Although I was born in Brashov," he said, "family records indicate that we had our beginnings elsewhere. You may think it snobbish, this delving into my background, but it is a hobby which has absorbed me for many years. I am not looking for glory; only for facts."

"Nothing wrong with that," Craig said. "I envy you your colorful past."

"Is yours so dull, then?"

"Not dull . . . the colors just aren't so nice. I grew up in the Atlanta slums. Things were pretty rough when I was a kid—"

"You weren't big enough to be tough."

Craig nodded, wondering why he didn't resent this second reference to his small size. He decided that it was because he liked the big man. Hofmanstahal wasn't insolent, just candid and direct.

"I read a lot," Craig went on. "My interest in astronomy led me into navigation while I was in the Navy. After I was mustered out I stayed at sea rather than go back to what I'd left."

They continued to converse in low, earnest voices for the remainder of the afternoon. Always above them the white gulls circled.

"Beautiful, aren't they?" asked Craig.

Hofmanstahal looked up. His pale eyes narrowed. "Scavengers! See the wicked eyes, the cruel beaks! Pah!"

Craig shrugged. "Let's eat. And hadn't you better do something for that cut under your eye?"

Hofmanstahal shook his massive head. "You eat, if you wish. I am not hungry." He touched his tongue to the dribble of blood that ran down his cheek.

They kept track of the days by cutting notches in the gunwale. There were two notches when Craig first began to wonder about Hofmanstahal.

They had arranged a system of rationing for food and water. It was far from being a strict ration, for there was plenty for both of them.

But Craig never saw Hofmanstahal eat.

The Rumanian, Craig thought, was a big man, he should certainly have an equally big appetite.

"I prefer," said Hofmanstahal, when Craig asked about it, "to take my meals at night."

Craig let it pass, assuming that the big man had a digestive disorder, or perhaps was one of those unfortunates who have inhibitions about eating in front of others. Not that the latter seemed likely, considering Hofmanstahal's amiably aggressive personality and the present unusual circumstances, but, on the other hand, what did it matter? Let him eat standing on his head if he wanted to.

Next morning, when Craig opened the food locker to get his share, the food supply was apparently undiminished.

The morning after that, the same thing.

Another notch. Five days, now. And Craig found something else to puzzle about. He was eating well; yet he felt himself sinking deeper and deeper into a strange, uncaring lethargy, as if he were well on his way toward starvation.

He took advantage of the abundance of food to eat more than was his wont. It didn't help.

Hofmanstahal, on the other hand, greeted each day with a sparkling eye and a spate of good-humored talk.

Both men by now had beards. Craig detested his, for it itched. Hofmanstahal was favoring his, combing it with his fingers, already training the mustache with insistent twiddlings of thumb and forefinger.

Craig lay wearily in the bow and watched.

"Hofmanstahal," he said. "You're not starving yourself on my account, are you? It isn't necessary, you know."

"No, my friend. I have never eaten better."

"But you've hardly touched the stores."

"Ah!" Hofmanstahal flexed his big muscles. "It is the inactivity. My appetite suffers."

Another notch. Craig continued to wonder. Each day, each hour, found him weaker, more listless. He lay in the bow of the boat, soaking in the warmth of the sun, his eyes opaque, his body limp. Sometimes he let one hand dangle in the cool water; but the appearance of ugly triangular shark fins put a stop to that.

"They are like all of nature, the sharks," Hofmanstahal said. "They rend and kill, and give nothing in return for the food they so brutally take. They can offer only their very bodies, which are in turn devoured by larger creatures. And on and on. The world is not a pretty place, my friend."

"Are men so different?"

"Men are the worst of all."

Seven notches, now. Craig was growing weaker. He was positive by now that Hofmanstahal was simply not eating.

There were nine notches on the gunwale when Craig found that Hofmanstahal *was* eating, after all.

It was night, and the sea was rougher than it had been. The *slap-slap* of waves against the hull wakened Craig from a deep, trancelike sleep. That, and the oppressive feeling of a nearby presence.

He stirred, felt the presence withdraw. Through half-shut eyes he saw Hofmanstahal, darkly silhouetted against a sky ablaze with stars.

"You were crying out in your sleep, my friend." The big man's voice was solicitous. "Nightmare?"

"My throat . . . stinging, burning. I . . ."

"The salt air. You will be all right in the morning."

Craig's face felt like a numb mask of clay. It was an effort to move his lips. "I think—I think I'm going—to die."

"No. You are not going to die. You must not. If you die, I die."

Craig thought about that. The rocking of the boat was gentle, soothing. A warmth stole over him, though the night was cool. He was weak, but comfortable; fearful, yet content. Head back, breathing easily, he let himself become aware of the glory of the heavens.

The constellation Perseus was slanting toward the western horizon, and Craig noted almost unconsciously, with the skill of long practice, that the variable star Algol was at its maximum brilliancy. Algol—the ghoul.

The thought lingered. It turned over and over in his mind, as his subconscious seemed to examine it for some hidden meaning.

Then, abruptly, the thought surged up into his conscious mind.

And he knew.

He lifted himself up to his elbows, supporting himself weakly.

"Hofmanstahal," he said, "you're a vampire. Aren't you?"

The other's chuckle was deep and melodious in the darkness.

"Answer me, Hofmanstahal. Aren't you a vampire?"

"Yes."

Craig had fainted. Now it was as if layer after layer of blackness were being removed, bringing him closer to the light with every moment. A tiny sullen orange disk glowed in the darkness, expanding, increasing in brightness until it filled the world.

The blackness was gone, and he was staring up into the blinding, brassy heart of the sun.

He gasped and turned his head away.

There was music. Someone whistling a German folk tune.

Hofmanstahal . . .

Hofmanstahal sat in the stern, his brawny gold-fuzzed forearms resting on his knees.

The whistling stopped.

"Good morning, my friend. You have had a good, long rest."

Craig stared, his lips working.

Far above a gull called harshly, and was answered by one skimming at water level.

Hofmanstahal smiled. "You mustn't look at me that way. I'm almost harmless. I assure you." He laughed gently. "Things could be much worse, you know. Suppose, for example, I had been a werewolf. Eh?" He waited a moment. "Oh, yes, Lycanthropy is real—as real as those gulls out there. Or—more fitting, perhaps—as real as those sharks. Once, in Paris, I lived for three months with a young woman who was a werewolf by night. How we both laughed when each discovered what the other was!"

Craig listened numbly, aware that Hofmanstahal was merely making idle talk. The story of the female werewolf turned into an anecdote, patently untrue. Hofmanstahal chuckled at it, and seemed disappointed when Craig did not. There was a certain sensitive shyness about the big Rumanian, Craig thought . . . a sensitive vampire! Aware of Craig's revulsion, he was camouflaging the situation with a flood of words.

"—And when the gendarme saw that the bullet which had killed her was an ordinary lead one, he said, 'Messieurs, you have done this *pauvre jeune fille* a grave injustice.' Ha! The moment was a sad one for me, but—"

"Stop it!" Craig gasped. "Go turn yourself into a bat or something and fly away. Just get out of my sight . . . my blood in your stomach . . ."

He tried to turn away, and his elbows slipped. His shoulderblades thumped the bottom of the boat. He lay there, eyes closed, and his throat thickened as if he wanted to laugh and vomit at the same time.

"I cannot turn myself into a bat, my friend. Ugly little creatures—" Hofmanstahal sighed heavily. "Nor do I sleep in a coffin. Nor does daylight kill me, as you can see. All that is superstition. Superstition! Do you know that my grandfather died with a white ash stake through his heart?" His beard tilted angrily. "Believe me, we variants have more to fear from the ignorant and superstitious than they from us. There are so many of them, and so few of us."

Craig said, "You won't touch me again!"

"Ah, but I must."

"I'm still strong enough to fight you off."

"But not strong enough to get at the food if I choose to prevent you."

Craig shook his head. "I'll throw myself overboard!"

"That I cannot permit. Now, why not submit to the inevitable. Each day, I will supply you with your ration of food; each night, you will supply me with mine. A symbiotic relationship. What could be fairer?"

"Beast! Monster! *I will not*—"

Hofmanstahal sighed, and looked out over the tossing sea. "Monster. Always they say that of us; they, who feed off the burned flesh of living creatures."

It was the face of his father, stern and reproving, that Craig always saw before him during those long nights in the lifeboat. His father, who had been a Baptist minister. When the lifeboat drifted on a sea that was like glass, reflecting the stars with such clarity that the boat might have been suspended in a vast star-filled sphere, and Craig felt the lips of the vampire at his throat—then conscience arose in the form of his father.

Well . . . he wasn't submitting willingly. Not at first. But the food had been withheld until his belly twisted with hunger and he cried out with parched lips for water. Then, shudderingly, he had allowed the vampire to feed.

It was not as bad as he had expected. An acute, stinging sensation as the sharp canines pricked the flesh (strange, that he had not noticed before how *sharp* they were); then numbness as the anesthetic venom did its work. The venom must have been a hypnotic. As the numbness spread toward his face, and his lips and cheeks became chill, strange colors danced before his eyes, blending and twining in cloudy patterns that sent his thoughts wandering down incomprehensible byways. He was part of Hofmanstahal. Hofmanstahal was part of him.

And each time it was less painful, less shocking, till finally it was mere routine.

Strangely, his conscience did not torment him during the day. The comfortable warmth and lassitude that before had only touched him now enveloped him completely. His thoughts were vague; memory tended to slip away from what had gone before, and to evade what was to come. The sea, the sky, the wheeling gulls were beautiful. And Hofmanstahal, vampire or not, was an interesting conversationalist.

"You are pale, friend Craig," he would say. "Perhaps I have been too greedy. Do you know, with that wan face and the beard, you remind me of a poet I knew in Austria. For a long time he was one of my favorite companions. But perhaps you did not know that we prefer certain donors to others. Believe me, we are not the indiscriminate gluttons that literature would have you think."

"How—did you become as you are?"

"How did I, Eric Hofmanstahal, become a vampire? That is a question with broad implications. I can tell you that my people were vampires, but that leaves unanswered the question of our origin. This I cannot tell you, though I have searched deeply into the matter. There are legends, of course, but they are contradictory." Hofmanstahal stroked his beard and seemed lost in thought.

"Some say," he went on, after a moment, "that when *homo sapiens* and the ape branched from a common ancestor, there was a third strain which was so despised by both that it was driven into obscurity. Others maintain that we came to Earth from another planet, in prehistoric times. There is even mention of a species which was quite different from man but which, because of man's dominance over the earth, imitated him until it developed a physical likeness to him. Then there is the fanciful notion that we are servants of the Devil—one battalion among his legions, created by him to spread sorrow and misery throughout the ages of the world.

"Legends! We have been persecuted, imprisoned, burned alive; we have been classified as maniacs and perverts—all because our body chemistry is unlike that of man. We drink from the fountain of life while man feasts at the fleshpots of the dead; yet we are called monsters." He crumpled a biscuit in his powerful hand and cast the pieces upon the water, which immediately boiled with sharks.

"Man!" he said softly.

Life went on. Craig ate. Hofmanstahal fed. And horror diminished with familiarity.

There were only the two of them, under the vast sky, rising and falling gently to the whim of the sea. The horizon was the edge of their world. No other existed. Night and day merged into gray sameness. Sea and sky were vague, warm reflections; the motion of the boat soothed. This was peace. There was no thought of resistance left in Craig. Hofmanstahal's "symbiosis" became a way of life; then life itself.

There was time in plenty to gaze up at the stars, a pleasure which everyday exigencies had so often denied him. And there was strange, dark companionship. It was peace. It was satisfaction. It was fulfilment. Fear was lost in stupor; revulsion, in a certain sensuality. Hofmanstahal's nightly visit was no longer a thing of horror, but the arrival of a friend whom he wanted to help with all his being, and who was in turn helping him. Night and day they exchanged life; and the life they nurtured became a single flow and purpose between them. Craig was the quiescent vessel of life, which Hofmanstahal filled every day, so that life might build itself against the coming of night and the return of its essence to Hofmanstahal.

Day and night marched above them toward the pale horizon that circumscribed their world. In their world values had changed, and the fact of change been forgotten.

Still, deep in his mind, Craig's conscience wailed. Legend, history, the church, all at one time or another had said that vampires were evil. He was submitting to a vampire; therefore, he was submitting to evil. Food or no food, the Reverend Craig would never have submitted. He would have sharpened a stake or cast a silver bullet—

But there were no such things here. His father's face rose before him to tell him that this did not matter. Craig sought to drive it away, but it remained. During the moments of nightly meeting, it glared down upon them brighter than the moon. But Hofmanstahal's back was always turned to it; and Craig, in all his weakness and indecision, did not mention it.

They had forgotten to carve the notches on the gunwale. Neither was certain now how long they had been adrift.

There came a day, however, when Hofmanstahal was forced to cut down Craig's ration of food.

"I am sorry," he said, "but you can see for yourself that it is necessary."

"We're so near the end of our supplies, then?"

"We are nearing the end of your supplies ... and if yours end, so will mine eventually."

"I don't really mind," Craig whispered. "I'm seldom really hungry now. At first, even the full rations left me unsatisfied, but now I don't even like the taste of the food. I suppose it's because I'm getting no exercise."

Hofmanstahal's smile was gentle. "Perhaps. Perhaps not. We must keep a sharp lookout for ships. If one does not come soon, we will starve, though of course I will now cut down my own rations as well as yours."

"I don't care."

"My poor Craig, when you regain your strength you will care very much. Like me, you will want to live and go on living."

"Maybe. But now I feel that dying would be easy and pleasant. Better, maybe, than going back to the world."

"The world is evil, yes; but the will to live in it drives all of us."

Craig lay motionless and wondered, with a clarity of mind he had not experienced in many, many days, whether he dreaded going back to the world because the world was evil, or whether it was because he felt that he himself was tainted, unfit to mix with human beings again.

. . . And Hofmanstahal might be a problem. Should he be reported to the authorities? No, for then they would know about . . . this.

But was all that had happened so disgraceful, so reprehensible? Had Craig had any other choice but to do what he had done?

None.

His conscience, in the form of his father, screamed in agony.

Well, then perhaps Hofmanstahal would try to force him to continue the relationship.

But surely gentle, considerate Hofmanstahal, the sensitive vampire, would not try to force—

Craig's mind rebelled against such practical thoughts. They required too much effort. It was easier not to think at all—to lie as he had lain for so many days, peaceful, relaxed, uncaring.

Clarity of mind faded into the gray sameness of day and night. He ate. Hofmanstahal fed.

He was scarcely conscious when Hofmanstahal spotted the smoke on the horizon. The big man lifted him up so that he could see it. It was a ship, and it was coming in their direction.

"So—now it is over." Hofmanstahal's voice was soft; his hands were warm on Craig's shoulders. "So it ends—our little idyll." The hands tightened. "My friend . . . my friend, before the ship comes, the men and the noise, the work and the worry and all that goes with it, let us for the last time—"

His head bent, his lips found Craig's throat.

Craig shivered. Over the Rumanian's shoulder he could see the ship approaching, a dot on the horizon. There would be men aboard.

Men! Normalcy and sanity, cities and machines and half-forgotten values, coming nearer and nearer over the tossing sea, beneath the brassy sky, from the real world of men that lay somewhere beyond the horizon . . .

Men! Like himself, like his father, who hovered shouting his disgust. And he, lying here. . . .

God, God, *what if they should see him!*

He kicked. He threw his arms about. He found strength he hadn't known he had, and threshed and flailed and shrieked with it.

The lifeboat rocked. A foot caught Hofmanstahal in the midriff. The vampire's arms flew wide and he staggered back with a cry:

"*Craig—*"

The backs of his knees struck the gunwale—the one with meaningless notches carved in it. His arms lashed as he strove to regain his balance. His eyes locked with Craig's, shock in them. Then he plunged backward into the sea.

The sharks rejected him as food, but not before they had killed him.

Craig found himself weeping in the bottom of the boat, his face in slime. And saying hoarsely again and again, "Eric, I'm sorry—"

It seemed a very long time before the ship came close enough for him to make out the moving figures on the deck. It seemed so long because of the thoughts and half-formed images that were racing through his brain.

A new awareness was coming over him in a hot flood, an awareness of—

Of the one thing popularly believed about vampires that must have solid foundation in fact.

Had the venom done it? He didn't know. He didn't care.

He lay weakly, watching the steamer through half-closed eyes. Sailors lined the rails, their field glasses trained on him.

He wondered if they could see his father. No, of course not—all that had been hallucination. Besides, a moment ago his father had fled.

It was a Navy ship, a destroyer. He was glad of that. He knew the Navy. The men would be healthy. Strenuous duty would make them sleep soundly.

And at the end of its voyage lay the whole pulsing world.

Craig licked his lips.

## FOR DISCUSSION: Share Alike

1. If Hofmanstahal had been named "Jones" by the author, do you think some of the mystique surrounding him might have been dispelled?
2. Can you point to remarks made by Hofmanstahal and Craig in the early part of the story which point to what is to follow in their relationship?
3. What is the dominant mood in the story as the days pass and rescue is not forthcoming?
4. Hofmanstahal is candid with Craig about being a vampire. Analyze Craig's reactions to this fact and indicate how his initial reactions and attitudes change by citing specific passages in the story.
5. Do the authors succeed in surprising you with the revelation that Craig has become a vampire?

# INTRODUCTION: The Amulet

Someone has written, "You can't cheat an honest man." As you read this story of a young man's encounter with two witches, bear the quotation in mind and consider how it relates to the personality and fate of the main character as he pits his wits against those of the two witch-women he meets.

# The Amulet
## Gordon R. Dickson

He had hit the kid too hard, there, back behind the tool shed—that was the thing. He should have let up a little earlier, but it had been fun working the little punk over. Too much fun; the kid had been all softness, all niceness—it had been like catnip to a cat and he had got all worked up over it, and then it had been too late. It had just been some drippy-nosed fifteen-year-old playing at running away from home, but the railroad bulls would be stumbling over what was left, back of the toolshed, before dawn.

That was why Clint had grabbed the first moving freight he could find in the yards instead of waiting for the northbound he was looking for. Now that the freight had lost itself in the Ozark backcountry, he slipped out of the boxcar on a slow curve and let the tangled wild grass of the hot Missouri summer take the bounce of his body as it rolled down the slope of the grading.

He came to a stop and sat up. The freight rattled by above him and was gone. He was a little jolted, that was all. He grinned into the insect-buzzing hush of the late afternoon. It took a young guy in shape to leave a moving freight. Any bum could hook on one. He considered his own blocky forearms, smooth with deep suntan and muscle, effortlessly propping him off the soft, crumbling earth; and he laughed out loud on the warm grass.

He felt cat-good, suddenly. Cat-good. It was the phrase he had for himself when things turned out well. Himself, the cat, landed on his feet again and ready to make out in the next back yard. What would the suckers be like this time? He rose, stretching and grinning, and looked over the little valley before him.

Below the ridge, it was more a small hollow than a true valley. The slope of the ridge came down sharp, covered with scrub pine, and leveled out suddenly into a little patch of plowed earth, just beginning to be nubbly with short new wands of grain. A small, brown shack sat at one end of the field, low-down from where he stood now, and in its yard an old granny in an ankle-length black skirt and brown sweater was chopping wood. He could see the flash of her ax through the far, clear air, and the *chop* sound came just behind. And for a moment, suddenly, for no reason at all, a strange feeling of unquiet touched him, like a dark moth wing of fear fluttering for a second in the deep back of his mind. Then he grinned again, and picked up his wrinkled suitcoat.

"Ma'm," he said in a soft shy voice, "Ma'm, could I get a drink of water from you, please?"

He chuckled, and went down the dip toward the field with easy, long-swinging strides. She was still chopping wood when he came into the yard. The long ax flashed with a practiced swing at the end of her thin, grasshopperlike arms, darkened by the sun even more deeply than his own. The ax split clean each time it came down, the wood falling neatly in two equal sections.

"Ma'm . . ." he said, stopping a few feet off from her and to one side.

She split one more piece of wood deliberately, then leaned the ax against the chopping block and turned to face him. Her face was as old as history and wrinkled like the plowed earth. Her age was unguessable, but a strange vitality seemed to smolder through the outer shell of her, like a fire under ashes, glowing still on some secret coal.

"What can I do for you?" she said. Her voice was cracked but strong, and the *you* of the question came out almost as *ye*. Yet her dark, steady eyes, under the puckered lids, seemed to mock him.

"Could I get a drink of water, ma'm?"

"Pump's over there."

He turned. He had seen the pump on the way in, and purposely entered from the other side of the yard. He went across to it and drank, holding his hand across the spout to block it so that the water would fountain up through the hole on top. He felt her gaze on him all the time he drank; and when he turned about she was still regarding him.

"Thank you, ma'm," he said. He smiled at her. "I wonder—I know it's a foolish question to ask, ma'm—but could you tell me where I am?"

"Spiney Holler," she said.

"Oh, my," he said. "I guessed I'd been going wrong."

"Where you headed?" she asked.

"Well—I was going home to Iowa, ma'm." His sheepish grin bared his foolishness to her laughter. "I know it sounds crazy. But I thought I was on a freight headed for Iowa. I was going home."

"You live in Iowa?"

"Just outside Des Moines." He sighed, letting his shoulders slump. "Can—can I sit down, ma'am? I'm just beat—don't know what to do."

"A big chunk like you? Sit down, boy—" her lean finger indicated the chopping block and he came across the yard as obediently as a child and dropped down on it. "How come you're here?"

"Well—" he hung his head. "I'm almost ashamed to say. My folks, they won't ever forgive me. I tell you, ma'm, it's about this pain in my side."

He felt, rather than saw, a dark flicker of interest in her eyes, but when he looked up, her wrinkled face was serene.

"—this pain, ma'm. I had it ever since I was a little kid. The doctors couldn't do nothing for it. And then, my cousin Lee—he's a salesman, gets all over—my cousin Lee wrote about this doctor in St. Louis. Well, the folks gave me the train fare and sent me down there. I got in on a Saturday and the doctor, he wasn't in his office. So I went to this hotel."

He looked at her. She waited, the little breeze blowing her skirt about her.

"Well, ma'm—" he faltered. "I know I should have known better. I was brought up right. But I got sick of that little hotel room and I went out Saturday night to see what St. Louis looked like and—well, ma'm, I got into trouble. It was liquor that did it—unless they put something in my drink—anyway, I woke up Monday morning feeling like the wrath of God and all my folks' money gone." He heaved a groaning sigh.

"And you ain't never going to do it again."

The open sneer in her voice brought his head up with a jerk. She stood, hands on hips above the tight-tucked skirt, grinning down at him. Sudden wrath and fear flamed up in him, but he hid them with the skill of long practice.

"Boy," she said. "You came to the wrong door with your story—set down!" she said sharply, as he started to rise, a wounded expression on his face. "You think I don't know one of old Scratch's[1] people when I meet 'em? Me—out of 'em all? Now how'd you like a drink?"

"A drink?" he said.

She turned and walked across to the half-open door of the house and came back with a fruit jar, partly filled. She handed it to him. He hesitated, then gulped. Wildcats clawed at his gullet.

She laughed at the tears in his eyes and took the jar from him. She drank in her turn, without any visible reaction, as if the liquid in the jar had been milk. Then she set the jar on the ground and fished a pack of cigarettes from her pocket. She lit herself one, without offering them to him, and stood smoking, gazing away over his head, out over the fields.

1. *Scratch*, the Devil.

"I sent for someone last Tuesday when my Charon[2] was spoiled," she said, musingly. "You can't be nobody but him."

He stared up at her, feeling as if his clothes had been stripped off him.

"You crazy?" he demanded roughly, to get a little of his own back. "You nuts or something?" She turned and grinned at him.

"Well, now, boy," she said. "You sound like you'd be some great comfort to a lone old woman on long winter nights and nothing to do. Quiet!" she snapped sharply, as he opened his mouth again. "Come on in the cabin with me," she said. "I got to check on this."

Warily, confused by a mixture of emotions inside him, yet curious, he rose and followed her in. The interior of the small house was murkily dark, a single room. Some straight-backed chairs stood about a polished wood floor decorated with throw rugs. There was a fireplace and a round-topped, four-legged table. The corners had things in them, but there the shadows were too deep for his sun-dazzled eyes to see. He thought he smelled cat, but there was no cat to be seen; only an owl—stuffed, it seemed—on the mantel over the fireplace.

She bent over. There was the scratch of a match and a candle sput-. tered alight, illuminating the tabletop and her face, but throwing the rest of the room deeper into darkness. A strange thrill trembled down his spine. He stared at the candle. It was only a candle. He stared at her face—but for all its strangeness, it was only a face.

"Money," she said. "That's what you think you want, eh, boy?"

"What else is there?" he retorted; but the loud notes of his voice rang thin at the end. She burst suddenly into harsh laughter.

"What else is there, he says!" she cried to the room about them. "What else?" The candle flared suddenly higher, dazzling him for a moment. When he could see again, he discovered two things on the table before him. One was a circle of leather string—like a boot shoelace with a small sack attached—and the other was a thin sheaf of twenty-dollar bills, crisp and new, bound about by a rubber band. He looked at the money and his mouth went dry, estimating there must be two or three hundred dollars in the stack. His hand twitched toward it; and he looked up at the old woman.

"Look it over, boy," she said. "Go ahead. Look at it."

He snatched it up and riffled through the stack. There were fourteen of the twenties. His eyes met hers across the table. He noticed again how thin she was, how old, how frail. Or was she frail?

"Only money, boy?" she sneered at him. "Only money? Well, then you got no trouble. You just run me an errand and all that's yours—and as much again when you come back!"

2. *Charon*, in mythology Charon ferried the souls of the dead across the river Styx to the Elysian fields.

Still he stood, looking at her.

"You want to know?" she said. "I'll tell you what you got to do for that money. You just go get my recipe book from my neighbor, Marie-Elaine."

His voice came hoarse and different from his throat.

"What's the gag?" he said.

"Why, boy, there's no gag," she said. "I done lent my recipe book to Marie-Elaine, that's all, and I want you to fetch it for me."

He considered, his mind turning this way and that like a hunting weasel; but each way it looked there was darkness and the unknown.

"Where does she live?" he asked.

"Her? Over the ridge." She looked at him and leaned toward him across the candle and the table. "Money, eh, boy? Just money?"

"I say—" he gasped, for the smoke of the candle came directly at him, almost choking him. "What else is there?"

"Something else, boy." Her eyes held him. They were all he could see, shining in the darkness. "Something in particular for you, boy, if you want it. You did a fine, dark thing last night; but it's not enough."

"What you talking about?"

"Talking about you. Marie-Elaine, she borrowed my book and my Charon; but she spoiled my Charon. Now she got to get me another, or I take her Azazel[3]—don't know what I'm talking about, do you, boy?"

"No—" he gasped.

"I got to play fair with you. Them's the rules. So you take up that amulet there afore you and wear it. No business of mine, if Marie-Elaine can get you to take it off. None of my doings, if you open the book."

His hand went out as if of its own will and picked up the string and sack. An odd, sour smell from it stung his nostrils.

"Why'd I want to open your book?" he managed.

"For the pride and the power, boy, the pride and the power." The candle flame flared up between them, blinding him. He heard her, intoning. "Once by call of flesh—once by burn and rash—once by darkness—she'll try you boy. But wear the amulet spite of her and me and the book won't tempt you. There, I've given you fair warning."

The candle flame sank to ordinary size again. Sight of the room came back to him. She stood watching him, a slight grin on her face.

He hesitated, standing with the limp, oily leather of the string in his hand. He had feelings about bad spots when he was getting into them— he'd been in enough. Cat-wise, he was. And there was something about this that was whispering at him to get out. Or was it just the moth-wing of fear he had felt as he looked over this hollow? He believed in nothing, not even in witches; but—all that money for a book—and not believing meant not disbelieving . . . and that made everything possible. If witches

3. *Azazel*, a Hebrew name symbolizing an evil spirit.

were so— A shiver ran down his back; but hot on 'it came the sullen bitter anger at this old granny who thought she could use him—*him!* *I'll show her*, he thought; and the blood pounded hot in his temples. He shoved the bills into his pocket, lifted the amulet, hung it around his neck, and tucked it out of sight into his shirt.

"Yeah. Leave it to me," he said. She laughed.

"That's the boy!" she crackled. "You can't miss it when you see it. A black book with a gold chain and a gold lock to the chain. You'll see it in plain sight. She's got no blindness on you."

"Sure," he said. "I'll get it."

He backed away, turned, and went out the door. He came out into rich, late sunlight. It lay full on the fields; and, in spite of the fact that it was near to sunset, he had to shut his eyes for a moment against its brilliance after the darkness inside.

He turned to the ridge, towering up black with scrub pines above him. A dusty footpath snaked off and up from the cabin and was lost. He was aware of the old woman watching from her cabin door.

"See you," he said. But she did not answer; and he turned sullenly away, burning, burning with his resentment.

The first cool breath of dying day filled his lungs as he climbed. He felt the goodness of being alive; and the money was comfortably pressed against his thigh—he could feel it through his pocket with each step up the ridge. But the sourness that had come upon him in his encounter with the old witch stayed with him. The path wound steeply, sometimes taking half-buried boulders like stone steps upward. It had not looked like a very high ridge; but the sun was barely above the horizon when he reached the top.

He stopped to catch his breath and consider whether he should go on, or take the money and cut back to the tracks. Another freight would come soon. Below him, down the way he had come, the shadows were long across the fields of the old woman and the slow curve of the railroad right of way. Before him, the further hollow was half in the shadow of the ridge, and only a small house, very like the old woman's but neater looking with a touch of something colorful at the windows, stood free of the dark. A sudden thrill of something that was fear, but yet was not fear, ran through him as he stood above the low lands drowning in the last of the twilight. This was country for witches. He could feel belief coming up into him from the earth under the soles of his surplus army boots. Something evil burnt in the far redness of the descending sun; and the growing breeze of night came out of the shadow of the pines and caressed his cheek with cool, exciting fingers of darkness.

He began with an odd eagerness to scramble down the path along the far side of the ridge.   He seemed to go rapidly, but the further hollow was all in twilight by the time he emerged from the pine trees into its open pasture.   Overhead, the sky was blood-red with sunset and the roof of the house was tinged with its ochre reflection.   A little light glowed yellow behind its windows.

He crossed the meadow and stumbled unexpectedly into a small stream.   Wading across, he came up a further slight slope and into the yard of the house.   When he was still a dozen feet from the door, it opened; and a woman stood suddenly revealed in silhouette, with the gloaming now too feeble to illuminate her face and the lamplight strong behind her.

He came up to the steps; and as he did so, something large and gray flitted by him and disappeared through the open doorway.   It had looked almost like an owl, but the young woman seemed to pay it no attention.   He looked up the steps.   There were three of them; and they put her head above his own.   She was quite young; and her thin summer dress clung to the close outline of her, revealing a slim, tautly proportioned body.

He stopped, looking up at her.

"Hi," he said.   "Say—" a sudden cunningness stilled his tongue as it was about to mention the book he had been sent for—"say, I seem to be lost.   Where am I?"

"Not far from Peterborough," she said.   She had a low, huskily musical voice.   "Come in."

He walked up the steps and she stepped back before him.   A light scent of some earthy perfume came to his nostrils and reminded him all at once of how he was a man and this was a woman.   The lamplight, as in the old woman's house, blinded him for a second.   But he recovered quickly; and when he looked up, it was to see her regarding him from beyond a small table not unlike that other, although this was smaller. There was no owl to be seen.   This room, like that in the c ᴵ woman's house, was full of shadows, the main difference being a large yellow cat that sat before a fireplace in which a small fire was burning against the quick coolness of evening.   On the mantelpiece above it was a large black book with a gold chain around it, secured by a small gold lock.   All this he saw in a glance, but it registered as nothing on his mind compared to the lamplit sight of the young woman.

He had never expected to find her beautiful.

She was tall for a woman, and sheer gray eyes looked at him from under slim black brows.   Her hair was the color of the deepest shadows and dropped thickly to curl in one smooth dark wave about her slim shoulders.   Her lips had their perfect redness without lipstick and the line of her jaw was delicately carved above the soft column of her neck. Her body was the kind men dream of.

"You're Marie-Elaine," he said, without thinking.

"They call me Marie-Elaine," she nodded.

"You've got a crazy neighbor over the ridge there," he said. "She—" caution suddenly placed its hand on his tongue—"told me your name— but she didn't tell me anything else about you." His voice came out a little thickly with the feeling inside him.

She laughed—not as the old woman had laughed; but softly and warmly.

"She's old," Marie-Elaine said. "She's real old."

"Hell, yes!" he said, continuing to stare at her. And then, slowly, again, he repeated it. "Hell . . . yes . . ."

"You're a stranger," she said.

"Call me Bill." He looked at her across the table. "I was hitching a ride on a freight and the brakeman saw me. I had to drop off by the old lady's place. I got a drink of water from her. She said it was this way to town."

"You must be tired." Her voice was as soft as cornsilk.

"I'm beat out."

"Sit down," she said. "I'll make some coffee."

"Thanks."

He looked about and saw a chair on two slim rockers, spindle-backed and with a thin dark cushion on the seat of it, standing beside the fire. He crossed and sat down in it gingerly—it held. There was a sound of water splashing; and Marie-Elaine came across the room with a kettle. She crouched on the opposite side of the fireplace to swing out a metal arm, hooked at the end, and suspend the kettle from the hook, over the flames. The red flickering light lit up the smooth line of her body all down the clean curve of back and thigh—and the wild blood stirred within him.

"What's Peterborough like?" he said, to be saying something.

"It's a town," she answered. Straightening up, she turned her head and smiled at him, a smile as red as the flames of the fire. "A small town. Strangers don't come, often."

"You like it that way?" he asked, boldly.

"No," she said softly, looking at him. "I like strangers." He felt his heart begin to pound slowly and heavily. "What'd she say about me?"

"Who?" he blinked at her. "Oh, the old bag? Not much." He spread his hands to the fire's warmth. "I didn't get the idea she liked you too well, though."

"She doesn't," Marie-Elaine said. "She hates me. And she's lost her Charon."

22

"Some of those old bags are that way."

It was a crazy conversation. He checked an impulse to shake his head and clear it. He could talk to a woman better than this. A clink of metal reached his ears. She was lifting the kettle off the hook. Was it boiling already? She carried it away to the further shadows.

He was aware of eyes watching him; and looked down to discover it was the cat. Tall and tawny, it sat upright before the fire, staring at him. Its eyes, half-closed, seemed dreamily to be passing judgment upon him.

"You live here all by yourself?" he asked.

"All by myself." Her voice came back to him and he peered into the dimness, trying to make her out. "Did she warn you about me?"

"Warn?" he said. The cat moved suddenly. He heard the soft sound of paws on the floor and it bounded into his lap. He jumped at the weight of it, then raised his hand to pet it. But it wrinkled its nose suddenly—and spat—and leaped back to the floor again.

"Warn?" he said. "No. What for?"

Marie-Elaine laughed.

"Just talk," she said. She came walking out of the shadows into the firelight, an odd-looking earthenware coffeepot in one hand and two black china cups in the other. She sat down on the settle opposite him, filled both cups and handed one across to him. He took it, hot in his hand.

"How come she's got it in for you?" he asked.

"Oh, it's business," she smiled a cat's creamy smile across the small flame-lit distance between them. "We sell our wares to the same people."

"Yeah," he said. "Your looks wouldn't have anything to do with it?" He watched her to see how the compliment registered. She tilted her face, framed by the dark hair, a little to one side and her shadowed eyes heated his blood.

"My looks?" she murmured.

"You're a doll," he told her, in that sudden harsh voice that usually worked so well for him with women. Her smile widened a little. That was all. But enough.

"Do you want some more coffee?" she asked.

"Pour me." He held out the cup. Her fingers caught and burned against his hand, holding it as she poured the brown liquid into his cup.

"Milk and sugar?" she said.

"Black." He shook his head and drank. The coffee was like nothing he had ever tasted before. Delicious. Staring at the curving china bottom, he realized he had drunk it all without taking his lips from the cup.

"More?" He nodded, and she poured again. He held the cup this time without drinking, warming both hands around it; and looked at her over it. With the coffee in him, the fire seemed brighter and she—standing before him, she had not moved, but now as he watched she seemed, without moving a muscle, to float nearer and nearer, calling to all his senses. His head swam. He smelled the wild, faint savor of her perfume; and, like the candle in the old woman's house, she blotted out everything.

"Tell me—" It was her voice, coming huskily at him.

"What?" he said, blindly staring.

"Would you do something for me?"

"Something? What?" he said. He would have risen and gone to her, but the amulet anchored him like some great weight around his neck.

"You shouldn't ask what," she breathed. "Just anything."

His head spun. He felt himself drifting away as if in some great drunkenness. "You got to tell me first—" he gasped.

Suddenly the enchantment was gone. The room was back to normal, and she was turning away from him with the coffeepot. He leaned a little forward in his chair, toward her, but something had come between them.

"They got a hotel in Peterborough?" he asked.

"No hotel," she shrugged, replacing the coffeepot. "Sleep here," she said indifferently. His chest itched suddenly; and, reaching up to scratch it, his fingers closed around the amulet, through his shirt. Hastily, he dropped his hand again.

"Well, that's nice of you," he said. "I sure appreciate that." The words came out clumsily, and he gulped his second cup of coffee to cover the excitement and confusion in him. The amulet, now that he had noticed it, was itching and burning like a live thing. There must be something in it that he was allergic to. He had got all puffed up from poison oak once, on a picnic. When he looked up from the coffee, he saw she was on her feet.

"Here," she said. She picked up the lamp from the table and it lit up a bed against the wall beyond her. "This is where I sleep. But I've another—over here." And she crossed the room, the shadows rolling back before her until against the opposite wall he saw a narrow bunk built of heavy wood and with slats across it, peeping out from under the edges of an old mattress. "I'll get you some bedding."

She turned and went toward a dark door opening in the rear wall of the room. The cat meowed suddenly from near the front door and she spoke over the shoulder. "Let him out for me." Then she had vanished through the rectangle of darkness.

He got up, feeling the relief as the amulet swung out and away from contact with his skin. He walked across to the door, and opened it.

"Here, cat," he said.

It did not come, immediately. Peering through the dimness, he discovered suddenly its green eyes staring at him, unwinkingly. "C'mon! Cat!"

The cool night air blew through the doorway into his face, chilling and antiseptic. Standing with his back to the inner room, he fumbled open the top buttons of his shirt and pulled the little weight of the amulet out. The fire flickered high for a moment behind him, painting the bare wooden door ajar before him and reflecting inward. Looking down, he saw a great, furious rash on his skin where the amulet had rested.

He heard the old witch again, in the back of his mind, chanting—*once by call of the flesh, once by burn and rash*—Sudden fury exploded in him. Did she think she'd frightened him with stuff like that? Did she think he wouldn't dare—?

He yanked, snarling, at the amulet. The cord broke; and he tossed it into outer darkness.

Sudden relief washed over him—and on the heels of it, suddenly, the night became alive. With a thousand voices, whispering, its clamor surged around him, advising him, counseling him, tempting him. But he was too sharp now to be tricked, too wise to be betrayed. Clever, clever, his mind curled and twisted and coiled about on itself like a snake hungry in the midst of plenty and waiting only to make its choice. The heat of his body was gone now, all the lust of his flesh for Marie-Elaine, and only the shrewd mind was left, working. He would show them. He would show them both.

He became aware, suddenly, that he was still standing in the open doorway.

"Cat?" he said. The green eyes had disappeared. He turned back into the house, closing the door behind him. She was fixing his bed.

"You let Azazel out?" she asked.

"Yes," he said. Something better than her, he thought, looking at her —something better here for me. I'll show you, who can handle who, he thought. She was smiling at him, for no reason he could see.

"Don't be hasty," she said, looking at him.

"Who's hasty?" he said.

"Not you," she said. And she had slipped away from him suddenly into the shadows around her bed.

"Turn out the lamp," her voice came back to him. His fingers fumbled with the hot little metal screw; and the brilliant, white-glowing mantel faded. He looked across again at the darkness where she lay, but the firelight danced like a bar between them.

He stepped backwards to his own bed and sat down on its hard, quilted surface. He took off his shoes and socks, listening for the sounds of her undressing—but he heard nothing. He slid in under the covers, still wearing pants and shirt—but after he was covered he thought better of it and stripped off his shirt and dropped it over the side of the bed, leaving his chest naked to the quilt.

He lay on his back, waiting for sleep. But he could not sleep.

The fire danced. He felt at once drugged from the coffee and quiveringly awake. With the throwing away of the amulet, a weird lightness and swiftness of thought had come upon him, and a sense of power. Witches or women, he thought, they couldn't match him. Women or witches . . . he almost laughed out loud in the darkness at the irresistible fury of his galloping thoughts. The events of the day flickered like a too-swift film before his eyes. He saw the kid, the freight, the old woman over the ridge. Again he climbed the stony, wooded slope and stood at its top, feeling the evil in the sunset. But now he no longer wondered about it. He accepted it, feeling it echo back from some eager sounding board within him.

The dark fish of his thoughts swam in the black flood of the silent hour surrounding him. The keen edge of his desire for Marie-Elaine, her woman-flesh, was gone. Now something deeper, further, stronger, attracted him. It was a taste, a feel, a hunger, a satisfaction—like that which the business of beating up the kid had brought him. It was as if a mouth within him whose presence he had never suspected, had now suddenly opened and was crying to be fed. Somewhere about him, now, was the food that would satisfy it, the drink that would slake it. He lay still in the darkness, listening.

From the far side of the room came the soft and steady breathing, a woman in sleep . . . His wide eyes roamed the blackness; and, as he watched, the room began to lighten.

At first he saw no reason for this brightening. And then he saw the faint outline of the room's two windows taking dim ghost-shape amidst the dark; and gazing through the nearest one, he saw that the moon was rising above the ridge. Its cold metal rim was just topping the crest of brush and rock; and he saw light spill like quicksilver from it, down the slope, picking out the points and branches of the dark pines.

He gazed back into the room. Dim it still was, all steeped in obscurity; but by some faint trick of the light, the book on the mantel lay plainly revealed against the wall's deep shadow. Its gold chain lustered in the gloom with some obscure element of reflected light.

The hunger and thirst came up in his throat. He felt a need to do great things, and a feeling of wild joy and triumph swung him from the bed. He stood upright in the room, then swiftly stooped to gather up socks, shoes, shirt and suitcoat and put them on. When he was ready to leave, the book lying above the mantelpiece drew his eye again, like a cask of gold. In three long strides he crossed the room to it and tucked it under his arm. It was heavy—heavier than he had thought; but he could have carried a dozen like it easily, with the wild energy now possessing him.

He went swiftly to the door, opened it a crack, and slipped out into the night. The moon was out, and it was like stepping into another day that was just the negative of the film that sunlight would print when the dark hours ended. Cold light flooded the low places and the hills, and before he had taken a dozen steps from the cabin his eyes had adjusted and he was at home in the night.

He went quickly, seeming to swim through it effortlessly on tiptoe and with the sharpness of the cool air in his lungs, a drunken headiness came on him. The book felt rich with its heaviness under his arm. A warmth from its thick leather binding seemed to burn through his shirt and side, infecting him with a strange and bright-fevered heat. He pressed its shape closer to him, so that the beating of his heart echoed back from it, giving blow for blow. Now running, he went up the ridge between the two hollows with their cabins—but all he did was without effort, as if this was no steep slope, but a plain. And at the top of the ridge he paused—not because he was out of breath, but because he had the book now, *and* the money, and the railroad tracks lay there before him in the moonlight and another freight would be along before the dark was gone. He had won, but at the same time, something pulled at him; and he was reluctant to go.

He stood, irresolute on top of the ridge. The night wind blew coldly in his face; and suddenly the fever that had brought him this far faded out of him, leaving him abruptly cold and clearheaded as if he had just risen from a long night's sleep.

Stunned, dismayed, deprived, he stood blinking. What had happened?

The plain earth, the plain moonlight, and the plain wind, gave him no answer. The dark magic that had lived in them was abruptly gone, snatched away from him as if it had never been; and he stood alone at night on an Ozark ridge with a worn and ancient book in his hands. With fingers that trembled, he tucked the book under one arm and reached into his hip pocket. Stiff paper crackled in his grasp; and he drew it forth to stare at it in the moonlight, slim twenty dollar bills.

"Money!" he muttered. And then, yelling out suddenly in furious disappointment and anger, "*Money!*" he flung it all suddenly from him, far and wide into the night wind. The bills fluttered, darkly falling in the moonlight, lost among the shadows of the two slopes. Snatching the book from under his arm he held it before him, closed, in both hands, heavy and warm from the heat of his body—in both hands. Was this it? Was this the way to their rich and secret life?

His heart beat.  In the depths of the hollow behind him, the cabin of Marie-Elaine sent small wisps of smoke from its chimney.  Before him the cabin of the older witch lay in equal silence and lightlessness.  Under the night sky, they and the whole countryside seemed to beat and shimmer to the beating of his own heart—and to the reverberations of some mighty soundless drum, now far off, but waiting.  The book burned his fingers.

"Why not?" he murmured.  "Why not?"  Slowly his one hand closed over the edge of the book's cover.  The taste that had been in his mouth as he clubbed the kid behind the tool shed was with him again.  The red fire of the hearth played once more over the curves of the crouching Marie-Elaine.  These waited for him behind the cover of the book.  He wrenched it open.

Black lightning leaped from the page before him, and blinded him.  He staggered back, dropping the book, yet crying out in ecstasy.  Blinded, he groped for it on all fours on the ground, mewing.

The distant drumming grew louder.  The drummer approached.  The landscape melted in the moonlight, swimming around him.  He was aware of strange perfumes and great things moving.  He crawled in the shadow of a robe and the two witches were somehow present, standing back.  But the blindness hid the book from him like a curtain of darkness, and out of that curtain came a Question.

"Yes!" he cried eagerly, yearningly.

And the Question was asked again.

"Yes, yes—" he cried.  "Anything!  Make me the smallest, make me the littlest—but make me one of you!"

And once more, the Question . . .

"I do!" he cried.  "I will!  Forever and ever—"

Then the darkness parted, accepting him.  And, even as he looked on the beginning of his road, he felt himself dwindling, shrinking.  For one last moment it came back to him, the big-muscled, sunburned arms and the proud body, lithe and clean, the strength and the freedom; and then his limbs were narrowed to bone and tendon, to thickset fur, his belly sucked in, and his haunches rose and a tail grew long.

And the two witches shrieked and howled with laughter.  They stood like sisters, arm in arm, sisters in malice, filling the night sky with their raucous, reveling laughter.

"Fool!" screeched the old one, letting go the other and swooping forward to fasten a leash and collar about his hairy cat's neck.  "Fool to think you could match your wits with ours!  Now you are my Charon, to fetch and run, an acolyte to our altars.  Fool that was once a man, did you think to feed before you had waited on table?"

# FOR DISCUSSION: The Amulet

1. At the beginning of the story the main character is described as "cat-good," landing on his feet again, and "stretching and grinning." How do these descriptions prepare you for the conclusion of the story?
2. Does the first witch whom the young man meets play fair with him? Does the second? Does the young man play fair with either witch? Based on your answers, what moral may the author be said to be drawing in presenting this story?
3. Which woman in the story seems more witch-like to you? Why?
4. What do you think the Question was?
5. The last sentence in the story reads, "Fool that was once a man, did you think to feed before you had waited on table?" Is the question a literal one? If not, what is its meaning?

# INTRODUCTION: The Werewolf

The werewolf is a terrifying creature. Particularly terrifying is the werewolf who remains unsuspected and gains power over the relatively helpless. Such is the case in this story of a werewolf, the spirits of the Hartz Mountains, and three children who find themselves at the mercy of supernatural forces they can neither comprehend nor cope with.

# The Werewolf
## H. B. Marryat

My father was not born, or originally a resident, in the Hartz Mountains; he was the serf of a Hungarian nobleman of great possessions in Transylvania; but although a serf, he was not by any means a poor or illiterate man. In fact, he was rich, and his intelligence and respectability were such that he had been raised by his lord to the stewardship; but whoever may happen to be born a serf, a serf must he remain, even though he become a wealthy man; such was the condition of my father. My father had been married for about five years and by his marriage had three children—my elder brother, Caesar, myself (Hermann), and a sister named Marcella. Latin is still the language spoken in that country, and that will account for our high-sounding names. My mother was a very beautiful woman, unfortunately more beautiful than virtuous: She was seen and admired by the lord of the soil; my father was sent away upon some mission; and during his absence, my mother, flattered by the attentions and won by the assiduities of this nobleman, yielded to his wishes. It so happened that my father returned very unexpectedly and discovered the intrigue. The evidence of my mother's shame was positive; he surprised her in the company of her seducer! Carried away by the impetuosity of his feelings, he watched the opportunity of a meeting taking place between them and murdered both his wife and her seducer. Conscious that, as a serf, not even the provocation which he had received would be allowed as a justification of his conduct, he hastily collected together what money he could lay his hands on, and as we were then in the depth of winter, he put his horses to the sleigh, and taking his children with him, he set off in the middle of the night and was far away before the tragical circumstance had become known. Aware that he would be pursued and that he had no chance of escape if he remained in any portion of his native country (in which the authorities could lay hold of him), he continued his flight without intermission until he had buried himself in the intricacies and seclusion of the Hartz Mountains. Of course, all that I have now told you I learned afterward. My oldest recollections are knit to a rude, yet comfortable, cottage in which I lived with my father, brother, and sister. It was on the confines of one of those vast forests which cover the northern part of Germany; around it were a few acres of ground, which, during the summer months, my father cultivated, and which, though they yielded a doubtful harvest, were sufficient for our support. In the winter we remained much indoors, for as my father followed the chase, we were left alone, and the wolves, during that season, incessantly prowled about. My father had purchased the cottage and land about it from one of the rude foresters, who gain their livelihood partly by hunting and partly by burning charcoal for the purpose of smelting the ore from the neighboring mines. It was distant about two miles from any other habitation. I can call to mind the whole landscape now: the tall pines which rose up on the mountain above us and the wide expanse of forest beneath, on the topmost boughs and heads of whose trees we looked down from our cottage, as the mountain below us rapidly descended into the distant valley. In summertime the prospect was beautiful, but during the severe winter, a more desolate scene could not well be imagined.

I said that in the winter my father occupied himself with the chase; every day he left us, and often would he lock the door, that we might not leave the cottage. He had no one to assist him or to take care of us—indeed, it was not easy to find a female servant who would live in such a solitude; but could he have found one, my father would not have received her, for he had imbibed a horror of the sex, as a difference of his conduct toward us, his two boys, and my poor little sister, Marcella, evidently proved. You may suppose we were sadly neglected; indeed, we suffered much, for my father, fearful that we might come to some harm, would not allow us fuel when he left the cottage; and we were obliged, therefore, to creep under the heaps of bearskins and there to keep ourselves as warm as we could until he returned in the evening, when a blazing fire was our delight. That my father chose this restless sort of life may appear strange, but the fact was that he could not remain quiet; whether from remorse for having committed murder or from the misery consequent on his change of situation or from both combined, he was never happy unless he was in a state of activity. Children, however, when left much to themselves, acquire a thoughtfulness not common to their age. So it was with us; and during the short cold days of winter we would sit silent, longing for the happy hours when the snow would melt and the leaves burst out and the birds begin their songs and when we should again be set at liberty.

Such was our peculiar and savage sort of life until my brother Caesar was nine, myself seven, and my sister five years old, when the circumstances occurred on which is based the extraordinary narrative which I am about to relate.

One evening my father returned home rather later than usual; he had been unsuccessful, and as the weather was very severe and many feet of snow were upon the ground, he was not only very cold, but in a very bad humor. He had brought in wood, and we were all three of us gladly assisting each other in blowing on the embers to create the blaze, when he caught poor little Marcella by the arm and threw her aside; the child fell, struck her mouth, and bled very much. My brother ran to raise her up. Accustomed to ill usage and afraid of my father, she did not dare to cry, but looked up in his face very piteously. My father drew his stool nearer to the hearth, muttered something in abuse of women, and busied himself with the fire, which both my brother and I had deserted when our sister was so unkindly treated. A cheerful blaze was soon the result of his exertions; but we did not, as usual, crowd around it. Marcella, still bleeding, retired to a corner, and my brother and I took our seats beside her, while my father hung over the fire gloomily and alone. Such had been our position for about half an hour, when the howl of a wolf, close under the window of the cottage, fell on our ears. My father started up and seized his gun; the howl was repeated, he examined the priming and then hastily left the cottage, shutting the door after him. We all waited (anxiously listening), for we thought that if he succeeded in shooting the wolf, he would return in a better humor; and although he was harsh to all of us, and particularly so to our little sister, still we loved our father and loved to see him cheerful and happy, for what else had we to look up to? And I may here observe that perhaps there never were three children who were fonder of each other; we did not, like other children, fight and dispute together; and if, by chance, any disagreement did arise between my brother and me, little Marcella would run to us, and kissing us both, seal, through her entreaties, the peace between us. Marcella was a lovely, amiable child; I can recall her beautiful features even now—Alas! poor little Marcella.

We waited for some time, but the report of the gun did not reach us, and my elder brother then said, "Our father has followed the wolf and will not be back for some time. Marcella, let us wash the blood from your mouth, and then we will leave this corner and go to the fire and warm ourselves."

We did so and remained there until near midnight, every minute wondering, as it grew later, why our father did not return. We had no idea that he was in any danger, but we thought that he must have chased the wolf for a very long time. "I will look out and see if father is coming," said my brother Caesar, going to the door. "Take care," said Marcella, "the wolves must be about now, and we cannot kill them, Brother." My brother opened the door very cautiously and but a few inches; he peeped out. "I see nothing," said he after a time, and once more he joined us at the fire. "We have had no supper," said I, for my father usually cooked the meat as soon as he came home, and during his absence we had nothing but the fragments of the preceding day.

"And if our father comes home after his hunt, Caesar," said Marcella, "he will be pleased to have some supper; let us cook it for him and for ourselves." Caesar climbed upon the stool and reached down some meat —I forget now whether it was venison or bear's meat; but we cut off the usual quantity and proceeded to dress it, as we used to do under our father's superintendence. We were all busied putting it into the platters before the fire to await his coming, when we heard the sound of a horn. We listened—there was a noise outside, and a minute afterward my father entered, ushering in a young female and a large dark man in a hunter's dress.

Perhaps I had better now relate what was only known to me many years afterward. When my father had left the cottage, he perceived a large white wolf about thirty yards from him; as soon as the animal saw my father, it retreated slowly, growling and snarling. My father followed; the animal did not run but always kept at some distance, and my father did not like to fire until he was pretty certain that his ball would take effect: Thus they went on for some time, the wolf now leaving my father far behind, and then stopping and snarling defiance at him, and then again, on his approach, setting off at speed.

Anxious to shoot the animal (for the white wolf is very rare), my father continued the pursuit for several hours, during which he continually ascended the mountain.

You must know that there are peculiar spots on those mountains which are supposed, and as my story will prove, truly supposed, to be inhabited by the evil influences; they are well known to the huntsmen, who invariably avoid them. Now one of these spots, an open space in the pine forests above us, had been pointed out to my father as dangerous on that account. But whether he disbelieved these wild stories or whether, in his eager pursuit of the chase, he disregarded them, I know not; certain, however, it is that he was decoyed by the white wolf to this open space, where the animal appeared to slacken her speed. My father approached, came close up to her, raised his gun to his shoulder, and was about to fire, when the wolf suddenly disappeared. He thought that the snow on the ground must have dazzled his sight, and he let down his gun to look for the beast —but she was gone; how she could have escaped over the clearance, without his seeing her, was beyond his comprehension. Mortified at the ill success of his chase, he was about to retrace his steps, when he heard the distant sound of a horn. Astonishment at such a sound—at such an hour —in such a wilderness, made him forget for the moment his disappointment, and he remained riveted to the spot. In a minute the horn was blown a second time and at no great distance; my father stood still and listened: A third time it was blown. I forget the term used to express it, but it was the signal which, my father well knew, implied that the party was lost in the woods. In a few minutes more my father beheld a man on horseback, with a female seated on the crupper, enter the cleared space and ride up to him. At first, my father called to mind the strange stories which he had heard of the supernatural beings who were said to frequent these mountains; but the nearer approach of the parties satisfied him that they were mortals like himself. As soon as they came up to him, the man who guided the horse accosted him. "Friend hunter, you are out late, the better fortune for us: We have ridden far and are in fear of our lives, which are eagerly sought after. These mountains have enabled us to elude our pursuers, but if we find not shelter and refreshment, that will avail us little, as we must perish from hunger and the inclemency of the night. My daughter, who rides behind me, is now more dead than alive—say, can you assist us in our difficulty?"

"My cottage is some few miles distant," replied my father, "but I have little to offer you besides a shelter from the weather; to the little I have you are welcome. May I ask whence you come?"

"Yes, friend, it is no secret now; we have escaped from Transylvania, where my daughter's honor and my life were equally in jeopardy!"

This information was quite enough to raise an interest in my father's heart. He remembered his own escape: He remembered the loss of his wife's honor and the tragedy by which it was wound up. He immediately, and warmly, offered all the assistance which he could afford them.

"There is no time to be lost, then, good sir," observed the horseman; "my daughter is chilled with the frost and cannot hold out much longer against the severity of the weather."

"Follow me," replied my father, leading the way toward home.

"I was lured away in pursuit of a large white wolf," observed my father; "it came to the very window of my hut, or I should not have been out at this time of night."

"The creature passed by us just as we came out of the wood," said the female in a silvery tone.

"I was nearly discharging my piece at it," observed the hunter; "but since it did us such good service, I am glad that I allowed it to escape."

34

In about an hour and a half, during which my father walked at a rapid pace, the party arrived at the cottage and, as I said before, came in.

"We are in good time, apparently," observed the dark hunter, catching the smell of the roasted meat, as he walked to the fire and surveyed my brother and sister and myself. "You have young cooks here, Mynheer." "I am glad that we shall not have to wait," replied my father. "Come, mistress, seat yourself by the fire; you require warmth after your cold ride." "And where can I put up my horse, Mynheer?" observed the huntsman. "I will take care of him," replied my father, going out of the cottage door.

The female must, however, be particularly described. She was young and apparently twenty years of age. She was dressed in a traveling dress, deeply bordered with white fur, and wore a cap of white ermine on her head. Her features were very beautiful, at least I thought so, and so my father has since declared. Her hair was flaxen, glossy, and shining, and bright as a mirror; and her mouth, although somewhat large when it was open, showed the most brilliant teeth I have ever beheld. But there was something about her eyes, bright as they were, which made us children afraid; they were so restless, so furtive; I could not at that time tell why, but I felt as if there were cruelty in her eye; and when she beckoned us to come to her, we approached her with fear and trembling. Still she was beautiful, very beautiful. She spoke kindly to my brother and myself, patted our heads, and caressed us; but Marcella would not come near her; on the contrary, she slunk away and hid herself in the bed and would not wait for supper, which half an hour before she had been so anxious for.

My father, having put the horse into a close shed, soon returned, and supper was placed upon the table. When it was over, my father requested that the young lady take possession of his bed, and he would remain at the fire and sit up with her father. After some hesitation on her part, this arrangement was agreed to, and I and my brother crept into the other bed with Marcella, for we had as yet always slept together.

But we could not sleep; there was something so unusual, not only in seeing strange people, but in having those people sleep at the cottage, that we were bewildered. As for poor little Marcella, she was quiet, but I perceived that she trembled during the whole night, and sometimes I thought that she was checking a sob. My father had brought out some spirits, which he rarely used, and he and the strange hunter remained drinking and talking before the fire. Our ears were ready to catch the slightest whisper—so much was our curiosity excited.

"You said you came from Transylvania?" observed my father.

"Even so, Mynheer," replied the hunter. "I was a serf to the noble house of ——; my master would insist upon my surrendering up my fair girl to his wishes; it ended in my giving him a few inches of my hunting knife."

"We are countrymen and brothers in misfortune," replied my father, taking the huntsman's hand and pressing it warmly.

"Indeed! Are you, then, from that country?"

"Yes; and I too have fled for my life. But mine is a melancholy tale."

"Your name?" inquired the hunter.

"Krantz."

"What! Krantz of—I have heard your tale; you need not renew your grief by repeating it now. Welcome, most welcome, Mynheer, and, I may say, my worthy kinsman. I am your second cousin, Wilfred of Barnsdorf," cried the hunter, rising up and embracing my father.

They filled their horn mugs to the brim and drank to one another, after the German fashion. The conversation was then carried on in a low tone; all that we could collect from it was that our new relative and his daughter were to take up their abode in our cottage, at least for the present. In about an hour they both fell back in their chairs and appeared to sleep.

"Marcella, dear, did you hear?" said my brother in a low tone.

"Yes," replied Marcella in a whisper, "I heard all. Oh! Brother, I cannot bear to look upon that woman—I feel so frightened."

My brother made no reply, and shortly afterward we were all three fast asleep.

When we awoke the next morning, we found that the hunter's daughter had risen before us. I thought she looked more beautiful than ever. She came up to Marcella and caressed her; the child burst into tears and sobbed as if her heart would break.

But not to detain you with too long a story, the huntsman and his daughter were accommodated in the cottage. My father and he went out hunting daily, leaving Christina with us. She performed all the household duties, was very kind to us children, and gradually the dislike even of little Marcella wore away. But a great change took place in my father; he appeared to have conquered his aversion to the sex and was most attentive to Christina. Often, after her father and we were in bed, would he sit up with her, conversing in a low tone by the fire. I ought to have mentioned that my father and the huntsman Wilfred slept in another portion of the cottage and the bed which he formerly occupied and which was in the same room as ours, had been given up to the use of Christina. These visitors had been about three weeks at the cottage, when one night, after we children had been sent to bed, a consultation was held. My father had asked Christina in marriage and had obtained both her own consent and that of Wilfred; after this a conversation took place, which was, as nearly as I can recollect, as follows:

"You may take my child, Mynheer Krantz, and my blessing with her, and I shall then leave you and seek some other habitation—it matters little where."

"Why not remain here, Wilfred?"

"No, no, I am called elsewhere; let that suffice, and ask no more questions. You have my child."

"I thank you for her and will duly value her; but there is one difficulty."

"I know what you would say; there is no priest here in this wild country: True, neither is there any law to bind; still must some ceremony pass between you, to satisfy a father. Will you consent to marry her after my fashion? If so, I will marry you directly."

"I will," replied my father.

"Then take her by the hand. Now, Mynheer, swear."

"I swear," repeated my father.

"By all the spirits of the Hartz Mountains—"

"Nay, why not by Heaven?" interrupted my father.

"Because it is not my humor," rejoined Wilfred; "if I prefer that oath, less binding perhaps, than another, surely you will not thwart me."

"Well, be it so then; have your humor. Will you make me swear by that in which I do not believe?"

"Yet many do so, who in outward appearance are Christians," rejoined Wilfred. "Say, will you be married, or shall I take my daughter away with me?"

"Proceed," replied my father impatiently.

"I swear by all the spirits of the Hartz Mountains, by all their power for good or for evil, that I take Christina for my wedded wife; that I will ever protect her, cherish her, and love her; that my hand shall never be raised against her to harm her."

My father repeated the words after Wilfred.

"And if I fail in this, my vow, may all the vengeance of the spirits fall upon me and upon my children; may they perish by the vulture, by the wolf or other beasts of the forest; may their flesh be torn from their limbs and their bones blanch in the wilderness; all this I swear."

My father hesitated as he repeated the last words; little Marcella could not restrain herself, and as my father repeated the last sentence, she burst into tears. This sudden interruption appeared to discompose the party, particularly my father; he spoke harshly to the child, who controlled her sobs, burying her face under the bedclothes.

Such was the second marriage of my father. The next morning the hunter Wilfred mounted his horse and rode away.

My father resumed his bed, which was in the same room as ours; and things went on much as before the marriage, except that our new stepmother did not show any kindness toward us; indeed, during my father's absence, she would often beat us, particularly little Marcella, and her eyes would flash fire as she looked eagerly upon the fair and lovely child.

One night, my sister awoke me and my brother.

"What is the matter?" said Caesar.

"She has gone out," whispered Marcella.

"Gone out!"

"Yes, gone out the door, in her night clothes," replied the child; "I saw her get out of bed, look at my father to see if he slept, and then she went out the door."

What could induce her to leave her bed, and all undressed to go out, in such bitter wintry weather, with the snow deep on the ground, was to us incomprehensible; we lay awake, and in about an hour we heard the growl of a wolf, close under the window.

"There is a wolf," said Caesar; "she will be torn to pieces."

"Oh no!" cried Marcella.

A few minutes afterward our stepmother appeared; she was in her nightdress, as Marcella had stated. She let down the latch of the door, so as to make no noise, went to a pail of water and washed her face and hands, and then slipped into the bed where my father lay.

We all three trembled, we hardly knew why, but we resolved to watch the next night: We did so—and not only on the ensuing night, but on many others, and always at about the same hour, would our stepmother rise from her bed and leave the cottage—and after she was gone, we invariably heard the growl of a wolf under our window and always saw her, on her return, wash herself before she retired to bed. We observed, also, that she seldom sat down to meals and that when she did, she appeared to eat with dislike; but when the meat was taken down, to be prepared for dinner, she would often furtively put a raw piece into her mouth.

My brother Caesar was a courageous boy; he did not like to speak to my father until he knew more. He resolved that he would follow her out and ascertain what she did. Marcella and I endeavored to dissuade him from this project, but he would not be controlled, and the very next night he lay down in his clothes, and as soon as our stepmother had left the cottage, he jumped up, took down my father's gun, and followed her.

You may imagine in what a state of suspense Marcella and I remained during his absence. After a few minutes, we heard the report of a gun. It did not awaken my father, and we lay trembling with anxiety. A minute afterward we saw our stepmother enter the cottage—her dress was bloody. I put my hand to Marcella's mouth to prevent her crying out, although I was myself in great alarm. Our stepmother approached my father's bed, looked to see if he was asleep, and then went to the chimney and blew the embers into a blaze.

"Who is there?" said my father, waking up.

"Lie still, dearest," replied my stepmother, "it is only me; I have lighted the fire to warm some water; I am not quite well."

My father turned around and was soon asleep, but we watched our stepmother. She changed her linen and threw the garments she had worn into the fire; and we then perceived that her right leg was bleeding profusely, as if from a gunshot wound. She bandaged it up, and then dressing herself, remained before the fire until the break of day.

Poor little Marcella, her heart beat quickly as she pressed me to her side—so indeed did mine. Where was our bother Caesar? How did my stepmother receive the wound unless from his gun? At last my father rose, and then for the first time I spoke, saying, "Father, where is my brother Caesar?"

"Your brother!" exclaimed he. "Why, where can he be?"

"Merciful Heaven! I thought as I lay very restless last night," observed our stepmother, "that I heard somebody open the latch of the door; and, dear me, Husband, what has become of your gun?"

My father cast his eyes up above the chimney and perceived that his gun was missing. For a moment he looked perplexed, then seizing a broad ax, he went out of the cottage without saying another word.

He did not remain away from us long: In a few minutes he returned, bearing in his arms the mangled body of my poor brother; he laid it down and covered up his face.

My stepmother rose up and looked at the body, while Marcella and I threw ourselves by its side, wailing and sobbing bitterly.

"Go to bed again, children," said she sharply. "Husband," continued she, "your boy must have taken the gun down to shoot a wolf, and the animal has been too powerful for him. Poor boy! He has paid dearly for his rashness."

My father made no reply; I wished to speak—to tell all—but Marcella, who perceived my intention, held me by the arm and looked at me so imploringly that I desisted.

My father, therefore, was left in his error; but Marcella and I, although we could not comprehend it, were conscious that our stepmother was in some way connected with my brother's death.

That day my father went out and dug a grave, and when he laid the body in the earth, he piled up stones over it, so that the wolves should not be able to dig it up. The shock of this catastrophe was to my poor father very severe; for several days he never went to the chase, although at times he would utter bitter anathemas and vengeance against the wolves.

But during this time of mourning on his part, my stepmother's nocturnal wanderings continued with the same regularity as before.

At last, my father took down his gun to repair to the forest; but he soon returned and appeared much annoyed.

"Would you believe it, Christina, that the wolves—perdition to the whole race—have actually contrived to dig up the body of my poor boy, and now there is nothing left of him but his bones?"

"Indeed!" replied my stepmother. Marcella looked at me, and I saw in her intelligent eyes all she would have uttered.

"A wolf growls under our window every night, Father," said I.

"Aye, indeed?—why did you not tell me, boy?—wake me the next time you hear it."

I saw my stepmother turn away; her eyes flashed fire, and she gnashed her teeth.

My father went out again and covered up with a larger pile of stones the little remnants of my poor brother which the wolves had spared. Such was the first act of the tragedy.

The spring now came on: The snow disappeared, and we were permitted to leave the cottage; but never would I quit, for one moment, my dear little sister, to whom, since the death of my brother, I was more ardently attached than ever; indeed, I was afraid to leave her alone with my stepmother, who appeared to have a particular pleasure in ill-treating the child. My father was now employed upon his little farm, and I was able to render him some assistance.

Marcella used to sit by us while we were at work, leaving my stepmother alone in the cottage. I ought to observe that, as the spring advanced, so did my stepmother decrease her nocturnal rambles, and that we never heard the growl of the wolf under the window after I had spoken of it to my father.

One day, when my father and I were in the field, Marcella being with us, my stepmother came out, saying that she was going into the forest to collect some herbs my father wanted and that Marcella must go to the cottage and watch the dinner. Marcella went, and my stepmother soon disappeared in the forest, taking a direction quite contrary to that in which the cottage stood, and leaving my father and me, as it were, between her and Marcella.

About an hour afterward we were startled by shrieks from the cottage, evidently the shrieks of little Marcella. "Marcella has burned herself, Father," said I, throwing down my spade. My father threw down his, and we both hastened to the cottage. Before we could gain the door, out darted a large white wolf, which fled with the utmost celerity. My father had no weapon; he rushed into the cottage and there saw poor little Marcella expiring; her body was dreadfully mangled, and the blood pouring from it had formed a large pool on the cottage floor. My father's first intention had been to seize his gun and pursue, but he was checked by this horrid spectacle; he knelt down by his dying child and burst into tears: Marcella could just look kindly on us for a few seconds, and then her eyes were closed in death.

My father and I were still hanging over my poor sister's body, when my stepmother came in. At the dreadful sight she expressed much concern, but she did not appear to recoil from the sight of blood, as most women do.

"Poor child!" said she. "It must have been that great white wolf which passed me just now and frightened me so—she's quite dead, Krantz."

"I know it—I know it!" cried my father in agony. I thought my father would never recover from the effects of this second tragedy: He mourned bitterly over the body of his sweet child and for several days would not consign it to its grave, although frequently requested by my stepmother to do so. At last he yielded and dug a grave for her close by that of my poor brother and took every precaution that the wolves should not violate her remains.

I was now really miserable as I lay alone in the bed which I had formerly shared with my brother and sister. I could not help thinking that my stepmother was implicated in both their deaths, although I could not account for the manner; but I no longer felt afraid of her: My little heart was full of hatred and revenge.

The night after my sister had been buried, as I lay awake, I perceived my stepmother get up and go out of the cottage. I waited for some time, then dressed myself and looked out through the door, which I half opened. The moon shone bright, and I could see the spot where my brother and my sister had been buried; and what was my horror, when I perceived my stepmother busily removing the stones from Marcella's grave.

She was in her white nightdress, and the moon shone full upon her. She was digging with her hands and throwing away the stones behind her with all the ferocity of a wild beast. It was some time before I could collect my senses and decide what to do. At last, I perceived that she had arrived at the body and raised it up to the side of the grave. I could bear it no longer; I ran to my father and awoke him.

"Father! Father!" cried I. "Dress yourself, and get your gun."

"What!" cried my father. "The wolves are there, are they?"

He jumped out of bed, threw on his clothes, and in his anxiety did not appear to perceive the absence of his wife. As soon as he was ready, I opened the door, he went out, and I followed him.

Imagine his horror, when (unprepared as he was for such a sight) he beheld as he advanced toward the grave, not a wolf, but his wife, in her nightdress on her hands and knees, crouching by the body of my sister and tearing off large pieces of the flesh and devouring them with all the avidity of a wolf. She was too busy to be aware of our approach. My father dropped his gun, his hair stood on end; so did mine; he breathed heavily, and then his breath for a time stopped. I picked up the gun and put it into his hand. Suddenly he appeared as if concentrated rage had restored him to double vigor; he leveled his piece, fired, and with a loud shriek, down fell the wretch whom he had fostered in his bosom.

"God of Heaven!" cried my father, sinking down upon the earth in a swoon as soon as he had discharged his gun.

I remained some time by his side before he recovered. "Where am I?" said he. "What has happened?—Oh!—yes, yes! I recollect now. Heaven forgive me!"

He rose, and we walked up to the grave; what again was our astonishment and horror to find that instead of the dead body of my stepmother, as we expected, there was lying over the remains of my poor sister, a large white she-wolf.

"The white wolf!" exclaimed my father. "The white wolf which decoyed me into the forest—I see it all now—I have dealt with the spirits of the Hartz Mountains."

For some time my father remained in silence and deep thought. He then carefully lifted up the body of my sister, replaced it in the grave, and covered it over as before, having struck the head of the dead animal with the heel of his boot, and raving like a madman. He walked back to the cottage, shut the door, and threw himself on the bed; I did the same, for I was in a stupor of amazement.

Early in the morning we were both roused by a loud knocking at the door, and in rushed the hunter Wilfred.

"My daughter!—man—my daughter!—where is my daughter!" cried he in a rage.

"Where the wretch, the fiend, should be, I trust," replied my father, starting up and displaying equal choler, "where she should be—in hell!—Leave this cottage or you may fare worse."

"Ha-ha!" replied the hunter. "Would you harm a potent spirit of the Hartz Mountains? Poor mortal, who must needs wed a werewolf."

"Out, demon! I defy thee and thy power."

"Yet shall you feel it; remember your oath—your solemn oath—never to raise your hand against her to harm her."

"I made no compact with evil spirits."

"You did; and if you failed in your vow, you were to meet the vengeance of the spirits. Your children were to perish by the vulture, the wolf—"

"Out, out, demon!"

"And their bones blanch in the wilderness. Ha!—Ha!"

My father, frantic with rage, seized his ax and raised it over Wilfred's head to strike.

"All this I swear," continued the huntsman, mockingly.

The ax descended; but it passed through the form of the hunter, and my father lost his balance and fell heavily on the floor.

"Mortal!" said the hunter, striding over my father's body. "We have power over only those who have committed murder. You have been guilty of double murder—you shall pay the penalty attached to your marriage vow. Two of your children are gone; the third is yet to follow —and follow them he will, for your oath is registered. Go—it were kindness to kill you—your punishment is—that you live!"

## FOR DISCUSSION: The Werewolf

1. Describe the father of the three children. What are his major characteristics? What is your attitude toward him?
2. Christina is described in the story as speaking "in a silvery tone." She is said to have worn a dress "deeply bordered with white fur" and "a cap of white ermine." How do these details prepare you for her real identity?
3. One way to help a reader identify with the central character in a story is to tell it in the first person. Do you think this narrative technique is successful in this case?
4. Werewolves, witches, magical experiences, remote settings, meetings in forests, and the like are common details in stories of the supernatural. Which of these details are present in this story? Which are present in other such stories you know such as "Hansel and Gretel" and "Jack and the Beanstalk?"
5. Wilfred, a spirit of the Hartz Mountains, points out to Krantz at the conclusion of the story that, "We have power over only those who have committed murder." What moral point is the author making by putting these words in Wilfred's mouth?
6. Speculate on the fate of the narrator, Hermann.

## INTRODUCTION: The Mark of the Beast

This story might well have been included in the next chapter on gods, devils, and damnations.  It is included here because its emphasis is on the werewolf theme.  Kipling has written other short stories dealing with supernatural themes, but perhaps none is so fully realized nor so skillfully executed as is this one in which an ordinary man desecrates a "heathen" god and is almost destroyed for his act.

# The Mark of the Beast
## Rudyard Kipling

> Your Gods and my Gods—
> do you or I know which are the stronger?
> *Native Proverb*

East of Suez, some hold, the direct control of Providence ceases; Man being there handed over to the power of the Gods and Devils of Asia, and the Church of England, Providence only exercising an occasional and modified supervision in the case of Englishmen.

This theory accounts for some of the more unnecessary horrors of life in India:  it may be stretched to explain my story.

My friend Strickland of the Police, who knows as much of the natives as is good for any man, can bear witness to the facts of the case. Dumoise, our doctor, also saw what Strickland and I saw.  The inference which he drew from the evidence was entirely incorrect.

When Fleete came to India he owned a little money and some land in the Himalayas, near a place called Dharmsala.  Both properties had been left him by an uncle, and he came out to finance them.  He was a big, heavy, genial, and inoffensive man.  His knowledge of natives was, of course, limited, and he complained of the difficulties of the language.

He rode in from his place in the hills to spend New Year in the station, and he stayed with Strickland.  On New Year's Eve there was a big dinner at the club, and the night was excusably wet.  When men foregather from the uttermost ends of the Empire, they have a right to be riotous. The frontier had sent down a contingent o' Catch-'em-Alive-O's who had not seen twenty white faces a year, and were used to ride fifteen miles to dinner at the next fort at the risk of a Khyberee bullet where there drinks should lie. They profited by their new security, for they tried to play pool with a curled-up hedgehog found in the garden, and one of them carried the marker round the room in his teeth. Half a dozen planters had come in from the south and were talking "horse" to the Biggest Liar in Asia, who was trying to cap all their stories at once. Everybody was there, and there was a general closing up of ranks and taking stock of our losses in dead or disabled that had fallen during the past year. It was a very wet night, and I remember that we sang "Auld Lang Syne" with our feet in the Polo Championship Cup, and our heads among the stars, and swore that we were all dear friends. Then some of us went away and annexed Burma, and some tried to open up the Sudan and were opened up by Fuzzies in that cruel scrub outside Suakin, and some found stars and medals, and some were married, which was bad, and some did other things which were worse, and others of us stayed in our chains and strove to make money on insufficient experiences.

Fleete began the night with sherry and bitters, drank champagne steadily up to the dessert, then raw, rasping Capri with all the strength of whisky, took Benedictine with his coffee, four or five whiskies and sodas to improve his pool strokes, beer and bones at half-past two, winding up with old brandy. Consequently, when he came out, at half-past three in the morning, into fourteen degrees of frost, he was very angry with his horse for coughing, and tried to leapfrog into the saddle. The horse broke away and went to his stables; so Strickland and I formed a Guard of Dishonour to take Fleete home.

Our road lay through the bazaar, close to a little temple of Hanuman, the Monkey-god, who is a leading divinity worthy of respect. All gods have good points, just as have all priests. Personally, I attach much importance to Hanuman, and am kind to his people—the great gray apes of the hills. One never knows when one may want a friend.

There was a light in the temple, and as we passed, we could hear voices of men chanting hymns. In a native temple, the priests rise at all hours of the night to do honour to their god. Before we could stop him, Fleete dashed up the steps, patted two priests on the back, and was gravely grinding the ashes of his cigar butt into the forehead of the red stone image of Hanuman. Strickland tried to drag him out, but he sat down and said solemnly:

"Shee that? Mark of the B—beasht! *I* made it. Ishn't it fine?"

In half a minute the temple was alive and noisy, and Strickland, who knew what came of polluting gods, said that things might occur. He, by virtue of his official position, long residence in the country, and weakness for going among the natives, was known to the priests and he felt unhappy. Fleete sat on the ground and refused to move. He said that "good old Hanuman" made a very soft pillow.

Then, without any warning, a Silver Man came out of a recess behind the image of the god. He was perfectly naked in that bitter, bitter cold, and his body shone like frosted silver, for he was what the Bible calls "a leper as white as snow." Also he had no face, because he was a leper of some years' standing and his disease was heavy upon him. We two stooped to haul Fleete up, and the temple was filling and filling with folk who seemed to spring from the earth, when the Silver Man ran in under our arms, making a noise exactly like the mewing of an otter, caught Fleete round the body and dropped his head on Fleete's breast before we could wrench him away. Then he retired to a corner and sat mewing while the crowd blocked all the doors.

The priests were very angry until the Silver Man touched Fleete. That nuzzling seemed to sober them.

At the end of a few minutes' silence one of the priests came to Strickland and said, in perfect English, "Take your friend away. He has done with Hanuman, but Hanuman has not done with him." The crowd gave room and we carried Fleete into the road.

Strickland was very angry. He said that we might all three have been knifed, and that Fleete should thank his stars that he had escaped without injury.

Fleete thanked no one. He said that he wanted to go to bed. He was gorgeously drunk.

We moved on, Strickland silent and wrathful, until Fleete was taken with violent shivering fits and sweating. He said that the smells of the bazaar were overpowering, and he wondered what slaughterhouses were permitted so near English residences. "Can't you smell the blood?" said Fleete.

We put him to bed at last, just as the dawn was breaking, and Strickland invited me to have another whisky and soda. While we were drinking he talked of the trouble in the temple, and admitted that it baffled him completely. Strickland hates being mystified by natives, because his business in life is to overmatch them with their own weapons. He has not yet succeeded in doing this, but in fifteen or twenty years he will have made some small progress.

"They should have mauled us," he said, "instead of mewing at us. I wonder what they meant. I don't like it one little bit."

I said that the Managing Committee of the temple would in all probability bring a criminal action against us for insulting their religion. There was a section of the Indian Penal Code which exactly met Fleete's offense. Strickland said he only hoped and prayed that they would do this.  Before I left I looked into Fleete's room, and saw him lying on his right side, scratching his left breast.  Then I went to bed cold, depressed, and unhappy, at seven o'clock in the morning.

At one o'clock I rode over to Strickland's house to inquire after Fleete's head.  I imagined that it would be a sore one.  Fleete was breakfasting and seemed unwell.  His temper was gone, for he was abusing the cook for not supplying him with an undone chop.  A man who can eat raw meat after a wet night is a curiosity.  I told Fleete this and he laughed.

"You breed queer mosquitoes in these parts," he said.  "I've been bitten to pieces, but only in one place."

"Let's have a look at the bite," said Strickland.  "It may have gone down since this morning."

While the chops were being cooked, Fleete opened his shirt and showed us, just over his left breast, a mark, the perfect double of the black rosettes—the five or six irregular blotches arranged in a circle—on a leopard's hide.  Strickland looked and said, "It was only pink this morning.  It's grown black now."

Fleete ran to a glass.

"By jove!"  he said, "this is nasty.  What is it?"

We could not answer.  Here the chops came in, all red and juicy, and Fleete bolted three in a most offensive manner.  He ate on his right grinders only, and threw his head over his right shoulder as he snapped the meat.  When he had finished, it struck him that he had been behaving strangely, for he said apologetically, "I don't think I ever felt so hungry in my life.  I've bolted like an ostrich."

After breakfast Strickland said to me, "Don't go.  Stay here, and stay for the night."

Seeing that my house was not three miles from Strickland's, this request was absurd.  But Strickland insisted, and was going to say something when Fleete interrupted by declaring in a shamefaced way that he felt hungry again.  Strickland sent a man to my house to fetch over my bedding and a horse, and we three went down to Strickland's stables to pass the hours until it was time to go out for a ride.  The man who has a weakness for horses never wearies of inspecting them; and when two men are killing time in this way they gather knowledge and lies the one from the other.

There were five horses in the stables, and I shall never forget the scene as we tried to look them over.  They seemed to have gone mad.  They reared and screamed and nearly tore up their pickets; they sweated and shivered and lathered and were distraught with fear.  Strickland's horses used to know him as well as his dogs; which made the matter more curious.  We left the stable for fear of the brutes throwing themselves in their panic. Then Strickland turned back and called me. The horses were still frightened, but they let us "gentle" and make much of them, and put their heads in our bosoms.

"They aren't afraid of *us*," said Strickland. "D'you know, I'd give three months' pay if *Outrage* here could talk."

But *Outrage* was dumb and could only cuddle up to his master and blow out his nostrils, as is the custom of horses when they wish to explain things but can't. Fleete came up when we were in the stalls, and as soon as the horses saw him, their fright broke out afresh. It was all that we could do to escape from the place unkicked. Strickland said, "They don't seem to love you, Fleete."

"Nonsense," said Fleete; "my mare will follow me like a dog." He went to her; she was in a loose box; but as he slipped the bars she plunged, knocked him down, and broke away into the garden. I laughed, but Strickland was not amused. He took his moustache in both fists and pulled at it till it nearly came out. Fleete, instead of going off to chase his property, yawned, saying that he felt sleepy. He went to the house to lie down, which was a foolish way of spending New Year's Day.

Strickland sat with me in the stables and asked if I had noticed anything peculiar in Fleete's manner. I said that he ate his food like a beast; but that this might have been the result of living alone in the hills out of the reach of society as refined and elevating as ours for instance. Strickland was not amused. I do not think that he listened to me, for his next sentence referred to the mark on Fleete's breast, and I said that it might have been caused by blister flies, or that it was possibly a birthmark newly born and now visible for the first time. We both agreed that it was unpleasant to look at, and Strickland found occasion to say that I was a fool.

"I can't tell you what I think now," said he, "because you would call me a madman; but you must stay with me for the next few days, if you can. I want you to watch Fleete, but don't tell me what you think till I have made up my mind."

"But I am dining out tonight," I said.

"So am I," said Strickland, "and so is Fleete. At least if he doesn't change his mind."

We walked about the garden smoking, but saying nothing—because we were friends, and talking spoils good tobacco—till our pipes were out. Then we went to wake up Fleete. He was wide awake and fidgeting about his room.

"I say, I want some more chops," he said. "Can I get them?"

We laughed and said, "Go and change. The ponies will be round in a minute."

"All right," said Fleete. "I'll go when I get the chops—underdone ones, mind."

He seemed to be quite in earnest. It was four o'clock, and we had had breakfast at one; still, for a long time, he demanded those underdone chops. Then he changed into riding clothes and went out into the veranda. His pony—the mare had not been caught—would not let him come near. All three horses were unmanageable—mad with fear—and finally Fleete said that he would stay at home and get something to eat. Strickland and I rode out wondering. As we passed the temple of Hanuman, the Silver Man came out and mewed at us.

"He is not one of the regular priests of the temple," said Strickland. "I think I should peculiarly like to lay my hands on him."

There was no spring in our gallop on the racecourse that evening. The horses were stale, and moved as though they had been ridden out.

"The fright after breakfast has been too much for them," said Strickland.

That was the only remark he made through the remainder of the ride. Once or twice I think he swore to himself; but that did not count.

We came back in the dark at seven o'clock, and saw that there were no lights in the bungalow. "Careless ruffians my servants are!" said Strickland.

My horse reared at something on the carriage drive, and Fleete stood up under its nose.

"What are you doing, groveling about the garden?" said Strickland.

But both horses bolted and nearly threw us. We dismounted by the stables and returned to Fleete, who was on his hands and knees under the orange bushes.

"What the devil's wrong with you?" said Strickland.

"Nothing, nothing in the world," said Fleete, speaking very quickly and thickly. "I've been gardening—botanizing you know. The smell of the earth is delightful. I think I'm going for a walk—a long walk—all night."

Then I saw that there was something excessively out of order somewhere, and I said to Strickland, "I am not dining out."

"Bless you!" said Strickland. "Here, Fleete, get up. You'll catch fever there. Come in to dinner and let's have the lamps lit. We'll all dine at home."

Fleete stood up unwillingly, and said, "No lamps—no lamps. It's much nicer here. Let's dine outside and have some more chops—lots of 'em and underdone—bloody ones with gristle."

Now a December evening in Northern India is bitterly cold, and Fleete's suggestion was that of a maniac. •

"Come in," said Strickland sternly. "Come in at once."

Fleete came, and when the lamps were brought, we saw that he was literally plastered with dirt from head to foot. He must have been rolling in the garden. He shrank from the light and went to his room. His eyes were horrible to look at. There was a green light behind them, not in them, if you understand, and the man's lower lip hung down.

Strickland said, "There is going to be trouble—big trouble—tonight. Don't you change your riding things."

We waited and waited for Fleete's reappearance, and ordered dinner in the meantime. We could hear him moving about his own room, but there was no light there. Presently from the room came the long-drawn howl of a wolf.

People write and talk lightly of blood running cold and hair standing up and things of that kind. Both sensations are too horrible to be trifled with. My heart stopped as though a knife had been driven through it, and Strickland turned as white as the tablecloth.

The howl was repeated, and was answered by another howl far across the fields.

That set the gilded roof on the horror. Strickland dashed into Fleete's room. I followed, and we saw Fleete getting out of the window. He made beast noises in the back of his throat. He could not answer us when we shouted at him. He spat.

I don't quite remember what followed, but I think that Strickland must have stunned him with the long bootjack or else I should never have been able to sit on his chest. Fleete could not speak, he could only snarl, and his snarls were those of a wolf, not of a man. The human spirit must have been giving way all day and have died out with the twilight. We were dealing with a beast that had once been Fleete.

The affair was beyond any human and rational experience. I tried to say "Hydrophobia," but the word wouldn't come, because I knew that I was lying.

We bound this beast with leather thongs of the punkah-rope, and tied its thumbs and big toes together, and gagged it with a shoehorn, which makes a very efficient gag if you know how to arrange it. Then we carried it into the dining room, and sent a man to Dumoise, the doctor, telling him to come over at once. After we had despatched the messenger and were drawing breath, Strickland said, "It's no good. This isn't any doctor's work." I, also, knew that he spoke the truth.

The beast's head was free, and it threw it about from side to side. Any one entering the room would have believed that we were curing a wolf's pelt. That was the most loathsome accessory of all.

Strickland sat with his chin in the heel of his fist, watching the beast as it wriggled on the ground, but saying nothing. The shirt had been torn open in the scuffle and showed the black rosette mark on the left breast. It stood out like a blister.

In the silence of the watching we heard something without mewing like a she-otter. We both rose to our feet, and, I answer for myself, not Strickland, felt sick—actually and physically sick. We told each other, as did the men in *Pinafore,* that it was the cat.

Dumoise arrived, and I never saw a little man so unprofessionally shocked. He said that it was a heart-rending case of hydrophobia, and that nothing could be done. At least any palliative measures would only prolong the agony. The beast was foaming at the mouth. Fleete, as we told Dumoise, had been bitten by dogs once or twice. Any man who keeps half a dozen terriers must expect a nip now and again. Dumoise could offer no help. He could only certify that Fleete was dying of hydrophobia. The beast was then howling, for it had managed to spit out the shoehorn. Dumoise said that he would be ready to certify to the cause of death, and that the end was certain. He was a good little man, and he offered to remain with us; but Strickland refused the kindness. He did not wish to poison Dumoise's New Year. He would only ask him not to give the real cause of Fleete's death to the public.

So Dumoise left, deeply agitated; and as soon as the noise of the cart-wheels had died away, Strickland told me, in a whisper, his suspicions. They were so wildly improbable that he dared not say them out loud; and I, who entertained all Strickland's beliefs, was so ashamed of owning to them that I pretended to disbelieve.

"Even if the Silver Man had bewitched Fleete for polluting the image of Hanuman, the punishment could not have fallen so quickly."

As I was whispering this the cry outside the house rose again, and the beast fell into a fresh paroxysm of struggling till we were afraid that the thongs that held it would give way.

"Watch!" said Strickland. "If this happens six times I shall take the law into my own hands. I order you to help me."

He went into his room and came out in a few minutes with the barrels of an old shotgun, a piece of fishing line, some thick cord, and his heavy wooden bedstead. I reported that convulsions had followed the cry by two seconds in each case, and the beast seemed perceptibly weaker.

Strickland muttered, "But he can't take away the life! He can't take away the life!"

I said, though I knew that I was arguing against myself, "It may be a cat. It must be a cat. If the Silver Man is responsible, why does he dare to come here?"

Strickland arranged the wood on the hearth, put the gun barrels into the glow of the fire, spread the twine on the table and broke a walking stick in two. There was one yard of fishing line, gut, lapped with wire, such as is used for *mahseer*-fishing, and he tied the two ends together in a loop.

Then he said, "How can we catch him? He must be taken alive and unhurt."

I said that we must trust in Providence, and go out softly with polo sticks into the shrubbery at the front of the house. The man or animal that made the cry was evidently moving round the house as regularly as a night watchman. We could wait in the bushes till he came by and knock him over.

Strickland accepted this suggestion, and we slipped out from a bathroom window into the front veranda and then across the carriage drive into the bushes.

In the moonlight we could see the leper coming round the corner of the house. He was perfectly naked, and from time to time he mewed and stopped to dance with his shadow. It was an unattractive sight, and thinking of poor Fleete, brought to such degradation by so foul a creature, I put away my doubts and resolved to help Strickland from the heated gun barrels to the loop of twine—from the loins to the head and back again—with all tortures that might be needful.

The leper halted in the front porch for a moment and we jumped out on him with the sticks. He was wonderfully strong, and we were afraid that he might escape or be fatally injured before we caught him. We had an idea that lepers were frail creatures, but this proved to be incorrect. Strickland knocked his legs from under him and I put my foot on his neck. He mewed hideously, and even through my riding boots I could feel that his flesh was not the flesh of a clean man.

He struck at us with his hand and feet stumps. We looped the lash of a dog whip round him, under the armpits, and dragged him backwards into the hall and so into the dining room where the beast lay. There we tied him with trunk straps. He made no attempt to escape, but mewed.

When we confronted him with the beast the scene was beyond description. The beast doubled backwards into a bow as though he had been poisoned with strychnine, and moaned in the most pitiable fashion. Several other things happened also, but they cannot be put down here.

"I think I was right," said Strickland. "Now we will ask him to cure this case."

But the leper only mewed. Strickland wrapped a towel round his hand and took the gun barrels out of the fire. I put the half of the broken walking stick through the loop of fishing line and buckled the leper comfortably to Strickland's bedstead. I understood then how men and women and little children can endure to see a witch burnt alive; for the beast was moaning on the floor, and though the Silver Man had no face, you could see horrible feelings passing through the slab that took its place, exactly as waves of heat play across red-hot iron—gun barrels for instance.

Strickland shaded his eyes with his hands for a moment and we got to work. This part is not to be printed.

The dawn was beginning to break when the leper spoke. His mewings had not been satisfactory up to that point. The beast had fainted from exhaustion and the house was very still. We unstrapped the leper and told him to take away the evil spirit. He crawled to the beast and laid his hand upon the left breast. That was all. Then he fell face down and whined, drawing in his breath as he did so.

We watched the face of the beast, and saw the soul of Fleete coming back into the eyes. Then a sweat broke out on the forehead and the eyes —they were human eyes—closed. We waited for an hour but Fleete still slept. We carried him to his room and bade the leper go, giving him the bedstead, and the sheet on the bedstead to cover his nakedness, the gloves and the towels with which we had touched him, and the whip that had been hooked round his body. He put the sheet about him and went out into the early morning without speaking or mewing.

Strickland wiped his face and sat down. A night gong, far away in the city, made seven o'clock.

"Exactly four-and-twenty hours!" said Strickland. "And I've done enough to ensure my dismissal from the service, besides permanent quarters in a lunatic asylum. Do you believe that we are awake?"

The red-hot gun barrel had fallen to the floor and was singeing the carpet. The smell was entirely real.

That morning at eleven we two together went to wake up Fleete. We looked and saw that the black leopard-rosette on his chest had disappeared. He was very drowsy and tired, but as soon as he saw us, he said, "Oh! Confound you fellows. Happy New Year to you. Never mix your liquors. I'm nearly dead."

"Thanks for your kindness, but you're over time," said Strickland. "Today is the morning of the second. You've slept the clock round with a vengeance."

The door opened, and little Dumoise put his head in. He had come on foot, and fancied that we were laying out Fleete.

"I've brought a nurse," said Dumoise. "I suppose that she can come in for . . . what is necessary."

"By all means," said Fleete cheerfully, sitting up in bed. "Bring on your nurses."

Dumoise was dumb. Strickland led him out and explained that there must have been a mistake in the diagnosis. Dumoise remained dumb and left the house hastily. He considered that his professional reputation had been injured, and was inclined to make a personal matter of the recovery. Strickland went out too. When he came back, he said that he had been to call on the Temple of Hanuman to offer redress for the pollution of the god, and had been solemnly assured that no white man had ever touched the idol and that he was an incarnation of all the virtues laboring under a delusion. "What do you think?" said Strickland.

I said, " 'There are more things . . .' "

But Strickland hates that quotation. He says that I have worn it threadbare.

One other curious thing happened which frightened me as much as anything in all the night's work. When Fleete was dressed he came into the dining room and sniffed. He had a quaint trick of moving his nose when he sniffed. "Horrid doggy smell, here," said he. "You should really keep those terriers of yours in better order. Try sulfur, Strick."

But Strickland did not answer. He caught hold of the back of a chair, and, without warning, went into an amazing fit of hysterics. It is terrible to see a strong man overtaken with hysteria. Then it struck me that we had fought for Fleete's soul with the Silver Man in that room, and had disgraced ourselves as Englishmen for ever, and I laughed and gasped and gurgled just as shamefully as Strickland, while Fleete thought that we had both gone mad. We never told him what we had done.

Some years later, when Strickland had married and was a church-going member of society for his wife's sake, we reviewed the incident dispassionately, and Strickland suggested that I should put it before the public.

I cannot myself see that this step is likely to clear up the mystery; because, in the first place, no one will believe a rather unpleasant story, and, in the second, it is well known to every right-minded man that the gods of the heathen are stone and brass, and any attempt to deal with them otherwise is justly condemned.

# FOR DISCUSSION: The Mark of the Beast

1. This story presents a variation on the classic werewolf theme in which a man is changed into a beast. What is that variation? In what ways does this story conform to the classic werewolf theme?
2. Kipling includes elements of humor in his story. Identify some of

them and discuss the ways in which they contribute to underscoring the horror of Fleete's transformation.

3. The doctor diagnoses Fleete's illness as a case of hydrophobia. Do you agree with the diagnosis or do you think there is a more supernatural explanation for Fleete's condition?

4. Permissiveness in the arts is a social issue today. In earlier times, certain things were considered too shocking to describe in detail in a story. Identify a case of the latter attitude in this story. Would you prefer to know exactly what was done to the leper to make him remove Fleete's affliction? Would such a description have made this a better story, in your opinion?

5. The narrator ends his tale with an ironic comment. What is that comment and how does it relate to the supernatural premise of the story?

Celebrated science fiction writer Ray Bradbury here explores a fantastic situation and an equally fantastic family with insight, compassion, and tenderness. The story is a splendid example of alienation told from a unique viewpoint and employing nearly all the legends concerning the terrible tribe whose stories make up this chapter.

# Homecoming
## Ray Bradbury

"Here they come," said Cecy, lying there flat in her bed.

"Where are they?" cried Timothy from the doorway.

"Some of them are over Europe, some over Asia, some of them over the Islands, some over South America!" said Cecy, her eyes closed, the lashes long, brown, and quivering.

Timothy came forward upon the bare plankings of the upstairs room. "Who are they?"

"Uncle Einar and Uncle Fry, and there's Cousin William, and I see Frulda and Helgar and Aunt Morgiana and Cousin Vivian, and I see Uncle Johann! They're all coming fast!"

"Are they up in the sky?" cried Timothy, his little gray eyes flashing. Standing by the bed, he looked no more than his fourteen years. The wind blew outside, the house was dark and lit only by starlight.

"They're coming through the air and traveling along the ground, in many forms," said Cecy, in her sleeping. She did not move on the bed; she thought inward on herself and told what she saw. "I see a wolflike thing coming over a dark river—at the shallows—just above a waterfall, the starlight shining up his pelt. I see a brown oak leaf blowing far up in the sky. I see a small bat flying. I see many other things, running through the forest trees and slipping through the highest branches; and they're *all* coming this way!"

"Will they be here by tomorrow night?" Timothy clutched the bedclothes. The spider on his lapel swung like a black pendulum, excitedly dancing. He leaned over his sister. "Will they all be here in time for the Homecoming?"

"Yes, yes, Timothy, yes," sighed Cecy. She stiffened. "Ask no more of me. Go away now. Let me travel in the places I like best."

"Thanks, Cecy," he said.  Out in the hall, he ran to his room.  He hurriedly made his bed.  He had just awakened a few minutes ago, at sunset, and as the first stars had risen, he had gone to let his excitement about the party run with Cecy.  Now she slept so quietly there was not a sound.  The spider hung on a silvery lasso about Timothy's slender neck as he washed his face.  "Just think, Spid, tomorrow night is Allhallows Eve!"

He lifted his face and looked into the mirror.  His was the only mirror allowed in the house.  It was his mother's concession to his illness.  Oh, if only he were not so afflicted!  He opened his mouth, surveyed the poor, inadequate teeth nature had given him.  No more than so many corn kernels—round, soft and pale in his jaws.  Some of the high spirit died in him.

It was now totally dark and he lit a candle to see by.  He felt exhausted.  This past week the whole family had lived in the fashion of the old country.  Sleeping by day, rousing at sunset to move about.  There were blue hollows under his eyes.  "Spid, I'm no good," he said, quietly, to the little creature.  "I can't even get used to sleeping days like the others."

He took up the candleholder.  Oh, to have strong teeth, with incisors like steel spikes.  Or strong hands, even, or a strong mind.  Even to have the power to send one's mind out, free, as Cecy did.  But, no, he was the imperfect one, the sick one.  He was even—he shivered and drew the candle flame closer—afraid of the dark.  His brothers snorted at him.  Bion and Leonard and Sam.  They laughed at him because he slept in a bed.  With Cecy it was different; her bed was part of her comfort for the composure necessary to send her mind abroad to hunt.  But Timothy, did he sleep in the wonderful polished boxes like the others?  He did not!  Mother let him have his own bed, his own room, his own mirror.  No wonder the family skirted him like a holy man's crucifix.  If only the wings would sprout from his shoulder blades.  He bared his back, stared at it.  And sighed again.  No chance.  Never.

Downstairs were exciting and mysterious sounds, the slithering black crepe going up in all the halls and on the ceilings and doors.  The sputter of burning black tapers in the banistered stairwell.  Mother's voice, high and firm.  Father's voice, echoing from the damp cellar.  Bion walking from outside the old country house lugging vast two-gallon jugs.

"I've just got to go to the party, Spid," said Timothy.  The spider whirled at the end of its silk, and Timothy felt alone.  He would polish cases, fetch toadstools and spiders, hang crepe, but when the party started he'd be ignored.  The less seen or said of the imperfect son the better.

All through the house below, Laura ran.

"The Homecoming!" she shouted gaily. "The Homecoming!" Her footsteps everywhere at once.

Timothy passed Cecy's room again, and she was sleeping quietly. Once a month she went belowstairs. Always she stayed in bed. Lovely Cecy. He felt like asking her, "Where are you now, Cecy? And *in* who? And what's happening? Are you beyond the hills? And what goes on there?" But he went on to Ellen's room instead.

Ellen sat at her desk, sorting out many kinds of blond, red and black hair and little scimitars of fingernail gathered from her manicurist job at the Mellin Village beauty parlor fifteen miles over. A sturdy mahogany case lay in one corner with her name on it.

"Go away," she said, not even looking at him. "I can't work with you gawking."

"Allhallows Eve, Ellen; just think!" he said, trying to be friendly.

"Hunh!" She put some fingernail clippings in a small white sack, labeled them. "What can it mean to you? What do you know of it? It'll scare the hell out of you. Go back to bed."

His cheeks burned. "I'm needed to polish and work and help serve."

"If you don't go, you'll find a dozen raw oysters in your bed tomorrow," said Ellen, matter-of-factly. "Good-bye, Timothy."

In his anger, rushing downstairs, he bumped into Laura.

"Watch where you're going!" she shrieked from clenched teeth.

She swept away. He ran to the open cellar door, smelled the channel of moist earthy air rising from below. "Father?"

"It's about time," Father shouted up the steps. "Hurry down, or they'll be here before we're ready!"

Timothy hesitated only long enough to hear the million other sounds in the house. Brothers came and went like trains in a station, talking and arguing. If you stood in one spot long enough the entire household passed with their pale hands full of things. Leonard with his little black medical case, Samuel with his large, dusty ebon-bound book under his arm, bearing more black crepe, and Bion excursioning to the car outside and bringing in many more gallons of liquid.

Father stopped polishing to give Timothy a rag and a scowl. He thumped the huge mahogany box. "Come on, shine this up, so we can start on another. Sleep your life away."

While waxing the surface, Timothy looked inside.

"Uncle Einar's a big man, isn't he, Papa?"

"Unh."

"How big is he?"

"The size of the box'll tell you."

"I was only asking. Seven feet tall?"

"You talk a lot."

About nine o'clock Timothy went out into the October weather. For two hours in the now-warm, now-cold wind he walked the meadows collecting toadstools and spiders. His heart began to beat with anticipation again. How many relatives had Mother said would come? Seventy? One hundred? He passed a farmhouse. If only you knew what was happening at our house, he said to the glowing windows. He climbed a hill and looked at the town, miles away, settling into sleep, the town hall clock high and round white in the distance. The town did not know, either. He brought home many jars of toadstools and spiders.

In the little chapel belowstairs a brief ceremony was celebrated. It was like all the other rituals over the years, with Father chanting the dark lines, Mother's beautiful white ivory hands moving in the reverse blessings, and all the children gathered except Cecy, who lay upstairs in bed. But Cecy was present. You saw her peering, now from Bion's eyes, now Samuel's, now Mother's, and you felt a movement and now she was in you, fleetingly and gone.

Timothy prayed to the Dark One with a tightened stomach. "Please, please, help me grow up, help me be like my sisters and brothers. Don't let me be different. If only I could put the hair in the plastic images as Ellen does, or make people fall in love with me as Laura does with people, or read strange books as Sam does, or work in a respected job like Leonard and Bion do. Or even raise a family one day, as Mother and Father have done. . . ."

At midnight a storm hammered the house. Lightning struck outside in amazing, snow-white bolts. There was a sound of an approaching, probing, sucking tornado, funneling and nuzzling the moist night earth. Then the front door, blasted half off its hinges, hung stiff and discarded, and in trooped Grandmama and Grandpapa, all the way from the old country!

From then on people arrived each hour. There was a flutter at the side window, a rap on the front porch, a knock at the back. There were fey noises from the cellar; autumn wind piped down the chimney throat, chanting. Mother filled the large crystal punch bowl with a scarlet fluid poured from the jugs Bion had carried home. Father swept from room to room lighting more tapers. Laura and Ellen hammered up more wolfsbane. And Timothy stood amidst this wild excitement, no expression to his face, his hands trembling at his sides, gazing now here, now there. Banging of doors, laughter, the sound of liquid pouring, darkness, sound of wind, the webbed thunder of wings, the padding of feet, the welcoming bursts of talk at the entrances, the transparent rattlings of casements, the shadows passing, coming, going, wavering.

"Well, well, and *this* must be Timothy!"

"What?"

A chilly hand took his hand. A long hairy face leaned down over him. "A good lad, a fine lad," said the stranger.

"Timothy," said his mother. "This is Uncle Jason."

"Hello, Uncle Jason."

"And over here——" Mother drifted Uncle Jason away. Uncle Jason peered back at Timothy over his caped shoulder, and winked.

Timothy stood alone.

From off a thousand miles in the candled darkness, he heard a high fluting voice; that was Ellen. "And my brothers, they *are* clever. Can you guess their occupations, Aunt Morgiana?"

"I have no idea."

"They operate the undertaking establishment in town."

"What!" A gasp.

"Yes!" Shrill laughter. "Isn't that priceless!"

Timothy stood very still.

A pause in the laughter. "They bring home sustenance for Mama, Papa and all of us," said Laura. "Except, of course, Timothy. . . ."

An uneasy silence. Uncle Jason's voice demanded. "Well? come now. What about Timothy?"

"Oh, Laura, your tongue," said Mother.

Laura went on with it. Timothy shut his eyes. "Timothy doesn't— well—doesn't *like* blood. He's delicate."

"He'll learn," said Mother. "He'll learn," she said very firmly. "He's my son, and he'll learn. He's only fourteen."

"But I was raised on the stuff," said Uncle Jason, his voice passing from one room on into another. The wind played the trees outside like harps. A little rain spatted on the windows—"raised on the stuff," passing away into faintness.

Timothy bit his lips and opened his eyes.

"Well, it was all my fault." Mother was showing them into the kitchen now. "I tried forcing him. You can't force children, you only make them sick, and then they never get a taste for things. Look at Bion, now, he was thirteen before he . . ."

"I understand," murmured Uncle Jason. "Timothy will come around."

"I'm sure he will," said Mother, defiantly.

Candle flames quivered as shadows crossed and recrossed the dozen musty rooms. Timothy was cold. He smelled the hot tallow in his nostrils and instinctively he grabbed at a candle and walked with it around and about the house, pretending to straighten the crepe.

"*Timothy*," someone whispered behind a patterned wall, hissing and sizzling and sighing the words, "*Timothy is afraid of the dark.*"

Leonard's voice. Hateful Leonard!

"I like the candle, that's all," said Timothy in a reproachful whisper.

More lightning, more thunder. Cascades of roaring laughter. Bang-ings and clickings and shouts and rustles of clothing. Clammy fog swept through the front door. Out of the fog, settling his wings, stalked a tall man.

"Uncle Einar!"

Timothy propelled himself on his thin legs, straight through the fog, under the green webbing shadows. He threw himself across Einar's arms. Einar lifted him.

"You've wings, Timothy!" He tossed the boy light as thistles. "Wings, Timothy: fly!" Faces wheeled under. Darkness rotated. The house blew away. Timothy felt breezelike. He flapped his arms. Einar's fingers caught and threw him once more to the ceiling. The ceiling rushed down like a charred wall. "Fly, Timothy!" shouted Einar, loud and deep. "Fly with wings! Wings!"

He felt an exquisite ecstasy in his shoulder blades, as if roots grew, burst to explode and blossom into new, moist membrane. He babbled wild stuff; again Einar hurled him high.

The autumn wind broke in a tide on the house, rain crashed down, shaking the beams, causing chandeliers to tilt their enraged candle lights. And the one hundred relatives peered out from every black, enchanted room, circling inward, all shapes and sizes, to where Einar balanced the child like a baton in the roaring spaces.

"Enough!" shouted Einar, at last.

Timothy, deposited on the floor timbers, exaltedly, exhaustedly fell against Uncle Einar, sobbing happily. "Uncle, uncle, uncle!"

"Was it good, flying? Eh, Timothy?" said Uncle Einar, bending down, patting Timothy's head. "Good, good."

It was coming toward dawn. Most had arrived and were ready to bed down for the daylight, sleep motionlessly with no sound until the follow-ing sunset, when they would shout out of their mahogany boxes for the revelry.

Uncle Einar, followed by dozens of others, moved toward the cellar. Mother directed them downward to the crowded row on row of highly polished boxes. Einar, his wings like sea-green tarpaulins tented behind him, moved with a curious whistling down the passageway; where his wings touched they made a sound of drumheads gently beaten.

Upstairs, Timothy lay wearily thinking, trying to like the darkness. There was so much you could do in darkness that people couldn't criticize you for, because they never saw you. He *did* like the night, but it was a qualified liking: sometimes there was so much night he cried out in rebellion.

In the cellar, mahogany doors sealed downward, drawn in by pale hands. In corners, certain relatives circled three times to lie, heads on paws, eyelids shut. The sun rose. There was a sleeping.

Sunset. The revel exploded like a bat nest struck full, shrieking out, fluttering, spreading. Box doors banged wide. Steps rushed up from cellar damp. More late guests, kicking on front and back portals, were admitted.

It rained, and sodden visitors laid their capes, their water-pelleted hats, their sprinkled veils upon Timothy who bore them to a closet. The rooms were crowd-packed. The laughter of one cousin, shot from one room, angled off the wall of another, ricocheted, banked and returned to Timothy's ears from a fourth room, accurate and cynical.

A mouse ran across the floor.

"I know you, Niece Leibersrouter!" exclaimed Father.

The mouse spiraled three women's feet and vanished into a corner. Moments later a beautiful woman rose up out of nothing and stood in the corner, smiling her white smile at them all.

Something huddled against the flooded pane of the kitchen window. It sighed and wept and tapped continually, pressed against the glass, but Timothy could make nothing of it, he saw nothing. In imagination he was outside staring in. The rain was on him, the wind at him, and the taper-dotted darkness inside was inviting. Waltzes were being danced; tall thin figures pirouetted to outlandish music. Stars of light flickered off lifted bottles; small clods of earth crumbled from casques, and a spider fell and went silently legging over the floor.

Timothy shivered. He was inside the house again. Mother was calling him to run here, run there, help, serve, out to the kitchen now, fetch this, fetch that, bring the plates, heap the food—on and on—the party happened around him but not to him. The dozens of towering people pressed in against him, elbowed him, ignored him.

Finally, he turned and slipped away up the stairs.

He called softly. "Cecy. Where are you now, Cecy?"

She waited a long while before answering. "In the Imperial Valley," she murmured faintly. "Beside the Salton Sea, near the mud pots and the steam and the quiet. I'm inside a farmer's wife. I'm sitting on a front porch. I can make her move if I want, or do anything or think anything. The sun's going down."

"What's it like, Cecy?"

"You can hear the mud pots hissing," she said, slowly, as if speaking in a church. "Little gray heads of steam push up the mud like bald men rising in the thick syrup, head first, out in the broiling channels. The gray heads rip like rubber fabric, collapse with noises like wet lips moving. And feathery plumes of steam escape from the ripped tissue. And there is a smell of deep sulfurous burning and old time. The dinosaur has been abroiling here ten million years."

"Is he done yet, Cecy?"

"Yes, he's done. Quite done." Cecy's calm sleeper's lips turned up. The languid words fell slowly from her shaping mouth. "Inside this woman's skull I am, looking out, watching the sea that does not move, and is so quiet it makes you afraid. I sit on the porch and wait for my husband to come home. Occasionally, a fish leaps, falls back, starlight edging it. The valley, the sea, the few cars, the wooden porch, my rocking chair, myself, the silence."

"What now, Cecy?"

"I'm getting up from my rocking chair," she said.

"Yes?"

"I'm walking off the porch, toward the mud pots. Planes fly over, like primordial birds. Then it is quiet, so quiet."

"How long will you stay inside her, Cecy?"

"Until I've listened and looked and felt enough: until I've changed her life some way. I'm walking off the porch and along the wooden boards. My feet knock on the planks, tiredly, slowly."

"And now?"

"Now the sulfur fumes are all around me. I stare at the bubbles as they break and smooth. A bird darts by my temple, shrieking. Suddenly I am in the bird and fly away! And as I fly, inside my new small glass-bead eyes I see a woman below me, on a boardwalk, take one two three steps forward into the mud pots. I hear a sound as of a boulder plunged into molten depths. I keep flying, circle back. I see a white hand, like a spider, wriggle and disappear into the gray lava pool. The lava seals over. Now I'm flying home, swift, swift, swift!"

Something clapped hard against the window, Timothy started.

Cecy flicked her eyes wide, bright, full, happy, exhilarated.

"Now I'm *home!*" she said.

After a pause, Timothy ventured, "The Homecoming's on. And everybody's here."

"Then why are you upstairs?" She took his hand. "Well, ask me." She smiled slyly. "Ask me what you came to ask."

"I didn't come to ask anything," he said. "Well, almost nothing. Well—oh, Cecy!" It came from him in one long rapid flow. "I want to do something at the party to make them look at me, something to make me good as them, something to make me belong, but there's nothing I can do and I feel funny and, well, I thought you might . . ."

"I might," she said, closing her eyes, smiling inwardly. "Stand up straight. Stand very still." He obeyed. "Now, shut your eyes and blank out your thought."

He stood very straight and thought of nothing, or at least thought of thinking nothing.

She sighed. "Shall we go downstairs now, Timothy?" Like a hand into a glove, Cecy was within him.

"Look everybody!" Timothy held the glass of warm red liquid. He held up the glass so that the whole house turned to watch him. Aunts, uncles, cousins, brothers, sisters!

He drank it straight down.

He jerked a hand at his sister Laura. He held her gaze, whispering to her in a subtle voice that kept her silent, frozen. He felt tall as the trees as he walked to her. The party now slowed. It waited on all sides of him, watching. From all the room doors the faces peered. They were not laughing. Mother's face was astonished. Dad looked bewildered, but pleased and getting prouder every instant.

He nipped Laura, gently, over the neck vein. The candle flames swayed drunkenly. The wind climbed around on the roof outside. The relatives stared from all the doors. He popped toadstools into his mouth, swallowed, then beat his arms against his flanks and circled. "Look, Uncle Einar! I can fly, at last!" Beat went his hands. Up and down pumped his feet. The faces flashed past him.

At the top of the stairs flapping, he heard his mother cry, "Stop, Timothy!" far below. "Hey!" shouted Timothy, and leaped off the top of the well, thrashing.

Halfway down, the wings he thought he owned dissolved. He screamed. Uncle Einar caught him.

Timothy flailed whitely in the receiving arms. A voice burst out of his lips, unbidden. "This is Cecy! This is Cecy! Come see me, all of you, upstairs, first room on the left!" Followed by a long trill of high laughter. Timothy tried to cut if off with his tongue.

Everybody was laughing. Einar set him down. Running through the crowding blackness as the relatives flowed upstairs toward Cecy's room to congratulate her, Timothy banged the front door open.

"Cecy, I hate you, I hate you!"

By the sycamore tree, in deep shadow, Timothy spewed out his dinner, sobbed bitterly and threshed in a pile of autumn leaves. Then he lay still. From his blouse pocket, from the protection of the matchbox he used for his retreat, the spider crawled forth. Spid walked along Timothy's arm. Spid explored up his neck to his ear and climbed in the ear to tickle it. Timothy shook his head. "Don't, Spid. Don't."

The feathery touch of a tentative feeler probing his eardrum set Timothy shivering. "Don't, Spid!" He sobbed somewhat less.

The spider traveled down his cheek, took a station under the boy's nose, looked up into the nostrils as if to seek the brain, and then clambered softly up over the rim of the nose to sit, to squat there peering at Timothy with green gem eyes until Timothy filled with ridiculous laughter. "Go away, Spid!"

Timothy sat up, rustling the leaves. The land was very bright with the moon. In the house he could hear the faint ribaldry as Mirror, Mirror was played. Celebrants shouted, dimly muffled, as they tried to identify those of themselves whose reflections did not, had not ever appeared in a glass.

"Timothy." Uncle Einar's wings spread and twitched and came in with a sound like kettledrums. Timothy felt himself plucked up like a thimble and set upon Einar's shoulder. "Don't feel badly, Nephew Timothy. Each to his own, each in his own way. How much better things are for you. How rich. The world's dead for us. We've seen so much of it, believe me. Life's best to those who live the least of it. It's worth more per ounce, Timothy, remember that."

The rest of the black morning, from midnight on, Uncle Einar led him about the house, from room to room, weaving and singing. A horde of late arrivals set the entire hilarity off afresh. Great-great-great-great and a thousand more great-greats Grandmother was there, wrapped in Egyptian cerements. She said not a word, but lay straight as a burnt ironing board against the wall, her eye hollows cupping a distant, wise, silent glimmering. At the breakfast, at four in the morning, one-thousand-odd-greats Grandmama was stiffly seated at the head of the longest table.

The numerous young cousins caroused at the crystal punch bowl. Their shiny olive-pit eyes, their conical, devilish faces and curly bronze hair hovered over the drinking table, their hard-soft, half-girl half-boy bodies wrestling against each other as they got unpleasantly, sullenly drunk. The wind got higher, the stars burned with fiery intensity, the noises redoubled, the dances quickened, the drinking became more positive. To Timothy there were thousands of things to hear and watch. The many darknesses roiled, bubbled, the many faces passed and repassed. . . .

"Listen!"

The party held its breath. Far away the town clock struck its chimes, saying six o'clock. The party was ending. In time to the rhythm of the striking clock, their one hundred voices began to sing songs that were four hundred years old, songs Timothy could not know. Arms twined, circling slowly, they sang, and somewhere in the cold distance of morning the town clock finished out its chimes and quieted.

Timothy sang. He knew no words, no tune, yet the words and tune came round and high and good. And he gazed at the closed door at the top of the stairs.

"Thanks Cecy," he whispered. "You're forgiven. Thanks."

Then he just relaxed and let the words move, with Cecy's voice, free from his lips.

Good-byes were said, there was a great rustling. Mother and Father stood at the door to shake hands and kiss each departing relative in turn. The sky beyond the open door colored in the east. A cold wind entered. And Timothy felt himself seized and settled in one body after another, felt Cecy press him into Uncle Fry's head so he stared from the wrinkled leather face, then leaped in a flurry of leaves up over the house and awakening hills. . . .

Then, loping down a dirt path, he felt his red eyes burning, his fur pelt rimed with morning, as inside Cousin William he panted through a hollow and dissolved away. . . .

Like a pebble in Uncle Einar's mouth, Timothy flew in a webbed thunder, filling the sky. And then he was back for all time, in his own body.

In the growing dawn, the last few were embracing and crying and thinking how the world was becoming less a place for them. There had been a time when they had met every year, but now decades passed with no reconciliation. "Don't forget," someone cried, "we meet in Salem in 1970!"

Salem. Timothy's numbed mind turned the words over. Salem, 1970. And there would be Uncle Fry and a thousand-times-great Grandmother in her withered cerements, and Mother and Father and Ellen and Laura and Cecy and all the rest. But would he be there? Could he be certain of staying alive until then?

With one last withering blast, away they all went, so many scarves, so many fluttery mammals, so many sere leaves, so many whining and clustering noises, so many midnights and insanities and dreams.

Mother shut the door. Laura picked up a broom. "No," said Mother. "We'll clean tonight. Now we need sleep." And the family vanished down cellar and upstairs. And Timothy moved in the crepe-littered hall, his head down. Passing a party mirror, he saw the pale mortality of his face all cold and trembling.

"Timothy," said Mother.

She came to touch her hand on his face. "Son," she said, "We love you. Remember that. We all love you. No matter how different you are, no matter if you leave us one day." She kissed his cheek. "And if and when you die, your bones will lie undisturbed, we'll see to that. You'll lie at ease forever, and I'll come visit every Allhallows Eve and tuck you in the more secure."

The house was silent. Far away the wind went over a hill with its last cargo of dark bats, echoing, chittering.

Timothy walked up the steps, one by one, crying to himself all the way.

## FOR DISCUSSION: Homecoming

1. In what ways does the author blend the commonplace and the supernatural in this story to make the reader gradually accept his fantastic premise as the story unfolds? Give examples.
2. In the introduction to this selection, we called it a story of alienation. Do you feel such a description is correct? Explain.
3. Although much of the behavior of the members of Timothy's family is shocking, the author presents it to us without deliberately emphasizing or over-dramatizing the shock value. An example: "Mother filled the large crystal punch bowl with a scarlet fluid poured from the jugs Bion had carried home." The scarlet fluid is, of course, human blood. Do you think the author should have said so directly or is his subtle technique more effective in creating the atmosphere present in the story?
4. Is there any trace of tragedy in this story?

# Gods, Devils, and Damnations — From the Darkness Next Door

# CHAPTER TWO

Imagine for a moment that you are a prehistoric man, living thirty thousand years ago. Your home is a cave. Beyond the cave lie dangers in the form of predatory beasts, other men, and nature itself. Suddenly one dark night, as rain begins to pelt down, the sky speaks. It is slit by white fire time and time again.

Remember now, you know nothing of thunder and lightning in terms of their natural causes. What do you, a prehistoric man, think as you shudder beneath the torn and noisy sky? Who has set the sky afire? Whose voice speaks in a language you cannot comprehend? What power is loose and roaming about in the night sky? You cry out in fear as a fiery lance strikes the enormous tree outside your cave and sends it careening to the ground with a crash.

From such occurrences did early man create his hierarchies of supernatural beings. Their whims and rages often wrought havoc and gave rise to man's fear of what he considered to be the supernatural in the world surrounding him. Many natural phenomena to him were supernatural events, and he created supernatural beings, gods, to explain these events.

Later, gods served a larger purpose than just giving explanations to the unexplainable. By the time of the pre-Christian era, men believed that gods controlled man's life after death and that they had the power to reward the good or to condemn the wicked to an unpleasant, gloomy afterlife.

Christianity embraced this belief and developed in explicit detail the structure of Hell and the penalties meted out there for various sins. Christians believed the Devil was present in life to tempt man away from the path leading to God. Of the many beliefs associated with the Devil were the common ones that the Devil could take over a person's body and that witches were his servants.

Few people today believe in witches or the possibility of the Devil taking over a person's body. But gods, devils, and damnations still form a major aspect of the supernatural in fiction as it is currently written. We are not so far removed from our prehistoric ancestors as we sometimes tend to think we are. Many of us still find things in the world that cannot be rationally explained unless we look to a divine being as the source of our sought after explanation, and many of us expect Satan to be waiting for us in the wings of eternity to punish us for misdeeds done during our lifetimes.

As you read the following stories, you will hear echoes of the fear that the prehistoric man must have felt as the lightning streaked the sky outside his cave and the thunder roared wildly at him.

Henry Slesar, in "The Jam," tells us of two very contemporary young men and the bizarre damnation they suffer. Sterling E. Lanier tells us of eldritch gods and their power in our world today. Sidney Carroll tells us about—

But read these stories of gods, devils, and damnations for yourself, secure in the knowledge that the great god Thor's hammer is not the cause of thunder. Nevertheless you will see that authors still concern themselves with gods and devils. They do so because we also concern ourselves with them. Clearly, supernatural literature is a vivid reflection of life.

All this with wond'ring eyes Aeneas view'd:
Each varying object his delight renew'd.
Eager to read the rest . . . Achates came,
And by his side the mad divining dame,
The priestess of the god, Deiphobe her name.
"Time suffers not," she said, "to feed your eyes
With empty pleasures: haste the sacrifice.
Sev'n bullocks, yet unyok'd, for Phoebus choose,
And for Diana sev'n unspotted ewes."
    This said, the servants urge the sacred rites,
While to the temple she the prince invites.
A spacious cave, within its farmost part,
Was hew'd and fashion'd by laborious art,
Through the hill's hollow sides: before the place,
A hundred doors a hundred entries grace:
As many voices issue, and the sound
Of Sibyl's words as many times rebound.
    Now to the mouth they come.   Aloud she cries,
"This is the time!   inquire your destinies!
He comes!   behold the god!"   Thus while she said,
(And shiv'ring at the sacred entry staid)
Her colour chang'd; her face was not the same;
And hollow groans from her deep spirit came.
Her hair stood up; convulsive rage possess'd
Her trembling limbs, and heav'd her lab'ring breast.
Greater than human kind she seem'd to look,
And, with an accent more than mortal, spoke.
Her staring eyes with sparkling fury roll;
When all the god came rushing on her soul.
Swiftly she turn'd, and, foaming as she spoke,
"Why this delay?"   she cry'd—"the pow'rs invoke.
Thy pray'rs alone can open this abode;
Else vain are my demands, and dumb the god."

*from* Aeneid, *Book VI—The Underworld, by* Virgil

# INTRODUCTION: The Jam

The author of this story obeys Edgar Allan Poe's dictum that a short story should have unity of time, place, and action. The time covered in this story is brief. The setting is a confined one. The action is minimal. But the power and effect of the story are enhanced by this very constriction of these three elements. Fate comes to the two boys in this story with the sureness and the swiftness of a hunting falcon.

# The Jam
## Henry Slesar

They left Stukey's pad around eight in the morning; that was the kind of weekend it had been. Early to bed, early to rise. Stukey laughed, squinting through the dirt-stained windshield of the battered Ford, pushing the pedal until the needle swung twenty, thirty miles over the speed limit. It was all Mitch's fault, but Mitch, curled up on the seat beside him like an embryo in a black leather womb, didn't seem to care. He was hurting too much, needing the quick jab of the sharp sweet point and the hot flow of the stuff in his veins. Man, what a weekend, Stukey thought, and it wasn't over yet. The fix was out there, someplace in the wilds of New Jersey, and Stukey, who never touched the filthy stuff himself, was playing good Samaritan. He hunched over the wheel like Indianapolis, pounding the horn with the heel of his right hand, shouting at the passing cars to *move over, move over meatball, watch where you're going, stupid, pull over, pull over, you lousy . . .*

"You tell 'em, man," Mitch said softly, "you tell 'em what to do."

Stukey didn't tell them, he showed them. He skinned the paint off a Buick as he snaked in and out of the line, and crowded so close to the tail of an MG that he could have run right over the little red wagon. Mitch began to giggle, urging him on, forgetting for the moment his destination and his need, delighting in the way Stukey used the car like a buzz saw, slicing a path through the squares in their Sunday driving stupor. "Look out, man," Mitch cackled, "here comes old Stukey, here comes nothin'."

The traffic artery was starting to clot at the entrance to the tunnel, and Stukey poured it on, jockeying the car first left and then right, grinning at the competitive game. Nobody had a chance to win with Stukey at the controls; Stukey could just shut his eyes and gun her; nobody else could do that. They made the tunnel entrance after sideswiping a big yellow Caddy, an episode that made Mitch laugh aloud with glee. They both felt better after that, and the tunnel was cool after the hot morning sun. Stukey relaxed a little, and Mitch stopped his low-pitched giggling, content to stare hypnotically at the blur of white tiles.

"I hope we find that fix, man," Mitch said dreamily. "My cousin, he says that's the place to go. How long you think, Stukey? How long?"

*Whish!* A Chevy blasted by him on the other lane, and Stukey swore. *Whish!* went an Oldsmobile, and Stukey bore down on the accelerator, wanting his revenge on the open road outside the tunnel. But the tunnel wound on, endlessly, longer than it ever had before. It was getting hot and hard to breathe; little pimples of sweat covered his face and trickled down into his leather collar; under the brass-studded coat, the sport shirt clung damply to his back and underarms. Mitch started to whine, and got that wide-eyed fishmouth look of his, and he gasped: "Man, I'm suffocating. I'm passing out . . ."

"What do you want me to do?" Stukey yelled. Still the tunnel wound on. *Whish!* went the cars in the parallel lane, and Stukey cursed his bad choice, cursed the heat, cursed Mitch, cursed all the Sundays that ever were. He shot a look at the balcony where the cops patrolled the traffic, and decided to take a chance. He slowed the car down to 35, and yanked the wheel sharply to the right to slip the car into a faster lane, right in front of a big, children-filled station wagon. Even in the tunnel roar they could hear its driver's angry shout, and Stukey told him what he could do with his station wagon and his children. Still the tunnel wound on.

They saw the hot glare of daylight at the exit. Mitch moaned in relief, but nothing could soften Stukey's ire. They came out of the tunnel and turned onto the highway, only to jerk to a halt behind a station wagon with a smelly exhaust. "Come on, come on!" Stukey muttered, and blew his horn. But the horn didn't start the cars moving, and Stukey, swearing, opened the door and had himself a look.

"Oh, man, man, they're stacked up for miles!" he groaned. "You wouldn't believe it, you wouldn't think it's possible . . ."

"What is it?" Mitch said, stirring in his seat. "What is it? An accident?"

"I dunno, I can't see a thing. But they just ain't movin', not a foot——"

"I'm sick," Mitch groaned. "I'm sick, Stukey."

"Shut up! Shut up!" Stukey said, hopping out of the car to stare at the sight again, at the ribbon of automobiles vanishing into a horizon ten, fifteen miles away. Like one enormous reptile it curled over the highway, a snake with multicolored skin, lying asleep under the hot sun. He climbed back in again, and the station wagon moved an inch, a foot, and greedily, he stomped the gas pedal to gobble up the gap. A trooper on a motorcycle bounced between the lanes, and Stukey leaned out of the window to shout at him, inquiring; he rumbled on implacably. The heat got worse, furnacelike and scorching, making him yelp when his hands touched metal. Savagely, Stukey hit the horn again, and heard a dim chorus ahead. Every few minutes, the station wagon jumped, and every few minutes, Stukey closed the gap. But an hour accumulated, and more, and they could still see the tunnel exit behind them. Mitch was whimpering now, and Stukey climbed in and out of the car like a madman, his clothes sopping with sweat, his eyes wild, cursing whenever he hit the gas pedal and crawled another inch, another foot forward...

"A cop! A cop!" he heard Mitch scream as a trooper, on foot, marched past the window. Stukey opened the car door and caught the uniformed arm. "Help us, will ya?" he pleaded. "What the hell's going on here? How do we get outa this?"

"You don't," the trooper said curtly. "You can't get off anyplace. Just stick it out, mac."

"We'll even leave the goddamn *car*. We'll *walk*, for God's sake. I don't care about the goddamn *car* ..."

"Sorry, mister. Nobody's allowed off the highway, even on foot. You can't leave this heap here, don't you know that?" He studied Stukey's sweaty face, and grinned suddenly. "Oh, I get it. You're new here, ain't you?"

"What do you mean, new?"

"I thought I never saw you in the Jam before, pal. Well, take it easy, fella."

"How long?" Stukey said hoarsely. "How long you think?"

"That's a stupid question," the trooper sneered. "Forever, of course. Eternity. Where the hell do you think you are?" He jabbed a finger into Stukey's chest. "But don't give *me* a hard time, buster. That was your *own* wreck back there."

"Wreck?" Mitch rasped from inside the car. "What wreck? What's he talkin' about, man?"

"The wreck you had in the tunnel." He waved his gloved hand toward the horizon. "That's where *all* these jokers come from, the tunnel wrecks. If you think this is bad, you ought to see the Jam on the turnpike."

"Wreck? Wreck?" Mitch screamed, as Stukey climbed behind the wheel. "What's he talking about wrecks for, Stukey?"

"Shut up, shut up!" Stukey sobbed, pounding his foot on the gas

74

pedal to gain yet another inch of road.  "We gotta get outa here, we gotta get out!"  But even when the station wagon jerked forward once more, he knew he was asking for too much, too late.

## FOR DISCUSSION: The Jam

1.  How does the author make the transition from the real to the super-natural in his story?
2.  Building tension and suspense is a necessary task if an author is to involve his reader in the tale he is telling.  How does this author use dialogue to increase the sense of tension and to build suspense?
3.  There are two distinct elements of horror in this story.  One is Mitch's physical agonies as his body demands heroin.  The other horror is spiritual.  Identify it.

## INTRODUCTION: The Kings of the Sea

Sit down with retired Brigadier Donald Ffellowes in his comfortable club, relax and let him tell you of his strange experience in the shadowy realm of the supernatural. You may not and need not believe what he tells you, but you will enjoy listening to him. And, if you don't believe him, try to find a natural explanation for what happened to him on a lonely section of the Swedish coast in 1938.

# The Kings of the Sea
### Sterling E. Lanier

I don't remember how magic came into the conversation at the club, but it had, somehow.

"Magic means rather different things to different people. To me..." Brigadier Donald Ffellowes, late of Her Majesty's forces, had suddenly begun talking. He generally sat, ruddy, very British and rather tired looking, on the edge of any circle. Occasionally he would add a date, a name, or simply nod, if he felt like backing up someone else's story. His own stories came at odd intervals and to many of us, frankly verged on the incredible, if not downright impossible. A retired artilleryman, Ffellowes now lived in New York, but his service had been all over the world, and in almost every branch of military life, including what seemed to be police or espionage work. That's really all there is to be said about either his stories or him, except that once he started one, no one ever interrupted him.

"I was attached to the embassy in Berlin in '38, and I went to Sweden for a vacation. Very quiet and sunny, because it was summer, and I stayed in Smaaland, on the coast, at a little inn. For a bachelor who wanted a rest, it was ideal, swimming every day, good food, and no newspapers, parades, crises or Nazis.

"I had a letter from a Swedish pal I knew in Berlin to a Swedish nobleman, a local landowner, a sort of squire in those parts. I was so absolutely happy and relaxed I quite forgot about going to see the man until the second week of my vacation, and when I did, I found he wasn't at home in any case.

"He owned a largish, old house about three miles from the inn, also on the coast road, and I decided to cycle over one day after lunch. The inn had a bike. It was a bright, still afternoon, and I wore my bathing trunks under my clothes, thinking I might get a swim either at the house or on the way back.

"I found the place easily enough, a huge, dark-timbered house with peaked roofs, which would look very odd over here, and even at home. But it looked fine there, surrounded by enormous old pine trees, on a low bluff over the sea. There was a lovely lawn, close cut, spread under the trees. A big lorry—you'd say a moving van—was at the door, and two men were carrying stuff out as I arrived. A middle-aged woman, rather smartly dressed, was directing the movers, with her back to me so that I had a minute or two to see what they were moving. One of them had just manhandled a largish black chair, rather archaic in appearance, into the lorry and then had started to lift a long, carved wooden chest, with a padlock on it, in after the chair. The second man, who must have been the boss mover, was arguing with the lady. I didn't speak too much Swedish, although I'm fair at German, but the two items I saw lifted into the van were apparently the cause of the argument, and I got the gist of it, you know.

" 'But Madame,' the mover kept on saying, 'Are you sure these pieces should be *destroyed*? They look very old.'

" 'You have been paid,' she kept saying, in a stilted way. 'Now get rid of it any way you like. Only take it away, now, at once.'

"Then she turned and saw me, and believe it or not, blushed bright red. The blush went away quickly, though, and she asked me pretty sharply what I wanted.

"I answered in English, that I had a letter to Baron Nyderstrom. She switched to English, which she spoke pretty well, and appeared a bit less nervous. I showed her the letter, which was a simple note of introduction, and she read it and actually smiled at me. She wasn't a bad-looking woman—about 45-48, somewhere in there, anyway—but she was dressed to the nines, and her hair was dyed an odd shade of metallic brown. Also, she had a really hard mouth and eyes.

" 'I'm so sorry,' she said, 'but the baron, who is my nephew, is away for a week and a half. I know he would have been glad to entertain an English officer friend of Mr.—' here she looked at the letter '—of Mr. Sorendson, but I'm afraid he is not around, while as you see, I am occupied. Perhaps another time?' She smiled brightly, and also rather nastily, I thought. 'Be off with you,' but polite.

"Well, really there was nothing to do except bow, and I got back on my bike and went wheeling off down the driveway.

"Halfway down the drive, I heard the lorry start, and I had just reached the road when it passed me, turning left, away from the direction of the inn, while I turned to the right.

"At that point something quite appalling happened. Just as the van left the drive, and also—as I later discovered—the estate's property line, something, a great weight, seemed to start settling over my shoulders, while I was conscious of a terrible cold, a cold which almost numbed me and took my wind away.

"I fell off the bike and half stood, half knelt over it, staring back after the dust of the lorry and completely unable to move. I remember the letters on the license and on the back of the van, which was painted a dark red. They said *Solvaag and Mechius, Stockholm.*

"I wasn't scared, mind you, because it was all too quick. I stood staring down the straight dusty road in the hot sun, conscious only of a terrible weight and the freezing cold, the weight pressing me down and the icy cold numbing me. It was as if time had stopped. And I felt utterly depressed, too, sick and, well, *hopeless.*

"Suddenly, the cold and the pressure stopped. They were just gone, as if they had never been, and I was warm, in fact, covered with sweat, and feeling like a fool there in the sunlight. Also, the birds started singing among the birches and pines by the road, although actually, I suppose they had been all along. I don't think the whole business took over a minute, but it seemed like hours.

"Well, I picked up the bike, which had scraped my shins, and started to walk along, pushing it. I could think quite coherently, and I decided I had had either a mild coronary or a stroke. I seemed to remember that you felt cold if you had a stroke. Also, I was really dripping with sweat by now and felt all swimmy; you'd say dizzy. After about five minutes, I got on the bike and began to pedal, slowly and carefully, back to my inn, deciding to have a doctor check me out at once.

"I had only gone about a third of a mile, numbed still by shock—after all I was only twenty-five, pretty young to have a heart attack or a stroke, either—when I noticed a little cove, an arm of the Baltic, on my right, which came almost up to the road, with tiny blue waves lapping at a small beach. I hadn't noticed it on the way to the baron's house, looking the other way, I guess, but now it looked like heaven. I was soaked with sweat, exhausted by my experience, and now had a headache. That cool sea water looked really marvelous, and as I said earlier, I had my trunks on under my clothes. There was even a towel in the bag strapped to the bike.

"I undressed behind a large pine tree ten feet from the road, and then stepped into the water. I could see white sand for about a dozen feet out, and then it appeared to get deeper quickly. I sat down in the shallow water, with just my neck sticking out, and began to feel human again. Even the headache receded into the background. There was no sound but the breeze soughing in the trees and the chirping of a few birds, plus the splash of little waves on the shore behind me. I felt at peace with everything and shut my eyes, half sitting, half floating in the water. The sun on my head was warm.

"I don't know what made me open my eyes, but I must have felt something watching, some presence. I looked straight out to sea, the entrance of the little cove, as I opened them, and stared into a face which was looking at me from the surface of the water about eight feet away, right where it began to get deeper."

No one in the room had moved or spoken once the story had started, and since Ffellowes had not stopped speaking since he began, the silence as he paused now was oppressive, even the muted sound of traffic outside seeming far off and unreal.

He looked around at us, then lit a cigarette and continued steadily.

"It was about two feet long, as near as I could tell, with two huge, oval eyes of a shade of amber yellow, set at the corners of its head. The skin looked both white and vaguely shimmery; there were no ears or nose that I could see, and there was a big, wide, flat mouth, opened a little, with blunt, shiny, rounded teeth. But what struck me most was the rage in the eyes. The whole impression of the face was vaguely— only vaguely, mind you—serpentine, snakelike, except for those eyes. They were mad, furious, raging, and not like an animal's at all, but like a man's. I could see no neck. The face 'sat' on the water, so to speak.

"I had only a split second to take all this in, mind you, but I was conscious at once that whatever this was, it was livid at *me* personally, not just at people. I suppose it sounds crazy, but I *knew* this right off.

"I hadn't even moved, hadn't had a chance, when something flickered under the head, and a grip like a steel cable clamped onto my hip. I dug my heels in the sand and grabbed down, pushing as hard as I could, but I couldn't shake that grip. As I looked down, I saw what had hold of me and damn near fainted, because it was a hand. It was double the size of mine, dead white, and had only two fingers and a thumb, with no nails, but it was a hand. Behind it was a boneless-looking white arm like a giant snake or an eel, stretching away back toward the head, which still lay on the surface of the water. At the same time I felt the air as cold, almost freezing, as if a private iceberg was following me again, although not to the point of making me numb. Oddly enough, the cold didn't seem to be *in* the water, though I can't explain this very well.

"I pulled back hard, but I might as well have pulled at a tree trunk for all the good it did. Very steadily the pressure on my hip was increasing, and I knew that in a minute I was going to be pulled out to that head. I was kicking and fighting, splashing the water and clawing at that hand, but in the most utter silence. The hand and arm felt just like rubber, but I could feel great muscles move under the hard skin.

"Suddenly I began to scream. I knew my foothold on the bottom sand was slipping and I was being pulled loose so that I'd be floating in a second. I don't remember what I screamed, probably just yelling with no words. I knew for a certainty that I would be dead in thirty seconds, you see." He paused, then resumed.

"My vision began to blur, and I seemed to be slipping, mentally, not physically, into a blind, cold world of darkness. But still I fought, and just as I began to be pulled loose from my footing, I heard two sounds. One was something like a machine gun, but ringing through it I heard a human voice shouting and, I thought, shouting one long word. The shout was very strong, ringing and resonant, so resonant that it pierced through the strange mental fog I was in, but the word was in no language I knew. Then I blacked out, and that was that.

"When I opened my eyes, I was in a spasm of choking. I was lying face down on the little beach, my face turned sideways on my crossed arms, and was being given artificial respiration. I vomited up more water and then managed to choke out a word or two, probably obscene. There was a deep chuckle, and the person who had been helping me turned me over, so that I could see him. He pulled me up to a sitting position and put a tweed-clad arm around my shoulders, giving me some support while I recovered my senses.

"Even kneeling as he was, when I turned to look at him, I could see he was a very tall man, in fact, a giant. He was wearing a brown tweed suit with knickerbockers, heavy wool knee socks and massive buckled shoes. His face was extraordinary. He was what's called an ash-blond, almost white-haired, and his face was very long, with high cheekbones, and also very white, with no hint of color in the cheeks. His eyes were green and very narrow, almost Chinese looking, and terribly piercing. Not a man you would ever forget if you once got a look at him. He looked about thirty-five, and was actually thirty, I later found out.

"I was so struck by his appearance, even though he was smiling gently, that I almost forgot what had happened to me. Suddenly I remembered though, and gave a convulsive start and tried to get up. As I did so, I turned to look at the water, and there was the cove, calm and serene, with no trace of that thing, or anything else.

"My new acquaintance tightened his grip on my shoulders and pulled me down to a sitting position, speaking as he did so.

" 'Be calm, my friend. You have been through a bad time, but it is gone now. You are safe.'

"The minute I heard his voice, I knew it was he who had shouted as I was being pulled under. The same timbre was in his speech now, so that every word rang like a bell, with a concealed purring under the words.

"I noticed more about him now. His clothes were soaked to the waist, and on one powerful hand he wore an immense ring set with a green seal stone, a crest. Obviously he had pulled me out of the water, and equally obviously, he was no ordinary person.

"'What was it,' I gasped finally, 'and how did you get me loose from it?'

"His answer was surprising. 'Did you get a good look at it?' He spoke in pure, unaccented 'British' English, I might add.

"'I did,' I said with feeling. 'It was the most frightful, bloody thing I ever saw, and people ought to be warned about this coast! When I get to a phone, every paper in Sweden *and* abroad will hear about it. They ought to fish this area with dynamite!'

"His answer was a deep sigh. Then he spoke. 'Face-to-face, you have seen one of Jormungandir's Children,' he said, 'and that is more than I or any of my family have done for generations.' He turned to face me directly and continued, 'And I must add, my friend, that if you tell a living soul of what you have seen, I will unhesitatingly pronounce you a liar or a lunatic. Further, I will say I found you alone, having a seeming fit in this little bay, and saved you from what appeared to me to be a vigorous attempt at suicide.'

"Having given me this bellypunch, he lapsed into a brooding silence, staring out over the blue water, while I was struck dumb by what I had heard. I began to feel I had been saved from a deadly sea monster only to be captured by an apparent madman.

"Then he turned back to me, smiling again. 'I am called Baron Nyderstrom,' he said, 'and my house is just a bit down the road. Suppose we go and have a drink, change our clothes and have a bit of a chat.'

"I could only stammer, 'But your aunt said you were away, away for more than a week. I came to see you because I have a letter to you.' I fumbled in my bathing suit, and then lurched over to my clothes under the trees. I finally found the letter, but when I gave it to him, he stuck it in his pocket. 'In fact I was just coming from your house when I decided to have a swim here. I'd had a sick spell as I was leaving your gate, and I thought the cool water would help.'

"'As you were leaving my gate?' he said sharply, helping me to get into my clothes. 'What do you mean "a sick spell," and what was that about my aunt?'

"As he assisted me, I saw for the first time a small, blue sports car, of a type unfamiliar to me, parked on the road at the head of the beach. It was in this, then, my rescuer had appeared. Half carrying, half leading me up the gentle slope, he continued his questioning, while I tried to answer him as best I could. I had just mentioned the lorry and the furniture as he got me into the left-hand bucket seat, having detailed in snatches my fainting and belief that I had had a mild stroke or heart spasm, when he got really stirred up.

"He levered his great body, and he must have been six-foot-five, behind the wheel like lightning, and we shot off in a screech of gears and spitting of gravel. The staccato exhaust told me why I thought I had heard a machine gun while fighting that incredible thing in the water.

"Well, we tore back up the road, into and up his driveway, and without a word, he slammed on the brakes and rushed into the house as if all the demons of hell were at his heels. I was left sitting stupefied in the car. I was not only physically exhausted and sick, but baffled and beginning again to be terrified. As I looked around the pleasant green lawn, the tall trees and the rest of the sunny landscape, do you know I wondered if through some error in dimensions, I had fallen out of my own proper space and landed in a world of monsters and lunatics!

"It could only have been a moment when the immense figure of my host appeared in the doorway. On his fascinating face was an expression which I can only describe as being mingled half sorrow, half anger. Without a word, he strode down his front steps and over to the car where, reaching in, he picked me up in his arms as easily as if I had been a doll instead of 175 pounds of British subaltern.

"He carried me up the steps and as he walked, I could hear him murmuring to himself in Swedish. It sounded to me like gibberish, with several phrases I could just make out being repeated over and over. 'What could they do, what else could they do! She would not be warned. What else could they do?'

"We passed through a vast dark hall, with great beams high overhead, until we came to the back of the house, and into a large sunlit room, overlooking the sea, which could only be the library or study. There were endless shelves of books, a huge desk, several chairs, and a long, low padded window seat on which the baron laid me down gently.

"Going over to a closet in the corner, he got out a bottle of aquavit and two glasses, and handed me a full one, taking a more modest portion for himself. When I had downed it—and I never needed a drink more— he pulled up a straight-backed chair and set it down next to my head. Seating himself, he asked my name in the most serious way possible, and when I gave it, he looked out of the window a moment.

" 'My friend,' he said finally, 'I am the last of the Nyderstroms. I mean that quite literally. Several rooms away, the woman you met earlier today is dead, as dead as you yourself would be, had I not appeared on the road, and from the same, or at least a similar cause. The only difference is that she brought this fate on herself, while you, a stranger, were almost killed by accident, and simply because you were present at the wrong time.' He paused and then continued with the oddest sentence, although, God knows, I was baffled already. 'You see,' he said, 'I am a kind of game warden and some of my charges are loose.'

"With that, he told me to lie quiet and started to leave the room. Remembering something, however, he came back and asked if I could remember the name of the firm which owned the mover's lorry I had seen. Fortunately I could, for as I told you earlier, it was seared on my brain by the strange attack I had suffered while watching it go up the road. When I gave it to him, he told me again not to move and left the room for another, from which I could hear him faintly using a telephone. He was gone a long time, perhaps half an hour, and by the time he came back, I was standing looking at his books. Despite the series of shocks I had gone through, I now felt fairly strong, but it was more than that. This strange man, despite his odd threat, had saved my life, and I was sure that I was safe from *him* at least. Also, he was obviously enmeshed in both sorrow and some danger, and I felt strongly moved to try and give him a hand.

"As he came back into the room, he looked hard at me, and I think he read what I was thinking, because he smiled, displaying a fine set of teeth.

" 'So—once again you are yourself. If your nerves are strong, I wish you to look on my late aunt. The police have been summoned and I need your help.'

"Just like that! A dead woman in the house and he needed my help!

"Well, if he was going to get rid of me, why call the police? Anyway, I felt safe as I told you, and you'd have to see the man, as I did, to know why.

"At any rate, we went down the great hall to another room, much smaller, and then through that again until we found ourselves in a little sewing room, full of women's stuff and small bits of fancy furniture. There in the middle of the room lay the lady whom I had seen earlier telling the movers to go away. She certainly appeared limp, but I knelt and felt her wrist because she was lying face down. Sure enough, no pulse at all and quite cold. But when I started to turn her over, a huge hand clamped on my shoulder and the baron spoke. 'I don't advise it,' he said warningly. 'Her face isn't fit to look at. She was frightened to death, you see.'

"I simply told him I had to, and he just shrugged his shoulders and stepped back. I got my hands under one shoulder and started to turn the lady, but my God, as the profile came into view, I dropped her and stood up like a shot. From the little I saw, her mouth was drawn back like an animal's, showing every tooth, and her eye was wide open and glaring in a ghastly manner. That was enough for me.

"Baron Nyderstrom led me from the room and back into the library, where we each had another aquavit in silence.

"I started to speak, but he held up his hand in a kind of command, and started talking.

" 'I shall tell the police that I passed you bathing on the beach, stopped to chat, and then brought you back for a drink. We found my aunt dead of heart failure and called the police. Now, sir, I like you, but if you will not attest to this same story, I shall have to repeat what I told you I would say at the beach, and I am well known in these parts. Also, the servants are away on holiday, and I think you can see that it would look ugly for you.'

"I don't like threats, and it must have showed, because although it would have looked bad as all hell, still I wasn't going to be a party to any murders, no matter how well-planned. I told him so, bluntly, and he looked sad and reflective, but not particularly worried.

" 'Very well,' he said at length, 'I can't really blame you, because you are in a very odd position.' His striking head turned toward the window in brief thought, and then he turned back to face me directly and spoke.

" 'I will make a bargain with you. Attest my statement to the police, and then let me have the rest of the day to talk to you. If, at the end of the day, I have not satisfied you about my aunt's death, you have my word, solemnly given, that I will go to the police station and attest *your* story, the fact that I have been lying and anything else you choose to say.'

"His words were delivered with great gravity, and it never for one instant occurred to me to doubt them. I can't give you any stronger statement to show you how the man impressed me. I agreed straightaway.

"In about ten minutes the police arrived, and an ambulance came with them. They were efficient enough, and very quick, but there was one thing that showed through the whole of the proceedings, and it was that the Baron Nyderstrom was *somebody!* All he did was state that his aunt had died of a heart attack and that was that! I don't mean the police were serfs, or crooks either for that matter. But there was an attitude of deference very far removed from servility or politeness. I doubt if royalty gets any more nowadays, even in England. When he had told me earlier that his name was 'known in these parts,' it was obviously the understatement of the decade.

"Well, the police took the body away in the ambulance, and the baron made arrangements for a funeral parlor and a church with local people over the telephone. All this took awhile, and it must have been 4:30 when we were alone again.

"We went back into the library. I should mention that he had gotten some cold meat, bread and beer from a back pantry, just after the police left, and so now we sat down and made ourselves some sandwiches. I was ravenous, but he ate quite lightly for a man of his size, in fact only about a third of what I did.

"When I felt full, I poured another glass of an excellent beer, lit a cigarette, sat back and waited. With this man, there was no need of unnecessary speech.

"He was sitting behind his big desk facing me, and once again that singularly attractive smile broke through.

" 'You are waiting for your story, my friend, if I may call you so. You shall have it, but I ask your word as a man of honor that it not be for repetition.' He paused briefly. 'I know it is yet a further condition, but if you do not give it, there is no recourse except the police station and jail for me. If you do, you will hear a story and perhaps— perhaps, I say, because I make no promises—see and hear something which no man has seen or heard for many, many centuries, save only for my family and not many of them. What do you say?'

"I never hesitated for a second. I said 'yes,' and I should add that I've never regretted it. No, never."

Ffellowes' thoughts seemed far away, as he paused and stared out into the murky New York night, dimly lit by shrouded street lamps, and the fog lights on passing cars. No one spoke, and no sound broke the silence of the room but a muffled cough. He continued.

"Nyderstrom next asked me if I knew anything about Norse mythology. Now this question threw me for an absolute loss. What did a dangerous animal and an awful death have to do with Norse mythology, to say nothing of a possible murder?

"However, I answered I'd read of Odin, Thor, and a few other gods as a child in school, the Valkyries, of course, and that was about it.

" 'Odin, Thor, the Valkyries, and a few others?' My host smiled, 'You must understand that they are rather late Norse and even late German adaptions of something much older. Much, much older, something with its roots in the dawn of the world.

" 'Listen,' he went on, speaking quietly but firmly, 'and when I have finished we will wait for that movers' truck to return. I was able to intercept it, and what it took, because of that very foolish woman, must be returned.'

"He paused as if at a loss how to begin, and then went on. His bell-like voice remained muted, but perfectly audible, while he detailed one of the damnedest stories I've ever heard. If I hadn't been through what I had that day, and if he hadn't been what he was, I could have thought I was listening to the Grand Master of all the lunatics I'd ever met.

" 'Long ago,' he said, 'my family came from inner Asia. They were some of the people the latercomers called *Aesir*, the gods of Valhalla, but they were not gods, only a race of wandering conquerors. They settled here, on this spot, despite warnings from the few local inhabitants, a small, dark, shore-dwelling folk. This house is built on the foundations of a fortress, a very old one, dating at the very least back to the second century B.C. It was destroyed later in the wars of the sixteenth century, but that is modern history.

" 'At any rate, my remote ancestors began soon to lose people. Women bathing, boys fishing, even full-grown warriors out hunting, they would vanish and never return. Children had to be guarded and so did the livestock, which had a way of disappearing also, although that of course was preferable to the children.

" 'Finally, for no trace of the mysterious marauders could be found, the chief of my family decided to move away. He had prayed to his gods and searched zealously, but the reign of silent, stealthy terror never ceased, and no human or other foe could be found.

" 'But before he gave up, the chief had an idea. He sent presents and a summons to the shaman, the local priest, not of our own people, but of the few, furtive, little shore folk, the strand people, who had been there when we came. We despised and avoided them, but we had never harmed them. And the bent little shaman came and answered the chief's questions.

" 'What he said amounted to this. We, that is my people, had settled on the land made sacred in the remote past to Jormungandir. Now Jormungandir in the standard Norse sagas and myths is the great, world-circling sea serpent, the son of the renegade Aesir Loki and a giantess. He is a monster who on the day of Ragnarok will arise to assault Asgard. But actually, these myths are based on something quite, quite different. The ancient Jormungandir was a god of the sea all right, but he was here before any Norsemen, and he had children, who were semimortal and very, very dangerous. All the Asgard business was invented later, by people who did not remember the reality, which was both unpleasant and a literal, living menace to ancient men.

" 'My ancestor, the first of our race to rule here, asked what he could do to abate the menace. Nothing, said the shaman, except go away. Unless, if the chief were brave enough, he, the shaman, could summon the Children of the God, and the chief could ask *them* how *they* felt!

" 'Well, my people were anything but Christians in those days, and they had some rather nasty gods of their own. Also, the old chief, my ancestor, was on his mettle, and he liked the land he and his tribe had settled. So—he agreed, and although his counselors tried to prevent him, he went alone at night to the shore with the old shaman of the shore people. And what is more, he returned.

" 'From that day to this we have always lived here on this stretch of shore. There is a vault below the deepest cellar where certain things are kept and a ceremony through which the eldest son of the house of Nyderstrom must pass. I will not tell you more about it save to say that it involves an oath, one we have never broken, and that the other parties to the oath would not be good for men to see. You should know, for you have seen one!'

"I had sat spellbound while this rigmarole went on, and some of the disbelief must have showed in my eyes, because he spoke rather sharply all at once.

" 'What do you think the Watcher in the Sea was, the "animal" that seized you? If it had been anyone else in that car but myself—!'

"I nodded, because after recalling my experience on my swim, I was less ready to dismiss his story, and I had been in danger of forgetting my adventure. I also apologized and he went on talking.

" 'The woman you spoke to was my father's much younger sister, a vain and arrogant woman of no brainpower at all. She lived a life in what is now thought of as society, in Stockholm, on a generous allowance from me, and I have never liked her. Somewhere, perhaps as a child, she learned more than she should about the family secret, which is ordinarily never revealed to our women.

" 'She wished me to marry and tried ceaselessly to entrap me with female idiots of good family whom she had selected.

" 'It is true that I must someday marry, but my aunt irritated me beyond measure, and I finally ordered her out of the house and told her that her allowance would cease if she did not stop troubling me. She was always using the place for house parties for her vapid friends, until I put a stop to it.

" 'I knew when I saw her body what she had done. She must have found out that the servants were away and that I would be gone for the day. She sent men from Stockholm. The local folk would not obey such an order from her, in my absence. She must have had duplicate keys, and she went in and down and had moved what she should never have seen, let alone touched. It was sacrilege, no less, and of a very real and dangerous kind. The fool thought the things she took held me to the house, I imagine.

" 'You see,' he went on, with more passion in his voice than I had previously heard. 'They are not responsible. They do not see things as we do. They regarded the moving of those things as the breaking of a trust, and they struck back. You appeared, because of the time element, to have some connection, and they struck at you. You do see what I mean, don't you?'

"His green eyes fixed themselves on me in an open appeal. He actually wanted sympathy for what, if his words were true, must be the damnedest set of beings this side of madness. And even odder, you know, he had got it. I had begun to make a twisted sense of what he said, and on that quiet evening in the big shadowed room, I seemed to feel an ancient and undying wrong, moreover one which badly needed putting right.

"He seemed to sense this and went on, more quietly.

" 'You know, I still need your help. Your silence later, but more immediate help now. Soon that lorry will be here and the things it took must be restored.

" 'I am not now sure if I can heal the breach. It will depend on the Others. If they believe me, all will go as before. If not—well, it was my family who kept the trust, but also who broke it. I will be in great danger, not only to my body but also to my soul. Their power is not all of the body.

" 'We have never known,' he went on softly, 'why they love this strip of coast. It is not used so far as we know, for any of their purposes, and they are not subject to our emotions or desires in any case. But they do, and so the trust is honored.'

"He looked at his watch and murmured 'six o'clock.' He got up and went to the telephone, but as his hand met the receiver, we both heard something.

"It was a distant noise, a curious sound, as if, far away somewhere, a wet piece of cloth were being dragged over stone. In the great silent house, the sound could not be localized, but it seemed to me to come from deep below us, perhaps in a cellar. It made my hair stiffen.

" 'Hah,' he muttered. 'They are stirring. I wonder—'

"As he spoke, we both became conscious of another noise, one which had been growing upon us for some moments unaware, that of a powerful motor engine. Our minds must have worked together for as the engine noise grew, our eyes met and we both burst into simultaneous gasps of relief. It could only be the furniture van, returning at last.

"We both ran to the entrance. The hush of evening lay over the estate, and shadows were long and dark, but the twin lights turning into the drive cast a welcome luminance over the entrance.

"The big lorry parked again in front of the main entrance, and the two workmen I had seen earlier got out. I could not really understand the rapid gunfire Swedish, but I gathered the baron was explaining that his aunt had made a mistake. At one point both men looked appalled, and I gathered that Nyderstrom had told them of his aunt's death. (He told me later that he had conveyed the impression that she was unsound mentally: it would help quiet gossip when they saw a report of the death).

"All four of us went around to the rear of the van, and the two men opened the doors. Under the baron's direction they carried out and deposited on the gravel the two pieces of furniture I had seen earlier. One was the curious chair. It did not look terribly heavy, but it had a box bottom, solid sides instead of legs and no arm rests. Carved on the oval-topped head was a hand grasping a sort of trident, and when I looked closely, I got a real jolt. The hand had only two fingers and a thumb, all without nails, and I suddenly felt in my bones the reality of my host's story.

"The other piece was the small, plain, rectangular chest, a bit like a large toy chest, with short legs ending in feet like a duck's. I mean three-toed and *webbed*, not the conventional 'duck foot' of the antique dealers.

"Both the chair and the chest were made of a dark wood, so dark it looked oily, and they had certainly not been made yesterday.

"Nyderstrom had the two men put the two pieces in the front hall and then paid them. They climbed back into their cab, so far as I could make out, apologizing continuously for any trouble they might have caused. We waved from the porch and then watched the lights sweep down the drive and fade into the night. It was fully dark now, and I suddenly felt a sense of plain old-fashioned fright as we stood in silence on the dark porch.

"'Come,' said the baron, suddenly breaking the silence, 'we must hurry. I assume you will help?'

"'Certainly,' I said. I felt I had to, you see, and had no lingering doubts at all. I'm afraid that if he'd suggested murdering someone, by this time I'd have agreed cheerfully. There was a compelling, hypnotic power about him. Rasputin was supposed to have had it and Hitler also, although I saw *him* plenty, and never felt it. At any rate, I just couldn't feel that anything this man wanted was wrong.

"We manhandled the chair and the chest into the back of the house, stopping at last in a back hall in front of a huge oaken door, which appeared to be set in a stone wall. Since the house was made of wood, this stone must have been part of the original building, the ancient fort, I guess, that he'd mentioned earlier.

"There were three locks on the door, a giant old padlock, a smaller newer one and a very modern-looking combination. Nyderstrom fished out two keys, one of them huge, and turned them. Then, with his back to me, he worked the combination. The old house was utterly silent, and there was almost an atmospheric hush, the kind you get when a bad thunderstorm is going to break.  Everything seemed to be waiting, waiting for something to happen.

"There was a click and Nyderstrom flung the great door open.  The first thing I noticed was that it was lined with steel on the other, inner side, and the second, that it opened on a broad flight of shallow steps leading down on a curve out of sight into darkness.  The third impression was not visual at all.  A wave of odor, strong but not unpleasant, of tide pools, seaweed and salt air poured out of the opening.  And there were several large patches of water on the highest steps, large enough to reflect the light.

"Nyderstrom closed the door again gently, not securing it, and turned to me.  He pointed, and I now saw on one wall of the corridor to the left of the door, about head height, a steel box, also with a combination lock.  A heavy cable led from it down to the floor.  Still in silence, he adjusted the combination and opened the box.  Inside was a knife switch, with a red handle.  He left the box open and spoke, solemnly and slowly.

" 'I am going down to a confrontation.  You must stay right here, with the door open a little, watching the steps.  I may be half an hour, but at most three quarters.  If I come up *alone*, let me out.  If I come up *not* alone, slam the door, turn the lock and throw that switch.  Also if anything *else* comes up, do so.  This whole house, under my direction, and at my coming of age, was extensively mined and you will have exactly two and a half minutes to get as far as possible from it.  Remember, at *most*, three quarters of an hour.  At the end of that time, even if nothing has happened, you will throw that switch and run . . .!'

"I could only nod.  There seemed to be nothing to say, really.

"He seemed to relax a little, patted me on the shoulders, and turned to unlock the strange chest.  Over his shoulder he talked to me as he took things out.  'You are going to see one thing at any rate, a true Sea King in full regalia.  Something, my friend, no one has seen who is not a member of my family since the late Bronze Age.'

"He stood up and began to undress quickly, until he stood absolutely naked.  I have never seen a more wonderful figure of a man, pallid as an ivory statue, but huge and splendidly formed.  On his head, from out of the stuff in the chest, he had set a narrow coronet, only a band in the back, but rising to a flanged peak in front.  Mounted in the front peak was a plaque on which the three-fingered hand and trident were outlined in purple gems.  The thing was solid gold.  Nyderstrom then stooped and pulled on a curious, short kilt, made of some scaly hide, like a lizard's and colored an odd green-gold.  Finally, he took in his right hand a short, curved, gold rod, ending in a blunt, stylized trident.

"We looked at each other a moment and then he smiled.  'My ancestors were very successful Vikings,' he said, still smiling. 'You see, they always could call on *help*.'

"With that, he swung the door open and went marching down the steps. I half shut it behind him and settled down to watch and listen.

"The sound of his footsteps receded into the distance, but I could still hear them in the utter silence for a long time. His family vault, which I was sure connected somehow with the sea, was a long way down. I crouched, tense, wondering if I would ever see him again. The whole business was utterly mad, and I believed every word of it. I still do.

"The steps finally faded into silence. I checked my watch and found ten minutes had gone by.

"Suddenly, as if out of an indefinite distance, I heard his voice. I recognized it instantly, for it was a long quavering call, sonorous and bell-like, very similar to what I had heard when he rescued me in the afternoon. The sound came from far down in the earth, echoing faintly up the dank stairs and died into silence. Then it came again, and when it died, yet again.

"My heart seemed to stop. I knew that this brave man was summoning something no man had a right to see and calling a council in which no one with human blood in his veins should sit.

"Silence, utter and complete, followed. I could hear nothing, save for an occasional faint drop of water falling somewhere out of my range of vision.

"I glanced at my watch. Twenty-one minutes had gone by. The minutes seemed to crawl endlessly, meaninglessly. I felt alone and in a strange dream, unable to move, frozen, an atom caught in a mesh beyond my comprehension.

"Then far away, I heard it, a faint sound. It was faint but regular, and increasing in volume, measured and remorseless. It was a tread, and it was coming up the stair in my direction.

"I glanced at my watch, thirty-four minutes. It could be my friend, still within his self-appointed limits of time. The step came nearer, nearer still. It was, so far as my straining ear could judge, a single step. It progressed further, and suddenly into the circle of light stepped Nyderstrom.

"He was alone and as he came up he waved in greeting. He was dripping wet and the light gleamed on his shining body. I threw the door wide and he stepped through.

"As his head emerged into the light, I stepped back, almost involuntarily. There was a look of exaltation and wonder on it, such as I have never seen on a human face. The strange green eyes flashed, and there was a faint flush on the high cheekbones.  He looked like a man who has seen a vision of Paradise.

"He walked rather wearily, but firmly, over to the switch box, which he closed and locked.  Then he turned to me, still with that blaze of radiance on his face.

" 'All is well, my friend.  They are again at peace with men.  They have accepted me and the story of what has happened.  All will be well now, with my house, and with me.'

"I stared at him hard, but he said no more and began to divest himself of his incredible regalia.  He had one more thing to say, and I can hear it still as if it were yesterday, spoken almost as an afterthought.

" 'They say the blood of the guardians is getting too thin again.  But that also is settled.  I have seen my bride.' "

## FOR DISCUSSION: The Kings of the Sea

1. Many late nineteenth- and early twentieth-century writers told their stories through the person of an adventurer sitting comfortably among friends in a pleasant club.  Do you like this method of story-telling?  What are its advantages?  Its disadvantages?
2. Talented authors can sometimes chill their readers in a very few words.  Such a chilling statement is presented in this story:  "You see, I am a kind of game warden and some of my charges are loose."  Discuss the effects, in terms of the story, of the phrase *game warden* and the word *charges*.
3. Which details in this story are taken from old Norse legends?  How does the author make use of these details?
4. Is Nyderstrom's bride-to-be a natural or supernatural being?

# INTRODUCTION: Flies

In the following blend of science and the supernatural, the author leads the reader slowly into a situation involving a modern scientist and an ancient demon. The story illustrates the fact that the supernatural in fiction can, in capable hands, do without such atmospheric effects as creaking shutters on a deserted house or apparitions on the stairs in the middle of the night.

The story takes place at a college reunion where three men meet after not having seen each other for twenty years. While the men are discussing their present careers, there are two instances when the scene switches back to the characters' college days. These switches are called *flashbacks*. A flashback can be confusing if you do not realize that it has occurred, but you can identify these flashbacks by the extra space before and after them.

# Flies
## by Isaac Asimov

"Flies!" said Kendell Casey, wearily. He swung his arm. The fly circled, returned and nestled on Casey's shirtcollar.

From somewhere there sounded the buzzing of a second fly.

Dr. John Polen covered the slight uneasiness of his chin by moving his cigarette quickly to his lips.

He said, "I didn't expect to meet you, Casey. Or you, Winthrop. Or ought I call you Reverend Winthrop?"

"Ought I call you Professor Polen?" said Winthrop, carefully striking the proper vein of rich-toned friendship.

They were trying to snuggle into the cast-off shell of twenty years back, each one of them. Squirming and cramming and not fitting.

Damn, thought Polen fretfully, why do people attend college reunions?

Casey's hot blue eyes were still filled with the aimless anger of the college sophomore who has discovered intellect, frustration, and the tag ends of cynical philosophy all at once.

Casey! Bitter man of the campus!

He hadn't outgrown that. Twenty years later and it was Casey, bitter ex-man of the campus! Polen could see that in the way his fingertips moved aimlessly and in the manner of his spare body.

As for Winthrop? Well, twenty years older, softer, rounder. Skin pinker, eyes milder. Yet no nearer the quiet certainty he would never find. It was all there in the quick smile he never entirely abandoned, as though he feared there would be nothing to take its place, that its absence would turn his face into a smooth and featureless flush.

Polen was tired of reading the aimless flickering of a muscle's end; tired of usurping the place of his machines; tired of the too much they told him.

Could they read him as he read them? Could the small restlessness of his own eyes broadcast the fact that he was damp with the disgust that had bred mustily within him?

Damn, thought Polen, why didn't I stay away?

They stood there, all three, waiting for one another to say something, to flick something from across the gap and bring it, quivering, into the present.

Polen tried it. He said, "Are you still working in chemistry Casey?"

"In my own way, yes," said Casey, gruffly. "I'm not the scientist you're considered to be. I do research on insecticides for E. J. Link at Chatham."

Winthrop said, "Are you really? You said you would work on insecticides. Remember, Polen? And with all that, the flies dare still be after you, Casey?"

Casey said, "Can't get rid of them. I'm the best proving ground in the labs. No compound we've made keeps them away when I'm around. Someone once said it was my odor. I attract them."

Polen remembered the someone who had said that.

Winthrop said, "Or else—"

Polen felt it coming. He tensed.

"Or else," said Winthrop, "it's the curse, you know." His smile intensified to show that he was joking, that he forgave past grudges.

Damn, thought Polen, they haven't even changed the words. And the past came back.

"Flies," said Casey, swinging his arm, and slapping. "Ever see such a thing? Why don't they light on you two?"

Johnny Polen laughed at him. He laughed often then. "It's something in your body odor, Casey. You could be a boon to science. Find out the nature of the odorous chemical, concentrate it, mix it with DDT, and you've got the best fly-killer in the world."

"A fine situation. What do I smell like? A lady fly in heat? It's a shame they have to pick on me when the whole damned world's a dung heap."

Winthrop frowned and said with a faint flavor of rhetoric, "Beauty is not the only thing, Casey, in the eye of the beholder."

Casey did not deign a direct response. He said to Polen, "You know what Winthrop told me yesterday? He said those damned flies were the curse of Beelzebub."[1]

"I was joking," said Winthrop.

"Why Beelzebub?" asked Polen.

"It amounts to a pun," said Winthrop. "The ancient Hebrews used it as one of their many terms of derision for alien gods. It comes from *Ba'al*, meaning *lord* and *zevuv*, meaning *fly*. The lord of flies."

Casey said, "Come on, Winthrop, don't say you don't believe in Beelzebub."

"I believe in the existence of evil," said Winthrop, stiffly.

"I mean Beelzebub. Alive. Horns. Hooves. A sort of competition deity."

"Not at all." Winthrop grew stiffer. "Evil is a short-term affair. In the end it must lose—"

Polen changed the subject with a jar. He said, "I'll be doing graduate work for Venner, by the way. I talked with him day before yesterday, and he'll take me on."

"No! That's wonderful." Winthrop glowed and leaped to the subject-change instantly. He held out a hand with which to pump Polen's. He was always conscientiously eager to rejoice in another's good fortune. Casey often pointed that out.

Casey said, "Cybernetics[2] Venner? Well, if you can stand him, I suppose he can stand you."

Winthrop went on. "What did he think of your idea? Did you tell him your idea?"

"What idea?" demanded Casey.

Polen had avoided telling Casey so far. But now Venner had considered it and had passed it with a cool, "Interesting!" How could Casey's dry laughter hurt it now?

Polen said, "It's nothing much. Essentially, it's just a notion that emotion is the common bond of life, rather than reason or intellect. It's practically a truism, I suppose. You can't tell what a baby thinks or even *if* it thinks, but it's perfectly obvious that it can be angry, frightened or contented even when a week old. See?

"Same with animals. You can tell in a second if a dog is happy or if a

1. *Beelzebub*, the prince of devils, sometimes considered as being next to Satan in importance.
2. *cybernetics*, comparative study of the automatic control system formed by the nervous system and brain and by mechanical-electrical communication systems.

cat is afraid. The point is that their emotions are the same as those we would have under the same circumstances."

"So?" said Casey. "Where does it get you?"

"I don't know yet. Right now, all I can say is that emotions are universals. Now suppose we could properly analyze all the actions of men and certain familiar animals and equate them with the visible emotion. We might find a tight relationship. Emotion A might always involve Motion B. Then we could apply it to animals whose emotions we couldn't guess at by common sense alone. Like snakes, or lobsters."

"Or flies," said Casey, as he slapped viciously at another and flicked its remains off his wrist in furious triumph.

He went on. "Go ahead, Johnny. I'll contribute the flies and you study them. We'll establish a science of flychology and labor to make them happy by removing their neuroses. After all, we want the greatest good of the greatest number, don't we? And there are more flies than men."

"Oh, well," said Polen.

Casey said, "Say, Polen, did you ever follow up that weird idea of yours? I mean, we all know you're a shining cybernetic light, but I haven't been reading your papers. With so many ways of wasting time, something has to be neglected, you know."

"What idea?" asked Polen, woodenly.

"Come on. You know. Emotions of animals and all that sort of gug. Boy, those were the days. I used to know madmen. Now I only come across idiots."

Winthrop said, "That's right, Polen. I remember it very well. Your first year in graduate school you were working on dogs and rabbits. I believe you even tried some of Casey's flies."

Polen said, "It came to nothing in itself. It gave rise to certain new principles of computing, however, so it wasn't a total loss."

Why did they talk about it?

Emotions! What right had anyone to meddle with emotions? Words were invented to conceal emotions. It was the dreadfulness of raw emotion that had made language a basic necessity.

Polen knew. His machines had bypassed the screen of verbalization and dragged the unconscious into the sunlight. The boy and the girl, the son and the mother. For that matter, the cat and the mouse or the snake and the bird. The data rattled together in its universality and it had all poured into and through Polen until he could no longer bear the touch of life.

In the last few years he had so painstakingly schooled his thoughts in other directions. Now these two came, dabbling in his mind, stirring up its mud.

Casey batted abstractedly across the tip of his nose to dislodge a fly. "Too bad," he said. "I used to think you could get some fascinating things out of, say, rats. Well, maybe not fascinating, but then not as boring as the stuff you would get out of our somewhat-human beings. I used to think—"

Polen remembered what he used to think.

Casey said, "Damn this DDT. The flies feed on it, I think. You know, I'm going to do graduate work in chemistry and then get a job on insecticides. So help me. I'll personally get something that *will* kill the vermin."

They were in Casey's room, and it had a somewhat keroseny odor from the recently applied insecticide.

Polen shrugged and said, "A folded newspaper will always kill."

Casey detected a nonexistent sneer and said instantly, "How would you summarize your first year's work, Polen? I mean aside from the true summary any scientist could state if he dared, by which I mean: 'Nothing.'"

"Nothing," said Polen. "There's your summary."

"Go on," said Casey. "You use more dogs than the physiologists do and I bet the dogs mind the physiological experiments less. I would."

"Oh, leave him alone," said Winthrop. "You sound like a piano with eighty-seven keys eternally out of order. You're a bore!"

You couldn't say that to Casey.

He said, with sudden liveliness, looking carefully away from Winthrop, "I'll tell you what you'll probably find in animals, if you look closely enough. Religion."

"What the dickens!" said Winthrop, outraged. "That's a foolish remark."

Casey smiled. "Now, now, Winthrop. *Dickens* is just a euphemism for *devil* and you don't want to be swearing."

"Don't teach me morals. And don't be blasphemous."

"What's blasphemous about it? Why shouldn't a flea consider the dog as something to be worshiped? It's the source of warmth, food, and all that's good for a flea."

"I don't want to discuss it."

"Why not? Do you good. You could even say that to an ant, an anteater is a higher order of creation. He would be too big for them to comprehend, too mighty to dream of resisting. He would move among them like an unseen, inexplicable whirlwind, visiting them with destruction and death. But that wouldn't spoil things for the ants. They would reason that destruction was simply their just punishment for evil. And the anteater wouldn't even know he was a deity. Or care."

Winthrop had gone white. He said, "I know you're saying this only to annoy me and I am sorry to see you risking your soul for a moment's amusement. Let me tell you this," his voice trembled a little, "and let me say it very seriously. The flies that torment you are your punishment in this life. Beelzebub, like all the forces of evil, may think he does evil, but it's only the ultimate good after all. The curse of Beelzebub is on you for *your* good. Perhaps it will succeed in getting you to change your way of life before it's too late."

He ran from the room.

Casey watched him go. He said, laughing, "I told you Winthrop believed in Beelzebub. It's funny the respectable names you can give to superstition." His laughter died a little short of its natural end.

There were two flies in the room, buzzing through the vapors toward him.

Polen rose and left in heavy depression. One year had taught him little, but it was already too much, and his laughter was thinning. Only his machines could analyze the emotions of animals properly, but he was already guessing too deeply concerning the emotions of men.

He did not like to witness wild murder-yearnings where others could see only a few words of unimportant quarrel.

Casey said, suddenly, "Say, come to think of it, you did try some of my flies, the way Winthrop says. How about that?"

"Did I? After twenty years, I scarcely remember," murmured Polen.

Winthrop said, "You must. We were in your laboratory and you complained that Casey's flies followed him even there. He suggested you analyze them and you did. You recorded their motions and buzzings and wing-wiping for half an hour or more. You played with a dozen different flies."

Polen shrugged.

"Oh, well," said Casey. "It doesn't matter. It was good seeing you, old man." The hearty handshake, the thump on the shoulder, the broad grin—to Polen it all translated into sick disgust on Casey's part that Polen was a "success" after all.

Polen said, "Let me hear from you sometimes."

The words were dull thumps. They meant nothing. Casey knew that. Polen knew that. Everyone knew that. But words were meant to hide emotion and when they failed, humanity loyally maintained the pretence.

Winthrop's grasp of the hand was gentler. He said, "This brought back old times, Polen. If you're ever in Cincinnati, why don't you stop in at the meetinghouse? You'll always be welcome."

To Polen, it all breathed of the man's relief at Polen's obvious depression. Science, too, it seemed, was not the answer, and Winthrop's basic and ineradicable insecurity felt pleased at the company.

"I will," said Polen. It was the usual polite way of saying, I won't.

He watched them thread separately to other groups.

Winthrop would never know. Polen was sure of that. He wondered if Casey knew. It would be the supreme joke if Casey did not.

He *had* run Casey's flies, of course, not that once alone, but many times. Always the same answer! Always the same unpublishable answer.

With a cold shiver he could not quite control, Polen was suddenly conscious of a single fly loose in the room, veering aimlessly for a moment, then beating strongly and reverently in the direction Casey had taken a moment before.

Could Casey *not* know? Could it be the essence of the primal punishment that he never learn he was Beelzebub?

Casey! Lord of the Flies!

## FOR DISCUSSION: Flies

1. The author presents several scientific theories as part of his fictional framework. Identify one of them and discuss how such theorizing heightens the impact of the supernatural in the story.
2. Intellectual play is presented very deftly in this story without slowing down the narrative or including extraneous material. One example of such wordplay is Casey's comment, "Why shouldn't a flea consider the dog as something to be worshiped?" Identify another similar example.
3. Do you think this story would properly fit into this chapter if Beelzebub were omitted? If you do, support your answer with evidence from the story.
4. What fact does the author withhold in the story and present at the conclusion to dramatize his supernatural theory?

## INTRODUCTION: Young Goodman Brown

From an early American master of the short story comes this startling tale of the devil, damnation, and a dreamlike experience in the supernatural world. Although to our ears Hawthorne's language may sound a bit antique, all the elements of good storytelling are present in his tale, a still-timely one of the ongoing war between good and evil.

# Young Goodman Brown
## Nathaniel Hawthorne

Young Goodman Brown came forth at sunset into the street at Salem village; but put his head back, after crossing the threshold, to exchange a parting kiss with his young wife. And Faith, as the wife was aptly named, thrust her own pretty head into the street, letting the wind play with the pink ribbons of her cap while she called to Goodman Brown.

"Dearest heart," whispered she, softly and rather sadly, when her lips were close to his ear, "prithee put off your journey until sunrise and sleep in your own bed tonight. A lone woman is troubled with such dreams and such thoughts that she's afeard of herself sometimes. Pray tarry with me this night, dear husband, of all nights in the year."

"My love and my Faith," replied young Goodman Brown, "of all nights in the year, this one night must I tarry away from thee. My journey, as thou callest it, forth and back again, must needs be done 'twixt now and sunrise. What, my sweet, pretty wife, dost thou doubt me already, and we but three months married?"

"Then God bless you!" said Faith, with the pink ribbons; "and may you find all well when you come back."

"Amen!" cried Goodman Brown. "Say thy prayers, dear Faith, and go to bed at dusk, and no harm will come to thee."

So they parted; and the young man pursued his way until, being about to turn the corner by the meetinghouse, he looked back and saw the head of Faith still peeping after him with a melancholy air, in spite of her pink ribbons.

"Poor little Faith!" thought he, for his heart smote him. "What a wretch am I to leave her on such an errand! She talks of dreams, too. Methought as she spoke there was trouble in her face, as if a dream had warned her what work is to be done tonight. But no, no; 't would kill her to think it. Well, she's a blessed angel on earth; and after this one night I'll cling to her skirts and follow her to heaven."

With this excellent resolve for the future, Goodman Brown felt himself justified in making more haste on his present evil purpose. He had taken a dreary road, darkened by all the gloomiest trees of the forest, which barely stood aside to let the narrow path creep through, and closed immediately behind. It was all as lonely as could be; and there is this peculiarity in such a solitude, that the traveler knows not who may be concealed by the innumerable trunks and the thick boughs overhead; so that with lonely footsteps he may yet be passing through an unseen multitude.

"There may be a devilish Indian behind every tree," said Goodman Brown to himself; and he glanced fearfully behind him as he added, "What if the devil himself should be at my very elbow!"

His head being turned back, he passed a crook of the road, and, looking forward again, beheld the figure of a man, in grave and decent attire, seated at the foot of an old tree. He arose at Goodman Brown's approach and walked onward side by side with him.

"You are late, Goodman Brown," said he. "The clock of the Old South was striking as I came through Boston, and that is full fifteen minutes agone."

"Faith kept me back a while," replied the young man, with a tremor in his voice, caused by the sudden appearance of his companion, though not wholly unexpected.

It was now deep dusk in the forest, and deepest in that part of it where these two were journeying. As nearly as could be discerned, the second traveler was about fifty years old, apparently in the same rank of life as Goodman Brown, and bearing a considerable resemblance to him, though perhaps more in expression than features. Still they might have been taken for father and son. And yet, though the elder person was as simply clad as the younger, and as simple in manner too, he had an indescribable air of one who knew the world, and who would not have felt abashed at the governor's dinner table or in King William's court, were it possible that his affairs should call him thither. But the only thing about him that could be fixed upon as remarkable was his staff, which bore the likeness of a great black snake, so curiously wrought that it might almost be seen to twist and wriggle itself like a living serpent. This, of course, must have been an ocular deception, assisted by the uncertain light.

"Come, Goodman Brown," cried his fellow traveler, "this is a dull pace for the beginning of a journey. Take my staff, if you are so soon weary."

"Friend," said the other, exchanging his slow pace for a full stop, "having kept covenant by meeting thee here, it is my purpose now to return whence I came. I have scruples touching the matter thou wot'st of."

"Sayest thou so?" replied he of the serpent, smiling apart. "Let us walk on, nevertheless, reasoning as we go; and if I convince thee not thou shalt turn back. We are but a little way in the forest yet."

"Too far! too far!" exclaimed the goodman, unconsciously resuming his walk. "My father never went into the woods on such an errand, nor his father before him. We have been a race of honest men and good Christians since the days of the martyrs; and shall I be the first of the name of Brown that ever took this path and kept—"

"Such company, thou wouldst say," observed the elder person, interpreting his pause. "Well said, Goodman Brown! I have been as well acquainted with your family as with ever a one among the Puritans; and that's no trifle to say. I helped your grandfather, the constable, when he lashed the Quaker woman so smartly through the streets of Salem; and it was I that brought your father a pitch-pine knot, kindled at my own hearth, to set fire to an Indian village, in King Philip's war. They were my good friends, both; and many a pleasant walk have we had along this path, and returned merrily after midnight. I would fain be friends with you for their sake."

"If it be as thou sayest," replied Goodman Brown, "I marvel they never spoke of these matters; or, verily, I marvel not, seeing that the least rumor of the sort would have driven them from New England. We are a people of prayer, and good works to boot, and abide no such wickedness."

"Wickedness or not," said the traveler with the twisted staff, "I have a very general acquaintance here in New England. The deacons of many a church have drunk the communion wine with me; the selectmen of divers towns make me their chairman; and a majority of the Great and General Court are firm supporters of my interest. The governor and I, too—But these are state secrets."

"Can this be so?" cried Goodman Brown, with a stare of amazement at his undisturbed companion. "Howbeit, I have nothing to do with the governor and council; they have their own ways, and are no rule for a simple husbandman like me. But, were I to go on with thee, how should I meet the eye of that good old man, our minister, at Salem village? Oh, his voice would make me tremble both Sabbath day and lecture day."

Thus far the elder traveler had listened with due gravity; but now burst into a fit of irrepressible mirth, shaking himself so violently that his snakelike staff actually seemed to wriggle in sympathy.

"Ha! ha! ha!" shouted he again and again; then composing himself, "Well, go on, Goodman Brown, go on; but, prithee, don't kill me with laughing."

"Well, then, to end the matter at once," said Goodman Brown, considerably nettled, "there is my wife, Faith. It would break her dear little heart; and I'd rather break my own."

"Nay, if that be the case," answered the other, "e'en go thy ways, Goodman Brown. I would not for twenty old women like the one hobbling before us that Faith should come to any harm."

As he spoke he pointed his staff at a female figure on the path, in whom Goodman Brown recognized a very pious and exemplary dame, who had taught him his catechism in youth, and was still his moral and spiritual adviser, jointly with the minister and Deacon Gookin.

"A marvel, truly, that Goody Cloyse should be so far in the wilderness at nightfall," said he. "But with your leave, friend, I shall take a cut through the woods until we have left this Christian woman behind. Being a stranger to you, she might ask whom I was consorting with and whither I was going."

"Be it so," said his fellow traveler. "Betake you the woods, and let me keep the path."

Accordingly the young man turned aside, but took care to watch his companion, who advanced softly along the road until he had come within a staff's length of the old dame. She, meanwhile, was making the best of her way, with singular speed for so aged a woman, and mumbling some indistinct words—a prayer, doubtless—as she went. The traveler put forth his staff and touched her withered neck with what seemed the serpent's tail.

"The devil!" screamed the pious old lady.

"Then Goody Cloyse knows her old friend?" observed the traveler, confronting her and leaning on his writhing stick.

"Ah, forsooth, and is it your worship indeed?" cried the good dame. "Yea, truly is it, and in the very image of my old gossip, Goodman Brown, the grandfather of the silly fellow that now is. But—would your worship believe it?—my broomstick hath strangely disappeared, stolen, as I suspect, by that unhanged witch, Goody Cory, and that, too, when I was all anointed with the juice of smallage, and cinquefoil, and wolfsbane—"

"Mingled with fine wheat and the fat of a newborn babe," said the shape of old Goodman Brown.

"Ah, your worship knows the recipe," cried the old lady, cackling aloud. "So, as I was saying, being all ready for the meeting, and no horse to ride on, I made up my mind to foot it; for they tell me there is a nice young man to be taken into communion tonight. But now your good worship will lend me your arm, and we shall be there in a twinkling."

"That can hardly be," answered her friend. "I may not spare you my arm, Goody Cloyse; but here is my staff, if you will."

So saying, he threw it down at her feet, where, perhaps, it assumed life, being one of the rods which its owner had formerly lent to the Egyptian magi. Of this fact, however, Goodman Brown could not take cognizance. He had cast up his eyes in astonishment, and, looking down again, beheld neither Goody Cloyse nor the serpentine staff, but this fellow traveler alone, who waited for him as calmly as if nothing had happened.

"That old woman taught me my catechism," said the young man; and there was a world of meaning in this simple comment.

They continued to walk onward, while the elder traveler exhorted his companion to make good speed and persevere in the path, discoursing so aptly that his arguments seemed rather to spring up in the bosom of his auditor than to be suggested by himself. As they went, he plucked a branch of maple to serve for a walking stick, and began to strip it of the twigs and little boughs, which were wet with evening dew. The moment his fingers touched them they became strangely withered and dried up as with a week's sunshine. Thus the pair proceeded, at a good free pace, until suddenly, in a gloomy hollow of the road, Goodman Brown sat himself down on the stump of a tree and refused to go any farther.

"Friend," said he, stubbornly, "my mind is made up. Not another step will I budge on this errand. What if a wretched old woman do choose to go to the devil when I thought she was going to heaven: is that any reason why I should quit my dear Faith and go after her?"

"You will think better of this by and by," said his acquaintance, composedly. "Sit here and rest yourself a while; and when you feel like moving again, there is my staff to help you along."

Without more words, he threw his companion the maple stick, and was as speedily out of sight as if he had vanished into the deepening gloom. The young man sat a few moments by the roadside, applauding himself greatly, and thinking with how clear a conscience he should meet the minister in his morning walk, nor shrink from the eye of good old Deacon Gookin. And what calm sleep would be his that very night, which was to have been spent so wickedly, but so purely and sweetly now, in the arms of Faith! Amidst these pleasant and praiseworthy meditations, Goodman Brown heard the tramp of horses along the road, and deemed it advisable to conceal himself within the verge of the forest, conscious of the guilty purpose that had brought him thither, though now so happily turned from it.

On came the hoof tramps and the voices of the riders, two grave old voices, conversing soberly as they drew near. These mingled sounds appeared to pass along the road, within a few yards of the young man's hiding place; but, owing doubtless to the depth of the gloom at that particular spot, neither the travelers nor their steeds were visible. Though their figures brushed the small boughs by the wayside, it could not be seen that they intercepted, even for a moment, the faint gleam from the strip of bright sky athwart which they must have passed. Goodman Brown alternately crouched and stood on tiptoe, pulling aside the branches and thrusting forth his head as far as he durst without discerning so much as a shadow. It vexed him the more, because he could have sworn, were such a thing possible, that he recognized the voices of the minister and Deacon Gookin, jogging along quietly, as they were wont to do, when bound to some ordination or ecclesiastical council. While yet within hearing, one of the riders stopped to pluck a switch.

"Of the two, reverend sir," said the voice like the deacon's, "I had rather miss an ordination dinner than tonight's meeting. They tell me that some of our community are to be here from Falmouth and beyond, and others from Connecticut and Rhode Island, besides several of the Indian powwows, who, after their fashion, know almost as much deviltry as the best of us. Moreover, there is a goodly young woman to be taken into communion."

"Mighty well, Deacon Gookin!" replied the solemn old tones of the minister. "Spur up, or we shall be late. Nothing can be done, you know, until I get on the ground."

The hoofs clattered again; and the voices, talking so strangely in the empty air, passed on through the forest, where no church had ever been gathered or solitary Christian prayed. Whither, then, could these holy men be journeying so deep into the heathen wilderness? Young Goodman Brown caught hold of a tree for support, being ready to sink down on the ground, faint and overburdened with the heavy sickness of his heart. He looked up to the sky, doubting whether there really was a heaven above him. Yet there was the blue arch, and the stars brightening in it.

"With heaven above and Faith below, I will yet stand firm against the devil!" cried Goodman Brown.

While he still gazed upward into the deep arch of the firmament and had lifted his hands to pray, a cloud, though no wind was stirring, hurried across the zenith and hid the brightening stars. The blue sky was still visible, except directly overhead, where this black mass of cloud was sweeping swiftly northward. Aloft in the air, as if from the depths of the cloud, came a confused and doubtful sound of voices. Once the listener fancied that he could distinguish the accents of townspeople of his own, men and women, both pious and ungodly, many of whom he had met at the communion table, and had seen others rioting at the tavern. The next moment, so indistinct were the sounds, he doubted whether he had heard aught but the murmur of the old forest, whispering without a wind. Then came a stronger swell of those familiar tones, heard daily in the sunshine at Salem village, but never until now from a cloud of night. There was one voice, of a young woman, uttering lamentations, yet with an uncertain sorrow, and entreating for some favor, which, perhaps, it would grieve her to obtain; and all the unseen multitude, both saints and sinners, seemed to encourage her onward.

"Faith!" shouted Goodman Brown, in a voice of agony and desperation; and the echoes of the forest mocked him, crying, "Faith! Faith!" as if bewildered wretches were seeking her all through the wilderness.

The cry of grief, rage, and terror was yet piercing the night, when the unhappy husband held his breath for a response. There was a scream, drowned immediately in a louder murmur of voices, fading into far-off laughter, as the dark cloud swept away, leaving the clear and silent sky above Goodman Brown. But something fluttered lightly down through the air and caught on the branch of a tree. The young man seized it, and beheld a pink ribbon.

"My Faith is gone!" cried he, after one stupefied moment. "There is no good on earth; and sin is but a name. Come, devil; for to thee is this world given."

And, maddened with despair, so that he laughed loud and long, did Goodman Brown grasp his staff and set forth again, at such a rate that he seemed to fly along the forest path rather than to walk or run. The road grew wilder and drearier and more faintly traced, and vanished at length, leaving him in the heart of the dark wilderness, still rushing onward with the instinct that guides mortal man to evil. The whole forest was peopled with frightful sounds—the creaking of the trees, the howling of wild beasts, and the yell of Indians; while sometimes the wind tolled like a distant church bell, and sometimes gave a broad roar around the traveler, as if all Nature were laughing him to scorn. But he was himself the chief horror of the scene, and shrank not from its other horrors.

"Ha! ha! ha!" roared Goodman Brown when the wind laughed at him. "Let us hear which will laugh loudest. Think not to frighten me with your deviltry. Come witch, come wizard, come Indian powwow, come devil himself, and here comes Goodman Brown. You may as well fear him as he fear you."

In truth, all through the haunted forest there could be nothing more frightful than the figure of Goodman Brown. On he flew among the black pines, brandishing his staff with frenzied gestures, now giving vent to an inspiration of horrid blasphemy, and now shouting forth such laughter as set all the echoes of the forest laughing like demons around him. The fiend in his own shape is less hideous than when he rages in the breast of man. Thus sped the demoniac on his course, until, quivering among the trees, he saw a red light before him, as when the felled trunks and branches of a clearing have been set on fire, and throw up their lurid blaze against the sky, at the hour of midnight. He paused, in a lull of the tempest that had driven him onward, and heard the swell of what seemed a hymn, rolling solemnly from a distance with the weight of many voices. He knew the tune; it was a familiar one in the choir of the village meetinghouse. The verse died heavily away, and was lengthened by a chorus, not of human voices, but of all the sounds of the benighted wilderness pealing in awful harmony together. Goodman Brown cried out, and his cry was lost to his own ear by its unison with the cry of the desert.

In the interval of silence he stole forward until the light glared full upon his eyes. At one extremity of an open space, hemmed in by the dark wall of the forest, arose a rock, bearing some rude, natural resemblance either to an altar or a pulpit, and surrounded by four blazing pines, their tops aflame, their stems untouched, like candles at an evening meeting. The mass of foliage that had overgrown the summit of the rock was all on fire, blazing high into the night and fitfully illuminating the whole field. Each pendant twig and leafy festoon was in a blaze. As the red light arose and fell, a numerous congregation alternately shone forth, then disappeared in shadow, and again grew, as it were, out of the darkness, peopling the heart of the solitary woods at once.

"A grave and dark-clad company," quoth Goodman Brown.

In truth they were such. Among them, quivering to and fro between gloom and splendor, appeared faces that would be seen next day at the council board of the province, and others which, Sabbath after Sabbath, looked devoutly heavenward, and benignantly over the crowded pews, from the holiest pulpits in the land. Some affirm that the lady of the governor was there. At least there were high dames well known to her, and wives of honored husbands, and widows, a great multitude, and ancient maidens, all of excellent repute, and fair young girls, who trembled lest their mothers should espy them. Either the sudden gleams of light flashing over the obscure field bedazzled Goodman Brown, or he recognized a score of the church members of Salem village famous for their especial sanctity. Good old Deacon Gookin had arrived, and waited at the skirts of that venerable saint, his revered pastor. But, irreverently consorting with these grave, reputable, and pious people, these elders of the church, these chaste dames and dewy virgins, there were men of dissolute lives and women of spotted fame, wretches given over to all mean and filthy vice, and suspected even of horrid crimes. It was strange to see that the good shrank not from the wicked, nor were the sinners abashed by the saints. Scattered also among their pale-faced enemies were the Indian priests, or powwows, who had often scared their native forest with more hideous incantations than any known to English witchcraft.

"But where is Faith?" thought Goodman Brown; and, as hope came into his heart, he trembled.

Another verse of the hymn arose, a slow and mournful strain, such as the pious love, but joined to words which expressed all that our nature can conceive of sin, and darkly hinted at far more. Unfathomable to mere mortals is the lore of fiends. Verse after verse was sung; and still the chorus of the desert swelled between like the deepest tone of a mighty organ; and with the final peal of that dreadful anthem there came a sound, as if the roaring wind, the rushing streams, the howling beasts, and every other voice of the unconcerted wilderness were mingling and according with the voice of guilty man in homage to the prince of all. The four blazing pines threw up a loftier flame, and obscurely discovered shapes and visages of horror on the smoke wreaths above the impious assembly. At the same moment the fire on the rock shot redly forth and formed a glowing arch above its base, where now appeared a figure. With reverence be it spoken, the figure bore no slight similitude, both in garb and manner, to some grave divine of the New England churches.

"Bring forth the converts!" cried a voice that echoed through the field and rolled into the forest.

At the word, Goodman Brown stepped forth from the shadow of the trees and approached the congregation, with whom he felt a loathful brotherhood by the sympathy of all that was wicked in his heart. He could have well-nigh sworn that the shape of his own dead father beckoned him to advance, looking downward from a smoke wreath, while a woman, with dim features of despair, threw out her hand to warn him back. Was it his mother? But he had no power to retreat one step, nor to resist, even in thought, when the minister and good old Deacon Gookin seized his arms and led him to the blazing rock. Thither came also the slender form of a veiled female, led between Goody Cloyse, that pious teacher of the catechism, and Martha Carrier, who had received the devil's promise to be queen of hell. A rampant hag was she. And there stood the proselytes beneath the canopy of fire.

"Welcome, my children," said the dark figure, "to the communion of your race. Ye have found thus young your nature and your destiny. My children, look behind you!"

They turned; and flashing forth, as it were, in a sheet of flame, the fiend worshipers were seen; the smile of welcome gleamed darkly on every visage.

"There," resumed the sable form, "are all whom ye have reverenced from youth. Ye deemed them holier than yourselves, and shrank from your own sin, contrasting it with their lives of righteousness and prayerful aspirations heavenward. Yet here are they all in my worshiping assembly. This night it shall be granted you to know their secret deeds: how hoary-bearded elders of the church have whispered wanton words to the young maids of their households; how many a woman, eager for widows' weeds, has given her husband a drink at bedtime and let him sleep his last sleep in her bosom; how beardless youths have made haste to inherit their fathers' wealth; and how fair damsels—blush not, sweet ones—have dug little graves in the garden, and bidden me, the sole guest, to an infant's funeral. By the sympathy of your human hearts for sin ye shall scent out all the places—whether in church, bedchamber, street, field, or forest—where crime has been committed, and shall exult to behold the whole earth one stain of guilt, one mighty blood spot. Far more than this. It shall be yours to penetrate, in every bosom, the deep mystery of sin, the fountain of all wicked arts, and which inexhaustibly supplies more evil impulses than human power—than my power at its utmost—can make manifest in deeds. And now, my children, look upon each other."

They did so; and, by the blaze of the hell-kindled torches, the wretched man beheld his Faith, and the wife her husband, trembling before that unhallowed altar.

"Lo, there ye stand, my children," said the figure, in a deep and solemn tone, almost sad with its despairing awfulness, as if his once angelic nature could yet mourn for our miserable race. "Depending upon one another's hearts, ye had still hoped that virtue were not all a dream. Now are ye undeceived. Evil is the nature of mankind. Evil must be your only happiness. Welcome again, my children, to the communion of your race."

"Welcome," repeated the fiend worshipers, in one cry of despair and triumph.

And there they stood, the only pair, as it seemed, who were yet hesitating on the verge of wickedness in this dark world. A basin was hollowed, naturally, in the rock. Did it contain water, reddened by the lurid light? or was it blood? or, perchance, a liquid flame? Herein did the shape of evil dip his hand and prepare to lay the mark of baptism upon their foreheads, that they might be partakers of the mystery of sin, more conscious of the secret guilt of others, both in deed and thought, than they could now be of their own. The husband cast one look at his pale wife, and Faith at him. What polluted wretches would the next glance show them to each other, shuddering alike at what they disclosed and what they saw!

"Faith! Faith!" cried the husband, "look up to heaven, and resist the wicked one."

Whether Faith obeyed he knew not. Hardly had he spoken when he found himself amid calm night and solitude, listening to a roar of the wind which died heavily away through the forest. He staggered against the rock, and felt it chill and damp; while a hanging twig, that had been all on fire, besprinkled his cheek with the coldest dew.

The next morning young Goodman Brown came slowly into the street of Salem village, staring around him like a bewildered man. The good old minister was taking a walk along the graveyard to get an appetite for breakfast and meditate his sermon, and bestowed a blessing, as he passed, on Goodman Brown. He shrank from the venerable saint as if to avoid an anathema. Old Deacon Gookin was at domestic worship, and the holy words of his prayer were heard through the open window. "What God doth the wizard pray to?" quoth Goodman Brown. Goody Cloyse, that excellent old Christian, stood in the early sunshine at her own lattice, catechizing a little girl who had brought her a pint of morning's milk. Goodman Brown snatched away the child as from the grasp of the fiend himself. Turning the corner by the meetinghouse, he spied the head of Faith, with the pink ribbons, gazing anxiously forth, and bursting into such joy at sight of him that she skipped along the street and almost kissed her husband before the whole village. But Goodman Brown looked sternly and sadly into her face, and passed on without a greeting.

Had Goodman Brown fallen asleep in the forest and only dreamed a wild dream of a witch-meeting?

Be it so if you will; but, alas! it was a dream of evil omen for young Goodman Brown. A stern, a sad, a darkly meditative, a distrustful, if not a desperate man did he become from the night of that fearful dream. On the Sabbath day, when the congregation were singing a holy psalm, he could not listen because an anthem of sin rushed loudly upon his ear and drowned all the blessed strain. When the minister spoke from the pulpit with power and fervid eloquence, and, with his hand on the open Bible, of the sacred truths of our religion, and of saintlike lives and triumphant deaths, and of future bliss or misery unutterable, then did Goodman Brown turn pale, dreading lest the roof should thunder down upon the gray blasphemer and his hearers. Often, awaking suddenly at midnight, he shrank from the bosom of Faith; and at morning or eventide, when the family knelt down at prayer, he scowled and muttered to himself, and gazed sternly at his wife, and turned away. And when he had lived long, and was borne to his grave a hoary corpse, followed by Faith, an aged woman, and children and grandchildren, a goodly procession, besides neighbors not a few, they carved no hopeful verse upon his tombstone, for his dying hour was gloom.

## FOR DISCUSSION: Young Goodman Brown

1. Did Goodman Brown actually see what he thought he did or was it some form of hallucination? Which details in the story support either of these interpretations?

2. Irony, a contradiction between what one expects something to be and what it actually turns out to be, is a key element in Hawthorne's story.  It extends even to the given name of Goodman Brown's wife. Explain.
3. Irony also touches the morality of Hawthorne's Salem.  To what extent are the people different from what they seem or from how they would wish us to see them?  How does the author make us feel about this discrepancy?
4. When the fiend worshipers cry "Welcome," why do you suppose the author calls it "one cry of despair and triumph"?  Is this not a contradiction in terms?
5. Can you find examples of humor on the part of the author in the story?  In what way do such light moments enhance or detract from the story?

# INTRODUCTION: None Before Me

In the previous story, we witnessed Nathaniel Hawthorne poking holes in the accepted fabric of morality as preached, if not practiced, in Salem village. Now we turn our attention to a more modern author who manages to have some fun despite his seriousness of purpose with the ideas of man, God, and their interrelationship. In this story, you will find many lines which have meanings on at least two levels. In some cases, more than two meanings can be ascribed to the lines. It is this deliberate ambiguity when used by a skilled author which enhances and enriches his seemingly simple story.

# None Before Me
## Sidney Carroll

John Olney Gresham had time, inclination, and money enough to be a connoisseur. He also had the correct instinct: He was a born miser. What he kept, he kept to himself alone. The privacy of property was his first passion and possibly his last. His earliest memories did not include a mother, father, sisters, brothers, nor even relatives of any proximity whatsoever. He had never had a sweetheart. Now in his last lonely days, he had neither wife nor kin. He had only his collection, his large house (somewhat on the baroque brownstone side), and servants. These were old and quiet and capable, never offering—never daring—to speak one unnecessary word to the master. Gresham timed his movement to the heavy gold watch in his pocket—a time for waking, a time for eating, a time for stepping from the dusty tranquillity of his den into the abominable traffic of the world and thence to the little shops where he did his trading, and a time for spending endless hours with his collection.

Gresham was a man who had improvised the main strategy of his life and then stuck ponderously to the stratagem. Connoisseurship had been a whim with him back in the long ago, and he had devoted his life to it. One nameless day in his monotone life he had seen an ivory figurine in a store window. Its simple symmetry had appealed to him. He had haggled over the price, bought the figurine, taken it home to study it, and he had suddenly become a collector of ivory. That had been the first whim. It had taken him for the first time out of the aimless rich young man's existence into the shops of the town. But once he invaded the shops he discovered a world far beyond the one he had bargained for. He discovered that ivory is a world unto itself, that as it gets more and more expensive it gets better and better. Immediately, therefore, Gresham acquired the most expensive piece of ivory carving in the world. Then he discovered that bagging the fox in the first five minutes destroys the very purpose—the thrill of the hunt. So the second whim seized him, in the form of the one inspiration of his life. Why not (it was such a simple notion after all—why had it never occurred to anybody else?) why not acquire the best single piece of anything in *any* line? Ivory was simply one kind of hunting; he had conquered it with one bold stroke. There were still diamonds to collect, and coral, and paintings, and tapestries, and—*pah!* there must be many things. So Gresham started to collect the best of anything in any line. His life was consecrated to it.

Thus it was that a certain Mr. Pegerine felt safe in his own mind one day when he called Gresham at the one time of the day when the servants were allowed to answer the phone. "I would speak to Mr. Gresham," said Pegerine, who was master of, among other things, the archaic speech of his calling. "Whom shall I say is on the telephone?" asked the servant. "Mr. Pegerine, dealer in Unusual Antiquities." Gresham came to the phone. "Yes? What is it?"

"Mr. Gresham, I have for you—something—the rarest, the most unusual. There is nothing like it in the entire world."

"What is it?"

"Mr. Gresham, I would really and truly prefer not to say. An item like this—it requires an effect of surprise. It must not be described beforehand."

"Bring it up. Tomorrow at four."

"Mr. Gresham, for this one time, you must come to my place. It is a large item. It is delicate. It is not possible to transport it indiscriminately. If it were not necessary, I would not—"

"Very well. Tomorrow at four. I'll be at your place."

"Thank you, Mr. Gresham."

When Gresham got to Pegerine's the next day, promptly, of course, on the stroke of four, old Pegerine led him into the back room. There it was. On an Empire table at which six people could eat with comfort, it stood.

It was the most magnificent doll's house in the world.

It was slightly under five feet high. Even to an innocent eye it was obviously perfect, marvelously perfect in every detail. It was an old European sort of house, almost square, with four doors and a gable roof covered with chimneys. A stork in a nest snuggled against one of the chimneys. The entire facade of the house had been swung open on hinges. Eighteen rooms were thus exposed, and the effect, on the closest scrutiny, was almost frightening in its perfection of detail. The tiny pictures on the walls, the silver service in the dining room, the linens in the closets, the rugs, the mullioned windows, the doors and the doorknobs— all these seemed to mock the perfection of the life-size world.

"The rugs were made by Aubusson," said Pegerine. "The little paintings—" He pointed at them with a slender gold pencil, "—are miniatures by Fragonard, Greuze, Watteau ... and here—just here—one by Vigée-Lebrun, the only miniature she ever painted. Worth a fortune in itself. Signed. The scale is actually one-twelfth actual size, one inch equals one foot. The house in reality would be approximately fifty feet high, ten feet to each floor and another ten for the roof. Each pane of glass in each window is bevelled, every mirror is in a solid gold frame, every gold frame is set with precious stones. Notice, please, where I point the pencil— the detail in the wallpaper. It should be examined with a glass. Now take the glassware. Crystal, every piece of it. The dishes were made originally for the second child of Marie Antoinette. I have the papers. Now notice the people. . . ."

And truly the little people in these little rooms were the most astonishing of all.

It is a perverse fact that of all the images man continues to make of man, the one which resembles him the least is the one which is intended to resemble him the most—namely, the doll. Nobody can make a doll that looks as if it breathes. But the artisan who had fashioned the tiny inhabitants of this extraordinary house had come close to the secret, small as his creatures were. In the living room on the ground floor, an aged grandmother sat in a rocking chair, with four children seated at her feet. The skin of the grandmother's face was veined at the temples. The wrinkles at her eyes had flickering shadows. She held a piece of knitting. Her hands were brown and waxen and bony, and the flesh and the grace of old fingers had been so scrupulously copied that they looked remarkably nimble; you would expect to hear, momentarily, the clicking of the knitting needles. The children around the grandmother, gazing up at her with loving admiration, were unique personalities, each with a different expression on his half-inch face. In an upstairs room an infant slept in a cradle shaped like a swan. The child slept; it truly slept. Flights of angels were painted on the walls of the room.

"Notice the wood paneling," said Pegerine, bending over. But by that time Pegerine knew there was really no need for him to play the guide on a conducted tour any longer. He had seen the expression on Gresham's face. He knew he had made the sale.

"Tell me," said Gresham, trying to stifle his excitement. "This sort of thing—I mean now—doll houses . . ."

"One of the oldest of the arts, Mr. Gresham. One of the most respected. Archeology shows that in the oldest civilizations the inhabitants of the earth built doll houses. Toys! This is the ultimate in toy making! Is there anyone who doubts that toy making is a major art?"

"I wouldn't know," Gresham snapped.

"It is true, sir. One of the oldest of the arts, and here, before you, the finest specimen ever made. Not the largest, that is obvious. Not the most ornate—there are complete models of Fontainebleau in existence. But the finest, beyond any doubt the finest."

"How would I know that?"

"I will guarantee it. Written down."

"All right, I'll buy it."

"Very good, Mr. Gresham."

"On one condition."

"Yes, Mr. Gresham?"

"If I ever find a better one I want my money back."

"With pleasure, Mr. Gresham."

It was transported, with infinite pains, to Gresham's house. He had it placed in the den, in the very center of the room.

The den was a museum to shame museums. It is unfortunate that after Gresham's death the room was disassembled piece by piece and raffled off to the bidders. The two hundred pieces it once contained now grace some two hundred dens and museums in two hundred parts of the world; the monstrous luxuriance of that room is lost forever. In its original entirety it was fantastic. Gresham had the world's most expensive pieces of ivory, a diamond the peer of the Koh-i-noor, an emerald statuette four inches high, a Da Vinci madonna, a Shakespeare quarto, and so forth and so forth. The priceless et cetera of Gresham's life was arranged in glass cases, or leather boxes, or under lock and key, and Gresham fondled them, one by one, every day of his life. He was everything the ideal connoisseur must be—rich man, miser, haggler. He was also (and this is important) a great lover. He fondled his pieces with his eyes, his hands, even his lips. Every morning he had flowers distributed through the den. The diamond, the emerald, the ivory gave him all the ecstasy of the blood his fat body could stand. Into the very middle of this inanimate harem Gresham placed the wonderful doll's house.

It was placed upon a sturdy table, so that anybody sitting in front of it had an excellent eye-level view of most of it. Its position in the center of the den was, in its singular way, symbolic. In very little time the doll's house became the center of Gresham's life.

He started by devoting the better part of a whole day to it. He sat in a chair with his hands clasped over his capacious middle, staring at the little objects one by one with placid and puffy eyes. The eyes moved slowly behind the eyeglasses, selecting the single objects to study, then focusing. He sat in the chair until he had memorized the position, the appearance, the personality of every object in every room.  He did not touch a thing.

On the second day he began to touch.  His short heavy fingers were not skillful in the ordinary uses of fingers.  In a word, he was clumsy.  Fortunately, he knew it.  He was careful.  Delicately, as delicately as he could, he reached out and felt the texture of the rugs, the surface of the wood paneling on the library walls, the silken edge of a fringe on a beautiful lamp.  His pudgy fingers floated through the exquisite rooms like pink balloons.  It was enough to frighten the little people.  He did not touch *them*.  He did not dare.  They were so fragile and so perfect.  He shrank from the terrible prospect of harming them in the least degree.

On the third day he began to touch the little people.

Now Pegerine counted it the finest day's work of his career when he sold the doll's house.  His profit from the deal was enormous.  He had wild thoughts that night.  Gresham was his client now, his friend.  He could sell the absurd old fat man many things now.  All a man like Pegerine needs is one such client.  Now, he could comb the cellars and the collections of the city, the world, and pick the finest and the best—and he could sell it all to Gresham.  A man who would spend that kind of money for a doll's house would spend money for anything.  Pegerine's dreams ran high that night.  He had no inkling of the fact that he had lost for all time the best customer he had ever had.

None of the dealers in the city ever knew what happened, least of all Pegerine.  Mr. Gresham suddenly stopped buying.  Whenever the dealers called the house at the appointed hour they were politely informed that Mr. Gresham was "not in the market for things, not any more, thank you."  Did that mean forever?  Yes, thank you, it meant forever.  No, Mr. Gresham was not ill.  No, he was not planning a trip.  Nobody could understand it, least of all Pegerine.  None of them ever had the slightest suspicion of the fact that it was Pegerine who had slain the goose.

For the truth of the matter is that when Gresham began to play with his doll's house, he found what he had been looking for all his life.  The search of the old orphan was over.  Here it was—a real home, and family, and children to do his bidding.  The more he played with the doll's house, that fat, ungenerous, niggardly old man, the more he reverted to childhood.

He locked the doors of his den, for he wanted no intruding servants to discover him at the game.  If a servant happened to discover him fondling a precious stone it would have caused him no embarrassment, but to have somebody find him playing with dolls would have thrown him into a fit.  So he would have his breakfast early, then go upstairs to the den, lock the door, pull the chair up to the doll's house, and begin to play.  At first he did it only in the mornings.  In the afternoons, after lunch, he would devote himself to the other parts of his collection. But the doll's house drew him more and more, and he became impatient with everything else, like a child who cannot eat lunch in the intensity of his desire to have done and get back to his toys, and soon he gave up the rest of the collection altogether. He now devoted himself, morning, noon, and night, to the doll's house. The diamond lay forgotten in its velvet bed, there were no more caresses for the ivory. Gresham's whole life was in the doll's house.

When his fingers became more accustomed to the little things, he let his fancy roam. For the first time in his life, Gresham played games. He began to rearrange the furniture, to rehang the pictures, to move the tiny rugs about. He exchanged andirons from the fireplace on the fourth floor with those from a fireplace on the second. But most of all and best of all he played with the little people. He moved the children in the parlor so that they all surrounded the grandmother instead of facing her. He liked it that way for a week, then he put them back again. In the kitchen a tiny buxom servant, all in white, stood bending over the wood stove. Gresham moved her so that she stood over the sink instead. He kept her there. The baby in the swan bed he did not touch at all. He liked it where it was, under the lovely flight of angels. There were other people in the other rooms, men and women and children. These he deployed and maneuvered. He became the ultimate in interior decorators: He could arrange the inhabitants of the house, put them and keep them where they looked best to him.

In a short time Gresham began to talk to himself. At least, the servants passing in the hall, passing swiftly and discreetly past the den, hearing his voice making an unaccustomed cooing sound, assumed he was talking to himself. This they did not take amiss. Anything might be expected from Mr. Gresham. Talking to himself in the privacy of his most private chamber was quickly and tacitly accepted as simply one more eccentricity. But the truth of the matter was that Gresham was not talking to himself. He was conversing with the little people.

"Now," he said, as he tipped the grandmother lightly back in her rocker and made her swing back and forth. "Isn't that comfy?" He sat there, tipping the rocker every time it gave signs of stopping in its arc. Slyly, swiftly, he would lift his eyes from the grandmother in the parlor, and aim his glance at the master bedroom. "What! Johnny, Mary— *kissing!* Soon as my back is turned?" With admonishments he would turn John and Mary back to back. "Don't want anybody hurt around here," he would say, slyly.

With the children he was just as solicitous. He soon gave names to each one of them, and he coddled them until they might have been the most spoiled brats in Christendom. "Emma," he would say, "did you enjoy your lunch today?" For he had gotten into the habit of moving the children and their elders into the dining room at meal hours, sitting them in their proper places, and changing the plates and removing the silver for every pretended course. He stopped short only at serving them food. He preserved his sanity to that extent. At night, however, he moved every one of the little people into beds in the various bedrooms, and in the morning he awakened them with a cheery "Gooood morning!"

Seven weeks of this and Gresham began to evolve his theory.

It was a simple theory. When one comes to examine it in the light of all pertinent facts, it was almost a natural theory. Gresham began to figure that he was God.

Why not? He had purchased, for an exorbitant fee, a world of his own. The creatures in it he owned body and soul. Over these creatures he exercised an authority complete, unquestioned, irrevocable. His hand moving among these walls was—why not?—the hand of Destiny.

What is the meaning of Destiny? Whatever the words that describe it, in whatever definition, it always has some secret concern with the future. Then the hand that controls the future—is it not the very hand of Destiny? Only in Gresham's brain, only on Gresham's sufferance, did the future of the little people exist. Gresham's pudgy fingers moved through the rooms, arranging furniture, and liaisons, and lives, with the tender mercy of a benevolent god. What *was* he, then, but God Almighty to this household, this world, this universe of his very own?

Thus the theory took shape, thus it rolled around in his brain, gathering momentum. He drew a picture for himself: he conceived of the world as a series of worlds one within the other, each with its own god, and the gods growing progressively larger, and interlocking, like one of those astounding Oriental balls within balls. Gresham was god of the doll's house, another was god of Gresham's world, and another was god of that god. No—it wasn't so much like an Oriental ball; it was more like a telescope. As he sat in his chair moving his little people backward and forward, upstairs and downstairs, controlling the present and the future of everything and everybody in that house, that world, that universe, he, Gresham, knew that he was God. It added a ticklish pleasure to the game. Now he had a divine scheme.

Now he created such a rigid routine for his people that he could not leave the room any more, except to retire to his bedroom for sleep. He dressed and undressed his creatures twice a day, read solemn bedtime stories to the children and conversed long hours with the adults. Now Gresham had all his meals sent to the den, and he was impatient with the servants when they took too long laying out the tray for him, or picking up the empty dishes after he had hurriedly dined. The moments were precious to him; he had so many things to do for his people.

Up to that point, up to the moment of the formation of his theory,

Gresham had been a benevolent god. Now, with his catechism set, he began to ponder the ways of all gods, and that started him exercising some of the little extra privileges of his class. After all, a god has to tinker. He began by inflicting certain discomforts, even pain, upon his creatures. One day he tipped the little grandmother so far back in her chair she fell out and lay in a heap on the floor. "See!" Gresham told her, "Life isn't *all* comfy!" Now, whenever one of the children was a little perverse in his movements, refusing to stand or sit in quite the manner Gresham had in mind, he took to spanking it. "Let that teach you a lesson!" he shouted. "Do as you're told! Conform!"

The change from benevolent to vindictive god grew with his growing realization of the absolute power he possessed. Up till now he had been charmed by his playthings and had acted like a father to an adopted family. Now, when the father became the heavenly father, he indulged himself in his omniscience. When the children weren't looking he stole toys from the playroom. He hid them in the kitchen. One day he took the knitting needles from the grandmother's hands. "Enough damn knitting!" he stormed at her. "Try working for a living! Sweat of your brow!" He took her, rocking chair and all, and dumped her in the kitchen. He even attacked the swan crib and the sleeping infant. He knocked the crib over and the infant came tumbling out, rolling over and over on the floor. "Train 'em young," said Gresham. "Teach 'em life's full of hard knocks." He let the infant lay on the floor for two days. He pretended to pay no attention to the wailing sound he heard.

They found Gresham later in a pool of blood, his head cracked in places like an egg tapped with a spoon. The glass of the window in the den had been smashed to bits.

The theory of the police was that Gresham had climbed to the window sill in order to throw himself out the window. That, being a fat and awkward man, he had bumped into the glass, shattering it. That he had then suffered some sort of attack, or had tripped, and had fallen over backward on his head. That was the way the police figured it out. But Gresham himself would have told them a different story about what happened that night.

He could have told them that he had had an extremely trying day with his flock. Nobody would stand up correctly. The furniture didn't look right. The baby wouldn't go to sleep. "Damn it!" he had screamed. "Shut up! All of you! Do as I say or—or—damn it, you'll roast in hell!" In his anger he kept moving things about with clumsy impatience—beds, chairs, rugs, pictures, people—and the index finger of his right hand, probing into the far corners of the infant's nursery, felt something it had never felt before. It was high up toward the ceiling in the room, which is why Gresham's eyes and fingers had never found it before. He had never stooped low enough to see the ceilings of the second floor. Now he bent over to look, and when he saw it he growled. He ripped it from a triangular shelf high up in the corner. It was a tiny religious figure. It might have been a madonna. He held it in the palm of his hand. It was all green and gold paint over plaster, and there was flowerlike calligraphy on the folds of its cloak and a benign expression upon a face as large as the head of a hatpin. He held it in his hand for some minutes. Then he had to loosen his tie. Then he held the thing between thumb and index finger and with one powerful squeeze he crushed it to powder. He flicked it from his fingertips.

"Fools!"

He rose from his chair and stood face to face with the house. He lifted his right hand clear over his left shoulder. His eyes were terrible. With one stroke of the arm he could end existence for all of them, then and there. He shuddered, a wrathful god. "No other gods before Me—!" he began. "No—" But the arm came slowly down to his side again. He quivered a little, but he did not strike. He subsided, a forgiving god.

That was the night Gresham could not sleep. Jealousy tore at his eyelids, gnawed inside of him. An ancient dyspepsia crept back in and gave him twinges, until he knew he could lie there no longer and simply stare at the ceiling.

"Idols," he murmured, "heathen idols!"

His pajamas were wet with sweat; jealousy seeped through his pores. He tossed on the damp sheets until he could stand it no more. He rose from the bed and strode with mighty steps out of the bedroom, into the hallway, into the den.

It was a dark night. No moonlight came through the windows. It was late, the blackest late part of night. He wanted no light for what he was about to do, so he did not turn on the switch. It took him minutes for his eyes to see through the darkness. The first thing they saw, of course, was the doll's house. He walked noiselessly, with a fat man's grace, up to it.

"I gave you life," he said in an even voice. "Now . . ."

Once more he raised his heavy right arm over his left shoulder. He raised himself on his toes. This time he brought the back of his hand down against the house with all his strength and what occurred first was the splintering of the wood where his hand hit—a split-second sound of splintering. The blow swept the whole marvelous house off the table, and it fell to the floor with a great crash. It was no sturdy framework that held that house together—too precise it was, and too delicate to be that strong. The framework caved in like glass. In a heap then, at Gresham's feet, lay a shattered mass of splinters, and bits of glass, and the irreplaceable furniture, and the little people, and torn pieces of the incomparable wallpaper, all in a rubble, like the rubble after a bombing.

120

"You fools!" Gresham shouted.

It was the back of Gresham's hand that had smote the building. Now the knuckles were bleeding. The hand was at his side and the blood dripped to the floor. "You fools," he shouted. "Never heard of a Day of Judgment? Wouldn't believe me when I warned you? The power of life is the power of death! I warned you—"

He raised the wounded hand and looked at it. The blood ran down his forearm. "Wash you in the blood—I'll wash you in the blood—you stupid, selfish, disobedient—*people!*"

He stood over the rubble and shouted, and exulted, and sweated. God—even a god—can not be entirely calm after producing an earthquake. Gresham could not keep his arms from shaking. But he knew he could go to sleep now. The evildoers had been slaughtered, vengeance had been wrought.

But first he walked to the window—first he wanted, for some strange reason, a look at the night sky. He walked to the window and leaned heavily upon the sill. He was still breathing hard, his throat and his brain felt curiously congested. He climbed up on the broad sill, as if, by getting closer to the window, he could suck in more air. He stood there on the sill, leaning his full weight against the window, panting hard. He looked up at the sky. It was the faintest pale blue of the very early dawn. Not a single cloud floated up there—nothing ... till Gresham saw. From the immense void, covering half the shoulder of the sky, the back of an enormous Hand was coming down at him—swiftly, powerfully, vengefully.

## FOR DISCUSSION: None Before Me

1. In our introduction to this story, we mentioned that many of the lines in the story above have more than one meaning. What meanings, in terms of the story's plot, can you find in Pegerine's remark, "Is there anyone who doubts that toy making is a major art?"
2. Gresham's interest in the doll house and its occupants quickly involves him completely. Examine the story and identify the developmental stages of Gresham's obsession.
3. What does the author mean when he says, "Now, with his catechism set, he began to ponder the ways of all the gods, and that started him exercising some of the little extra privileges of his class"?
4. Why does the author capitalize the word "Hand" in the last sentence in the story?
5. Explain Gresham's theory of the Oriental balls or telescope. In what way does the fate he suffers confirm his theory? Would you say his fate was deserved?

## INTRODUCTION: Burnt Toast

Throughout the world's literature, we find stories of men bargaining with the Devil. The men in these stories are willing to exchange their souls for whatever it is they want that the Devil can supply. The theme is one that has intrigued writers and readers for centuries because it touches on man's fantasy life in which he yearns for power or riches and, in that same fantasy life, knows that a sometimes high price must be paid for what he wishes. In this story, a man gambles with the Devil, and the author applies his ingenuity to the situation to create a clever plot with a surprising conclusion—one told in an amusingly ironic style.

# Burnt Toast
## Mack Reynolds

"We have here a table bearing thirteen cocktails," the demon said. "And now into one I add a touch from this vial."

"What zat?"

"Poison. Now I switch the glasses about. Truly, you couldn't remember into which glass I emptied the vial, could you?"

"What's the gag, buddy?"

"The proposition," the demon said, "is quite simple. You take your pick and drink it. For your first choice I give you exactly one hundred dollars."

Alan Sheriff shook his head in an attempt to clear away the fog. "You said, minute ago, you put poison..."

"In just one. There are thirteen in all. You choose a glass, you drink it, and I award you with a hundred dollars. If you wish to try again, you receive two hundred, next award is four hundred, and so on. If you lose, the forfeit is your life and your ... soul."

It took a long moment to assimilate that. "Let's see the century," Sheriff muttered.

The demon brought forth a wallet and selected a bill which he laid on the table, then looked at the other in anticipation.

Sheriff said thickly, "Nothing to lose anyway." He took up the nearest glass, fished the olive out and threw it aside.

The demon smiled politely.

"*Bottoms up!*" Sheriff said, tossing it off with the practiced stiffwristed motion of the drinker.  He put the glass down, stood swaying in silence.

"Not bad liquor," he said finally.  "I needed that."

"The hundred dollars is yours.  Would you like to try for two hundred?"

Sheriff looked at the bill.  "This is good, eh?"

The demon shifted his shoulders in impatience.  "Of course."

Sheriff said, "Suppose I could ask you what this is all about, but the hell with it.  So long, sucker."

"I'll still be here tomorrow, Alan Sheriff."


There was a knock and the demon said, "Come in."

Sheriff closed the door behind him.  His blood-veined eyes went about the barren hotel room; magnet-drawn, they came to the small table.  Twelve cocktail glasses, sweated with cold, sat upon it.

He said tentatively, "I was tight last night . . ."

"The night before last," the demon corrected.

". . . but I wasn't *that* tight.  I couldn't have dreamed it, especially the hundred bucks."

"Already gone, I assume," the demon said.  "You came to try again?"

"Why'd you give me that hundred?  Listen, you haven't got a drink around the place have you?"

The other seated himself in the room's sole chair, put the tips of his fingers together.  "You won the hundred dollars on a wager.  As far as a drink is concerned, I am afraid all I have is there."  He indicated the table with its burden of twelve glasses.

Sheriff's eyes went from him to the table, back again.  He hadn't shaved since last he had been here and the pallor and odor of long weeks of alcohol were on him.  He wavered.  "I don't remember too well."

"Briefly," the demon said, "I represent interests that desire your immortal soul."  He made again the proposition of the previous evening while Sheriff stared at him.  When he was finished, his visitor's eyes went again to the table with its twelve glasses.

"Let's see your money," Sheriff said, shaky and unbelieving.

The demon brought forth his wallet, extracted two bills.

Sheriff stepped to the table, reached for a drink.  *"Prosit!"* he grunted, bolting it.  He waited, then with satisfaction, "Wrong one."

The demon shrugged.

Sheriff said, "If I take another one, how much do I get?"

"Four hundred dollars.  You wish to try again?"

"There's eleven glasses left.  One poison, eh?"

"That is correct.  The odds are with you."

Sheriff grinned sourly, two broken front teeth becoming evident.

"Best odds I ever had." He reached out quickly, took up another glass, held it in his hand for a moment then drank it as he had the other one with one quick motion. "Four hundred more," he demanded, and received it.

"And now for eight?" the demon prodded.

"Not till I get this spent," Sheriff chortled. "Then I'll be back, sucker." He held up the $600 he had won, stared at it unbelievingly, clenched it in his fist and stumbled from the room.

The demon looked after him.

"Eight hundred this time," the demon said, the sum ready in his hand, "and the odds are one in ten."

*Here's to glory!* Sheriff toasted.

When Alan Sheriff returned, four days later, he was shaven, bathed, attired in gray flannel, his teeth had known a dentist's attention and the shaking of his hands was all but imperceptible.

"You're sober," the demon said.

Sheriff looked at him. The other was medium sized, dressed conservatively. Sheriff said, "You don't look like the Devil."

"How am I supposed to look?"

Sheriff scowled at him. "Listen, I sobered myself up, but it's temporary. Just long enough to find out what the hell's going on. What'd you give me that money for?"

The demon explained, still again, the wagers they had made.

Afterward Sheriff said, wonderingly, "My soul, eh? Tell the truth, I didn't think there was any such thing."

"It has been greatly debated," the demon agreed.

"What I can't understand," Sheriff said, "is all this trouble you're going to. You picked me out of the gutter. You would've got my ... soul ... anyway."

"You underestimate the efforts of our opposition," the demon sighed. "And you must realize victory is never absolutely assured until the last second of life. Ten minutes after I approached you, you might have decided upon reform." He twisted his mouth sardonically.

Sheriff shook his head while saying, "I still don't get this ... this system of trying to get my ... soul."

The demon had seated himself in the armchair, now he shrugged. "Each person in his time is confronted with his decision. Most, admittedly, not quite so directly as this."

"But all that dough for a down-and-out bum. Already I've got fifteen hundred, and the next chance more than doubles it."

The demon nodded. "Your next try is for one thousand, six hundred. But the amount is meaningless. The, ah, commodity cannot be evaluated in terms of money. One of our most prized specimens cost but thirty pieces of silver." He added absently, "In that particular case he didn't know it was his soul he was selling."

Alan Sheriff looked down at the table. There were nine glasses remaining. He said, "For sixteen hundred bucks, eh?"

The demon nodded, his eyes shining.

Sheriff's hand snaked out, took up a glass and brought it half way to his lips. His eyes went to the demon's.

The other smiled.

Alan Sheriff put the glass down quickly, took up another. He held it for a moment. The demon still smiled.

Sheriff's mouth tightened. "*Salud!*" he said, bolting the cocktail. He closed his eyes and waited. When he opened them, the other was extending a sheaf of bills.

Sheriff said, "You'll still be here later in the week?"

"For you I shall always be here, night or day. There are eight glasses left. Your next wager will involve three thousand, two hundred."

Sheriff said flatly, "I gave up two weeks ago. Lots of dough for liquor, good food, gambling, makes the going easier but I'm not changing my mind about calling life quits. I'll be back when I've spent this."

"Very sound judgment," the demon nodded. "Until then."

"So soon?" the demon said. "However, the wager is now three thousand, two hundred."

Sheriff said, "This is the last time."

"Ah?"

"This time I'm using the dough for a new start. I'm getting a job."

"Admirable motive, I understand—from the human viewpoint. However, we shall see." The demon changed the subject. "If I understand correctly the laws of chance, this is your crucial test."

"How's that?" Sheriff's eyes came up from the glasses to the other's face.

"When we began, there were thirteen glasses, one of which was poisoned. However, we are nearly half through now and your good luck cannot last forever. Taking the averages, you should miss this time."

Sheriff shook his head. "Each time is a separate time. You don't use up your luck, there is no such thing. The odds aren't as good as they were, but they're still seven to one in my favor."

"Very well, let us see."

Alan Sheriff, sweat on his forehead, reached out slowly for one of the martinis. "*Here's looking at you,*" he said.

The demon answered the door and smiled to see his visitor.

"Alan Sheriff! But I thought your last visit was to be just that."

Sheriff's face was tight. "I'm not here for myself, damn you. It's for somebody else."

"Somebody else?" the demon said. "I don't understand."

"A girl," Sheriff snapped. "It's none of your business. You wouldn't ever have seen me again except for Muriel. She needs five thousand; medical bills for her old lady, sanitarium. Never mind. The thing is I'll take another one of those drinks."

The demon pinched his lip thoughtfully. "I don't know."

"Damn it, what difference does it make what I want the dough for?"

"Ummm. Your motive for taking the wager disturbs me. Some centuries ago a somewhat similar case precipitated a *cause célèbre*. Chap named Johann Faust. Matter had to be taken to the, ah, higher authorities. However, let us see what develops. There are seven glasses and your odds are six to one with the prize amounting to exactly six thousand, four hundred dollars."

Sheriff took up a glass at random, toasted defiantly, *"Here's to the ladies!"*

"Very sentimental," the demon nodded.

Sheriff banged on the door heavily, and, before it could be answered, banged again.

The demon opened it, his face quizzical. "Ah, our Alan Sheriff."

Sheriff lurched to the table. The martini glasses stood as before, six of them remaining. They appeared chill and as fresh as the first time he had seen them, months ago.

"What's the bet now?" he slurred.

"The wager is twelve thousand, eight hundred against your life and soul." The demon's voice was soft.

"OK. *Here's how!*"

The demon nodded pleasantly.

"Beat you again," Sheriff sneered, "Give me the dough. I'm on my way to show up a wise guy. Show him what a real spender can do for a girl." The alcohol was heavy on his breath. "What'd be a classy present for Muriel? Show her what a real guy does for a dame..."

The demon ran a thoughtful thumbnail along his trimmed mustache. "I understand mink is highly thought of," he murmured.

"Ah," the demon said. "Here we are, once again."

Sheriff looked about the room, unchanged from the last time he had been here except there were but five glasses on the small table. He wondered vaguely what had happened to the eight glasses he had emptied in turn.

"You know," he said, "each time I come here I have to be convinced all over again that it's true."

"Indeed?  As I recall, on your last visit you were in the midst of a somewhat feverish romantic situation.  Did you take my advice as to the desirability of mink?"

Sheriff was gazing in fascination at the glasses.  He said, "What?  Oh, yeah.  This here wise guy boyfriend of hers, old high school sweetheart kind of crap, was trying to beat my time."  He chuckled thickly.  "But I gave her the old rush job, wound up in Miami Beach for a week.  Quite a town."

"Isn't it though?  And where is Muriel these days?"

Sheriff was tired of the subject.  "She's around somewhere.  Got on my nerves finally.  What's the bet now?  I'm thinking of going into the restaurant business—with my kid brother, he needs the dough to get started."

"Twenty-five thousand, six hundred," the demon said briefly.

"Well, *here's mud in your eye*," Sheriff said.

"Fifty-one thousand, two hundred," the demon said.  "The new business doesn't seem to prosper?"

"The kid doesn't realize there's angles to every business.  He's too slow for me.  We need this dough to put in a bar and maybe a few tables and some slots in the back, maybe some rooms upstairs where a guy can take a dame or maybe throw a little reefer party."

"There are now four glasses," the demon said.

"*Skoal!*"

The demon opened the door at the knock and admitted the burly, heavy-faced man.  "It's been a long time," he said simply.

"Yeah," Sheriff said.  He looked about the small room.  "But you haven't changed much.  Neither has this room.  I wasn't sure it'd still be here."

"Some things are changeless," the demon said.

"Three glasses left, eh?  My luck's really been with me so far.  You know, it's been so long since I been here.  What's the bet now?"

"You would win one hundred and two thousand, four hundred dollars, my friend."

"Two chances out of three.  It's still a good percentage and I'm branching out into new territory and need the dough."  He stared down at the identical glasses, still retaining their appearance of chill freshness.

"And how is your brother these days?"

"Bill? The hell with him. I had to bounce him out. Too square for the business I'm in. You know," he bragged, "I'm a pretty big shot in some of the rackets these days."

"Ah? I see."

Sheriff took up one of the glasses, looked over its edge at his opponent. "Well, *first one today with this hand,*" he muttered, downing it. He waited for a moment then took up the money, stuffed it into his overcoat pocket and left without a backward glance.

The knock at the door was hurried, anxious.

The demon opened it and said, "Yes?"

Sheriff hastened in, looked about quickly. "I'm safe here?"

The demon chuckled. "Really, Alan Sheriff!"

"They're after me. The cops . . ."

"Ah?"

Sheriff's eyes went to the small table. "Two glasses left," he muttered. "I could hire Liber for a lawyer, grease a few palms. With more than two hundred grand I could beat this rap, or, for that matter, I could go on down to Mexico, live there the rest of my life."

"It's been done," the demon agreed.

"Fifty-fifty chance," Sheriff hissed in sudden decision. He lifted one of the glasses from the table, said *"Cheers,"* downed it and stood back to wait, his face empty and white. Nothing happened.

He turned to the other. "Give me the money," he said triumphantly. "You know what, sucker? It's like you once said. It's never too late to change. I beat you all the way down the line, but I know when I've pushed my luck as far as it'll go. After I've got myself out of this jam, I'm going to straighten up, see?"

"I doubt it," the demon murmured.

"Yes I am, buster. You've lost this boy."

The demon said, "I suggest you drink the other martini."

The other stared at him. "That's the one with the poison."

The demon shook his head gently. "I suggest you take the thirteenth glass, Alan Sheriff. It might help you somewhat in the tribulations that lie ahead. After all, it *is* the very best of gin and vermouth."

Sheriff chuckled his contempt. "Give me my dough, sucker. I'm getting out."

The demon said, "What gave you the impression that the poison was a quick acting one, Alan Sheriff?"

Sheriff blinked at him. "Huh?"

"I don't remember informing you that death was to be instantaneous following your choice of the wrong glass."

"I ... I don't get it ..."

"But of course you got it," the demon said smoothly. "The poison was odorless and tasteless and you got it on your eighth try. Since then your life and soul have been mine to collect at will. The fact that I haven't done so sooner was my own whim—and excellent business, as it developed. Surely in the past few years you have done more for the, ah, *cause* I serve than you would have had I collected my wager immediately."

After a long moment Sheriff picked up the last glass. "Maybe you're right. I might be needing this, and they *are* good martinis.

*"One for the road,"* he toasted with attempted bravado.

*"Down the hatch,"* the demon corrected.

## FOR DISCUSSION: Burnt Toast

1. What assumption does Alan Sheriff (and the reader) make which is the key element that lends impact to the story's conclusion?
2. Sheriff makes a series of toasts throughout the story as he takes each succeeding drink. How does this device contribute to the power of the story's concluding two lines? How does it relate to the story's title?
3. What comments can you make concerning the kind of person Alan Sheriff is based on the evidence supplied by the author? How does the author make you feel about him?
4. Suppose Alan Sheriff had managed to avoid drinking the poisoned martini. Do you feel that the story would remain effective or do you feel it has more drama as constructed? Why?

# Ghost Stories— The Haunted House of Man's Mind

# CHAPTER THREE

Ghost stories existed in the literatures of the Egyptians, the Greeks, the Romans, the Chinese, and the Arabs. In the Middle Ages and even during the Renaissance, people believed in ghosts, and authors were not challenged to apply a great deal of literary artistry to make their ghost stories believable. But writers of a later period, when scepticism was the order of the day, were required to sharpen their literary techniques to make the reader accept supernatural premises. Accordingly, they developed artistic styles, skill in creating atmosphere, narrative power, and, in many cases, a relatively sophisticated understanding of human psychology.

The present-day writer of the ghost story must make his reader accept things and events that the reader's rationality makes him reject. Ghost stories offer a serious challenge to the author's art for this reason. If the reader smiles or chuckles when the ghost puts in its appearance in a story, the writer has failed and so has the story.

In the ghost story, the student of supernatural literature can find developed to their fullest extent such literary techniques as the development of an effective climax, the creation of mood, the skillful blending of the commonplace with the fantastic, and, most important, the building of suspense.

All these elements are, of course, to be found in good fiction of any kind. But within the genre of the ghost story, these techniques must be particularly well handled or the reader will reject the story as ridiculous.

One need not believe in ghosts to enjoy a good ghost story. Most of us still have a sufficient if somewhat submerged reservoir of what may be called a sense of the primitive to enjoy tales of spectral visitations.

There are all kinds of ghosts with all kinds of missions and intentions. Ghosts manifest themselves to the living in different ways. You will find ghosts of many different kinds in these stories, some in contemporary settings and some in quainter locales, but all interesting as only the manifestations of the supernatural can be to the mind still capable of appreciating the marvelous.

Unfortunately, there is a meager market today for the well-told ghost story. Perhaps many of us are too aware of other frightening aspects of our modern world to have any fear left for the insubstantial shape glimpsed on a darkened staircase or the haunted face outside the window beneath a midnight moon. However, just before and just after the turn of this century, there were literary giants abroad in the land of the supernatural tale. We refer to such men as Algernon Blackwood, Arthur Machen, Sheridan Le Fanu, Oliver Onions, Henry James, and others.

As previously noted, good ghost stories today are almost as rare as the ghosts they tell us about. This, to one who appreciates the genuinely fine examples of literature available within this genre, is regrettable. We can only hope that someday writers will again turn their literary attentions to the ghost story and will, in the words of the ghost of Hamlet's murdered father, "a tale unfold whose lightest word would harrow up thy soul, freeze thy young blood, make thy two eyes like stars start from their spheres, thy knotted and combined locks to part, and each particular hair to stand on end, like quills upon the fretful porcupine."

"Now it so happened, long ere it was day,
This fellow had a dream, and as he lay
In bed it seemed he heard his comrade call,
'Help! I am lying in an ox's stall
And shall tonight be murdered as I lie.
Help me, dear brother, help or I shall die!
Come in all haste!' Such were the words he spoke;
The dreamer, lost in terror, then awoke

But once awake he paid it no attention,
Turned over and dismissed it as invention,
It was a dream, he thought, a fantasy.
And twice he dreamt this dream successively.

"Yet a third time his comrade came again,
Or seemed to come, and said, 'I have been slain.
Look, look!  my wounds are bleeding wide and deep.
Rise early in the morning, break your sleep
And go to the west gate.  You there shall see
A cart all loaded up with dung,' said he,
'And in that dung my body has been hidden.
Boldly arrest that cart as you are bidden,
It was my money that they killed me for.'

"He told him every detail, sighing sore,
And pitiful in feature, pale of hue.
This dream, believe me, Madam, turned out true;
For in the dawn, as soon as it was light,
He went to where his friend had spent the night
And when he came upon the cattle-stall
He looked about him and began to call.

"The innkeeper, appearing thereupon,
Quickly gave answer, 'Sir, your friend has gone.
He left the town a little after dawn.'
The man began to feel suspicious, drawn
By memories of his dream—the western gate,
The dung-cart—off he went, he would not wait,
Towards the western entry.  There he found,
Seemingly on its way to dung some ground,
A dung-cart loaded on the very plan
Described so closely by the murdered man.
So he began to shout courageously
For right and vengeance on the felony,
'My friend's been killed!  There's been a foul attack,
He's in that cart and gaping on his back!
Fetch the authorities, get the sheriff down
—Whosoever job it is to run the town—
Help!  My companion's murdered, sent to glory!'

"What need I add to finish off the story?
People ran out and cast the cart to ground,
And in the middle of the dung they found
The murdered man.  The corpse was fresh and new."

*from "The Nun's Priest's Tale,"* The Canterbury Tales

In the epigraph for this chapter, Chanticleer tells the story of how a murdered man urges his friend to reveal the crime and seek retribution.   Chanticleer's story from *The Canterbury Tales* by Geoffrey Chaucer is an ancient one.   Here is a somewhat similar but more modern tale of murder and the role of the supernatural in uncovering the crime and the one who committed it.   Both stories illustrate the sensitivity to the supernatural possessed by writers separated by many centuries.

# The Haunted Woodshed
## Harold R. Daniels

Through thirty years of schoolteaching, Mary Comstock dreamed of the day she could retire to a small New England village and live out her remaining years quietly raising dahlias.   She might even, she dreamed, be accepted into some small intellectual group so that there would be evenings of good conversation and music.

The house that she actually bought was not in a village but was located half a mile from it.   It had been a farm and the price was far less than a similar house in town would have cost.   Even so, it took more of her small savings than she would have liked.   Two acres of land went with the house.   She would, she told herself, raise her own vegetables and perhaps have a few left over for sale at the roadside.

She bought the house after two weekend inspection visits.   Mr. Purcell, the real estate agent who went with her on the visits, wasted much time fussily pointing out the merits of the house—wasted it because Mary was in love with the house from the moment she saw it.   It was a dignified little white saltbox in excellent condition.   Having seen it, Mary knew that no other house could possibly meet her needs so exactly.

Except for the woodshed.

She didn't like that from the start and actually came to fear it.   The fear began a week after she said her goodbyes to her fellow teachers—they gave her a silver-plated tea set—and moved to Morrow Corners.

Mary Comstock, at that time, was in her late fifties—a small, indomitable figure of a woman not given to foolish fears.   She had faced down too many classes of bullying boys, too many stuffed-shirt school boards, to be a coward.

The woodshed was perhaps twenty feet long by fifteen feet wide. It was made of heavy unpainted planks that had mellowed and silvered with the seasons. There was a wide, heavy door in the front and a tiny window in the back. It was actually a rather picturesque little building and Mary did not understand quite what it was that she disliked about it. Certainly the proportions were neat enough.

She had glanced into it on her first visit to the farm, but she did not go inside it until a week after she had moved and had finished setting up her own furniture. She told herself that she was not really avoiding the woodshed—there were simply too many other things to attend to.

At the end of the first week she went out to inspect it.

There was a crude bar-and-socket arrangement on the door, so arranged that the bar would ride up on a sloping wedge and drop into the socket if the door were slammed hard enough. She lifted the free end of the bar from the socket and pulled the door back. It creaked and held back against her pull, as if reluctant to open. When she released the door it swung back as if to close again. She said in small impatience, "Darned thing," and pulled it all the way open so that it banged against the shed wall and shivered to a standstill.

Mary was a sensitive and imaginative woman. When she stepped from the brillant sunshine into the gloom of the woodshed she was almost overwhelmed by a feeling of melancholy so tangible that it was almost like a blow. She recoiled from it and only a fine sense of the ridiculous kept her from retreating back to the sunlight that now seemed the brighter by contrast.

She said aloud—and her own voice startled her—"Pshaw, Mary Comstock. It's only an old woodshed. You act as if it were Madame Tussaud's." But she had to force herself to remain in the building.

It seemed almost bucolicly harmless. The floor was of hard-packed dirt embedded with countless wood chips and scraps of bark. Thin light came through the tiny window high up on the wall. Dust motes danced in a bright bar of sunlight. A lonesome bluebottle fly droned wearily against the dusty glass, butting his head against it fatalistically.

She stayed in the shed for ten minutes or so, planning its possible rearrangement into a potting shed. She left it before she was done with her planning and she scolded herself for this as she slammed the heavy door.

"Poltergeists. Witches. Haunts. You should be ashamed of yourself! Next you'll be looking for elves down in the orchard."

Nevertheless, she did not go near the woodshed for another week— because, she told herself, she was much too busy. From time to time she would glance at the woodshed from the house or the yard and each time she shivered and felt cold.

Shame made her visit the building again. When she opened the door she felt the same sense of overpowering, lurking evil. She stayed only five minutes on that second occasion and it took all her considerable will power to make her remain that long . . .

The next time she drove into Morrow Corners in the little coupe that had been a personal friend for a dozen years, she stopped in at the office of Ben Purcell, the real estate man who had sold her the house.

He seemed nervous when she sat down across the desk from him. "I hope everything is going well, Mrs. Comstock," he said. "No leaks in the roof or anything like that?"

"It hasn't rained since I bought the house," she reminded him. "And it's Miss Comstock, as you should remember from the deed papers. I wish you'd stop fidgeting, Mr. Purcell. I bought the house and I'm perfectly happy with it. I merely want to know who lived there before I did."

Purcell looked relieved. "Why, Henry Wienowski had the place before you did, Miss Comstock. Of course, he deeded it over to the bank to sell for him two years ago—when he moved to the big Platt farm he bought. Mighty good farmer, Henry is. I don't care what the talk was."

"What talk?"

Purcell mopped his forehead with an outsize handkerchief. "Oh—just talk. Didn't amount to anything."

Mary leaned forward. "I taught school for thirty years, Mr. Purcell. I'm not an easy woman for even a grown man to fool. What are you hiding back about my house? Did some tragedy take place there?"

Purcell said anxiously, "No tragedy, exactly. It's just that Mrs. Wienowski disappeared. "Let's see—that was five years ago. There was a lot of talk that Henry did away with her. Nothing was ever proved, though."

"Did they arrest him?"

"Sure. Held him for a while but they couldn't find any evidence. So they had to let him go. He went straight back to his place—your place, now—and lived on there until he bought the Platt farm." Purcell paused. "I hope you don't think I wouldn't have told you all this if you'd asked, Miss Comstock."

She stood up to leave. "I'm sure you would," she said dryly.

Because she was reasonably stubborn, Mary Comstock went into the woodshed three times within the next week. Each time the inherent evil of the place drove her out. By this time she was thoroughly angry with herself and with the woodshed.

"I suppose," she told herself, "you think that poor woman's body is buried under the dirt. I suppose you don't think that that's the very first place the police would look if they thought a murder had been committed."

The week went slowly. She had already made the little house immaculate. Now she looked for things to do. From a bolt of butcher's linen that she found in the cellar she made drapes for her bedroom. She painted. She scrubbed. She planted a small garden. And for the sake of economy she bought a young pig, planning to have it butchered and stored in the cooperative freezer plant. When she visited the plant, a pleasant young man named Barney Pace gave her the key to her private locker.

"That will be four dollars," he told her. "The plant is always open, but any time you want butchering done you'll have to come around in the daytime. I'll be here, or my dad."

They walked back into the cool depths of the freezer plant. Barney borrowed her key back and opened her locker for her. "I'll probably butcher your shoat in the cool of the evening," he told her. "The meat will go in here."

The locker was about the size of a file-cabinet drawer. When Barney opened it, a wisp of white vapor curled out. "My," she said. "It's certainly cold enough." She glanced around. "What in the world do you keep in those big lockers?"

The big lockers were similar to her own but many times larger. "Farmers rent them," Barney told her. "They can store whole beef carcasses in them. In the old days they used to butcher at home and pickle the beef for the winter. Now they have prime meat the year round. Any time they want a roast or a steak they just come in and get it. People in town do the same thing. Buy beef when it's cheap and store it."

On her next trip to town Mary stopped at the library. With her teaching background she was able to establish an immediate and warm friendship with the librarian, whose name was Margaret Miller. They chatted for two hours in between the book borrowers.

Mrs. Miller was voluble, frankly delighted that a genuine booklover had moved to Morrow Corners. Yes, she agreed, it was a lovely little house. And yes, she remembered when Mrs. Wienowski disappeared. Everyone was sure that the terrible-tempered Henry had murdered her— such a pity that nothing could be done about it. He used to beat her terribly, people said. Yes, she had known her. A thin little woman, always looking over her shoulder. Always afraid. And yes, she would be delighted to come and visit with Mary. This last was when Mary Comstock finally got up to leave.

From the library Mary went straight to the Sheriff's substation. The deputy in charge was a big, slow-moving man with a red face and sympathetic eyes. His name was Redfield. He pulled out a chair for Mary and sat down across from her.

"Now then," he said pleasantly, "what can I do for you, Mrs. Comstock?"

She said absently, "Miss. And before I tell you anything at all, I want you to know that I am not a silly or a timid woman."

He said reassuringly, "Wouldn't occur to me at all, Miss Comstock."

She told him about her sensations whenever she went into the woodshed. When she finished, she half expected to find him smiling at her, humoring her. He wasn't smiling.

He shook his head slowly. "There isn't any body under that woodshed—if that's what you're thinking. I know because I helped dig it up. You see, ma'am, we're all pretty sure that Henry Weinowski killed his wife. But being sure and proving it are two different matters."

Redfield leaned back in his chair. "About that feeling you get when you go into the woodshed—well, I just don't know. I sure wouldn't laugh at you for it though. An old farmer by the name of Hansen hung himself in his own barn not far from my place. I helped cut him down. I still get gooseflesh when I go near his place—and I'm a pretty hardheaded man."

Mary asked, "That man—that Wienowski—he's still walking around as free as a bird?"

"As free as a bird. Makes me want to turn in my badge."

"She never told any of her friends that she was afraid her husband would kill her? I mean, if she did, couldn't you arrest him on suspicion?"

"She never had any friends. Henry wouldn't let her. No, she just disappeared from the face of the earth. She used to deliver eggs to a dozen customers here in town. One day she just didn't show up. The next day Henry brought the eggs around himself and said his wife had gone home to visit her folks for a spell. They're Polish people—live in a town in Minnesota."

"Did you write to see if she ever got there?" Mary asked.

"Did better than that. I telephoned. Cost the town a few dollars, I guess. You see, Henry had been in trouble with me before. Once he beat his wife so bad she had to be put in the hospital. Brought her in himself and damned if he didn't want to know how much it was going to cost before he'd leave her. She wouldn't make a complaint against him though. Too scared. Said she fell down the cellar stairs—and her with fist and boot marks all over her. After she turned up missing I went out there and nosed around. Couldn't do too much without evidence but I got her people's address from Henry and I called them right away. They hadn't heard from her in years. I asked Henry how she left town. He told me she went on a Greyhound bus. I checked at the depot and they hadn't sold a ticket to anywhere in Minnesota for months. So I arrested Henry right then and there. That's when we searched the place. And we really searched it. We poked into every foot of ground with iron rods. Used bloodhounds too. Dug up the cellar. Dug up your woodshed—every inch of it. But she wasn't there."

Mary, pitying the vanished Mrs. Wienowski, said, "The poor creature. What do you suppose he did with her?"

Redfield shrugged. "Don't know, ma'am. Maybe drove off in the woods somewhere and buried her. I just hope that some day her body— what's left of it—will turn up. I'd like to see Henry hang."

After leaving the Sheriff's office, Mary drove down the street to the freezer locker to pick up chops for supper. Young Barney Pace was at the meat block. He smiled as she came in. "Good day, Miss Comstock. Get something from your locker for you?"

She handed him the key. "Please, Barney. Cut me off two nice rib chops if you will."

"Sure, ma'am."

She watched him cut the young pig's carcass. "I wish I could afford to rent a bigger locker and buy a quarter of beef," she said pensively. "Though I suppose it would be foolish to have that much meat stored away just for myself."

Barney wrapped her chops in brown paper and handed them to her. "Not if you bought a rib quarter. You might think about it, Miss Comstock. Beef's a lot cheaper that way."

A tall, stoop-shouldered man pushed past the meat block into the locker storage room. He wore faded denims and a much-washed blue shirt that stretched tautly across his hulking frame. Barney said in a low voice, "That's the man who used to own your place. You know him?"

"You mean that's Mr. Wienowski?"

"That's him. Killed his wife and got away with it."

Mary listened to Barney's chatter with only half an ear. She had glimpsed Henry Wienowski's face. She had seen the brutal jaw and the narrowed, avaricious eyes. All her life she had prided herself in not judging people by appearances, but now she had seen a face that she knew was capable of murder.

After a minute or two Wienowski came stalking back from the locker room. Over his shoulder he had slung the carcass of a sheep. Wrapped in butcher linen, the frozen flesh showed dark red through the cloth. The legs of the carcass stuck rigidly out in all directions. Mary Comstock breathed a soft, "Oh, no!" and hurried to her car.

She found Deputy Redfield dozing at his desk and was impatient with him. "Sheriff," she said, "Henry Wienowski has one of those big lockers at the freezer plant."

"I can't arrest him for that. Every farmer in the valley has a locker."

She bent toward him throwing the words like darts. "Did you look *in his locker* when his wife disappeared?"

Redfield swallowed. "Lord," he said. "No." He stood up, no longer looking kindly but grim and purposeful. "Miss Comstock," he said. "I'm three kinds of a fool. It's just that a thing like that wouldn't occur— You'd better stay here."

She shook her head. "I'm going with you."

Barney Pace smiled again when Deputy Redfield walked in with Mary behind him. He saw the expression on Redfield's face and stopped smiling. "What's the matter, Ed?"

"Have you got a duplicate key to Henry Wienowski's locker?"

"No. I've got a key to the regular lock but Henry put his own padlock on when he rented it."

"Never mind. Give me the key you've got and fetch a flashlight."

Barney opened Wienowski's locker with the duplicate key. The padlock was attached to a chain and there was enough slack so that the door could be opened about an inch. A wisp of cold vapor ghosted out and Mary drew back a step in spite of herself. Redfield looked at the padlock. "Cheap job," he grunted, and sent Barney to fetch a hammer and screwdriver.

The deputy placed the screwdriver in the staple of the padlock and struck the base with the hammer. At the second blow the staple snapped open. "Glad I didn't have to break it," Redfield said. He opened the door wide and focused Barney's flashlight.

Inside the locker were nearly a dozen objects, the lower ones blurred by heavy coats of frost. They were lumpy, amorphous, unrecognizable. Redfield dragged one out. It went *thump* on the floor and Mary gasped.

Barney said, "Hog." He said later, "Another hog. Sheep. Side of beef."

The last of the cloth-wrapped bundles was frozen solidly to the floor of the locker. Barney had to help Redfield tug and haul at it until it slid, finally, out onto the floor.

It was long and there was a round protuberance at one end.

Mary looked away. A head, she thought, a woman's head. She decided that she was going to be sick.

And then Redfield grunted again. "Veal carcass. That's all. Shove them back in, will you, Barney? Try to get 'em in the same order we took them out."

To Mary Comstock he said, "I'm almost glad we didn't find anything. I've got some beef of my own in this room. Don't think I'd care to eat any of it if we'd—well, you know what I mean."

She said in a small voice, "I suppose you think I'm a perfect simpleton."

"Don't think anything of the kind. You were dead-right. It had to be checked out."

In the days that followed, Mary's love for the little saltbox house deepened in direct proportion to her revulsion for the woodshed. More and more she was drawn to the place in spite of her abhorrence—just as a motorist will glance and glance again at the bloody and crumpled victims of an accident seen in passing.

Mary's new friend, the librarian, visited her frequently now. Deputy Redfield dropped in twice for iced tea—and if he was a mite disappointed that Mary kept no beer on ice for visiting lawmen, he nevertheless came the second time.

She was happy, she told herself. The woodshed was only the minor flaw that set off the perfection of the whole. She was frankly interested in the Wienowski case and she pumped Redfield about it shamelessly on both his visits. Once he became a little annoyed.

"This is a country village, Mary," he told her, "but we've got access to the State Bureau of Investigation and those are crack men. I held Henry Wienowski for four days after I first picked him up and those men helped me search the place. There wasn't any loose soil. There weren't any bloodstains in the house or in Henry's truck—and I mean to tell you, those State detectives went over everything with microscopes. It wasn't just a matter of a hick sheriff like me making a halfway search."

"I'm sorry, Ed," she told him. "I didn't mean to sound as if I thought you weren't capable. Have some more tea and we'll talk about something else."

A few days after Redfield's second visit, Mary set out half a dozen pots of impatiens in the front garden. When she was finished, she picked up the empty pots and started for the house. On the way to the back door she stopped.

"You've got a perfectly good shed for these things," she told herself, "and you're not going to let your imagination keep you from using it."

She turned toward the woodshed.

As she came closer to it she felt the familiar loathing. The day was perfectly still and hot. When she opened the door a bluebottle fly—it could have been the same one she had seen weeks earlier—was still bumbling against the window. Folding the door all the way back, she stepped aside—into the same aura of brooding melancholy that she had felt before.

"Now don't just set those pots down and run," she told herself firmly. "You take your time and stack them neatly in the corner where they belong."

As she stepped toward the corner she felt a rush of air. Turning, with an involuntary cry of fright, she saw the heavy door slam to behind her, cutting off most of the light so that she stood in semidarkness. In near-panic she ran to the door. There was a wooden latchpiece stuck through it from the outside that was supposed to make it possible to lift the heavy wooden bar from the inside. She pried up on it too quickly and it snapped in her hands with a powdery puff of dry rot.

"Don't panic," she whispered. "Keep a grip on yourself. Get a stick or something and stick it through the latch hole."

There was no stick small enough to go through the hole. The door was solid and tight-fitting. Mary tried for ten minutes to get it open before she stopped to catch her breath.

Standing in the dark, panting, she glanced down at the floor. Of course. She could dig her way out. She searched for a small log and found one. It was beveled at the point where some forgotten woodsman had chopped it. The point sank easily into the dirt close to the wall and she remembered what Redfield had said. "We dug every inch of that woodshed up."

When she had loosened a quantity of the dry soil, she scooped it aside with her hands and scraped some more with the sharp stick. She had made a hole almost two feet deep when she came across the butcher linen.

The bones that were wrapped in the linen were dirt-stained. She thought at first that they were wood chips—except that no wood chip should be shaped like a human skull . . .

Half an hour later she broke through the ground outside the woodshed. It was typical of Mary Comstock that she stopped to wash and put on a clean dress before she went to fetch Deputy Redfield.

Later he told her about it. "We went out and got him this afternoon. He was like an animal. It took three of us to wrestle him down and then we had to chain him up with cow chain."

It was evening now and a coolness sifted itself over them as they sat on her front porch. "Then it *was* Mrs. Wienowski's body?"

"No doubt about it. With the bones in her throat crushed where he strangled her."

Mary shivered. "Poor woman."

"Henry was pretty clever at that. If you can ever call a murderer clever. He killed her and put her body in the freezer locker just like you figured. Then he sat back and laughed while we tore up the ground out here looking for her. Then he figured the safest place in the world was a place we had already searched. He was right about that too. Or he would have been if you hadn't got trapped in there."

Mary warmed his coffee. "I wonder, though, why he sold the place. You'd think he'd want to stay where he could keep his eye on it."

"You know how that woodshed spooked you, Mary. Maybe it had the same effect on him. And he had no reason to believe anyone would go digging the shed up.  Like I say, if you hadn't got trapped in there—say, how did that happen anyway?"

Mary said slowly, "The wind, I guess.  I had the door swung all the way back so it couldn't have closed by itself."

Redfield frowned.  "I do a little farming, Mary, so I watch the weather.  There wasn't enough wind today to move the wheat, let alone a heavy door."

"I know," she said softly.

In the morning she went out to the woodshed to see how well Redfield's men had filled in the hole they had made in exhuming poor Mrs. Wienowski's body.  They had leveled it and tramped the dirt back down so that it looked as it had looked before.  Inside it was cool and faintly musty and nothing more.

It felt exactly as a woodshed should feel . . .

## FOR DISCUSSION: The Haunted Woodshed

1. The character of Mary Comstock is important in her unearthing of the mystery and in providing a foil—or counterbalance—to the otherworldly.  What qualities of personality help her through this extraordinary experience?

2. This narrative is as much a detective story as a tale of the supernatural.  What aspects of the story would be basic elements in a crime detecting mystery?

3. What do you believe the author intends the reader to believe concerning the reason for Mary Comstock's temporary imprisonment in the woodshed?  Support your answer with quotes from the story.

## INTRODUCTION: The Furnished Room

O. Henry set many of his stories in New York City, which he referred to as Bagdad-on-the-Subway. New York is the setting for this story— a place of restlessness and rootlessness for many people which relates to the lives of the man and woman who are the major characters in this tale of love, death, and a supernatural manifestation in an ordinary furnished room.

# The Furnished Room
## O. Henry

Restless, shifting, fugacious as time itself is a certain vast bulk of the population of the red brick district of the lower West Side. Homeless, they have a hundred homes. They flit from furnished room to furnished room, transients forever—transients in abode, transients in heart and mind. They sing "Home, Sweet Home" in ragtime; they carry their *lares et penates* in a bandbox; their vine is entwined about a picture hat; a rubber plant is their fig tree.

Hence the houses of this district, having had a thousand dwellers, should have a thousand tales to tell, mostly dull ones, no doubt; but it would be strange if there could not be found a ghost or two in the wake of all these vagrant guests.

One evening after dark a young man prowled among these crumbling red mansions, ringing their bells. At the twelfth he rested his lean hand baggage upon the step and wiped the dust from his hatband and fore- head. The bell sounded faint and far away in some remote, hollow depths.

To the door of this, the twelfth house whose bell he had rung, came a housekeeper who made him think of an unwholesome, surfeited worm that had eaten its nut to a hollow shell and now sought to fill the vacancy with edible lodgers.

He asked if there was a room to let.

"Come in," said the housekeeper. Her voice came from her throat; her throat seemed lined with fur. "I have the third-floor-back, vacant since a week back. Should you wish to look at it?"

The young man followed her up the stairs. A faint light from no particular source mitigated the shadows of the halls. They trod noise- lessly upon a stair carpet that its own loom would have forsworn. It seemed to have become vegetable; to have degenerated in that rank, sunless air to lush lichen or spreading moss that grew in patches to the staircase and was viscid under the foot like organic matter. At each turn of the stairs were vacant niches in the wall. Perhaps plants had once been set within them. If so they had died in that foul and tainted air. It may be that statues of the saints had stood there, but it was not difficult to conceive that imps and devils had dragged them forth in the darkness and down to the unholy depths of some furnished pit below.

"This is the room," said the housekeeper, from her furry throat. "It's a nice room. It ain't often vacant. I had some most elegant people in it last summer—no trouble at all, and paid in advance to the minute. The water's at the end of the hall. Sprowls and Mooney kept it three months. They done a vaudeville sketch. Miss B'retta Sprowls—you may have heard of her—oh, that was just the stage names—right there over the dresser is where the marriage certificate hung, framed. The gas is here, and you see there is plenty of closet room. It's a room everybody likes. It never stays idle long."

"Do you have many theatrical people rooming here?" asked the young man.

"They comes and goes. A good proportion of my lodgers is connected with the theaters. Yes, sir, this is the theatrical district. Actor people never stays long anywhere. I get my share. Yes, they comes and they goes."

He engaged the room, paying for a week in advance. He was tired, he said, and would take possession at once. He counted out the money. The room had been made ready, she said, even to towels and water. As the housekeeper moved away he put, for the thousandth time, the question that he carried at the end of his tongue.

"A young girl—Miss Vashner—Miss Eloise Vashner—do you remember such a one among your lodgers? She would be singing on the stage, most likely. A fair girl, of medium height and slender, with reddish, gold hair and a dark mole near her left eyebrow."

"No, I don't remember the name. Them stage people has names they change as often as their rooms. They comes and they goes. No, I don't call that one to mind."

No. Always no. Five months of ceaseless interrogation and the inevitable negative. So much time spent by days in questioning managers, agents, schools and choruses; by night among the audiences of theaters from all-star casts down to music halls so low that he dreaded to find what he most hoped for. He who had loved her best had tried to find her. He was sure that since her disappearance from home this great, water-girt city held her somewhere, but it was like a monstrous quicksand, shifting its particles constantly, with no foundation, its upper granules of today buried tomorrow in ooze and slime.

The furnished room received its latest guest with a first glow of pseudo hospitality, a hectic, haggard, perfunctory welcome like the specious smile of a demirep. The sophistical comfort came in reflected gleams from the decayed furniture, the ragged brocade upholstery of a couch and two chairs, a foot-wide cheap pier glass between the two windows, from one or two gilt picture frames and a brass bedstead in a corner.

The guest reclined, inert, upon a chair, while the room, confused in speech as though it were an apartment in Babel, tried to discourse to him of its divers tenantry.

A polychromatic rug like some brilliant-flowered rectangular, tropical islet lay surrounded by a billowy sea of soiled matting. Upon the gay-papered wall were those pictures that pursue the homeless one from house to house—The Huguenot Lovers, The First Quarrel, The Wedding Breakfast, Psyche at the Fountain. The mantel's chastely severe outline was ingloriously veiled behind some pert drapery drawn rakishly askew like the sashes of the Amazonian ballet. Upon it was some desolate flotsam cast aside by the room's marooned when a lucky sail had borne them to a fresh port—a trifling vase or two, pictures of actresses, a medicine bottle, some stray cards out of a deck.

One by one, as the characters of a cryptograph become explicit, the little signs left by the furnished room's procession of guests developed a significance. The threadbare space in the rug in front of the dresser told that lovely women had marched in the throng. The tiny fingerprints on the wall spoke of little prisoners trying to feel their way to sun and air. A splattered stain, raying like the shadow of a bursting bomb, witnessed where a hurled glass or bottle had splintered with its contents against the wall. Across the pier glass had been scrawled with a diamond in staggering letters the name "Marie." It seemed that the succession of dwellers in the furnished room had turned in fury—perhaps tempted beyond forebearance by its garish coldness—and wreaked upon it their passions. The furniture was chipped and bruised; the couch, distorted by bursting springs, seemed a horrible monster that had been slain during the stress of some grotesque convulsion. Some more potent upheaval had cloven a great slice from the marble mantel. Each plank in the floor owned its particular cant and shriek as from a separate and individual agony. It seemed incredible that all this malice and injury had been wrought upon the room by those who had called it for a time their home; and yet it may have been the cheated home instinct surviving blindly, the resentful rage at false household gods that had kindled their wrath. A hut that is our own we can sweep and adorn and cherish.

The young tenant in the chair allowed these thoughts to file, soft shod, through his mind, while there drifted into the room furnished sounds and furnished scents. He heard in one room a tittering and incontinent, slack laughter; in others the monologue of a scold, the rattling of dice, a lullaby, and one crying dully; above him a banjo tinkled with spirit. Doors banged somewhere; the elevated trains roared intermittently; a cat yowled miserably upon a back fence. And he breathed the breath of the house—a dank savor rather than a smell—a cold, musty effluvium as from underground vaults mingled with the reeking exhalations of linoleum and mildewed and rotten woodwork.

Then suddenly, as he rested there, the room was filled with the strong, sweet odor of mignonette. It came as upon a single buffet of wind with such sureness and fragrance and emphasis that it almost seemed a living visitant. And the man cried aloud: "What, dear?" as if he had been called, and sprang up and faced about. The rich odor clung to him and wrapped him around. He reached out his arms for it, all his senses for the time confused and commingled. How could one be peremptorily called by an odor? Surely it must have been a sound. But, was it not the sound that had touched, that had caressed him?

"She has been in this room," he cried, and he sprang to wrest from it a token, for he knew he would recognize the smallest thing that had belonged to her or that she had touched. This enveloping scent of mignonette, the odor that she had loved and made her own—whence came it?

The room had been but carelessly set in order. Scattered upon the flimsy dresser scarf were half a dozen hairpins—those discreet, indistinguishable friends of womankind, feminine of gender, infinite of mood and uncommunicative of tense. These he ignored, conscious of their triumphant lack of identity. Ransacking the drawers of the dresser he came upon a discarded, tiny, ragged handkerchief. He pressed it to his face. It was racy and insolent with heliotrope; he hurled it to the floor. In another drawer he found odd buttons, a theater program, a pawnbroker's card, two lost marshmallows, a book on the divination of dreams. In the last was a woman's black satin hair bow, which halted him, poised between ice and fire. But the black satin hair bow also is femininity's demure, impersonal common ornament and tells no tales.

And then he traversed the room like a hound on the scent, skimming the walls, considering the corners of the bulging matting on his hands and knees, rummaging mantel and tables, the curtains and hangings, the drunken cabinet in the corner, for a visible sign, unable to perceive that she was there beside, around, against, within, above him, clinging to him, wooing him, calling him so poignantly through the finer senses that even his grosser ones became cognizant of the call. Once again he answered loudly: "Yes, dear!" and turned, wild-eyed, to gaze on vacancy, for he could not yet discern form and color and love and outstretched arms in the odor of mignonette. Oh, God! whence that odor, and since when have odors had a voice to call? Thus he groped.

He burrowed in crevices and corners, and found corks and cigarettes. These he passed in passive contempt. But once he found in a fold of the matting a half-smoked cigar, and this he ground beneath his heel with a green and trenchant oath. He sifted the room from end to end. He found dreary and ignoble small records of many a peripatetic tenant; but of her whom he sought, and who may have lodged there, and whose spirit seemed to hover there, he found no trace.

And then he thought of the housekeeper.

He ran from the haunted room downstairs and to a door that showed a crack of light. She came out to his knock. He smothered his excitement as best he could.

"Will you tell me, madam," he besought her, "who occupied the room I have before I came?"

"Yes, sir. I can tell you again. 'Twas Sprowls and Mooney, as I said. Miss B'retta Sprowls it was in the theaters, but Missis Mooney she was. My house is well known for respectability. The marriage certificate hung, framed, on a nail over—"

"What kind of a lady was Miss Sprowls—in looks, I mean?"

"Why, black-haired, sir, short, and stout, with a comical face. They left a week ago Tuesday."

"And before they occupied it?"

"Why, there was a single gentleman connected with the draying business. He left owing me a week. Before him was Missis Crowder and her two children, that stayed four months; and back of them was old Mr. Doyle, whose sons paid for him. He kept the room six months. That goes back a year, sir, and further I do not remember."

He thanked her and crept back to his room. The room was dead. The essence that had vivified it was gone. The perfume of mignonette had departed. In its place was the old, stale odor of moldy house furniture, of atmosphere in storage.

The ebbing of his hope drained his faith. He sat staring at the yellow, singing gaslight. Soon he walked to the bed and began to tear the sheets into strips. With the blade of his knife he drove them tightly into every crevice around windows and door. When all was snug and taut he turned out the light, turned the gas full on again, and laid himself gratefully upon the bed.

It was Mrs. McCool's night to go with the can for beer. So she fetched it and sat with Mrs. Purdy in one of those subterranean retreats where housekeepers foregather and the worm dieth seldom.

"I rented out my third-floor-back this evening," said Mrs. Purdy, across a fine circle of foam. "A young man took it. He went up to bed two hours ago."

"Now, did ye, Mrs. Purdy, ma'am?" said Mrs. McCool, with intense admiration. "You do be a wonder for rentin' rooms of that kind. And did ye tell him, then?" she concluded in a husky whisper laden with mystery.

"Rooms," said Mrs. Purdy, in her furriest tones, "are furnished for to rent. I did not tell him, Mrs. McCool."

" 'Tis right ye are, ma'am; 'tis by renting rooms we kape alive. Ye have the rale sense for business, ma'am. There be many people will rayjict the rentin' of a room if they be tould a suicide has been after dyin' in the bed of it."

"As you say, we has our living to be making," remarked Mrs. Purdy.

"Yis, ma'am; 'tis true. 'Tis just one wake ago this day I helped ye lay out the third-floor-back. A pretty slip of a colleen she was to be killin' herself wid the gas—a swate little face she had, Mrs. Purdy, ma'am."

"She'd a-been called handsome, as you say," said Mrs. Purdy, assenting but critical, "but for that mole she had a-growin' by her left eyebrow. Do fill up your glass again, Mrs. McCool."

## FOR DISCUSSION: The Furnished Room

1. O. Henry characterizes the furnished room in his story as successfully as he does his people. Describe the character of the furnished room.
2. O. Henry has the young man in his story respond to the fragrance of mignonette as if it were a call. Does this deliberate confusion of sense impressions contribute in any way to the development of the supernatural element in the story?
3. Authors can sometimes successfully characterize a person in a single sentence or even in a phrase. O. Henry, speaking of the housekeeper, says, "... her throat seemed lined with fur." Later, when the house-keeper speaks, it is "from her furry throat." What impression do you receive of this woman from the repeated use of this image?
4. Does the housekeeper have a reason for not telling the young man the whole truth about the tenants of the furnished room? Is it a valid reason in terms of her character?
5. There is one fact in the story that proves that the young man was right in believing that the girl he loved had once lived in the fur-nished room. What is it?
6. One of the characteristics of O. Henry's skill as an author is his ability to understate an important event, thereby dramatizing it. This skill is displayed in the way O. Henry writes of the young man's ultimate fate which occurs in the furnished room. Explain.

## INTRODUCTION: Was It a Dream?

In O. Henry's story we were told of a man and woman in love and how that love endured after the death of one of the lovers. The story is imbued with grief and a hopeless sense of longing. The same plot, atmosphere, and emotional elements are to be found in de Maupassant's story which follows. In addition, both stories incorporate a somewhat cynical point of view concerning human behavior. The two stories have both similarities and differences. They vividly illustrate the ways in which two different authors choose to treat the same basic theme.

# Was It a Dream?
### Guy de Maupassant

I had loved her madly!

Why does one love? Why does one love? How queer it is to see only one being in the world, to have only one thought in one's mind, only one desire in the heart and only one name on the lips— a name which comes up continually, rising, like the water in a spring, from the depths of the soul to the lips, a name which one repeats over and over again, which one whispers ceaselessly, everywhere, like a prayer.

I am going to tell you our story, for love has only one, which is always the same. I met her and lived on her tenderness, on her caresses, in her arms, in her dresses, on her words, so completely wrapped up, bound and absorbed in everything which came from her that I no longer cared whether it was day or night, or whether I was dead or alive, on this old earth of ours.

And then she died. How? I do not know; I no longer know anything. But one evening she came home wet, for it was raining heavily, and the next day she coughed, and she coughed for about a week and took to her bed. What happened I do not remember now, but doctors came, wrote, and went away. Medicines were brought, and some women made her drink them. Her hands were hot, her forehead was burning, and her eyes were bright and sad. When I spoke to her she answered me, but I do not remember what we said. I have forgotten everything, everything, everything! She died, and I very well remember her slight, feeble sigh. The nurse said: "Ah!" and I understood; I understood!

I knew nothing more, nothing. I saw a priest who said: "Your mistress?" And it seemed to me as if he were insulting her. As she was dead, nobody had the right to say that any longer, and I turned him out. Another came who was very kind and tender, and I shed tears when he spoke to me about her.

They consulted me about the funeral, but I do not remember anything that they said, though I recollect the coffin and the sound of the hammer when they nailed her down in it. Oh! God, God!

She was buried! Buried! She! In that hole! Some people came—female friends. I made my escape and ran away. I ran and then walked through the streets, went home and the next day started on a journey.

Yesterday I returned to Paris, and when I saw my room again—our room, our bed, our furniture, everything that remains of the life of a human being after death—I was seized by such a violent attack of fresh grief that I felt like opening the window and throwing myself out into the street. I could not remain any longer among these things, between these walls which had inclosed and sheltered her, which retained a thousand atoms of her, of her skin and of her breath, in their imperceptible crevices. I took up my hat to make my escape, and just as I reached the door I passed the large glass in the hall, which she had put there so that she might look at herself every day from head to foot as she went out, to see if her toilet looked well and was correct and pretty, from her little boots to her bonnet.

I stopped short in front of that looking glass in which she had so often been reflected—so often, so often, that it must have retained her reflection. I was standing there trembling, with my eyes fixed on the glass—on that flat, profound, empty glass—which had contained her entirely and had possessed her as much as I, as my passionate looks had. I felt as if I loved that glass. I touched it; it was cold. Oh, the recollection! Sorrowful mirror, burning mirror, horrible mirror, to make men suffer such torments! Happy is the man whose heart forgets everything that it has contained, everything that has passed before it, everything that has looked at itself in it or has been reflected in its affection, in its love! How I suffer!

I went out without knowing it, without wishing it, and toward the cemetery. I found her simple grave, a white marble cross, with these few words:

*She loved, was loved, and died.*

She is there below, decayed! How horrible! I sobbed with my forehead on the ground, and I stopped there for a long time, a long time.

Then I saw that it was getting dark, and a strange, mad wish, the wish of a despairing lover, seized me. I wished to pass the night, the last night, in weeping on her grave. But I should be seen and driven out. How was I to manage? I was cunning and got up and began to roam about in that city of the dead. I walked and walked. How small this city is in comparison with the other, the city in which we live. And yet how much more numerous the dead are than the living. We need high houses, wide streets and much room for the four generations which see the daylight at the same time, drink water from the spring and wine from the vines, and eat bread from the plains.

And for all the generations of the dead, for all that ladder of humanity that has descended down to us, there is scarcely anything, scarcely anything! The earth takes them back, and oblivion effaces them. Adieu!

At the end of the cemetery, I suddenly perceived that I was in its oldest part, where those who had been dead a long time are mingling with the soil, where the crosses themselves are decayed, where possibly newcomers will be put tomorrow. It is full of untended roses, of strong and dark cypress trees—a sad and beautiful garden, nourished on human flesh.

I was alone, perfectly alone. So I crouched under a green tree and hid myself there completely amid the thick and somber branches. I waited, clinging to the trunk as a shipwrecked man does to a plank.

When it was quite dark I left my refuge and began to walk softly, slowly, inaudibly, through that ground full of dead people. I wandered about for a long time, but could not find her tomb again. I went on with extended arms, knocking against the tombs with my hands, my feet, my knees, my chest, even with my head, without being able to find her. I groped about like a blind man seeking his way; I felt the stones, the crosses, the iron railings, the metal wreaths and the wreaths of faded flowers! I read the names with my fingers, by passing them over the letters. What a night! What a night! I could not find her again!

There was no moon. What a night! I was frightened, horribly frightened in those narrow paths between two rows of graves. Graves! Graves! Graves! Nothing but graves! On my right, on my left, in front of me, around me, everywhere there were graves! I sat down on one of them, for I could not walk any longer; my knees were so weak. I could hear my heart beat! And I heard something else as well. What? A confused, nameless noise. Was the noise in my head, in the impenetrable night, or beneath the mysterious earth, the earth sown with human corpses? I looked all around me, but I cannot say how long I remained there; I was paralyzed with terror, cold with fright, ready to shout out, ready to die.

Suddenly it seemed to me that the slab of marble on which I was sitting was moving. Certainly it was moving, as if it were being raised. With a bound I sprang onto the neighboring tomb, and I saw, yes, I distinctly saw the stone which I had just quitted rise upright. Then the dead person appeared, a naked skeleton, pushing the stone back with its bent back. I saw it quite clearly, although the night was so dark. On the cross I could read:

*Here lies Jacques Olivant, who died at the age of fifty-one. He loved his family, was kind and honorable, and died in the grace of the Lord.*

The dead man also read what was inscribed on the tombstone; then he picked up a stone off the path, a little, pointed stone, and began to scrape the letters carefully. He slowly effaced them, and with the hollows of his eyes he looked at the place where they had been engraved. Then, with the tip of the bone that had been his forefinger, he wrote in luminous letters, like those lines which boys trace on walls with the tip of a lucifer match:

*Here reposes Jacques Olivant, who died at the age of fifty-one. He hastened his father's death by his unkindness, as he wished to inherit his fortune; he tortured his wife, tormented his children, deceived his neighbors, robbed everyone he could, and died wretched.*

When he had finished writing, the dead man stood motionless, looking at his work. On turning around I saw that all the graves were open, that all the dead bodies had emerged from them and that all had effaced the lines inscribed on the gravestones by their relations, substituting the truth instead. And I saw that all had been the tormentors of their neighbors—malicious, dishonest, hypocrites, liars, rogues, calumniators, envious; that they had stolen, deceived, performed every disgraceful, every abominable action, these good fathers, these faithful wives, these devoted sons, these chaste daughters, these honest tradesmen, these men and women who were called irreproachable. They were all writing at the same time, on the threshold of their eternal abode, the truth, the terrible and the holy truth, of which everybody was ignorant, or pretended to be ignorant, while they were alive.

I thought that *she* also must have written something on her tombstone; and now, running without any fear among the half-open coffins, among the corpses and skeletons, I went toward her, sure that I should find her immediately. I recognized her at once without seeing her face, which was covered by the winding sheet; and on the marble cross where shortly before I had read:

*She loved, was loved, and died.*

I now saw:

*Having gone out in the rain one day in order to deceive her lover, she caught cold and died.*

It appears that they found me at daybreak, lying on the grave unconscious.

## FOR DISCUSSION: Was It a Dream?

1. What similarities of plot, atmosphere and emotion can you discover in the O. Henry and the de Maupassant stories? What differences?
2. There is a similarity between de Maupassant's view of human behavior as expressed in his story and that of Hawthorne in his story *Young Goodman Brown*. What is the specific similarity of viewpoint that they share?
3. Does de Maupassant succeed in making the narrator's feelings of love and grief seem real to you? Whether your answer is affirmative or negative, support it by quoting from the story.
4. De Maupassant's title for his story suggests that there may be an explanation for the events seen by the narrator in the graveyard which does not involve the supernatural. Do you believe he intended the narrator's experience to have been a supernatural one or a dream—possibly a hallucination?

## INTRODUCTION: The Ghost Ship

Ghosts have chilled skins and halted hearts throughout the ages. They have sought revenge against the living. They have caused people's deaths. But not all ghosts have been malign, nor have they always frightened the people among whom they appeared. In the story that follows, you will meet a group of ghosts who may be said to be not merely friendly but, indeed, convivial.

# The Ghost Ship
## Richard Middleton

Fairfield is a little village lying near the Portsmouth Road about half-way between London and the sea. Strangers who find it by accident now and then call it a pretty, old-fashioned place; we who live in it and call it home don't find anything very pretty about it, but we should be sorry to live anywhere else. Our minds have taken the shape of the inn and the church and the green, I suppose. At all events, we never feel comfortable out of Fairfield.

Of course the Cockneys, with their vasty houses and noise-ridden streets, can call us rustics if they choose, but for all that Fairfield is a better place to live in than London. Doctor says that when he goes to London his mind is bruised with the weight of the houses, and he was a Cockney born. He had to live there himself when he was a little chap, but he knows better now. You gentlemen may laugh—perhaps some of you come from London way—but it seems to me that a witness like that is worth a gallon of arguments.

Dull? Well, you might find it dull, but I assure you that I've listened to all the London yarns you have spun tonight and they're absolutely nothing to the things that happen at Fairfield. It's because of our way of thinking and minding our own business. If one of your Londoners were set down on the green of a Saturday night when the ghosts of the lads who died in the war keep tryst with the lasses who lie in the churchyard, he couldn't help being curious and interfering, and then the ghosts would go somewhere where it was quieter. But we just let them come and go and don't make any fuss, and in consequence Fairfield is the ghostliest place in all England. Why, I've seen a headless man sitting on the edge of the well in broad daylight, and the children playing about his feet as if he were their father. Take my word for it, spirits know when they are well off as much as human beings.

Still, I must admit that the thing I'm going to tell you about was queer even for our part of the world, where three packs of ghost-hounds hunt regularly during the season, and blacksmith's great-grandfather is busy all night shoeing the dead gentlemen's horses. Now that's a thing that wouldn't happen in London, because of their interfering ways, but black-smith he lies up aloft and sleeps as quiet as a lamb. Once when he had a bad head he shouted down to them not to make so much noise, and in the morning he found an old guinea left on the anvil as an apology. He wears it on his watch chain now. But I must get on with my story; if I start telling you about the queer happenings at Fairfield I'll never stop.

It all came of the great storm in the spring of '97, the year that we had two great storms. This was the first one, and I remember it very well, because I found in the morning that it had lifted the thatch of my pigsty into the widow's garden as clean as a boy's kite. When I looked over the hedge, widow—Tom Lamport's widow that was—was prodding for her nasturtiums with a daisy-grubber. After I had watched her for a little I went down to the "Fox and Grapes" to tell landlord what she had said to me. Landlord he laughed, being a married man and at ease with the sex. "Come to that," he said, "the tempest has blowed something into my field. A kind of a ship I think it would be."

I was surprised at that until he explained that it was only a ghost ship and would do no hurt to the turnips. We argued that it had been blown up from the sea at Portsmouth, and then we talked of something else. There were two slates down at the parsonage and a big tree in Lumley's meadow. It was a rare storm.

I reckon the wind had blown our ghosts all over England. They were coming back for days afterwards with foundered horses and as footsore as possible, and they were so glad to get back to Fairfield that some of them walked up the street crying like little children. Squire said that his great-grandfather's great-grandfather hadn't looked so deadbeat since the Battle of Naseby, and he's an educated man.

What with one thing and another, I should think it was a week before we got straight again, and then one afternoon I met the landlord on the green and he had a worried face. "I wish you'd come and have a look at that ship in my field," he said to me; "it seems to me it's leaning real hard on the turnips. I can't bear thinking what the missus will say when she sees it."

I walked down the lane with him, and sure enough there was a ship in the middle of his field, but such a ship as no man had seen on the water for three hundred years, let alone in the middle of a turnip field.

It was all painted black and covered with carvings, and there was a great bay window in the stern for all the world like the Squire's drawing room. There was a crowd of little black cannon on deck and looking out of her portholes, and she was anchored at each end to the hard ground. I have seen the wonders of the world on picture postcards, but I have never seen anything to equal that.

"She seems very solid for a ghost ship," I said, seeing the landlord was bothered.

"I should say it's a betwixt and between," he answered, puzzling it over, "but it's going to spoil a matter of fifty turnips, and missus she'll want it moved." We went up to her and touched the side, and it was as hard as a real ship. "Now there's folks in England would call that very curious," he said.

Now I don't know much about ships, but I should think that that ghost ship weighed a solid two hundred tons, and it seemed to me that she had come to stay, so that I felt sorry for the landlord, who was a married man. "All the horses in Fairfield won't move her out of my turnips," he said, frowning at her.

Just then we heard a noise on her deck, and we looked up and saw that a man had come out of her front cabin and was looking down at us very peaceably. He was dressed in a black uniform set out with rusty gold lace, and he had a great cutlass by his side in a brass sheath. "I'm Captain Bartholomew Roberts," he said, in a gentleman's voice, "put in for recruits. I seem to have brought her rather far up the harbor."

"Harbor!" cried landlord; "why, you're fifty miles from the sea."

Captain Roberts didn't turn a hair. "So much as that, is it?" he said coolly. "Well, it's of no consequence."

Landlord was a bit upset at this. "I don't want to be unneighborly," he said, "but I wish you hadn't brought your ship into my field. You see, my wife sets great store on these turnips."

The Captain took a pinch of snuff out of a fine gold box that he pulled out of his pocket, and dusted his fingers with a silk handkerchief in a very genteel fashion. "I'm only here for a few months," he said; "but if a testimony of my esteem would pacify your good lady I should be content," and with the words he loosed a great gold brooch from the neck of his coat and tossed it down to landlord.

Landlord blushed as red as a strawberry. "I'm not denying she's fond of jewelry," he said, "but it's too much for half a sackful of turnips." And indeed it was a handsome brooch.

The Captain laughed. "Tut, man," he said, "it's a forced sale, and you deserve a good price. Say no more about it." And nodding good-day to us, he turned on his heel and went into the cabin. Landlord walked back up the lane like a man with a weight off his mind. "That tempest has blowed me a bit of luck," he said; "the missus will be main pleased with that brooch. It's better than blacksmith's guinea, any day."

Ninety-seven was Jubilee year, the year of the second Jubilee, you remember, and we had great doings at Fairfield, so that we hadn't much time to bother about the ghost ship, though anyhow it isn't our way to meddle in things that don't concern us. Landlord, he saw his tenant once or twice when he was hoeing his turnips and passed the time of day, and landlord's wife wore her new brooch to church every Sunday. But we didn't mix much with the ghosts at any time, all except an idiot lad there was in the village, and he didn't know the difference between a man and a ghost, poor innocent! On Jubilee Day, however, somebody told Captain Roberts why the church bells were ringing, and he hoisted a flag and fired off his guns like a loyal Englishman. 'Tis true the guns were shotted, and one of the round shot knocked a hole in Farmer Johnstone's barn, but nobody thought much of that in such a season of rejoicing.

It wasn't till our celebrations were over that we noticed that anything was wrong in Fairfield. 'Twas shoemaker who told me first about it one morning at the "Fox and Grapes." "You know my great-great-uncle?" he said to me.

"You mean Joshua, the quiet lad," I answered, knowing him well.

"Quiet!" said shoemaker indigantly. "Quiet you call him, coming home at three o'clock every morning as drunk as a magistrate and waking up the whole house with his noise."

"Why, it can't be Joshua!" I said, for I knew him for one of the most respectable young ghosts in the village.

"Joshua it is," said shoemaker; "and one of these nights he'll find himself out in the street if he isn't careful."

This kind of talk shocked me, I can tell you, for I don't like to hear a man abusing his own family, and I could hardly believe that a steady youngster like Joshua had taken to drink. But just then in came butcher Aylwin in such a temper that he could hardly drink his beer. "The young puppy! the young puppy!" he kept on saying; and it was some time before shoemaker and I found out that he was talking about his ancestor that fell at Senlac.

"Drink?" said shoemaker hopefully, for we all like company in our misfortunes, and butcher nodded grimly.

"The young noodle," he said, emptying his tankard.

Well, after that I kept my ears open, and it was the same story all over the village. There was hardly a young man among all the ghosts of Fairfield who didn't roll home in the small hours of the morning the worse for liquor. I used to wake up in the night and hear them stumble past my house, singing outrageous songs. The worst of it was that we couldn't keep the scandal to ourselves, and the folk at Greenhill began to talk of "sodden Fairfield," and taught their children to sing a song about us:

*"Sodden Fairfield, sodden Fairfield, has no use for bread-and-butter;*
*Rum for breakfast, rum for dinner, rum for tea, and rum for supper!"*

We are easygoing in our village, but we didn't like that.

Of course we soon found out where the young fellows went to get the drink, and landlord was terribly cut up that his tenant should have turned out so badly, but his wife wouldn't hear of parting with the brooch, so that he couldn't give the Captain notice to quit. But as time went on, things grew from bad to worse, and at all hours of the day you would see those young reprobates sleeping it off on the village green. Nearly every afternoon a ghost wagon used to jolt down to the ship with a lading of rum, and though the older ghosts seemed inclined to give the Captain's hospitality the go-by, the youngers were neither to hold nor to bind.

So one afternoon when I was taking my nap I heard a knock at the door, and there was parson looking very serious, like a man with a job before him that he didn't altogether relish. "I'm going down to talk to the Captain about all this drunkenness in the village, and I want you to come with me," he said straight out.

I can't say that I fancied the visit much myself, and I tried to hint to parson that as, after all, they were only a lot of ghosts, it didn't very much matter.

"Dead or alive, I'm responsible for their good conduct," he said, "and I'm going to do my duty and put a stop to this continued disorder. And you are coming with me, John Simmons." So I went, parson being a persuasive kind of man.

We went down to the ship, and as we approached her, I could see the Captain tasting the air on deck. When he saw parson he took off his hat very politely, and I can tell you that I was relieved to find that he had a proper respect for the cloth. Parson acknowledged his salute and spoke out stoutly enough. "Sir, I should be glad to have a word with you."

"Come on board, sir; come on board," said the Captain, and I could tell by his voice that he knew why we were there. Parson and I climbed up an uneasy kind of ladder, and the Captain took us into the great cabin at the back of the ship, where the bay window was. It was the most wonderful place you ever saw in your life, all full of gold and silver plate, swords with jeweled scabbards, carved oak chairs, and great chests that looked as though they were bursting with guineas. Even parson was surprised, and he did not shake his head very hard when the Captain took down some silver cups and poured us out a drink of rum. I tasted mine, and I don't mind saying that it changed my view on things entirely. There was nothing betwixt and between about that rum, and I felt that it was ridiculous to blame the lads for drinking too much of stuff like that. It seemed to fill my veins with honey and fire.

Parson put the case squarely to the Captain, but I didn't listen much to what he said; I was busy sipping my drink and looking through the window at the fishes swimming to and fro over landlord's turnips. Just then it seemed the most natural thing in the world that they should be there, though afterwards, of course, I could see that that proved it was a ghost ship.

But even then I thought it was queer when I saw a drowned sailor float by in the thin air with his hair and beard all full of bubbles. It was the first time I had seen anything quite like that at Fairfield.

All the time I was regarding the wonders of the deep, parson was telling Captain Roberts how there was no peace or rest in the village owing to the curse of drunkenness, and what a bad example the youngsters were setting to the older ghosts. The Captain listened very attentively, and only put in a word now and then about boys being boys and young men sowing their wild oats. But when parson had finished his speech he filled up our silver cups and said to parson, with a flourish, "I should be sorry to cause trouble anywhere where I have been made welcome, and you will be glad to hear that I put to sea tomorrow night. And now you must drink me a prosperous voyage." So we all stood up and drank the toast with honor, and that noble rum was like hot oil in my veins.

After that Captain showed us some of the curiosities he had brought back from foreign parts, and we were greatly amazed, though afterwards I couldn't clearly remember what they were. And then I found myself walking across the turnips with parson, and I was telling him of the glories of the deep that I had seen through the window of the ship. He turned on me severely. "If I were you, John Simmons," he said, "I should go straight home to bed." He has a way of putting things that wouldn't occur to an ordinary man, has parson, and I did as he told me.

Well, next day it came on to blow, and it blew harder and harder, till about eight o'clock at night I heard a noise and looked out into the garden. I dare say you won't believe me, it seems a bit tall even to me, but the wind had lifted the thatch of my pigsty into the widow's garden a second time. I thought I wouldn't wait to hear what widow had to say about it, so I went across the green to the "Fox and Grapes," and the wind was so strong that I danced along on tiptoe like a girl at the fair. When I got to the inn landlord had to help me shut the door; it seemed as though a dozen goats were pushing against it to come in out of the storm.

"It's a powerful tempest," he said, drawing the beer. "I hear there's a chimney down at Dickory End."

"It's a funny thing how these sailors know about the weather," I answered. "When Captain said he was going tonight, I was thinking it would take a capful of wind to carry the ship back to sea, but now here's more than a capful."

"Ah, yes," said landlord, "it's tonight he goes true enough, and, mind you, though he treated me handsome over the rent, I'm not sure it's a loss to the village. I don't hold with gentrice who fetch their drink from London instead of helping local traders to get their living."

"But you haven't got any rum like his," I said, to draw him out.

His neck grew red above his collar, and I was afraid I'd gone too far; but after a while he got his breath with a grunt.

"John Simmons," he said, "if you've come down here this windy night to talk a lot of fool's talk, you've wasted a journey."

Well, of course, then I had to smooth him down with praising his rum, and Heaven forgive me for swearing it was better than Captain's. For the like of that rum no living lips have tasted save mine and parson's. But somehow or other I brought landlord round, and presently we must have a glass of his best to prove its quality.

"Beat that if you can!" he cried, and we both raised our glasses to our mouths, only to stop halfway and look at each other in amaze. For the wind that had been howling outside like an outrageous dog had all of a sudden turned as melodious as the carol-boys of a Christmas Eve.

"Surely that's not my Martha," whispered landlord; Martha being his great-aunt that lived in the loft overhead.

We went to the door, and the wind burst it open so that the handle was driven clean into the plaster of the wall. But we didn't think about that at the time; for over our heads, sailing very comfortably through the windy stars, was the ship that had passed the summer in landlord's field. Her portholes and her bay window were blazing with lights, and there was a noise of singing and fiddling on her decks. "He's gone," shouted landlord above the storm, "and he's taken half the village with him!" I could only nod in answer, not having lungs like bellows of leather.

In the morning we were able to measure the strength of the storm, and over and above my pigsty there was damage enough wrought in the village to keep us busy. True it is that the children had to break down no branches for the firing that autumn, since the wind had strewn the woods with more than they could carry away. Many of our ghosts were scattered abroad, but this time very few came back, all the young men having sailed with Captain; and not only ghosts, for a poor half-witted lad was missing, and we reckoned that he had stowed himself away or perhaps shipped as cabin boy, not knowing any better.

What with the lamentations of the ghost-girls and the grumblings of families who had lost an ancestor, the village was upset for a while, and the funny thing was that it was the folk who had complained most of the carryings-on of the youngsters, who made most noise now that they were gone. I hadn't any sympathy with shoemaker or butcher, who ran about saying how much they missed their lads, but it made me grieve to hear the poor bereaved girls calling their lovers by name on the village green at nightfall. It didn't seem fair to me that they should have lost their men a second time, after giving up life in order to join them, as like as not. Still, not even a spirit can be sorry for ever, and after a few months we made up our mind that the folk who had sailed in the ship were never coming back, and we didn't talk about it any more.

And then one day, I dare say it would be a couple of years after, when the whole business was quite forgotten, who should come traipsing along the road from Portsmouth but the daft lad who had gone away with the ship, without waiting till he was dead to become a ghost. You never saw such a boy as that in all your life. He had a great rusty cutlass hanging to a string at his waist, and he was tattooed all over in fine colors, so that even his face looked like a girl's sampler. He had a handkerchief in his hand full of foreign shells and old-fashioned pieces of small money, very curious, and he walked up to the well outside his mother's house and drew himself a drink as if he had been nowhere in particular.

The worst of it was that he had come back as soft-headed as he went, and try as we might we couldn't get anything reasonable out of him. He talked a lot of gibberish about keelhauling and walking the plank and crimson-murders—things which a decent sailor should know nothing about, so that it seemed to me that for all his manners Captain had been more of a pirate than a gentleman mariner. But to draw sense out of that boy was as hard as picking cherries off a crabtree. One silly tale he had that he kept on drifting back to, and to hear him you would have thought that it was the only thing that happened to him in his life. "We was at anchor," he would say, "off an island called the Basket of Flowers, and the sailors had caught a lot of parrots and we were teaching them to swear. Up and down the decks, up and down the decks, and the language they used was dreadful. Then we looked up and saw the masts of the Spanish ship outside the harbor. Outside the harbor they were, so we threw the parrots into the sea and sailed out to fight. And all the parrots were drownded in the sea and the language they used was dreadful." That's the sort of boy he was, nothing but silly talk of parrots when we asked him about the fighting. And we never had a chance of teaching him better, for two days after he ran away again, and hasn't been seen since.

That's my story, and I assure you that things like that are happening at Fairfield all the time. The ship has never come back, but somehow as people grow older they seem to think that one of these windy nights she'll come sailing in over the hedges with all the lost ghosts on board. Well, when she comes, she'll be welcome. There's one ghost-lass that has never grown tired of waiting for her lad to return. Every night you'll see her out on the green, straining her poor eyes with looking for the mast-lights among the stars. A faithful lass you'd call her, and I'm thinking you'd be right.

Landlord's field wasn't a penny the worse for the visit, but they do say that since then the turnips that have been grown in it have tasted of rum.

## FOR DISCUSSION: The Ghost Ship

1. Ghosts have always been assumed to be "different" from living beings. In what ways are the ghosts in this story different from or similar to the human characters? How do these ghosts compare with other ghosts you have read about?
2. Human beings frequently have a way of muddling their affairs. So do ghosts, according to this author. Give an example of such ghostly muddling from the story.
3. The author adds an interesting dimension to his story by having the local male ghosts of Fairfield ship out on the ghost ship. How does the author make this event real to the reader in emotional terms?
4. The author adds a few final fascinating touches to his narrative by bringing back "the daft lad" and letting him speak of his adventures on the ghost ship. Do you think the boy was merely "daft," or did he actually visit such places as "the Basket of Flowers"?
5. Landlord explains that the ghost ship "would do no hurt to the turnips." Did it?

# INTRODUCTION: Hey, Look at Me!

Ghosts have walked and wailed, rattled their chains, and gone about their occasionally grisly business in countless stories. Many of them have been bound to earth for a particular task as was the ghost of Hamlet's murdered father. Here we encounter the ghost of a writer, Maxwell Kingery, who was also bound to earth for a particularly compelling reason. Because of the author's sensitive and skillful telling of his tale, the reader is likely to find himself feeling a deep compassion for the ghost of Maxwell Kingery as it wanders the streets of a small California town, desperately intent on trying to achieve after death what it had failed to accomplish in life.

# Hey, Look at Me!
## Jack Finney

About six months after Maxwell Kingery died, I saw his ghost walking along Miller Avenue in Mill Valley, California. It was 2:20 in the afternoon, a clear sunny day, and I saw him from a distance which I later paced off; it was less than fifteen feet. There is no possibility that I was mistaken about who—or what—I saw, and I'll tell you why I'm sure.

My name is Peter Marks, and I'm the book editor of a San Francisco newspaper. I live in Mill Valley a dozen miles from San Francisco, and I work at home most days; from about nine till around two or three in the afternoon. My wife is likely to need something from the store by then, so I generally walk downtown, nearly always stopping in at Myer's bakery, which has a lunch counter. Until he died, I often had coffee there with Max Kingery, and we'd sit at the counter for half an hour and talk.

He was a writer, so it was absolutely inevitable that I'd be introduced to him soon after he came to Mill Valley. A lot of writers live here, and whenever a new one arrives people love to introduce us and then stand back to see what will happen. Nothing much ever does, though once a man denounced me right out on the sidewalk in front of the Redhill liquor store. "Peter Marks? The book critic?" he said, and when I nodded, he said, "You, sir, are a puling idiot who ought to be writing 'News of Our Pets' for *The Carmel Pine Cone* instead of criticizing the work of your betters." Then he turned, and—this is the word—stalked off, while I stood staring after him, smiling. I'd panned two of his books, he'd been waiting for Peter Marks ever since, and was admirably ready when his moment came.

But all Max Kingery said, stiffly, the day we were introduced, was, "How do you do," then he stood there nodding rapidly a number of times, finally remembering to smile; and that's all I said to him. It was in the spring, downtown in front of the bank, I think, and Max was bare-headed, wearing a light-brown shabby-looking topcoat with the collar turned up. He was a black-haired, black-eyed man with heavy black-rimmed glasses, intense and quick-moving; it was hard for him to stand still there. He was young but already stooped, his hair thinning. I could see this was a man who took himself seriously, but his name rang no bell in my mind and we spoke politely and parted quickly; probably forever if we hadn't kept meeting in the bakery after that. But we both came in for coffee nearly every afternoon, and after we'd met and nodded half a dozen times we were almost forced to sit together at the counter and try to make some conversation.

So we slowly became friends; he didn't have many. After I knew him I looked up what he'd written, naturally, and found it was a first novel which I'd reviewed a year before. I'd said it showed promise, and that I thought it was possible he'd write a fine novel someday, but all in all it was the kind of review usually called *mixed,* and I felt awkward about it.

But I needn't have worried. I soon learned that what I or anyone else thought of his book was of no importance to Max; he knew that in time I and everyone else would have to say that Maxwell Kingery was a very great writer. Right now not many people, even here in town, knew he was a writer at all, but that was OK with Max; he wasn't ready for them to know. Someday not only every soul in Mill Valley but the inhabitants of remote villages in distant places would know he was one of the important writers of his time, and possibly of all time. Max never said any of this, but you learned that he thought so and that it wasn't egotism. It was just something he knew, and maybe he was right. Who knows how many Shakespeares have died prematurely, how many young geniuses we've lost in stupid accidents, illnesses and wars?

Cora, my wife, met Max presently, and because he looked thin, hungry and forlorn—as he was—she had me ask him over for a meal, and pretty soon we were having him often. His wife had died about a year before we met him. (The more I learned about Max, the more it seemed to me that he was one of those occasional people who, beyond all dispute, are plagued by simple bad luck all their lives.) After his wife died, and his book had failed, he moved from the city to Mill Valley, and now he lived alone working on the novel which, with the others to follow, was going to make him famous. He lived in a mean, cheap little house he'd rented, walking downtown for meals. I never knew where he got whatever money he had; it wasn't much. So we had him over often so Cora could feed him, and, once he was sure he was welcome, he'd stop in of his own accord, if his work was going well. And nearly every day I saw him downtown, and we'd sit over coffee and talk.

It was seldom about writing. All he'd ever say about his own work when we met was it was going well or that it was not, because he knew I was interested. Some writers don't like to talk about what they're doing, and he was one; I never even knew what his book was about. We talked about politics, the possible futures of the world, and whatever else people on the way to becoming pretty good friends talk about. Occasionally he read a book I'd reviewed, and we'd discuss it and my review. He was always polite enough about what I did, but his real attitude showed through. Some writers are belligerent about critics, some are sullen and hostile, but Max was just contemptuous. I'm sure he believed that all writers outranked all critics—well or badly, they actually do the deed which we only sit and carp about. And sometimes Max would listen to an opinion of mine about someone's book, then he'd shrug and say, "Well, you're not a writer," as though that severely limited my understanding. I'd say, "No, I'm a critic," which seemed a good answer to me, but Max would nod as though I'd agreed with him. He liked me, but to Max my work made me only a hanger-on, a camp follower, almost a parasite. That's why it was all right to accept free meals from me; I was one of the people who live off the work writers do, and I'm sure he thought it was only my duty, which I wouldn't deny, to help him get his book written. Reading it would be my reward.

But, of course, I never read Max's next book or the others that were to follow it; he died that summer, absolutely pointlessly. He caught flu or something; one of those nameless things everyone gets occasionally. But Max didn't always eat well or live sensibly, and it hung on and turned into pneumonia, though he didn't know that. He lay in that little house of his waiting to get well, and didn't. By the time he got himself to a doctor, and the doctor got him to a hospital and got some penicillin in him, it was too late and Max died in Marin General Hospital that night.

What made it even more shocking to Cora and me was the way we learned about it. We were out of town on vacation 600 miles away in Utah when it happened, and didn't know about it. (We've thought over and again, of course, that if only we'd been home when Max took sick we'd have taken him to our house and he'd never have gotten pneumonia, and I'm sure it's true; Max was just an unlucky man.) When we got home, not only did we learn that Max was dead but even his funeral, over ten days before, was already receding into the past.

So there was no way for Cora and me to make ourselves realize that

Max was actually gone forever. You return from a vacation and slip back into an old routine so easily sometimes it hardly seems you'd left. It was like that now, and walking into the bakery again for coffee in the afternoons it seemed only a day or so since I'd last seen Max here, and whenever the door opened I'd find myself glancing up.

Except for a few people who remembered seeing me around town with Max, and who spoke to me about him now, shaking their heads, it didn't seem to me that Max's death was even discussed. I'm sure people had talked about it to some extent at least, although not many had known him well or at all. But other events had replaced that one by some days. So to Cora and me Max's absence from the town didn't seem to have left any discernible gap in it.

Even visiting the cemetery didn't help. It's in San Rafael, not Mill Valley, and the grave was in a remote corner; we had to climb a steep hill to reach it. But it hardly seemed real; there was no marker, and we had to count in from the road to even locate it. Standing there in the sun with Cora, I felt a flash of resentment against his relatives, but then I knew I shouldn't. Max had a few scattered cousins or something in New Jersey and Pennsylvania. The last time he'd known any of them at all well they'd been children, and he hadn't corresponded with them since. Now they'd sent a minimum of money to California to pay expenses, more from family pride than for Max, I expect, and none of them had come themselves. You couldn't blame them, it was a long way and expensive, but it was sad; there'd been only five people at the funeral. Max had never been in or even seen this cemetery, and standing at the unmarked grave, the new grass already beginning, I couldn't get it through my head that it had anything much to do with him.

He just vanished from the town, that's all. His things—a half-finished manuscript, portable typewriter, some clothes and half a ream of unused yellow paper—had been shipped to his relatives. And Max, with a dozen great books hidden in his brain, who had been going to become famous, was now just gone, hardly missed and barely remembered.

Time is the great healer, it makes you forget; sometimes it makes you forget literally and with great cruelty. I knew a man whose wife ran away, and he never saw her again. He missed her so much he thought he could never for a moment forget it. A year later, reading in his living room at night, he became so absorbed in his book that when he heard a faint familiar noise in the kitchen he called out without looking up from his book and asked his wife to bring him a cup of tea when she came back into the room. Only when there was no answer did he look up from his complete forgetfulness; then his loss swept over him worse than ever.

About six months after Max died, I finished my day's work and walked downtown. This was in January, and we'd just had nearly a month of rain, fog and wet chill. Then California did what it does several times every winter and for which I always forgive it anything. The rain stopped, the sun came out, the sky turned an unclouded blue, and the temperature went up into the high 70s. Everything was lush from the winter rains and there was no way to distinguish those three or four days from summer, and I walked into town in shirt-sleeves. And when I started across Miller Avenue by the bus station heading for Myer's bakery across the street and saw Max Kingery over there walking toward the corner of Throckmorton just ahead, I wasn't surprised but just glad to see him. I think it was because this was like a continuation of the summer I'd known him, the interval following it omitted; and because I'd never really had proof that he died. So I walked on, crossing the street and watching Max, thin, dark and intense; he didn't see me. I was waiting till I got close enough to call to him and I reached the middle of the street and even took a step or two past it before I remembered that Max Kingery was dead. Then I just stood there, my mouth hanging open, as Max or what seemed to be Max walked on to the corner, turned, and moved on out of sight.

I went on to the bakery then and had my coffee; I had to have something. I don't know if I could have spoken, but I didn't have to; they always set a cup of coffee in front of me when I came in. My hand shook when I lifted the cup, and I spilled some, and if it had occurred to me I'd have gone to a bar instead and had several drinks.

If you ever have some such experience you'll learn that people resist believing you as they resist nothing else; you'll resist it yourself. I got home and told Cora what had happened; we sat in the living room and this time I did have a drink in my hand. She listened; there really wasn't much to say, I found, except that I'd seen Max Kingery walking along Miller Avenue. I couldn't blame Cora; my words sounded flat and foolish as I heard them. She nodded and said that several times she'd seen dark, preoccupied, thin young men downtown who reminded her a little of Max. It was only natural; it was where we'd so often run into him.

Patiently I said, "No; listen to me, Cora. It's one thing to see someone who reminds you of someone else; from a distance, or from the back, or just as he disappears in a crowd. But you cannot possibly mistake a stranger when you see him close up and see his face in full daylight for someone you know well and saw often. With the possible exception of identical twins, there are no such resemblances between people. That was Max, Cora, Max Kingery and no one else in the world."

Cora just sat there on the davenport continuing to look at me; she didn't know what to say. I understood, and felt half sorry for her, half irritated. Finally—she had to say *something*—she said, "Well...what was he wearing?"

I had to stop and think. Then I shrugged. "Well, just some kind of pants; I didn't notice the shoes; a dark shirt of some kind, maybe plaid, I don't know. And one of those round straw hats."

"Round straw hats?"

"Yeah, you know. You see people wearing them in the summer. I think they buy them at carnivals or somewhere. With a peak. Shaped like a baseball cap only they're made of some kind of shiny yellow straw. Usually the peak is stitched around the rim with a narrow strip of red cloth or braid. This one was, and it had a red button on top, and"—I remembered this suddenly, triumphantly—"it had his initials on the front! Big red initials, *M.K.*, about three inches high, stitched into the straw just over the peak in red thread or braid or something."

Cora was nodding decisively. "That proves it."

"Of course! It——"

"No, no," she said irritably. "It proves that it *wasn't* Max; it couldn't be!"

I don't know why we were so irritable; fear of the unnatural, I suppose. "And just how does it prove that?"

"Oh, Pete! Can you *imagine* Max Kingery of all people wearing a hat like that? You've got to be"—she shrugged, hunting for the word— "some kind of extrovert to wear silly hats. Of all people in the world who would *not* wear a straw baseball cap with a red button on the top and three-inch-high *initials* on the front..." She stopped, looking at me anxiously, and after a moment I had to agree.

"Yeah," I said slowly. "He'd be the last guy in the world to wear one of those." I gave in then; there wasn't anything else to do. "It must have been someone else. I probably got the initials wrong; I saw what I thought they ought to be instead of what they were. It would *have* to be someone else, naturally, cap or no cap." Then the memory of what I'd seen rose up in my mind again clear as a sharply detailed photograph, and I said slowly, "But I just hope you see him sometime, that's all. Whoever he is."

She saw him ten days later. There was a movie at the Sequoia we wanted to see, so we got our sitter, then drove downtown after supper; the weather was clear and dry but brisk, temperature in the middle or high thirties. When we got to the box office, the picture was still on with twenty minutes to go yet, so we took a little walk first.

Except for the theater and a bar or two, downtown Mill Valley is locked up and deserted at night. But most of the display windows are left lighted, so we strolled along Throckmorton Avenue and began looking into them, beginning with Gomez Jewelry. We were out of sight of the theater here, and as we moved slowly along from window to window there wasn't another human being in sight, not a car moving, and our own footsteps on the sidewalk—unusually loud—were the only sound. We were at The Men's Shop looking in at a display of cuff links, Cora urging me once more to start wearing shirts with French cuffs so I could wear links in my sleeves, when I heard footsteps turn a corner and begin approaching us on Throckmorton, and I knew it was Max.

I used to say that I'd like to have some sort of psychical experience, that I'd like to see a ghost, but I was wrong. I think it must be one of the worst kinds of fear. I now believe it can drive men insane and whiten their hair, and that it has. It's a nasty fear, you're so helpless, and it began in me now, increasing steadily, and I wanted to spare Cora the worst of it.

She was still talking, pointing at a pair of cuff links made from old cable-car tokens. I knew she'd become aware of the footsteps in a moment and turn to see whoever was passing. I had to prepare her before she turned and saw Max full in the face without warning, and—not wanting to—I turned my head slowly. A permanent awning projects over the storefronts along here, and the light from the windows seemed to be confined under it, not reaching the outer edge of the walk beyond the awning. But there was a three-quarter moon just rising above the trees that surround the downtown area, and by that pale light I saw Max walking briskly along that outer edge of sidewalk beside the curb, only a dozen yards away now. He was bareheaded and I saw his face sharp and clear, and it was Max beyond all doubt. There was no way to say anything else to myself.

I slipped my hand under Cora's coat sleeve and began squeezing her upper arm, steadily harder and harder, till it must have approached pain—and she understood, becoming aware of the footsteps. I felt her body stiffen and I wished she wouldn't but knew she had to—she turned. Then we stood there as he walked steadily toward us in the moonlight. My scalp stirred, each hair of my head moved and tried to stand. The skin all over my body chilled as the blood receded from it. Beside me Cora stood shivering, violently, and her teeth were chattering, the only time in my life I've ever heard the sound. I believe she would have fallen except for my grip on her arm.

Courage was useless, and I don't claim I had any, but it seemed to me that to save Cora from some unspeakable consequence of fear beyond ability to bear it that I had to speak and that I had to do it casually. I can't say why I thought that, but as Max approached—his regular steadily advancing steps the only sound left in the world now, his white face in the moonlight not ten feet away—I said, "Hello, Max."

*170*

At first I thought he wasn't going to answer or respond in any way. He walked on, eyes straight ahead, for at least two more steps, then his head turned very slowly as though the effort were enormous, and he looked at us as he passed with a terrible sadness lying motionless in his eyes. Then, just as slowly, he turned away again, eyes forward, and he was actually a pace or two beyond us when his voice—a dead monotone, the effort tremendous—said, "Hello," and it was the voice of despair, absolute and hopeless.

The street curves just ahead, he would disappear around its bend in a moment, and as I stared after him, in spite of the fear and sorrow for Max, I was astounded at what I saw now. There is a kind of jacket which rightly or wrongly I associate with a certain kind of slouching, thumbs-hooked-in-the-belt juvenile exhibitionist. They are made of some sort of shiny sateen-like cloth, always in two bright and violently contrasting colors—the sleeves yellow, the body of a chemical green, for example—and usually a name of some sort is lettered across the back. Teenage gangs wear them, or used to.

Max wore one now. It was hard to tell colors in the moonlight, but I think it was orange with red sleeves, and stitched on the back in a great flowing script that nearly covered it was *Max K.* Then he was gone, around the corner, his fading footsteps continuing two, three, four or five more times as they dwindled into silence.

I had to support Cora, and her feet stumbled as we walked to the car. In the car she began to cry, rocking back and forth, her hands over her face. She told me later that she'd cried from grief at feeling such fear of Max. But it helped her, and I drove us to lights and people then; to a crowded bar away from Mill Valley in Sausalito a few miles off. We sat and drank then, several brandies each, and talked and wondered and asked each other the same questions but had no answers.

I think other people saw Max in Mill Valley during those days. One of the local cabdrivers who park by the bus station walked up to me one day; actually he strolled, hands in pockets, making a point of seeming very casual. He said, "Say, that friend of yours, that young guy used to be around town that died?" There was caution in his voice, and he stood watching me closely as I answered. I nodded and said yeah to show that I understood who he meant. "Well, did he have a brother or something?" the driver said, and I shook my head and said not that I knew of. He nodded but was unsatisfied, still watching my face and waiting for me to offer something more but I didn't. And I knew he'd seen Max. I'm sure others saw him and knew who it was, as Cora and I did; it isn't something you mention casually. And I suppose there were those who saw him and merely recognized him vaguely as someone they'd seen around town before.

I walked over to Max's old house a day or so after we'd seen him; by that time, of course, I knew why he'd come back. The real estate office that had it listed for rental again would have let me have the key if I'd asked; they knew me. But I didn't know what I could tell them as a reason for going in. It was an old house, run down, too small for most people; not the kind that rents quickly or that anyone bothers guarding too diligently. I felt sure I could get in somewhere, and on the tiny back porch, shielded from view, I tried the kitchen window and it opened and I climbed in.

The few scraps of furniture that had come with the place were still there, in the silence: a wooden table and two chairs in the tiny kitchen which Max had hardly used; the iron single bed in the bedroom; the worn-out musty-smelling davenport and matching chair in the living room and the rickety card table beside the front windows where Max had worked. What little I found, I found lying on the floor beside the table; two crumpled-up wads of the yellow copy paper Max had used.

I opened them up, but it's hard to describe what was written on them. There were single words and what seemed to be parts of words and fragments of sentences and completely unreadable scribblings, all written in pencil. There was a word that might have been *forest* or *foreign;* the final letters degenerated into a scrawl as though the hand holding the pencil had begun to fall away from the paper before it could finish. There was an unfinished sentence beginning, *She ran to,* and the stroke crossing the *t* wavered on partway across and then down the sheet till it ran off the bottom. There is no use describing in detail what is on those two crumpled sheets; there's no sense to be made of it, though I've often tried. It looks, I imagine, like the scrawlings of a man weak from fever and in delirium; as though every squiggle and wobbly line were made with almost-impossible effort. And I'm sure they were. It is true that they might be notes jotted down months earlier when Max was alive and which no one bothered to pick up and remove; but I know they aren't. They're the reason Max came back. They're what he tried to do, and failed.

I don't know what ghosts are or why, in rare instances, they appear. Maybe all human beings have the power, if they have the will, to reappear as Max and a few others have done occasionally down through the centuries. But I believe that to do so takes some kind of terrible and unimaginable expenditure of psychic energy. I think it takes such a fearful effort of will that it is beyond our imagining; and that only very rarely is such an incredible effort made.

I think a Shakespeare killed before *Hamlet, Othello* and *Macbeth* were written might have put forth such effort and returned. And I know that

Max Kingery did. But there was almost nothing left over to do what he came back for. Those meaningless fragments were the utmost he could accomplish. His appearances were at the cost of tremendous effort, and I think that to even turn his head and look at us in addition, as he did the night we saw him, and then to actually pronounce an audible word besides, were efforts no one alive can understand.

It was beyond him, he could not return and then write the books that were to have made the name of Max Kingery what he'd been certain it was destined to be. And so he had to give up; we never saw Max again, though we saw two more places he'd been.

Cora and I were driving to San Rafael over the county road. You can get there on a six-lane highway now, 101, that slices straight through the hills, but this was once part of the only road between the two towns and it winds a lot around and between the Marin County hills, under the trees. It's a pleasant narrow little two-lane road, and we like to take it once in a while; I believe it's still the shortest route to San Rafael, winding though it is. This was the end of January or early in February, I don't remember. It was early in the week, I'd taken the day off, and Cora wanted something at Penney's so we drove over.

Twenty or thirty feet up on the side of a hill about a mile outside Mill Valley there's an outcropping of smooth-faced rock facing the road, and Cora glanced at it, exclaimed and pointed, and I jammed on the brakes and looked up where she was pointing. There on the rock facing the public road, painted in great four-foot letters, was *Max Ki,* the lines crude and uneven, driblets of paint running down past the bottoms of letters, the final stroke continuing on down the face of the rock until the paint or oil on the brush or stick had run thin and faded away. We knew Max had painted it—his name or as much of it as he could manage—and staring up at it now, I understood the loud jacket with *Max K* on its back, and the carnival straw hat with the big red initials.

For who *are* the people who paint their names or initials in public places and on the rocks that face our highways? Driving from San Francisco to Reno through the Donner Pass you see them by the hundreds, some painted so high that the rocks must have been scaled, dangerously, to do it. I used to puzzle over them; to paint your name or initials up there in the mountains wasn't impulse. It took planning. You'd have to drive over a hundred miles with the can of paint on the floor of the car. Who would do that? And who would wear the caps stitched with initials and the jackets with names on their backs? It was plain to me now; they are the people, of course, who feel that they have no identity. And who are fighting for one.

They are unknown, nearly invisible, so they feel; and their names or initials held up to the uninterested eyes of the world are silent shouts of, 'Hey, look at me!' Children shout it incessantly while acquiring their identities, and if they never acquire one maybe they never stop shouting. Because the things they do must always leave them with a feeling of emptiness. Initials on their caps, names on their jackets, or even painted high on a cliff visible for miles, they must always feel their failure to leave a real mark, and so they repeat it again and again. And Max who had to be someone, who *had* to be, did as they did, finally, from desperation. To have never been anyone and to be forgotten completely was not to be borne. At whatever cost he too had to try to leave his name behind him, even if he were reduced to painting it on a rock.

I visited the cemetery once more that spring; plodding up the hill, eyes on the ground. Nearing the crest I looked up, then stopped in my tracks, astounded. There at the head of Max's grave stood an enormous gray stone, the biggest by far of any in sight, and it was made not of concrete or pressed stone but of the finest granite. It would last a thousand years, and cut deeply into its face in big letters was MAXWELL KINGERY, AUTHOR.

Down in his shop outside the gates I talked to the middle-aged stonecutter in the little office at the front of the building; he was wearing a work apron and cap. He said, "Yes, certainly I remember the man who ordered it; black hair and eyes, heavy glasses. He told me what it should say, and I wrote it down. Your name's Peter Marks, isn't it?" I said it was, and he nodded as though he knew it. "Yes, he told me you'd be here, and I knew you would. Hard for him to talk; had some speech impediment, but I understood him." He turned to a littered desk, leafed through a little stack of papers, then found the one he wanted, and slid it across the counter to me. "He said you'd be in and pay for it; here's the bill. It's expensive but worth it, a fine stone and the only one here I know of for an author."

For several moments I just stood there staring at the paper in my hand. Then I did the only thing left to do, and got out one of the checks I carry in my wallet. Waiting while I wrote, the stonecutter said politely, "And what do you do, Mr. Marks; you an author, too?"

"No," I said, signing the check, then I looked up smiling. "I'm just a critic."

## FOR DISCUSSION: Hey, Look at Me!

1.  Authors attempt to arouse the interest of their readers from the very first sentence of their stories. What does the author of this story do to gain your attention?

2. Why do you suppose the author places Max's grave in a remote part of the cemetery?  In what way does this element contribute to the central point of the tale?

3. The relationship between Max and the narrator of the story is tenuous, but it involves trust on Max's part.  Identify the major element in the story that proves that Max trusted Peter Marks.

4. At what point in the story did you begin to understand why Max had returned as a ghost?  How many "clues" to Max's reason does the author give?  Trace the musings of the narrator in relation to the "clues" given in order to analyze the subtle way in which the author develops his essentially fantastic premise while making it, nevertheless, believable.

5. Peter Marks ultimately understands what forced Max to return from the dead.  It is a force which motivates all human beings, and it is stated quite simply in the narrative.  What is it?

6. Peter Marks, in the last line of the story, says, in answer to the stonecutter's question, "No, I'm just a critic."  What, if any, is the significance of the word "just" in his response?

# INTRODUCTION: Running Wolf

Algernon Blackwood is considered by many literary critics to be without peer as a creator of the supernatural story. He was writing at the time when other great authors were producing superb short stories of the supernatural—such men as Henry James and Sheridan Le Fanu. *Running Wolf* is a fine example of the kind of supernatural stories Blackwood created during his career. It is a tale that amply reveals why its author has achieved such critical acclaim within the field of the supernatural story.

# Running Wolf
## Algernon Blackwood

The man who enjoys an adventure outside the general experience of the race, and imparts it to others, must not be surprised if he is taken for either a liar or a fool, as Malcolm Hyde, hotel clerk on a holiday, discovered in due course. Nor is "enjoy" the right word to use in describing his emotions; the word he chose was probably "survive."

When he first set eyes on Medicine Lake he was struck by its still, sparkling beauty, lying there in the vast Canadian backwoods; next, by its extreme loneliness; and, lastly—a good deal later, this—by its combination of beauty, loneliness, and singular atmosphere, due to the fact that it was the scene of his adventure.

"It's fairly stiff with big fish," said Morton of the Montreal Sporting Club. "Spend your holidays there—up Mattawa way, some fifteen miles west of Stony Creek. You'll have it all to yourself except for an old Indian who's got a shack there. Camp on the east side—if you'll take a tip from me." He then talked for half an hour about the wonderful sport; yet he was not otherwise very communicative, and did not suffer questions gladly, Hyde noticed. Nor had he stayed there very long himself. If it was such a paradise as Morton, its discoverer and the most experienced rod in the province, claimed, why had he himself spent only three days there?

"Ran short of grub," was the explanation offered; but to another friend he had mentioned briefly, "flies" and to a third, so Hyde learned later, he gave the excuse that his half-breed "took sick," necessitating a quick return to civilization.

Hyde, however, cared little for the explanations; his interest in these came later. "Stiff with fish" was the phrase he liked. He took the Canadian Pacific train to Mattawa, laid in his outfit at Stony Creek, and set off thence for the fifteen-mile canoe trip without a care in the world.

Traveling light, the portages did not trouble him; the water was swift and easy, the rapids negotiable; everything came his way, as the saying is. Occasionally he saw big fish making for the deeper pools, and was sorely tempted to stop; but he resisted. He pushed on between the immense world of forests that stretched for hundreds of miles, known to deer, bear, moose, and wolf, but strange to any echo of human tread, a deserted and primeval wilderness. The autumn day was calm, the water sang and sparkled, the blue sky hung cloudless over all, ablaze with light. Toward evening he passed an old beaver dam, rounded a little point, and had his first sight of Medicine Lake. He lifted his dripping paddle; the canoe shot with silent glide into calm water. He gave an exclamation of delight, for the loveliness caught his breath away.

Though primarily a sportsman, he was not insensible to beauty. The lake formed a crescent, perhaps four miles long, its width between a mile and half a mile. The slanting gold of sunset flooded it. No wind stirred its crystal surface. Here it had lain since the redskins' god first made it; here it would lie until he dried it up again. Towering spruce and hemlock trooped to its very edge, majestic cedars leaned down as if to drink, crimson sumacs shone in fiery patches, and maples gleamed orange and red beyond belief. The air was like wine, with the silence of a dream.

It was here the red men formerly "made medicine," with all the wild ritual and tribal ceremony of an ancient day. But it was of Morton, rather than of Indians, that Hyde thought. If this lonely, hidden paradise was really stiff with big fish, he owed a lot to Morton for the information. Peace invaded him, but the excitement of the hunter lay below.

He looked about him with quick, practiced eye for a camping place before the sun sank below the forests and the half-lights came. The Indian's shack, lying in full sunshine on the eastern shore, he found at once; but the trees lay too thick about it for comfort, nor did he wish to be so close to its inhabitant. Upon the opposite side, however, an ideal clearing offered. This lay already in shadow, the huge forest darkening it toward evening; but the open space attracted. He paddled over quickly and examined it. The ground was hard and dry, he found, and a little brook ran tinkling down one side of it into the lake. This outfall, too, would be a good fishing spot. Also it was sheltered. A few low willows marked the mouth.

An experienced camper soon makes up his mind. It was a perfect site, and some charred logs, with traces of former fires, proved that he was not the first to think so. Hyde was delighted. Then, suddenly, disappointment came to tinge his pleasure. His kit was landed, and preparations for putting up the tent were begun, when he recalled a detail that excitement had so far kept in the background of his mind— Morton's advice. But not Morton's only, for the storekeeper at Stony Creek had reinforced it. The big fellow with straggling moustache and stooping shoulders, dressed in shirt and trousers, had handed him out a final sentence with the bacon, flour, condensed milk, and sugar. He had repeated Morton's half-forgotten words:

"Put yer tent on the east shore, I should," he had said at parting.

He remembered Morton, too, apparently. "A shortish fellow, brown as an Indian and fairly smelling of the woods. Traveling with Jake, the half-breed." That assuredly was Morton. "Didn't stay long, now, did he," he added to himself in a reflective tone.

"Going Windy Lake way, are yer? Or Ten Mile Water, maybe?" he had first inquired of Hyde.

"Medicine Lake."

"Is that so?" the man said, as though he doubted it for some obscure reason. He pulled at his ragged moustache a moment. "Is that so, now?" he repeated. And the final words followed him downstream after a considerable pause—the advice about the best shore on which to put his tent.

All this now suddenly flashed back upon Hyde's mind with a tinge of disappointment and annoyance, for when two experienced men agreed, their opinion was not to be lightly disregarded. He wished he had asked the storekeeper for more details. He looked about him, he reflected, he hesitated. His ideal camping-ground lay certainly on the forbidden shore. What in the world, he wondered, could be the objection to it?

But the light was fading; he must decide quickly one way or the other. After staring at his unpacked dunnage, and the tent, already half erected, he made up his mind with a muttered expression that consigned both Morton and the storekeeper to less pleasant places. "They must have *some* reason," he growled to himself; "fellows like that usually know what they're talking about. I guess I'd better shift over to the other side—for tonight, at any rate."

He glanced across the water before actually reloading. No smoke rose from the Indian's shack. He had seen no sign of a canoe. The man, he decided, was away. Reluctantly, then, he left the good camping-ground and paddled across the lake, and half an hour later his tent was up, firewood collected, and two small trout were already caught for supper. But the bigger fish, he knew, lay waiting for him on the other side by the little outfall, and he fell asleep at length on his bed of balsam boughs, annoyed and disappointed, yet wondering how a mere

178

sentence could have persuaded him so easily against his own better judgment. He slept like the dead; the sun was well up before he stirred.

But his morning mood was a very different one. The brilliant light, the peace, the intoxicating air, all this was too exhilarating for the mind to harbor foolish fancies, and he marveled that he could have been so weak the night before. No hesitation lay in him anywhere. He struck camp immediately after breakfast, paddled back across the strip of shining water, and quickly settled in upon the forbidden shore, as he now called it, with a contemptuous grin. And the more he saw of the spot, the better he liked it. There was plenty of wood, running water to drink, an open space about the tent, and there were no flies. The fishing, moreover, was magnificent. Morton's description was fully justified, and "stiff with big fish" for once was not an exaggeration.

The useless hours of the early afternoon he passed dozing in the sun, or wandering through the underbrush beyond the camp. He found no sign of anything unusual. He bathed in a cool, deep pool; he reveled in the lonely little paradise. Lonely it certainly was, but the loneliness was part of its charm; the stillness, the peace, the isolation of this beautiful backwoods lake delighted him. The silence was divine. He was entirely satisfied.

After a brew of tea, he strolled toward evening along the shore, looking for the first sign of a rising fish. A faint ripple on the water, with the lengthening shadows, made good conditions. *Plop* followed *plop*, as the big fellows rose, snatched at their food, and vanished into the depths. He hurried back. Ten minutes later he had taken his rods and was gliding cautiously in the canoe through the quiet water.

So good was the sport, indeed, and so quickly did the big trout pile up in the bottom of the canoe, that despite the growing lateness, he found it hard to tear himself away. "One more," he said, "and then I really will go." He landed that "one more," and was in the act of taking off the hook, when the deep silence of the evening was curiously disturbed. He became abruptly aware that some one watched him. A pair of eyes, it seemed, were fixed upon him from some point in the surrounding shadows.

Thus, at least, he interpreted the odd disturbance in his happy mood; for thus he felt it. The feeling stole over him without the slightest warning. He was not alone. The slippery big trout dropped from his fingers. He sat motionless, and stared about him.

Nothing stirred; the ripple on the lake had died away; there was no wind; the forest lay a single purple mass of shadow; the yellow sky, fast fading, threw reflections that troubled the eye and made distances uncertain. But there was no sound, no movement; he saw no figure anywhere. Yet he knew that some one watched him, and a wave of quite unreasoning terror gripped him. The nose of the canoe was against the bank. In a moment, and instinctively, he shoved it off and paddled into deeper water. The watcher, it came to him also instinctively, was quite close to him upon that bank. But where? And who? Was it the Indian?

Here, in deeper water, and some twenty yards from the shore, he paused and strained both sight and hearing to find some possible clue. He felt half ashamed, now that the first strange feeling passed a little. But the certainty remained. Absurd as it was, he felt positive that some one watched him with concentrated and intent regard. Every fiber in his being told him so; and though he could discover no figure, no new outline on the shore, he could even have sworn in which clump of willow bushes the hidden person crouched and stared. His attention seemed drawn to that particular clump.

The water dripped slowly from his paddle, now lying across the thwarts. There was no other sound. The canvas of his tent gleamed dimly. A star or two were out. He waited. Nothing happened.

Then, as suddenly as it had come, the feeling passed, and he knew that the person who had been watching him intently had gone. It was as if a current had been turned off; the normal world flowed back; the landscape emptied as if some one had left a room. The disagreeable feeling left him at the same time, so that he instantly turned the canoe in to the shore again, landed, and, paddle in hand, went over to examine the clump of willows he had singled out as the place of concealment. There was no one there, of course, nor any trace of recent human occupancy. No leaves, no branches stirred, nor was a single twig displaced; his keen and practiced sight detected no sign of tracks upon the ground. Yet, for all that, he felt positive that a little time ago someone had crouched among these very leaves and watched him. He remained absolutely convinced of it. The watcher, whether Indian hunter, stray lumberman, or wandering half-breed, had now withdrawn, a search was useless, and dusk was falling. He returned to his little camp, more disturbed perhaps than he cared to acknowledge. He cooked his supper, hung up his catch on a string, so that no prowling animal could get at it during the night, and prepared to make himself comfortable until bedtime. Unconsciously, he built a bigger fire than usual, and found himself peering over his pipe into the deep shadows beyond the firelight, straining his ears to catch the slightest sound. He remained generally on the alert in a way that was new to him.

A man under such conditions and in such a place need not know discomfort until the sense of loneliness strikes him as too vivid a reality. Loneliness in a backwoods camp brings charm, pleasure, and a happy sense of calm until, and unless, it comes too near. It should remain an ingredient only among other conditions; it should not be directly, vividly noticed. Once it has crept within short range, however, it may easily cross the narrow line between comfort and discomfort, and darkness is an undesirable time for the transition. A curious dread may easily follow—the dread lest the loneliness suddenly be disturbed, and the solitary human feel himself open to attack.

For Hyde, now, this transition had been already accomplished; the too intimate sense of his loneliness had shifted abruptly into the worst condition of no longer being quite alone. It was an awkward moment, and the hotel clerk realized his position exactly. He did not quite like it. He sat there, with his back to the blazing logs, a very visible object in the light, while all about him the darkness of the forest lay like an impenetrable wall. He could not see a yard beyond the small circle of his campfire; the silence about him was like the silence of the dead. No leaf rustled, no wave lapped; he himself sat motionless as a log.

Then again he became suddenly aware that the person who watched him had returned, and that same intent and concentrated gaze as before was fixed upon him where he lay. There was no warning; he heard no stealthy tread or snapping of dry twigs, yet the owner of those steady eyes was very close to him, probably not a dozen feet away. This sense of proximity was overwhelming.

It is unquestionable that a shiver ran down his spine. This time, moreover, he felt positive that the man crouched just beyond the firelight, the distance he himself could see being nicely calculated, and straight in front of him. For some minutes he sat without stirring a single muscle, yet with each muscle ready and alert, straining his eyes in vain to pierce the darkness, but only succeeding in dazzling his sight with the reflected light. Then, as he shifted his position slowly, cautiously, to obtain another angle of vision, his heart gave two big thumps against his ribs and the hair seemed to rise on his scalp with the sense of cold that gave him gooseflesh. In the darkness facing him he saw two small and greenish circles that were certainly a pair of eyes, yet not the eyes of an Indian hunter, or of any human being. It was a pair of animal eyes that stared so fixedly at him out of the night. And this certainty had an immediate and natural effect upon him.

For, at the menace of those eyes, the fears of millions of long dead hunters since the dawn of time woke in him. Hotel clerk though he was, heredity surged through him in an automatic wave of instinct. His hand groped for a weapon. His fingers fell on the iron head of his small camp ax, and at once he was himself again. Confidence returned; the vague, superstitious dread was gone. This was a bear or wolf that smelt his catch and came to steal it. With beings of that sort he knew instinctively how to deal, yet admitting, by this very instinct, that his original dread had been of quite another kind.

"I'll damned quick find out what it is," he exclaimed aloud, and snatching a burning brand from the fire, he hurled it with good aim straight at the eyes of the beast before him.

The bit of pitch pine fell in a shower of sparks that lit the dry grass this side of the animal, flared up a moment, then died quickly down again. But in that instant of bright illumination he saw clearly what his unwelcome visitor was. A big timber wolf sat on its hindquarters, staring steadily at him through the firelight. He saw its legs and shoulders, he saw its hair, he saw also the big hemlock trunks lit up behind it, and the willow scrub on each side. It formed a vivid, clear-cut picture shown in clear detail by the momentary blaze. To his amazement, however, the wolf did not turn and bolt away from the burning log, but withdrew a few yards only, and sat there again on its haunches, staring, staring as before. Heavens, how it stared! He "shoo-ed" it, but without effect; it did not budge. He did not waste another good log on it, for his fear was dissipated now; a timber wolf was a timber wolf, and it might sit there as long as it pleased, provided it did not try to steal his catch. No alarm was in him any more. He knew that wolves were harmless in the summer and autumn, and even when "packed" in the winter, they would attack a man only when suffering desperate hunger. So he lay and watched the beast, threw bits of stick in its direction, even talked to it, wondering only that it never moved. "You can stay there for ever, if you like," he remarked to it aloud, "for you cannot get at my fish, and the rest of the grub I shall take into the tent with me!"

The creature blinked its bright green eyes, but made no move.

Why, then, if his fear was gone, did he think of certain things as he rolled himself in the Hudson Bay blankets before going to sleep? The immobility of the animal was strange, its refusal to turn and bolt was still stranger. Never before had he known a wild creature that was not afraid of fire. Why did it sit and watch him, as with purpose in its gleaming eyes? How had he felt its presence earlier and instantly? A timber wolf, especially a solitary wolf, was a timid thing, yet this one feared neither man nor fire. Now, as he lay there wrapped in his blankets inside the cozy tent, it sat outside beneath the stars, beside the fading embers, the wind chilly in its fur, the ground cooling beneath its planted paws, watching him, steadily watching him, perhaps until the dawn.

It was unusual, it was strange. Having neither imagination nor tradition, he called upon no store of racial visions. Matter of fact, a hotel clerk on a fishing holiday, he lay there in his blankets, merely wondering and puzzled. A timber wolf was a timber wolf and nothing more. Yet this timber wolf—the idea haunted him—was different. In a word, the deeper part of his original uneasiness remained. He tossed about, he shivered sometimes in his broken sleep; he did not go out to see, but he woke early and unrefreshed.

Again with the sunshine and the morning wind, however, the incident of the night before was forgotten, almost unreal. His hunting zeal was uppermost. The tea and fish were delicious, his pipe had never tasted so good, the glory of this lonely lake amid primeval forests went to his head a little; he was a hunter before the Lord, and nothing else. He tried the edge of the lake, and in the excitement of playing a big fish, knew suddenly that *it*, the wolf, was there. He paused with the rod, exactly as if struck. He looked about him, he looked in a definite direction. The brilliant sunshine made every smallest detail clear and sharp—boulders of granite, burned stems, crimson sumac, pebbles along the shore in neat, separate detail—without revealing where the watcher hid. Then, his sight wandering farther inshore among the tangled undergrowth, he suddenly picked up the familiar, half-expected outline. The wolf was lying behind a granite boulder, so that only the head, the muzzle, and the eyes were visible. It merged in its background. Had he not known it was a wolf, he could never have separated it from the landscape. The eyes shone in the sunlight.

There it lay. He looked straight at it. Their eyes, in fact, actually met full and square. "Great Scott!" he exclaimed aloud, "why, it's like looking at a human being!"

From that moment, unwittingly, he established a singular personal relation with the beast. And what followed confirmed this undesirable impression, for the animal rose instantly and came down in leisurely fashion to the shore, where it stood looking back at him. It stood and stared into his eyes like some great wild dog, so that he was aware of a new and almost incredible sensation—that it courted recognition.

"Well! well!" he exclaimed again, relieving his feelings by addressing it aloud, "if this doesn't beat everything I ever saw! What d'you want, anyway?"

He examined it now more carefully. He had never seen a wolf so big before; it was a tremendous beast, a nasty customer to tackle, he reflected, if it ever came to that. It stood there absolutely fearless, and full of confidence. In the clear sunlight he took in every detail of it— a huge, shaggy, lean-flanked timber wolf, its wicked eyes staring straight into his own, almost with a kind of purpose in them. He saw its great jaws, its teeth, and its tongue hung out, dropping saliva a little. And yet the idea of its savagery, its fierceness, was very little in him.

He was amazed and puzzled beyond belief. He wished the Indian would come back. He did not understand this strange behavior in an animal. Its eyes, the odd expression in them, gave him a queer, unusual, difficult feeling. Had his nerves gone wrong, he almost wondered.

The beast stood on the shore and looked at him. He wished for the first time that he had brought a rifle. With a resounding smack he brought his paddle down flat upon the water, using all his strength, till the echoes rang as from a pistol shot that was audible from one end of the lake to the other. The wolf never stirred. He shouted, but the beast remained unmoved. He blinked his eyes, speaking as to a dog, a domestic animal, a creature accustomed to human ways. It blinked its eyes in return.

At length, increasing his distance from the shore, he continued fishing, and the excitement of the marvelous sport held his attention—his surface attention, at any rate. At times he almost forgot the attendant beast; yet whenever he looked up, he saw it there. And worse; when he slowly paddled home again, he observed it trotting along the shore as though to keep him company. Crossing a little bay, he spurted, hoping to reach the other point before his undesired and undesirable attendant. Instantly the brute broke into that rapid, tireless lope that, except on ice, can run down anything on four legs in the woods. When he reached the distant point, the wolf was waiting for him. He raised his paddle from the water, pausing a moment for reflection; for his very close attention—there were dusk and night yet to come—he certainly did not relish. His camp was near; he had to land; he felt uncomfortable even in the sunshine of broad day, when, to his keen relief, about half a mile from the tent, he saw the creature suddenly stop and sit down in the open. He waited a moment, then paddled on. It did not follow. There was no attempt to move; it merely sat and watched him. After a few hundred yards, he looked back. It was still sitting where he left it. And the absurd, yet significant, feeling came to him that the beast divined his thought, his anxiety, his dread, and was now showing him, as well as it could, that it entertained no hostile feeling and did not meditate attack.

He turned the canoe toward the shore; he landed; he cooked his supper in the dusk; the animal made no sign. Not far away it certainly lay and watched, but it did not advance. And to Hyde, observant now in a new way, came one sharp, vivid reminder of the strange atmosphere into which his commonplace personality had strayed: he suddenly recalled that his relations with the beast, already established, had progressed distinctly a stage further. This startled him, yet without the accompanying alarm he must certainly have felt twenty-four hours before. He had an understanding with the wolf. He was aware of friendly thoughts toward it. He even went so far as to set out a few big fish on the spot where he had first seen it sitting the previous night. "If he comes," he thought, "he is welcome to them, I've got plenty, anyway." He thought of it now as "he."

Yet the wolf made no appearance until he was in the act of entering his tent a good deal later. It was close on ten o'clock, whereas nine was his hour, and late at that, for turning in. He had, therefore, unconsciously been waiting for him. Then, as he was closing the flap, he saw the eyes close to where he had placed the fish.   He waited, hiding himself, and expecting to hear sounds of munching jaws; but all was silence. Only the eyes glowed steadily out of the background of pitch darkness. He closed the flap.   He had no slightest fear.   In ten minutes he was sound asleep.

He could not have slept very long, for when he woke up he could see the shine of a faint red light through the canvas, and the fire had not died down completely.   He rose and cautiously peeped out.   The air was very cold, he saw his breath.   But he also saw the wolf, for it had come in, and was sitting by the dying embers, not two yards away from where he crouched behind the flap.   And this time, at these very close quarters, there was something in the attitude of the big wild thing that caught his attention with a vivid thrill of startled surprise and a sudden shock of cold that held him spellbound.   He stared, unable to believe his eyes; for the wolf's attitude conveyed to him something familiar that at first he was unable to explain.   Its pose reached him in the terms of another thing with which he was entirely at home.   What was it?   Did his senses betray him?   Was he still asleep and dreaming?

Then, suddenly, with a start of uncanny recognition, he knew.   Its attitude was that of a dog.   Having found the clue, his mind then made an awful leap.   For it was, after all, no dog its appearance aped, but something nearer to himself, and more familiar still.   Good heavens!   It sat there with the pose, the attitude, the gesture in repose of something almost human.   And then, with a second shock of biting wonder, it came to him like a revelation.   The wolf sat beside that campfire as a man might sit.

Before he could weigh his extraordinary discovery, before he could examine it in detail or with care, the animal, sitting in this ghastly fashion, seemed to feel his eyes fixed on it.   It slowly turned and looked him in the face, and for the first time Hyde felt a fullblooded superstitious fear flood through his entire being.   He seemed transfixed with that nameless terror that is said to attack human beings who suddenly face the dead, finding themselves bereft of speech and movement.   This moment of paralysis certainly occurred.   Its passing, however, was as singular as its advent.   For almost at once he was aware of something beyond and above this mockery of human attitude and pose, something that ran along unaccustomed nerves and reached his feeling, even perhaps his heart.   The revulsion was extraordinary, its result still more extraordinary and unexpected.   Yet the fact remains.   He was aware of another thing that had the effect of stilling his terror as soon as it was born.   He was aware of appeal, silent, half expressed, yet vastly pathetic. He saw in the savage eyes a beseeching, even a yearning, expression that changed his mood as by magic from dread to natural sympathy.   The great gray brute, symbol of cruel ferocity, sat there beside his dying fire and appealed for help.

The gulf betwixt animal and human seemed in that instant bridged. It was, of course, incredible. Hyde, sleep still possibly clinging to his inner being with the shades and half shapes of dream yet about his soul, acknowledged, how he knew not, the amazing fact. He found himself nodding to the brute in half consent, and instantly, without more ado, the lean gray shape rose like a wraith and trotted off swiftly, but with stealthy tread, into the background of the night.

When Hyde woke in the morning his first impression was that he must have dreamed the entire incident. His practical nature asserted itself. There was a bite in the fresh autumn air; the bright sun allowed no half lights anywhere; he felt brisk in mind and body. Reviewing what had happened, he came to the conclusion that it was utterly vain to speculate; no possible explanation of the animal's behavior occurred to him: he was dealing with something entirely outside his experience. His fear, however, had completely left him. The odd sense of friendliness remained. The beast had a definite purpose, and he himself was included in that purpose. His sympathy held good.

But with the sympathy there was also an intense curiosity. "If it shows itself again," he told himself, "I'll go up close and find out what it wants." The fish laid out the night before had not been touched.

It must have been a full hour after breakfast when he next saw the brute; it was standing on the edge of the clearing, looking at him in the way now become familiar. Hyde immediately picked up his ax and advanced toward it boldly, keeping his eyes fixed straight upon its own. There was nervousness in him, but kept well under; nothing betrayed it; step by step he drew nearer until some ten yards separated them. The wolf had not stirred a muscle as yet. Its jaws hung open, its eyes observed him intently; it allowed him to approach without a sign of what its mood might be. Then, with these ten yards between them, it turned abruptly and moved slowly off, looking back first over one shoulder and then over the other, exactly as a dog might do, to see if he was following.

A singular journey it was they then made together, animal and man. The trees surrounded them at once, for they left the lake behind them, entering the tangled bush beyond. The beast, Hyde noticed, obviously picked the easiest track for him to follow; for obstacles that meant nothing to the four-legged expert, yet were difficult for a man, were carefully avoided with an almost uncanny skill, while yet the general direction was accurately kept. Occasionally there were windfalls to be surmounted; but though the wolf bounded over these with ease, it was always waiting for the man on the other side after he had laboriously climbed over. Deeper and deeper into the heart of the lonely forest they penetrated in this singular fashion, cutting across the arc of the lake's crescent, it seemed to Hyde; for after two miles or so, he recognized the big rocky bluff that overhung the water at its northern end. This outstanding bluff he had seen from his camp, one side of it falling sheer into the water; it was probably the spot, he imagined, where the Indians held their medicine-making ceremonies, for it stood out in isolated fashion, and its top formed a private plateau not easy of access. And it was here, close to a big spruce at the foot of the bluff upon the forest side, that the wolf stopped suddenly and for the first time since its appearance gave audible expression to its feeling. It sat down on its haunches, lifted its muzzle with open jaws, and gave vent to a subdued and long-drawn howl that was more like the wail of a dog than the fierce barking cry associated with a wolf.

By this time Hyde had lost not only fear, but caution too; nor, oddly enough, did this warning howl revive a sign of unwelcome emotion in him. In that curious sound he detected the same message that the eyes conveyed—appeal for help. He paused, nevertheless, a little startled, and while the wolf sat waiting for him, he looked about him quickly. There was young timber here; it had once been a small clearing, evidently. Ax and fire had done their work, but there was evidence to an experienced eye that it was Indians and not white men who had once been busy here. Some part of the medicine ritual, doubtless, took place in the little clearing, thought the man, as he advanced again toward his patient leader. The end of their queer journey, he felt, was close at hand.

He had not taken two steps before the animal got up and moved very slowly in the direction of some low bushes that formed a clump just beyond. It entered these, first looking back to make sure that its companion watched. The bushes hid it; a moment later it emerged again. Twice it performed this pantomime, each time, as it reappeared, standing still and staring at the man with as distinct an expression of appeal in the eyes as an animal may compass, probably. Its excitement, meanwhile, certainly increased, and this excitement was, with equal certainty, communicated to the man. Hyde made up his mind quickly. Gripping his ax tightly, and ready to use it at the first hint of malice, he moved slowly nearer to the bushes, wondering with something of a tremor what would happen.

If he expected to be startled, his expectation was at once fulfilled; but it was the behavior of the beast that made him jump. It positively frisked about him like a happy dog. It frisked for joy. Its excitement was intense, yet from its open mouth no sound was audible. With a sudden leap, then, it bounded past him into the clump of bushes, against whose very edge he stood, and began scraping vigorously at the ground.

Hyde stood and stared, amazement and interest now banishing all his nervousness, even when the beast, in its violent scraping, actually touched his body with its own. He had, perhaps, the feeling that he was in a dream, one of those fantastic dreams in which things may happen without involving an adequate surprise; for otherwise the manner of scraping and scratching at the ground must have seemed an impossible phenomenon. No wolf, no dog certainly, used its paws in the way those paws were working. Hyde had the odd, distressing sensation that it was hands, not paws, he watched. And yet, somehow, the natural, adequate surprise he should have felt was absent. The strange action seemed not entirely unnatural. In his heart some deep hidden spring of sympathy and pity stirred instead. He was aware of pathos.

The wolf stopped in its task and looked up into his face. Hyde acted without hesitation then. Afterwards he was wholly at a loss to explain his own conduct. It seemed he knew what to do, divined what was asked, expected of him. Between his mind and the dumb desire yearning through the savage animal there was intelligent and intelligible communication. He cut a stake and sharpened it, for the stones would blunt his ax-edge. He entered the clump of bushes to complete the digging his four-legged companion had begun. And while he worked, though he did not forget the close proximity of the wolf, he paid no attention to it; often his back was turned as he stooped over the laborious clearing away of the hard earth; no uneasiness or sense of danger was in him any more. The wolf sat outside the clump and watched the operations. Its concentrated attention, its patience, its intense eagerness, the gentleness and docility of the gray, fierce, and probably hungry brute, its obvious pleasure and satisfaction, too, at having won the human to its mysterious purpose—these were colors in the strange picture that Hyde thought of later when dealing with the human herd in his hotel again. At the moment he was aware chiefly of pathos and affection. The whole business was, of course, not to be believed, but that discovery came later, too, when telling it to others.

The digging continued for fully half an hour before his labor was rewarded by the discovery of a small whitish object. He picked it up and examined it—the finger-bone of a man. Other discoveries then followed quickly and in quantity. The cache was laid bare. He collected nearly the complete skeleton. The skull however, he found last, and might not have found at all but for the guidance of his strangely alert companion. It lay some few yards away from the central hole now dug, and the wolf stood nuzzling the ground with its nose before Hyde understood that he was meant to dig exactly in that spot for it. Between the beast's very paws his stake struck hard upon it. He scraped the earth from the bone and examined it carefully. It was perfect, save for the fact that some wild animal had gnawed it, the teeth-marks being still plainly visible. Close beside it lay the rusty iron head of a tomahawk. This and the smallness of the bones confirmed him in his judgment that it was the skeleton not of a white man, but of an Indian.

During the excitement of the discovery of the bones one by one, and finally of the skull, but, more especially, during the period of intense interest while Hyde was examining them, he had paid little if any attention to the wolf. He was aware that it sat and watched him, never moving its keen eyes for a single moment from the actual operations, but sign or movement it made none at all. He knew that it was pleased and satisfied, he knew also that he had now fulfilled its purpose in a great measure. The further intuition that now came to him, derived, he felt positive, from his companion's dumb desire, was perhaps the cream of the entire experience to him. Gathering the bones together in his coat, he carried them, together with the tomahawk, to the foot of the big spruce where the animal had first stopped. His leg actually touched the creature's muzzle as he passed. It turned its head to watch, but did not follow, nor did it move a muscle while he prepared the platform of boughs upon which he then laid the poor worn bones of an Indian who had been killed, doubtless, in sudden attack or ambush, and to whose remains had been denied the last grace of proper tribal burial. He wrapped the bones in bark; he laid the tomahawk beside the skull; he lit the circular fire round the pyre, and the blue smoke rose upward into the clear bright sunshine of the Canadian autumn morning till it was lost among the mighty trees far overhead.

In the moment before actually lighting the little fire he had turned to note what his companion did. It sat five yards away, he saw, gazing intently, and one of its front paws was raised a little from the ground. It made no sign of any kind. He finished the work, becoming so absorbed in it that he had eyes for nothing but the tending and guarding of his careful ceremonial fire. It was only when the platform of boughs collapsed, laying their charred burden gently on the fragrant earth among the soft wood ashes, that he turned again, as though to show the wolf what he had done, and seek, perhaps, some look of satisfaction in its curiously expressive eyes. But the place he searched was empty. The wolf had gone.

He did not see it again; it gave no sign of its presence anywhere; he was not watched.. He fished as before, wandered through the bush about his camp, sat smoking round his fire after dark, and slept peacefully in his cozy little tent. He was not disturbed. No howl was ever audible in the distant forest, no twig snapped beneath a stealthy tread, he saw no eyes. The wolf that behaved like a man had gone for ever.

It was the day before he left that Hyde, noticing smoke rising from the shack across the lake, paddled over to exchange a word or two with the Indian, who had evidently now returned. The Redskin came down to meet him as he landed, but it was soon plain that he spoke very little English. He emitted the familiar grunts at first; then bit by bit Hyde stirred his limited vocabulary into action. The net result, however, was slight enough, though it was certainly direct:

"You camp there?" the man asked, pointing to the other side.

"Yes."

"Wolf come?"

"Yes."

"You see wolf?"

"Yes."

The Indian stared at him fixedly a moment, a keen, wondering look upon his coppery, creased face.

"You 'fraid wolf?" he asked after a moment's pause.

"No," replied Hyde, truthfully. He knew it was useless to ask questions of his own, though he was eager for information. The other would have told him nothing. It was sheer luck that the man had touched on the subject at all, and Hyde realized that his own best role was merely to answer, but to ask no questions. Then, suddenly, the Indian became comparatively voluble. There was awe in his voice and manner.

"Him no wolf. Him big medicine wolf. Him spirit wolf."

Whereupon he drank the tea the other had brewed for him, closed his lips tightly, and said no more. His outline was discernible on the shore, rigid and motionless, an hour later, when Hyde's canoe turned the corner of the lake three miles away, and landed to make the portages up the first rapid of his homeward stream.

It was Morton who, after some persuasion, supplied further details of what he called the legend. Some hundred years before, the tribe that lived in the territory beyond the lake began their annual medicine-making ceremonies on the big rocky bluff at the northern end; but no medicine could be made. The spirits, declared the chief medicine man, would not answer. They were offended. An investigation followed. It was discovered that a young brave had recently killed a wolf, a thing strictly forbidden, since the wolf was the totem animal of the tribe. To make matters worse, the name of the guilty man was Running Wolf. The offense being unpardonable, the man was cursed and driven from the tribe:

"Go out. Wander alone among the woods, and if we see you we slay you. Your bones shall be scattered in the forest, and your spirit shall not enter the Happy Hunting Grounds till one of another race shall find and bury them."

"Which meant," explained Morton laconically, his only comment on the story, "probably forever."

## FOR DISCUSSION: Running Wolf

1. One of the ways an author can draw his readers into a story of the supernatural is to precede and surround the supernatural event with a wealth of ordinary detail. How does Blackwood use this technique in *Running Wolf*?
2. We have pointed out in the general introduction to this anthology that mankind's interest in the supernatural may be accounted for by ancient fears which still linger on the subconscious level in modern minds. This point is made by the author of this story. Identify the passage which contains the theory.
3. The hero of this story assumes at first that the one watching him is a human being. He later learns that it is a wolf. How does this erroneous assumption prepare the reader for the wolf's supernatural role in the story? What occurs between Hyde and the wolf at the moment of Hyde's recognition of the animal? Of what importance to the story is this occurrence?
4. Trace the changes in the hero's attitude toward the wolf.

# Spells and Sorcery– Odd Doings and Strange Dooms

# CHAPTER FOUR

If someone were to ask you if you believe in the ability of certain persons to cast a spell upon you or if you were queried concerning your belief in sorcery, you might be inclined in this modern and scientifically sophisticated age to answer, "Certainly not!"

But later, you might find that you joke with a friend as a black cat crosses your path. "Bad luck," you might say, and laugh. Or you might win a lottery drawing and point out to your friends that the number of your ticket was seventy-seven and seven was always your "lucky number."

These hypothetical illustrations are presented here for a specific purpose—to draw your attention to the continuing serio-comic regard in which many of us today hold certain superstitions. There is a relationship between the ability to believe in superstitions and the ability to believe in the supernatural power of certain persons to cast spells upon people. Superstition is defined as any belief inconsistent with the known laws of science. The supernatural can be defined in the same words. It is little wonder then that sorcery enlists the belief of many people when we consider the rather widespread belief in certain superstitions.

Sorcerers who can cast spells and make all kinds of magic have long been key figures in the literature of the supernatural. For example, Prospero, in Shakespeare's *The Tempest,* could command the winds. There was the magician Merlin associated with King Arthur's court. You may be familiar with the story of *The Sorcerer's Apprentice* who tried to imitate his master's skills with near-disastrous results.

In the stories that follow, you will meet other sorcerers. In the story which opens this chapter, for example, the sorcerer is a young boy who wields fantastic powers. Poe's story in this chapter describes mesmerism, which, despite its scientific overtones, is really nothing more or less than a relatively modern kind of spell, as is hypnosis. The monkey's paw in W. W. Jacobs's story is a talisman with magical powers, a kind of sorcerer's inanimate apprentice.

As you read these stories, you will meet interesting people caught in the webs that sorcerers have woven or subject to the spells cast upon them by some of the most interesting characters in supernatural literature.

Ye elves of hills, brooks, standing lakes, and groves:
And ye that on the sands with printless foot
Do chase the ebbing Neptune, and do fly him
When he comes back; you demi-puppets that
By moonshine do the green sour ringlets make,
Whereof the ewe not bites; and you whose pastime
Is to make midnight mushrooms, that rejoice
To hear the solemn curfew; by whose aid—
Weak masters though ye be—I have bedimm'd
The noontide sun, call'd forth the mutinous winds,
And 'twixt the green sea and the azured vault
Set roaring war: to the dread rattling thunder
Have I given fire, and rifted Jove's stout oak
With his own bolt; the strong-based promontory
Have I made shake, and by the spurs pluck'd up
The pine and cedar: graves at my command
Have waked their sleepers, oped, and let 'em forth
By my so potent art.   But this rough magic
I here abjure; and, when I have required
Some heavenly music,—which even now I do,—
To work mine end upon their senses, that
This airy charm is for, I'll break my staff,
Bury it certain fathoms in the earth,
And deeper than did ever plummet sound
I'll drown my book.

*from* The Tempest, *by Shakespeare.*

# INTRODUCTION: It's a Good Life

The following story takes place in a rural setting—in a village called Peaksville, population 46. That's all we can definitely tell you about the locale because, thanks to young Anthony and his strange supernatural powers, Peaksville can no longer be located by the traveler.

# It's a Good Life
## Jerome Bixby

Aunt Amy was out on the front porch, rocking back and forth in the highbacked chair and fanning herself, when Bill Soames rode his bicycle up the road and stopped in front of the house.

Perspiring under the afternoon "sun," Bill lifted the box of groceries out of the big basket over the front wheel of the bike, and came up the front walk.

Little Anthony was sitting on the lawn, playing with a rat. He had caught the rat down in the basement—he had made it think that it smelled cheese, the most rich-smelling and crumbly-delicious cheese a rat had ever thought it smelled, and it had come out of its hole, and now Anthony had hold of it with his mind and was making it do tricks.

When the rat saw Bill Soames coming, it tried to run, but Anthony thought at it, and it turned a flip-flop on the grass and lay trembling, its eyes gleaming in small black terror.

Bill Soames hurried past Anthony and reached the front steps, mumbling. He always mumbled when he came to the Fremont house, or passed it by, or even thought of it. Everybody did. They thought about silly things, things that didn't mean very much, like two-and-two-is-four-and-twice-is-eight and so on; they tried to jumble up their thoughts and keep them skipping back and forth, so Anthony couldn't read their minds. The mumbling helped. Because if Anthony got anything strong out of your thought, he might take a notion to do something about it—like curing your wife's sick headaches or your kid's mumps, or getting your old milk cow back on schedule, or fixing the privy. And while Anthony mightn't actually mean any harm, he couldn't be expected to have much notion of what was the right thing to do in such cases.

That was if he liked you. He might try to help you, in his way. And that could be pretty horrible.

If he didn't like you . . . well, that could be worse.

Bill Soames set the box of groceries on the porch railing, and stopped his mumbling long enough to say, "Everythin' you wanted, Miss Amy."

"Oh, fine William," Amy Fremont said lightly. "My ain't it terrible hot today?"

Bill Soames almost cringed. His eyes pleaded with her. He shook his head violently *no*, and then interrupted his mumbling again, though obviously he didn't want to: "Oh don't say that, Miss Amy . . . it's fine, just fine. A real *good* day!"

Amy Fremont got up from the rocking chair, and came across the porch. She was a tall woman, thin, a smiling vacancy in her eyes. About a year ago, Anthony had gotten mad at her, because she'd told him he shouldn't have turned the cat into a cat-rug, and although he had always obeyed her more than anyone else, which was hardly at all, this time he'd snapped at her. With his mind. And that had been the end of Amy Fremont's bright eyes, and the end of Amy Fremont as everyone had known her. And that was when word got around in Peaksville (population: 46) that even the members of Anthony's own family weren't safe. After that, everyone was twice as careful.

Someday Anthony might undo what he'd done to Aunt Amy. Anthony's Mom and Pop hoped he would. When he was older, and maybe sorry. If it was possible, that is. Because Aunt Amy had changed a lot, and besides, now Anthony wouldn't obey anyone.

"Land alive, William," Aunt Amy said, "you don't have to mumble like that. Anthony wouldn't hurt you. My goodness, Anthony likes you!" She raised her voice and called to Anthony, who had tired of the rat and was making it eat itself. "Don't you, dear? Don't you like Mr. Soames?"

Anthony looked across the lawn at the grocery man—a bright, wet, purple gaze. He didn't say anything. Bill Soames tried to smile at him. After a second Anthony returned his attention to the rat. It had already devoured its tail, or at least chewed it off—for Anthony had made it bite faster than it could swallow, and little pink and red furry pieces lay around it on the green grass. Now the rat was having trouble reaching its hindquarters.

Mumbling silently, thinking of nothing in particular as hard as he could, Bill Soames went stiff-legged down the walk, mounted his bicycle and pedaled off.

"We'll see you tonight, William," Aunt Amy called after him.

As Bill Soames pumped the pedals, he was wishing deep down that he could pump twice as fast, to get away from Anthony all the faster, and away from Aunt Amy, who sometimes just forgot how *careful* you had to be. And he shouldn't have thought that. Because Anthony caught it. He caught the desire to get away from the Fremont house as if it was something *bad*, and his purple gaze blinked, and he snapped a small, sulky thought after Bill Soames—just a small one, because he was in a good mood today, and besides, he liked Bill Soames, or at least didn't dislike him, at least today. Bill Soames wanted to go away—so, petulantly, Anthony helped him.

Pedaling with superhuman speed—or rather, appearing to, because in reality the bicycle was pedaling *him*—Bill Soames vanished down the road in a cloud of dust, his thin, terrified wail drifting back across the summerlike heat.

Anthony looked at the rat. It had devoured half its belly, and had died from pain. He thought it into a grave out deep in the cornfield— his father had once said, smiling, that he might as well do that with the things he killed—and went around the house, casting his odd shadow in the hot, brassy light from above.

In the kitchen, Aunt Amy was unpacking the groceries. She put the Mason-jarred goods on the shelves, and the meat and milk in the icebox, and the beet sugar and coarse flour in big cans under the sink. She put the cardboard box in the corner, by the door, for Mr. Soames to pick up next time he came. It was stained and battered and torn and worn fuzzy, but it was one of the few left in Peaksville. In faded red letters it said *Campbell's Soup*. The last cans of soup, or of anything else, had been eaten long ago, except for a small communal hoard which the villagers dipped into for special occasions—but the box lingered on, like a coffin, and when it and the other boxes were gone, the men would have to make some out of wood.

Aunt Amy went out in back, where Anthony's Mom—Aunt Amy's sister —sat in the shade of the house, shelling peas. The peas, every time Mom ran a finger along a pod, went *lollop-lollop-lollop* into the pan on her lap.

"William brought the groceries," Aunt Amy said. She sat down wearily in the straight-backed chair beside Mom, and began fanning herself again. She wasn't really old; but ever since Anthony had snapped at her with his mind, something had seemed to be wrong with her body as well as her mind, and she was tired all the time.

"Oh, good," said Mom. *Lollop* went the fat peas into the pan.

Everybody in Peaksville always said "Oh fine," or "Good," or "Say, that's swell!" when almost anything happened or was mentioned—even unhappy things like accidents or even deaths. They'd always say "Good," because if they didn't try to cover up how they really felt, Anthony might overhear with his mind and then nobody knew what might happen. Like the time Mrs. Kent's husband, Sam, had come walking back from the graveyard, because Anthony liked Mrs. Kent and had heard her mourning.

*Lollop.*

"Tonight's television night," said Aunt Amy. "I'm glad. I look forward to it so much every week. I wonder what we'll see tonight?"

"Did Bill bring the meat?" asked Mom.

"Yes." Aunt Amy fanned herself, looking up at the featureless brassy glare of the sky. "Goodness, it's so hot! I wish Anthony would make it just a little cooler—"

"*Amy!*"

"Oh!" Mom's sharp tone had penetrated, where Bill Soames' agonized expression had failed. Aunt Amy put one thin hand to her mouth in exaggerated alarm. "Oh ... I'm sorry, dear." Her pale blue eyes shuttled around, right and left, to see if Anthony was in sight. Not that it would make any difference if he was or wasn't—he didn't have to be near you to know what you were thinking. Usually, though, unless he had his attention on somebody, he would be occupied with thoughts of his own.

But some things attracted his attention—you could never be sure just what.

"This weather's just *fine*," Mom said.

*Lollop.*

"Oh, yes," Aunt Amy said. "It's a wonderful day. I wouldn't want it changed for the world!"

*Lollop.*

*Lollop.*

"What time is it?" Mom asked.

Aunt Amy was sitting where she could see through the kitchen window to the alarm clock on the shelf above the stove. "Four-thirty," she said.

*Lollop.*

"I want tonight to be something special," Mom said. "Did Bill bring a good lean roast?"

"Good and lean, dear. They butchered just today, you know, and sent us over the best piece."

"Dan Hollis will be *so* surprised when he finds out that tonight's television party is a birthday party for him too!"

"Oh *I* think he will! Are you sure nobody's told him?"

"Everybody swore they wouldn't."

"That'll be real nice," Aunt Amy nodded, looking off across the cornfield. "A birthday party."

"Well—" Mom put the pan of peas down beside her, stood up and brushed her apron. "I'd better get the roast on. Then we can set the table." She picked up the peas.

Anthony came around the corner of the house. He didn't look at them, but continued on down through the carefully kept garden—*all* the gardens in Peaksville were carefully kept, very carefully kept—and went past the rusting, useless hulk that had been the Fremont family car, and went smoothly over the fence and out into the cornfield.

"Isn't this a lovely day!" said Mom, a little loudly, as they went toward the back door.

Aunt Amy fanned herself. "A beautiful day, dear. Just *fine!*"

Out in the cornfield, Anthony walked between the tall, rustling rows of green stalks. He liked to smell the corn. The alive corn overhead, and the old dead corn underfoot. Rich Ohio earth, thick with weeds and brown, dry-rotting ears of corn, pressed between his bare toes with every step—he had made it rain last night so everything would smell and feel nice today.

He walked clear to the edge of the cornfield, and over to where a grove of shadowy green trees covered cool, moist, dark ground and lots of leafy undergrowth and jumbled moss-covered rocks and a small spring that made a clear, clean pool. Here Anthony liked to rest and watch the birds and insects and small animals that rustled and scampered and chirped about. He liked to lie on the cool ground and look up through the moving greenness overhead, and watch the insects flit in the hazy soft sunbeams that stood like slanting, glowing bars between ground and tree-tops. Somehow, he liked the thoughts of the little creatures in this place better than the thoughts outside; and while the thoughts he picked up here weren't very strong or very clear, he could get enough out of them to know what the little creatures liked and wanted, and he spent a lot of time making the grove more like what they wanted it to be. The spring hadn't always been here; but one time he had found thirst in one small furry mind, and had brought subterranean water to the surface in a clear cold flow, and had watched blinking as the creature drank, feeling its pleasure. Later he had made the pool, when he found a small urge to swim.

He had made rocks and trees and bushes and caves, and sunlight here and shadows there, because he had felt in all the tiny minds around him the desire—or the instinctive want—for this kind of resting place, and that kind of mating place, and this kind of place to play, and that kind of home.

And somehow the creatures from all the fields and pastures around the grove had seemed to know that this was a good place, for there were always more of them coming in—every time Anthony came out here there were more creatures than the last time, and more desires and needs to be tended to. Every time there would be some kind of creature he had never seen before, and he would find its mind, and see what it wanted, and then give it to it.

He liked to help them. He liked to feel their simple gratification.

Today, he rested beneath a thick elm, and lifted his purple gaze to a red and black bird that had just come to the grove. It twittered on a branch over his head, and hopped back and forth, and thought its tiny thoughts, and Anthony made a big, soft nest for it, and pretty soon it hopped in.

A long, brown, sleek-furred animal was drinking at the pool. Anthony found its mind next. The animal was thinking about a smaller creature that was scurrying along the ground on the other side of the pool, grubbing for insects. The little creature didn't know that it was in danger. The long, brown animal finished drinking and tensed its legs to leap, and Anthony thought it into a grave in the cornfield.

He didn't like those kinds of thoughts. They reminded him of the thoughts outside the grove. A long time ago some of the people outside had thought that way about *him,* and one night they'd hidden and waited for him to come back from the grove—and he'd just thought them all into the cornfield. Since then, the rest of the people hadn't thought that way —at least, very clearly. Now their thoughts were all mixed up and confusing whenever they thought about him or near him, so he didn't pay much attention.

He liked to help them, too, sometimes—but it wasn't simple, or very gratifying either. They never thought happy thoughts when he did—just the jumble. So he spent more time out here.

He watched all the birds and insects and furry creatures for a while, and played with a bird, making it soar and dip and streak madly around tree trunks until, accidentally, when another bird caught his attention for a moment, he ran it into a rock. Petulantly, he thought the rock into a grave in the cornfield; but he couldn't do anything more with the bird. Not because it was dead, though it was; but because it had a broken wing. So he went back to the house. He didn't feel like walking back through the cornfield, so he just *went* to the house, right down into the basement.

It was nice down here. Nice and dark and damp and sort of fragrant, because once Mom had been making preserves in a rack along the far wall and then she'd stopped coming down ever since Anthony had started spending time here, and the preserves had spoiled and leaked down and spread over the dirt floor, and Anthony like the smell.

He caught another rat, making it smell cheese, and after he played with it, he thought it into a grave right beside the long animal he'd killed in the grove. Aunt Amy hated rats, and so he killed a lot of them, because he liked Aunt Amy most of all and sometimes did things that Aunt Amy wanted. Her mind was more like the little furry minds out in the grove. She hadn't thought anything bad at all about him for a long time.

After the rat, he played with a big black spider in the corner under the stairs, making it run back and forth until its web shook and shimmered in the light from the cellar window like a reflection in silvery water. Then he drove fruit flies into the web until the spider was frantic trying to wind them all up. The spider liked flies, and its thoughts were stronger than theirs, so he did it. There was something bad in the way it liked flies, but it wasn't clear—and besides, Aunt Amy hated flies too.

He heard footsteps overhead—Mom moving around in the kitchen. He blinked his purple gaze, and almost decided to make her hold still—but instead he went up to the attic, and, after looking out the circular window for a while at the front lawn and the dusty road and Henderson's tip-waving wheat field beyond, he curled into an unlikely shape and went partly to sleep.

Soon people would be coming for television, he heard Mom think.

He went more to sleep. He liked television night. Aunt Amy had always liked television a lot, so one time he had thought some for her, and a few other people had been there at the time, and Aunt Amy had felt disappointed when they wanted to leave. He'd done something to them for that—and now everybody came to television.

He liked all the attention he got when they did.

Anthony's father came home around six-thirty, looking tired and dirty and bloody. He'd been over in Dunn's pasture with the other men, helping pick out the cow to be slaughtered this month and doing the job, and then butchering the meat and salting it away in Soames's icehouse. Not a job he cared for, but every man had his turn. Yesterday, he had helped scythe down old McIntyre's wheat. Tomorrow, they would start threshing. By hand. Everything in Peaksville had to be done by hand.

He kissed his wife on the cheek and sat down at the kitchen table. He smiled and said, "Where's Anthony?"

"Around someplace," Mom said.

Aunt Amy was over at the wood-burning stove, stirring the big pot of peas. Mom went back to the oven and opened it and basted the roast.

"Well, it's been a *good* day," Dad said. By rote. Then he looked at the mixing bowl and breadboard on the table. He sniffed at the dough. "M'm," he said. "I could eat a loaf all by myself, I'm so hungry."

"No one told Dan Hollis about its being a birthday party, did they?" his wife asked.

"Nope. We kept as quiet as mummies."

"We've fixed up such a lovely surprise!"

"Um? What?"

"Well ... you know how much Dan likes music. Well, last week Thelma Dunn found a *record* in her attic!"

"No!"

"Yes! And we had Ethel sort of ask—you know, without really *asking* —if he had that one. And he said no. Isn't that a wonderful surprise?"

"Well, now, it sure is. A record, imagine! That's a real nice thing to find! What record is it?"

"Perry Como, singing *You Are My Sunshine.*"

"Well, I'll be darned. I always liked that tune." Some raw carrots were lying on the table. Dad picked up a small one, scrubbed it on his chest, and took a bite. "How did Thelma happen to find it?"

"Oh, you know—just looking around for new things."

"M'm." Dad chewed the carrot. "Say, who has that picture we found a while back? I kind of like it—that old clipper sailing along—"

"The Smiths. Next week the Sipichs get it and they give the Smiths old McIntyre's music-box, and we give the Sipichs—" And she went down the tentative order of things that would exchange hands among the women at church this Sunday.

He nodded. "Looks like we can't have the picture for a while, I guess. Look, honey, you might try to get that detective book back from the Reillys. I was so busy the week we had it, I never got to finish all the stories."

"I'll try," his wife said doubtfully. "But I hear the van Husens have a stereoscope they found in the cellar." Her voice was just a little accusing. "They had it two whole months before they told anybody about it—"

"Say," Dad said, looking interested. "That'd be nice, too. Lots of pictures?"

"I suppose so. I'll see on Sunday. I'd like to have it—but we still owe the van Husens for their canary. I don't know why that bird had to pick *our* house to die . . . it must have been sick when we got it. Now there's just no satisfying Betty van Husen—she even hinted she'd like our *piano* for a while!"

"Well, honey, you try for the stereoscope—or just anything you think we'll like." At last he swallowed the carrot. It had been a little young and tough. Anthony's whims about the weather made it so that people never knew what crops would come up, or what shape they'd be in if they did. All they could do was plant a lot; and always enough of something came up any one season to live on. Just once there had been a grain surplus; tons of it had been hauled to the edge of Peaksville and dumped off into the nothingness. Otherwise, nobody could have breathed when it started to spoil.

"You know," Dad went on. "It's nice to have the new things around. It's nice to think that there's probably still a lot of stuff nobody's found yet, in cellars and attics and barns and down behind things. They help, somehow. As much as anything can help—"

"Sh-h!" Mom glanced nervously around.

"Oh," Dad said, smiling hastily. "It's all right! The new things are *good!* It's *nice* to be able to have something around you've never seen before, and know that something you've given somebody else is making them happy . . . that's a real *good* thing."

"A good thing," his wife echoed.

"Pretty soon," Aunt Amy said, from the stove, "there won't be any more new things. We'll have found everything there is to find. Goodness, that'll be too bad—"

"*Amy!*"

"Well—" Her pale eyes were shallow and fixed, a sign of her recurrent vagueness. "It will be kind of a shame—no new things—"

"Don't *talk* like that," Mom said, trembling. "Amy, be *quiet!*"

"It's *good,*" said Dad, in the loud, familiar, wanting-to-be-overheard tone of voice. "Such talk is *good.* It's okay, honey—don't you see? It's good for Amy to talk any way she wants. It's good for her to feel bad. Everything's good. Everything *has* to be good . . ."

Anthony's mother was pale. And so was Aunt Amy—the peril of the moment had suddenly penetrated the clouds surrounding her mind. Sometimes it was difficult to handle words so that they might not prove disastrous. You just never *knew.* There were so many things it was wise not to say, or even think—but remonstration for saying or thinking them might be just as bad, if Anthony heard and decided to do anything about it. You could just never tell what Anthony was liable to do.

Everything had to be good. Had to be fine just as it was, even if it wasn't. Always. Because any change might be worse. So terribly much worse.

"Oh, my goodness, yes, of course it's good," Mom said. "You talk any way you want to, Amy, and it's just fine. Of course, you want to remember that some ways are *better* than others . . ."

Aunt Amy stirred the peas, fright in her pale eyes.

"Oh, yes," she said. "But I don't feel like talking right now. It . . . it's *good* that I don't feel like talking."

Dad said tiredly, smiling, "I'm going out and wash up."

They started arriving around eight o'clock. By that time, Mom and Aunt Amy had the big table in the dining room set, and two more tables off to the side. The candles were burning, and the chairs situated, and Dad had a big fire going in the fireplace.

The first to arrive were the Sipichs, John and Mary. John wore his best suit, and was well-scrubbed and pink-faced after his day in McIntyre's pasture. The suit was neatly pressed, but getting threadbare at elbows and cuffs. Old McIntyre was working on a loom, designing it out of schoolbooks, but so far it was slow going. McIntyre was a capable man with wood and tools, but a loom was a big order when you couldn't get metal parts. McIntyre had been one of the ones who, at first, had wanted to try to get Anthony to make things the villagers needed, like clothes and canned goods and medical supplies and gasoline. Since then, he felt that what had happened to the whole Terrance family and Joe Kinney was his fault, and he worked hard trying to make it up to the rest of them. And since then, no one had tried to get Anthony to do anything.

Mary Sipich was a small, cheerful woman in a simple dress. She immediately set about helping Mom and Aunt Amy put the finishing touches on the dinner.

The next arrivals were the Smiths and Dunns, who lived right next to each other down the road, only a few yards from the nothingness. They drove up in the Smiths' wagon, drawn by their old horse.

Then the Reillys showed up, from across the darkened wheatfield, and the evening really began. Pat Reilly sat down at the big upright in the front room, and began to play from the popular sheet music on the rack. He played softly, as expressively as he could—and nobody sang. Anthony liked piano playing a whole lot, but not singing; often he would come up from the basement, or down from the attic, or just *come*, and sit on top of the piano, nodding his head as Pat played *Lover* or *Boulevard of Broken Dreams* or *Night and Day*. He seemed to prefer ballads, sweet-sounding songs—but the one time somebody had started to sing, Anthony had looked over from the top of the piano and done something that made everybody afraid of singing from then on. Later they'd decided that the piano was what Anthony had heard first, before anybody had ever tried to sing, and now anything else added to it didn't sound right and distracted him from his pleasure.

So, every television night, Pat would play the piano, and that was the beginning of the evening. Wherever Anthony was, the music would make him happy, and put him in a good mood, and he would know that they were gathering for television and waiting for him.

By eight-thirty everybody had shown up, except for the seventeen children and Mrs. Soames who was off watching them in the schoolhouse at the far end of town. The children of Peaksville were never, never allowed near the Fremont house—not since little Fred Smith had tried to play with Anthony on a dare. The younger children weren't even told about Anthony. The others had mostly forgotten about him, or were told that he was a nice, nice goblin but they must never go near him.

Dan and Ethel Hollis came late, and Dan walked in not suspecting a thing. Pat Reilly had played the piano until his hands ached—he'd worked pretty hard with them today—and now he got up, and everybody gathered around to wish Dan Hollis a happy birthday.

*204*

"Well, I'll be darned," Dan grinned. "This is swell, I wasn't expecting this at all ... gosh, this is *swell!*"

They gave him his presents—mostly things they had made by hand, though some were things that people had possessed as their own and now gave him as his. John Sipich gave him a watch charm, hand-carved out of a piece of hickory wood. Dan's watch had broken down a year or so ago, and there was nobody in the village who knew how to fix it, but he still carried it around because it had been his grandfather's and was a fine old heavy thing of gold and silver. He attached the charm to the chain, while everybody laughed and said John had done a nice job of carving. Then Mary Sipich gave him a knitted necktie, which he put on, removing the one he'd worn.

The Reillys gave him a little box they had made, to keep things in. They didn't say what things, but Dan said he'd keep his personal jewelry in it. The Reillys had made it out of a cigar box, carefully peeled of its paper and lined on the inside with velvet. The outside had been polished, and carefully if not expertly carved by Pat—but his carving got complimented too. Dan Hollis received many other gifts—a pipe, a pair of shoelaces, a tie pin, a knit pair of socks, some fudge, a pair of garters made from old suspenders.

He unwrapped each gift with vast pleasure, and wore as many of them as he could right there, even the garters. He lit up the pipe, and said he'd never had a better smoke, which wasn't quite true, because the pipe wasn't broken in yet. Pete Manners had had it lying around ever since he'd received it as a gift four years ago from an out-of-town relative who hadn't known he'd stopped smoking.

Dan put the tobacco into the bowl very carefully. Tobacco was precious. It was only pure luck that Pat Reilly had decided to try to grow some in his backyard just before what had happened to Peaksville had happened. It didn't grow very well, and then they had to cure it and shred it and all, and it was just precious stuff. Everybody in town used wooden holders old McIntyre had made, to save on butts.

Last of all, Thelma Dunn gave Dan Hollis the record she had found.

Dan's eyes misted even before he opened the package. He knew it was a record.

"Gosh," he said softly. "What one is it? I'm almost afraid to look ..."

"You haven't got it, darling," Ethel Hollis smiled. "Don't you remember, I asked about *You Are My Sunshine?*"

"Oh, gosh," Dan said again. Carefully he removed the wrapping and stood there fondling the record, running his big hands over the worn grooves with their tiny, dulling crosswise scratches. He looked around the room, eyes shining, and they all smiled back, knowing how delighted he was.

"Happy birthday, darling!" Ethel said, throwing her arms around him and kissing him.

He clutched the record in both hands, holding it off to one side as she pressed against him. "Hey," he laughed, pulling back his head. "Be careful . . . I'm holding a priceless object!" He looked around again, over his wife's arms, which were still around his neck. His eyes were hungry. "Look . . . do you think we could play it? Lord, what I'd give to hear some new music . . . just the first part, the orchestra part, before Como sings?"

Faces sobered. After a minute, John Sipich said, "I don't think we'd better, Dan. After all, we don't know just where the singer comes in— it'd be taking too much of a chance. Better wait till you get home."

Dan Hollis reluctantly put the record on the buffet with all his other presents. "It's *good*," he said automatically, but disappointedly, "that I can't play it here."

"Oh, yes," said Sipich. "It's good." To compensate for Dan's disappointed tone, he repeated, "It's *good*."

They ate dinner, the candles lighting their smiling faces, and ate it all right down to the last delicious drop of gravy. They complimented Mom and Aunt Amy on the roast beef, and the peas and carrots, and the tender corn on the cob. The corn hadn't come from the Fremont's cornfield, naturally—everybody knew what was out there, and the field was going to weeds.

Then they polished off the dessert—homemade ice cream and cookies. And then they sat back, in the flickering light of the candles, and chatted waiting for television.

There never was a lot of mumbling on television night—everybody came and had a good dinner at the Fremonts', and that was nice, and afterwards there was television, and nobody really thought much about that—it just had to be put up with. So it was a pleasant enough get-together, aside from your having to watch what you said just as carefully as you always did everyplace. If a dangerous thought came into your mind, you just started mumbling, even right in the middle of a sentence. When you did that, the others just ignored you until you felt happier again and stopped.

Anthony liked television night. He had done only two or three awful things on television night in the whole past year.

Mom had put a bottle of brandy on the table, and they each had a tiny glass of it. Liquor was even more precious than tobacco. The villagers could make wine, but the grapes weren't right, and certainly the techniques weren't, and it wasn't very good wine. There were only a few bottles of real liquor left in the village—four rye, three Scotch, three brandy, nine real wine and half a bottle of Drambuie belonging to old

206

McIntyre (only for marriages)—and when those were gone, that was it.

Afterward, everybody wished that the brandy hadn't been brought out. Because Dan Hollis drank more of it than he should have, and mixed it with a lot of the home-made wine. Nobody thought anything about it at first, because he didn't show it much outside, and it was his birthday party and a happy party, and Anthony liked these get-togethers and shouldn't see any reason to do anything even if he was listening.

But Dan Hollis got high, and did a fool thing. If they'd seen it coming, they'd have taken him outside and walked him around.

The first thing they knew, Dan stopped laughing right in the middle of the story about how Thelma Dunn had found the Perry Como record and dropped it and it hadn't broken because she'd moved faster than she ever had before in her life and caught it. He was fondling the record again, and looking longingly at the Fremonts' gramophone over in the corner, and suddenly he stopped laughing and his face got slack, and then it got ugly, and he said, "Oh, *Christ!*"

Immediately the room was still. So still they could hear the whirring movement of the grandfather's clock out in the hall. Pat Reilly had been playing the piano, softly. He stopped, his hands poised over the yellowed keys.

The candles on the dining room table flickered in a cool breeze that blew through the lace curtains over the bay window.

"Keep playing, Pat," Anthony's father said softly.

Pat started again. He played *Night and Day*, but his eyes were sideways on Dan Hollis, and he missed notes.

Dan stood in the middle of the room, holding the record. In his other hand he held a glass of brandy so hard his hand shook.

They were all looking at him.

"*Christ,*" he said again, and he made it sound like a dirty word.

Reverend Younger, who had been talking with Mom and Aunt Amy by the dining-room door, said "Christ" too—but he was using it in a prayer. His hands were clasped, and his eyes were closed.

John Sipich moved forward. "Now, Dan . . . it's *good* for you to talk that way. But you don't want to talk too much, you know."

Dan shook off the hand Sipich put on his arm.

"Can't even play my record," he said loudly. He looked down at the record, and then around at their faces. "Oh my *God . . .*"

He threw the glassful of brandy against the wall. It splattered and ran down the wallpaper in streaks.

Some of the women gasped.

"Dan," Sipich said in a whisper. "Dan, cut it out—"

Pat Reilly was playing *Night and Day* louder, to cover up the sounds of the talk. It wouldn't do any good, though, if Anthony was listening.

Dan Hollis went over to the piano and stood by Pat's shoulder, swaying a little.

"Pat," he said. "Don't play *that*. Play *this*." And he began to sing. Softly, hoarsely, miserably: "Happy birthday to me. . . . *Happy birthday to me . . .*"

"*Dan!*" Ethel Hollis screamed. She tried to run across the room to him. Mary Sipich grabbed her arm and held her back. "Dan," Ethel screamed again. "Stop—"

"My God, be quiet!" hissed Mary Sipich, and pushed her toward one of the men, who put his hand over her mouth and held her still.

"—Happy Birthday, dear Danny," Dan sang. "Happy birthday to me!" He stopped and looked down at Pat Reilly. "Play it, Pat. Play it, so I can sing right . . . you know I can't carry a tune unless somebody plays it!"

Pat Reilly put his hands on the keys and began *Lover*—in a low waltz tempo, the way Anthony liked it. Pat's face was white. His hands fumbled.

Dan Hollis stared over at the dining room door. At Anthony's mother, and at Anthony's father who had gone to join her.

"You had him," he said. Tears gleamed on his cheeks as the candlelight caught them. "*You* had to go and *have* him . . ."

He closed his eyes, and the tears squeezed out. He sang loudly, "You are my sunshine . . . my only sunshine . . . you make me happy . . . when I am blue . . ."

Anthony came into the room.

Pat stopped playing. He froze. Everybody froze. The breeze rippled the curtains. Ethel Hollis couldn't even try to scream—she had fainted.

"Please don't take my sunshine . . . away . . . " Dan's voice faltered into silence. His eyes widened. He put both hands out in front of him, the empty glass in one, the record in the other. He hiccupped, and said, "*No*—"

"Bad man," Anthony said, and thought Dan Hollis into something like nothing anyone would have believed possible, and then he thought the thing into a grave deep, deep in the cornfield.

The glass and record thumped on the rug. Neither broke.

Anthony's purple gaze went around the room.

Some of the people began mumbling. They all tried to smile. The sound of mumbling filled the room like a far-off approval. Out of the murmuring came one or two clear voices:

"Oh, it's a very *good* thing," said John Sipich.

"A good thing," said Anthony's father, smiling. He'd had more practice in smiling than most of them. "A wonderful thing."

"It's swell . . . just swell," said Pat Reilly, tears leaking from eyes and nose, and he began to play the piano again, softly, his trembling hands feeling for *Night and Day*.

Anthony climbed up on top of the piano, and Pat played for two hours.

Afterward, they watched television. They all went into the front room, and lit just a few candles, and pulled up chairs around the set. It was a small-screen set, and they couldn't all sit close enough to it to see, but that didn't matter. They didn't even turn the set on. It wouldn't have worked anyway, there being no electricity in Peaksville.

They just sat silently, and watched the twisting, writhing shapes on the screen, and listened to the sounds that came out of the speaker, and none of them had any idea of what it was all about. They never did. It was always the same.

"It's real nice," Aunt Amy said once, her pale eyes on the meaningless flickers and shadows. "But I liked it a little better when there were cities outside and we could get real—"

"Why, Amy!" said Mom. "It's good for you to say such a thing. Very good. But how can you mean it? Why, this television is *much* better than anything we ever used to get!"

"Yes," chimed in John Sipich. "It's fine. It's the best show we've ever seen!"

He sat on the couch, with two other men, holding Ethel Hollis flat against the cushions, holding her arms and legs and putting their hands over her mouth, so she couldn't start screaming again.

"It's really *good!*" he said again.

Mom looked out of the front window, across the darkened road, across Henderson's darkened wheat field to the vast, endless, gray nothingness in which the little village of Peaksville floated like a soul—the huge nothingness that was most evident at night, when Anthony's brassy day had gone.

It did no good to wonder where they were . . . no good at all. Peaksville was just someplace. Someplace away from the world. It was wherever it had been since that day three years ago when Anthony had crept from her womb and old Doc Bates—God rest him—had screamed and dropped him and tried to kill him, and Anthony had whined and done the thing. Had taken the village someplace. Or had destroyed the world and left only the village, nobody knew which.

It did no good to wonder about it. Nothing at all did any good—except to live as they must live. Must always, always live, if Anthony would let them.

These thoughts were dangerous, she thought.

She began to mumble. The others started mumbling too. They had all been thinking, evidently.

The men on the couch whispered and whispered to Ethel Hollis and when they took their hands away, she mumbled too.

While Anthony sat on top of the set and made television, they sat around and mumbled and watched the meaningless, flickering shapes far into the night.

Next day it snowed, and killed off half the crops—but it was a *good* day.

## FOR DISCUSSION: It's a Good Life

1. Why do you think the author chose this particular title for the story?
2. Discuss the character of Anthony in terms of his virtues and his vices. Use illustrations from the story.
3. The residents of Peaksville have made certain adjustments to the bizarre situation in which they find themselves. Does this fact indicate anything about human nature under stress?
4. What do you find most shocking or horrifying about this story? Why?

## INTRODUCTION: The Canvas Bag

Because of the rich imagination of the author of this story, the sorcerer who is the central character does not fit the stereotyped images of the aged alchemist or the evil magician. Here we encounter a man named Joe Baker in a contemporary setting, and we find that Joe is very much like a number of other young men. But there is one major difference that sets Joe apart from other men. Joe is a sorcerer, and the talent of the author who created him has made him a very interesting and very human one.

# The Canvas Bag
## Alan E. Nourse

The telephone jangled just as Joe Baker got himself settled in the bathtub. He growled something poisonous and dashed the length of the rooming house hallway to his bare little room at the end, bathrobe flying, spattering water far and wide as he reached for the offending instrument. Then Jeannie's voice was tinkling in his ear; his annoyance vanished, and his heart skipped twice in dreadful premonition.

Jeannie was laughing. "I must have dragged you out of the shower! You sound like you've hurdled barriers."

"Many barriers," said Joe, slapping at the trickle of water meandering down his leg. His feet were planted in an expanding puddle. "There's nothing wrong—is there?"

"Nothing drastic." Jeannie's voice was warm. "I'll have to be late tonight, is all. Maybe an hour or more—I don't know. Frankie's decided that *this* is the night to finish the inventory. No other night will do. And you know Frankie."

Joe shook the water out of his ears and consigned Frankie to the eighth circle of the nether world. A chill of disappointment stabbed through him all out of proportion to the importance of an hour's delay in their dinner date. But then, he was sure he heard the same disappointment in Jeannie's voice and felt somewhat mollified. It was almost as if she knew what a special date it was going to be. "How about nine, then? I'll meet you there."

"We should be finished by then. I'll be hungry, too."

"Sky's the limit tonight. Even on barriers to hurdle." He wondered vaguely how a girl who spent all day dishing out food could bear to look at it at night, much less eat it.

Jeannie's laugh was echoing in his ears as he hung up. He blinked sourly around the room. An *extra* hour to kill. He could hardly bear it. It was a drab room with a single window that stared out on the main street catching the hot Indiana sun. Not a bad room if you liked cheap boarding houses. From the window he could see the whole town before him. He stared down for a moment or two before turning away, allowing his mind to drift back to his first impression of it the day he'd dropped off the freight car six weeks before.

A grubby little dump town, he had thought. A good place to stop for the night and move on. They probably wouldn't favor gentlemen of the road around here anyway. Nothing unusual, his thinking that—the usual chain of thoughts that went through his mind when he hit a little Midwest town with its dusty streets and its dirty frame houses. It was even an ordinary-looking diner where he had been sitting, deciphering the hectographed bill-of-fare when the girl behind the counter had come over, and he had looked up and seen Jeannie.

He gave a little laugh now and fished clean clothes from the bureau. A starched shirt had always been a trial for Joe; he struggled into it manfully, grinning at himself in the mirror. So very much could happen in six short weeks! One's ideas of towns and people and everything could change so rapidly. He whistled a little tune, regarding his broad tanned face and unkempt brown hair as he whirled the tie. Not a bad face, Joe Baker. Not bad at all. You could see how a gal might go for it. And tonight she simply *had* to go for it. He'd never asked a girl to marry him before in his whole life. She couldn't refuse, not tonight.

But the thought of marriage made him feel a bit strange. It was bound to happen sometime, he had told himself. A man can't tramp the roads forever. Someday the time would come to stop. It had always been sometime in the dim, distant future with Joe. But it wasn't any more. Tonight the time had come.

And then his eye fell on the little blue canvas bag on the floor in the corner.

He blinked at the bag. The bag blinked back at him. He gave a nervous laugh and kicked the bag. It went skidding across the floor.

"Good-by, Bag," he said gleefully. "I won't need *you* any more. Our drifting days are over."

For a girl who had inventoried all evening, Jeannie was bright and chipper when Joe met her coming out of the diner. She was one of those curious girls who seem to have totally unlimited energy and become the more beautiful the wearier they are. She was slender and dark with wide gray eyes set in a narrow elfin face. Like a queen, Joe thought, as she came down the steps, or at least a princess. She kissed him lightly, and he slipped his arm around her as they walked around back to her old coupé. "He's an old tyrant, that Frankie," she was saying.

"Let me take you away from all this," said Joe gallantly. "Let me take you on the wings of the wind. The Pleasure Palace awaits."

She laughed, and Joe slipped easily into the driver's seat.

"The Spoon for dinner?" Jeannie asked.

"The Spoon? Not tonight. This is *our* night, kiddie, nothing but the best." He looked down at her and kissed her on the nose. "You know that place on the point—down by the bend of the river? Steaks an inch thick, they say, and dancing on the terrace." He slid the car out into the road traffic. "Tonight we celebrate."

"It's very, very expensive, I've heard."

"Eat, drink, and be merry."

Worry flickered in her gray eyes. "You're—you're not heading out again, are you, Joe?"

He smiled. "'Fraid not. Not a chance. I'm thinking of retiring from the road."

She snuggled closer and threw her head back happily. "For good?"

"For good."

"Then we *do* have something to celebrate."

The place was crowded when they arrived, but the waiter found them a table for two looking out on the broad river. Across the room the orchestra was playing quietly when they ordered, and soon they were in each other's arms, whirling gracefully to the music. It was a strange world for Joe—a warm, soft world of love and sweet smells and great cleanliness, and he could hardly focus his thoughts as the girl pressed her soft cheek to his. He had missed so much, all these years of drifting from town to town, never satisfied, never stopping. He had waited for years, and now he was sure, beyond doubt, that the long years of waiting had been entirely worth it. "I've got a secret, Jeannie," he whispered as they moved into the shadows of the terrace.

"Don't tell me," she whispered back.

"Why not?"

"Because then it wouldn't be a secret, would it?"

"But some secrets are for two people, they aren't any good for just one." Her ear was inches from his lips. "I love you, Jeannie. Did you know that?"

She nodded.

"I want you to marry me."

He thought he felt her arms tighten for a moment, and they danced silently, close together in a wonderful haze that required no words. But when she turned her face up to him, her eyes were sober and troubled. "Are you sure you want that?" she asked.

"I'm not fooling, Jeannie."

She turned her face away. "Oh, I know you're not, Joe, but do you *know* what you want to do? Do you really want to stop drifting, take a house, settle down for good? Do you really think you could do that?"

"I wouldn't be asking you if I hadn't thought it through, would I?" There was a puzzled note in his voice, and he frowned. Something deep inside him had gone cold, a strange sort of pain he had never felt before. "I've been on the road for a long time, I know; but a man gets tired of drifting after a while. Sooner or later he finds a girl that makes it all seem silly." His words faltered; somehow, he couldn't get the right ones to come out. The coldness in his chest deepened. "Look, Jeannie, the road is a hard life, there isn't any softness or friendship or happiness out there. Why would anybody choose it? Why should I ever want to go back?"

He broke off, realizing that he was raising his voice. He blinked at Jeannie in dismay, and she looked away, shaking her head and guiding them back to their seats. She looked up at him strangely. "You don't have to convince me, Joe. I believe it." She paused. "I wonder if *you* believe it."

His voice choked in his throat. "I only know how I feel, and I know it's true. I wouldn't have asked you otherwise."

She nodded, staring at the checkered tablecloth. Then she looked him straight in the eyes. "I want you to tell me something, Joe," she said quietly. "I want you to tell me how old you are."

Joe stared at her and very slowly set down his glass. Something was drumming in his head, a frightful deafening sound that chilled him to the bone. "Why, I'm . . . thirty-ish, or so," he said vaguely, wrinkling his forehead. "Thirty-one, I think, or thirty-two." He blinked at her. "I don't know, it's somewhere around there."

"But can't you *remember*, Joe?" Her eyes were wide.

"Well, of course I can, I suppose! I had a birthday last February." The drumming in his ears grew louder. "No, that was Pete Hower's birthday. We were on the road together. Funny guy, Pete, he—"

"*Please*, Joe!"

A chill ran up his back. It was as if he had suddenly glanced over his shoulder and seen a vast pit opening up behind him. He saw Jeannie's worried face, and he wracked his brains trying to remember, but his mind met with nothing save abysmal blankness. He stared at her in alarm. "Jeannie, *I can't remember!*"

"Oh, Joe! Think! You've got to!"

"But what difference does it make?"

"Joe—" The girl's voice was trembling, close to tears. "Think, Joe. Go back. Back to where you were before you came here, and where you went before that. Here—here's some paper. Write it down. Try to remember, Joe."

He took the pencil numbly. Slowly, from the drumming in his head things were beginning to creep into his mind, incredible things. "I—I just came East from Fargo six weeks ago," he faltered. "Hopped a freight. Ran into some trouble with the cops and had a fight. And then I'd been in Minot for a while before that."

"How long?"

"Couple of months. I was working my way East, thought I'd work the docks for a while."

"And where were you before Minot?"

"Santa Monica. Cab-driving job. I almost got killed; that chilled me on the coast. Came up from San Diego before that; hit Dago on a tramp steamer that had come through the canal from Vera Cruz. And then before that there was the war."

A horrible thought flashed through Joe Baker's mind. A fiendish voice was screaming in his ear: *Which war, Joe, which war?*

Suddenly, in a terrifying flash, he remembered. The muddy fog cleared from his mind, and his memory whirled back and back, and his face went white.

There was the fighting in Anzio, and the storming of Monte Casino—

And there was the girl in Pittsburgh who'd cleaned him out that night at Jardine's—that seemed like a century ago! And the logging up in Canada before that—

And the long depression years before that in the hobo jungles—

And the job he'd lost when his boss went down in the crash—

And the run-in with the Boston cops in the boot-legging deal which couldn't go wrong—

And the cattle-herding jaunt down through Wyoming and Colorado and Oklahoma before that—how long was that trip? Four years? Must have been, with all the time he'd wasted in Denver—

Joe Baker stared at the girl across the table from him, his mind screaming. He could almost see the blue canvas bag by his side, he could feel the excitement again as he had packed it full, ready for another move, and another, and another. . . . With a sudden horrified rush he picked up the paper and pencil and began scratching down places, times, distances, something clutching in his chest as he wrote:

The mustering out after the armistice, and the long trip home from France—

The days of drifting through Europe after the turn of the century—

The shouting, savage cavalry charges against the Spanish in Cuba—

The bitter hatred of the Kansas farmers when the railroads went through—

The hum of hoofbeats on the Nevada prairie, the wild screams of the Indian raiders—

The crash of artillery, the bitter sharp voice of the long-rifles at Chickamauga—

*He remembered them. He remembered them all.*

Joe Baker sat back in his chair finally, his hands trembling. It was utterly incredible, of course. But it was true. He'd just never thought of it before. He'd drifted from town to town, from job to job, anywhere the moment seemed to suggest. Drifted, and stopped for a while, and drifted again. He'd never thought of the past, for the past was filled with pain and loneliness, and such things seldom encourage reminiscing. It had simply never occurred to him to stop and think how long he'd drifted, nor what might happen if he ever tried to stop.

*And he had drifted for a hundred and fifty years.*

He stared at the girl's frightened face. "You knew—somehow you knew."

She nodded. "I didn't know what it was. I knew you were *different,* somehow. At first I thought it was just that you'd been traveling a long time, that it was a part of a personality you'd built up on the road. I felt it the first moment I saw you. And then I began to realize that the difference was something else. But I didn't realize how long you've been going—"

"But my face!" he cried. "My body! How could it be possible? Why is it that I'm not old, shriveled, dead?"

"I don't know."

"But it couldn't happen!"

Jeannie shook her head weakly. "There's something else far more important."

"What's that?"

"What makes you do it."

"I tell you *I don't know.*"

"But you *must* have remembered the time passing!" she burst out.

Joe shook his head. "I just never stopped to think. Why should I have? There've never been friends, or family, or anyone to hang onto along the way. It never mattered what time it was, or what day it was. All that mattered was whether it was winter or summer, whether it was hot or cold, whether I was full or hungry. Jeannie, does it matter now? I love you, I want to stop, now, I want to marry you."

They were dancing again, and she was fighting to hold back the tears, clinging to him like a lost child. "Yes, yes—tomorrow, Joe—We can get the papers. Don't ever go away from me, Joe. Oh, I'm afraid."

"Don't be, don't be."

"I can't help it. I'm afraid tomorrow—"

He put a finger to her lips. "Tomorrow we'll get a license. Then we'll be married. I've never wanted to stop before. But I do now, more than anything on Earth. And I will."

The drive back into town was very quiet.

It was late when he returned to his room. He dreaded to return. If there were only something they could *do*, some place to go *now*, while he knew he could! But there was nothing to do until tomorrow, and he was cold with fear. He walked into the room and snapped on the lights and the coldness tightened in his chest.

His eyes fell on the blue canvas bag.

It was old and threadbare and exceedingly dusty. The dust from a thousand long roads of a thousand countries was ground into its fiber, and it seemed a thing alive, a living entity with a power of its own worn deep into its creases and leatherwork. An ordinary old-fashioned traveling bag, really; over the years he had become attached to it with an unreasoning fondness. It was his home, his only solid, dependable connection with the world through which he had been drifting like a ghost. A sound, sturdy friend, always there, carrying his few possessions. He had tramped miles, once, to recover it when it had been left behind. Once it had been stolen, and he had killed a man to get it back.

And now he hated it.

Even as he looked at it, the drums were beating in his ears again—his own pulse? He didn't know. He stared at the bag, and phantoms began to flicker through his mind tormenting him. The miles had been long and dusty, but they had been free miles. He had been lonely, desperately lonely, but always, he had been free. And now....

He took the bag up on his lap, unzippered it, and watched it fall open into the familiar creases. Once there had been buttons on it, long ago. Now a zipper replaced the buttons, but it was still the same old bag. Inside there were odds and ends. A pack of cigarettes, slightly mildewed, and an ancient straight-razor. A couple of unused rifle shells, a pair of stick-on rubber soles for his shoes, a shabby torn bandanna. Like an overpowering wind the memories filtered through his mind, the call of the road, the long dark nights under the glistening star blanket. And now he would stop, throw away the bag, go off and settle down in a house, take work in the quarry outside town every day.... Once stopped, he could never drift again.

The coldness deepened. Nervously he dropped the bag on the floor, kicked it across the room. It was nonsense to think that way. He hated the road and all the loneliness it had meant. He *wouldn't* go back, not with a girl like Jeannie to keep him from ever being lonely again.

The chill grew into panic. He sat down on the bed, trembling. He was afraid. He was fighting now, and a voice was whispering in his ear, *You've got to go, Joe, you can't stop, never, never—run now, before you hurt her any more! You can never stop drifting, Joe.*

He gripped the bedstead until his knuckles turned white. Why? He strained his memory trying to think back, trying to remember how it had started so long ago. It was as though a great hand were pushing him, drawing him toward the canvas bag, urging him to pack it up, take it and race away, like the wind, onto the road again. But he didn't want to go; he wanted a wife, a home.

*Home, Joe? You hated your home!*

No, no, he thought. A line of sweat was standing out on his upper lip. I didn't hate it, I was young, I didn't understand, I didn't know.

*You threw a curse on your home, Joe. Remember? You screamed it in your mother's face, you reviled her and packed your canvas bag.*

I didn't know what I was doing, he thought. I was foolish. I couldn't have known.

*But you said it, Joe. Remember what you said?*

No!

*I'll never come home if I live a thousand years.*

He clutched at the bag. His hand anchored on the grip, and he felt it start tugging at him. He let out a cry and threw it on the floor. Frantically he jerked the telephone from the hook, dialed Jeannie's number and heard her sleepy voice.

"Jeannie, you've got to help me," he choked. "Come over, please, I can't help myself."

There had been other times he'd tried. He remembered them now, horrible struggles that had nearly killed him with torment until he gave up. He had never believed in ghosts and witchcraft and curses, but something was forcing him now, something within him so cold, so dark and powerful that he could never hope to fight it. He sat on the edge of the bed, gritting his teeth, and the voice was crying louder and louder, *You can never stop, Joe, no matter what happens, you'll never have a home again, never, never, never.*

The room was empty when she arrived. She choked back a sob, closed the door behind her, and leaned exhausted against the wall. She was too late. The dresser drawers were ripped open, a dirty sock lay under the bed, a handkerchief was crumpled on the bureau. He was gone, and so was the canvas bag.

Her eye fell on a folded white paper on the floor. She picked it up with trembling fingers and recognized it. With a little cry she plunged it into her pocket and fled down the front stairs, her coat flying behind her as she ran.

The street was dark and deserted. A light shone across the street, and another, up near the end of town, made a baleful yellow blotch in the darkness. She ran faster, her heels snapping harshly on the dry pavement, until she turned into a lighted building at the end of the street.

A sleepy clerk looked up at her and blinked.

"Was—was a young man in here?"

The clerk nodded suspiciously. "Bus to Chicago. Getting ready to leave."

She threw her money down, and snatched up the little white ticket. Seconds later she was running down the bus lane to the large coach with CHICAGO across the front. She stumbled up the steps, and then she saw him.

He was sitting near the back, eyes closed, face deathly white. In his arms he was clutching his blue canvas bag, and his whole body was trembling. Slowly she moved back, sank down in the seat beside him. "Oh, Joe, Joe—"

"Jeannie, I'm sorry, I just can't help it."

"I know, Joe."

He looked at her, his eyes widening. She shook her head, and took his heavy hand in hers. Then he saw the ticket.

"Jeannie—"

"Hush. Don't say it."

"But you don't know what you're doing! We can never have a home, darling, *never*. No matter how hard we try. Think of the long, homeless roads, Jeannie, all over the world, on and on, maybe even to the stars."

She smiled, nodding gently. "But at least you won't be lonely now."

"Jeannie, *you can't.*"

"I can," she said and rested her head quietly against his shoulder.

# FOR DISCUSSION: The Canvas Bag

1.  We have referred to Joe Baker as a sorcerer. Do you think the reference is a valid one now that you have read the story?
2.  Why did Joe telephone Jeannie and ask for her help and then leave before she arrived at his room? What does his behavior tell you about Joe?
3.  Given the supernatural premise in this story, what will happen to Joe in the future? To Jeannie?
4.  We have all read many kinds of love stories. Many, if not most of them, have happy endings. Would you say that the ending to this story is a happy one?

## INTRODUCTION: The Monkey's Paw

Many stories have been written concerning the supernatural situation in which an individual is granted any three wishes of his own choosing. This story deals with the same idea but in a rather unique fashion. The author succeeds in dealing with very human and very deep emotions as he tells his story of the talisman that had the power to grant its possessor any three wishes in the world. Before you decide that you would like to have the monkey's paw for yourself, read the story. *Then* decide.

# The Monkey's Paw
## W. W. Jacobs

Without, the night was cold and wet, but in the small parlor of Lakesnam Villa the blinds were drawn and the fire burned brightly. Father and son were at chess, the former, who possessed ideas about the game involving radical changes, putting his king into such sharp and unnecessary perils that it even provoked comment from the white-haired old lady knitting placidly by the fire.

"Hark at the wind," said Mr. White, who, having seen a fatal mistake after it was too late, was amiably desirous of preventing his son from seeing it.

"I'm listening," said the latter, grimly surveying the board as he stretched out his hand. "Check."

"I should hardly think that he'd come tonight," said his father, with his hand poised over the board.

"Mate," replied the son.

"That's the worst of living so far out," bawled Mr. White, with sudden and unlooked-for violence; "of all the beastly, slushy out-of-the-way places to live in, this is the worst. Pathway's a bog, and the road's a torrent. I don't know what people are thinking about. I suppose because only two houses on the road are let, they think it doesn't matter."

"Never mind, dear," said his wife soothingly; "perhaps you'll win the next one."

Mr. White looked up sharply, just in time to intercept a knowing glance between mother and son. The words died away on his lips, and he hid a guilty grin in his thin gray beard.

"There he is," said Herbert White, as the gate banged to loudly and heavy footsteps came toward the door.

The old man rose with hospitable haste, and opening the door, was heard condoling with the new arrival. The new arrival also condoled with himself, so that Mrs. White said, "Tut, tut!" and coughed gently as her husband entered the room, followed by a tall burly man, beady of eye and rubicund of visage.

"Sergeant Major Morris," he said, introducing him.

The sergeant major shook hands, and taking the proffered seat by the fire, watched contentedly while his host got out whisky and tumblers and stood a small copper kettle on the fire.

At the third glass his eyes got brighter, and he began to talk, the little family circle regarding with eager interest this visitor from distant parts, as he squared his broad shoulders in the chair and spoke of strange scenes and doughty deeds, of wars and plagues and strange peoples.

"Twenty-one years of it," said Mr. White, nodding at his wife and son. "When he went away he was a slip of a youth in the warehouse. Now look at him."

"He don't look to have taken much harm," said Mrs. White politely.

"I'd like to go to India myself," said the old man, "just to look round a bit, you know."

"Better where you are," said the sergeant major, shaking his head. He put down the empty glass and, sighing softly, shook it again.

"I should like to see those old temples and fakirs and jugglers," said the old man. "What was that you started telling me the other day about a monkey's paw or something, Morris?"

"Nothing," said the soldier hastily. "Leastways, nothing worth hearing."

"Monkey's paw?" said Mrs. White curiously.

"Well, it's just a bit of what you might call magic, perhaps," said the sergeant major offhandedly.

His three listeners leaned forward eagerly. The visitor absent-mindedly put his empty glass to his lips and then set it down again. His host filled it for him.

"To look at," said the sergeant major, fumbling in his pocket, "it's just an ordinary little paw, dried to a mummy."

He took something out of his pocket and proffered it. Mrs. White drew back with a grimace, but her son, taking it, examined it curiously.

"And what is there special about it?" inquired Mr. White, as he took it from his son and, having examined it, placed it upon the table.

"It had a spell put on it by an old fakir," said the sergeant major, "a very holy man. He wanted to show that fate ruled people's lives, and that those who interfered with it did so to their sorrow. He put a spell on it so that three separate men could have three wishes from it."

His manner was so impressive that his hearers were conscious that their light laughter jarred somewhat.

"Well, why don't you have three, sir?" said Herbert White cleverly.

The soldier regarded him in the way that middle age is wont to regard presumptuous youth. "I have," he said quietly, and his blotchy face whitened.

"And did you really have the three wishes granted?" asked Mrs. White.

"I did," said the sergeant major, and his glass tapped against his strong teeth.

"And has anybody else wished?" inquired the old lady.

"The first man had his three wishes, yes," was the reply. "I don't know what the first two were, but the third was for death. That's how I got the paw."

His tones were so grave that a hush fell upon the group.

"If you've had your three wishes, it's no good to you now, then, Morris," said the old man at last. "What do you keep it for?"

The soldier shook his head. "Fancy, I suppose," he said slowly. "I did have some idea of selling it, but I don't think I will. It has caused enough mischief already. Besides, people won't buy. They think it's a fairy tale, some of them, and those who do think anything of it want to try it first and pay me afterward."

"If you could have another three wishes," said the old man, eyeing him keenly, "would you have them?"

"I don't know," said the other. "I don't know."

He took the paw, and dangling it between his front finger and thumb, suddenly threw it upon the fire. White, with a slight cry, stooped down and snatched it off.

"Better let it burn," said the soldier solemnly.

"If you don't want it, Morris," said the old man, "give it to me."

"I won't," said his friend doggedly. "I threw it on the fire. If you keep it, don't blame me for what happens. Pitch it on the fire again, like a sensible man."

The other shook his head and examined his new possession closely. "How do you do it?" he inquired.

"Hold it up in your right hand and wish aloud," said the sergeant major, "but I warn you of the consequences."

"Sounds like the *Arabian Nights*," said Mrs. White, as she rose and began to set the supper. "Don't you think you might wish for four pairs of hands for me?"

Her husband drew the talisman from his pocket and then all three burst into laughter as the sergeant major, with a look of alarm on his face, caught him by the arm.

"If you must wish," he said gruffly, "wish for something sensible."

Mr. White dropped it back into his pocket, and placing chairs, motioned his friend to the table. In the business of supper the talisman was partly forgotten, and afterward the three sat listening in an enthralled fashion to a second installment of the soldier's adventures in India.

"If the tale about the monkey's paw is not more truthful than those he has been telling us," said Herbert, as the door closed behind their guest, just in time for him to catch the last train, "we shan't make much out of it."

"Did you give him anything for it, father?" inquired Mrs. White, regarding her husband closely.

"A trifle," said he, coloring slightly. "He didn't want it, but I made him take it. And he pressed me again to throw it away."

"Likely," said Herbert, with pretended horror. "Why, we're going to be rich, and famous, and happy. Wish to be an emperor, father, to begin with; then you can't be henpecked."

He darted round the table, pursued by the maligned Mrs. White armed with an antimacassar.

Mr. White took the paw from his pocket and eyed it dubiously. "I don't know what to wish for, and that's a fact," he said slowly. "It seems to me I've got all I want."

"If you only cleared the house, you'd be quite happy, wouldn't you?" said Herbert, with his hand on his shoulder. "Well, wish for two hundred pounds, then; that'll just do it."

His father, smiling shamefacedly at his own credulity, held up the talisman, as his son, with a solemn face somewhat marred by a wink at his mother, sat down at the piano and struck a few impressive chords.

"I wish for two hundred pounds," said the old man distinctly.

A fine crash from the piano greeted the words, interrupted by a shuddering cry from the old man. His wife and son ran toward him.

"It moved," he cried, with a glance of disgust at the object as it lay on the floor. "As I wished it twisted in my hands like a snake."

"Well, I don't see the money," said his son, as he picked it up and placed it on the table, "and I bet I never shall."

"It must have been your fancy, father," said his wife, regarding him anxiously.

He shook his head. "Never mind, though; there's no harm done, but it gave me a shock all the same."

They sat down by the fire again while the two men finished their pipes. Outside, the wind was higher than ever, and the old man started nervously at the sound of a door banging upstairs. A silence unusual and depressing settled upon all three, which lasted until the old couple rose to retire for the night.

"I expect you'll find the cash tied up in a big bag in the middle of your bed," said Herbert, as he bade them good night, "and something horrible squatting up on top of the wardrobe watching you as you pocket your ill-gotten gains."

In the brightness of the wintry sun next morning as it streamed over the breakfast table, Herbert laughed at his fears. There was an air of prosaic wholesomeness about the room which it had lacked on the previous night, and the dirty, shriveled little paw was pitched on the sideboard with a carelessness which betokened no great belief in its virtues.

"I suppose all old soldiers are the same," said Mrs. White. "The idea of our listening to such nonsense! How could wishes be granted in these days? And if they could, how could two hundred pounds hurt you, father?"

"Might drop on his head from the sky," said the frivolous Herbert.

"Morris said the things happened so naturally," said his father, "that you might if you so wished attribute it to coincidence."

"Well, don't break into the money before I come back," said Herbert, as he rose from the table. "I'm afraid it'll turn you into a mean, avaricious man, and we shall have to disown you."

His mother laughed, and following him to the door, watched him down the road, and returning to the breakfast table, was very happy at the expense of her husband's credulity. All of which did not prevent her from scurrying to the door at the postman's knock, nor prevent her from referring somewhat shortly to retired sergeant majors of bibulous habits when she found that the post brought a tailor's bill.

"Herbert will have some more of his funny remarks, I expect, when he comes home," she said, as they sat at dinner.

"I dare say," said Mr. White, pouring himself out some beer; "but for all that, the thing moved in my hand; that I'll swear to."

"You thought it did," said the old lady soothingly.

"I say it did," replied the other. "There was no thought about it; I had just—What's the matter?"

His wife made no reply. She was watching the mysterious movements of a man outside, who, peering in an undecided fashion at the house, appeared to be trying to make up his mind to enter. In mental connection with the two hundred pounds, she noticed that the stranger was well-dressed and wore a silk hat of glossy newness. Three times he paused at the gate, and then walked on again. The fourth time he stood with his hand upon it, and then with sudden resolution flung it open and walked up the path. Mrs. White at the same moment placed her hands behind her, and hurriedly unfastening the strings of her apron, put that useful article of apparel beneath the cushion of her chair.

She brought the stranger, who seemed ill at ease, into the room. He gazed furtively at Mrs. White, and listened in a preoccupied fashion as the old lady apologized for the appearance of the room, and her husband's coat, a garment which he usually reserved for the garden. She then waited as patiently as her sex would permit for him to broach his business, but he was at first strangely silent.

"I—was asked to call," he said at last, and stooped and picked a piece of cotton from his trousers. "I come from Maw and Meggins."

The old lady started. "Is anything the matter?" she asked breathlessly. "Has anything happened to Herbert? What is it? What is it?"

Her husband interposed. "There, there, mother," he said hastily. "Sit down, and don't jump to conclusions. You've not brought bad news, I'm sure, sir," and he eyed the other wistfully.

"I'm sorry—" began the visitor.

"Is he hurt?" demanded the mother.

The visitor bowed in assent. "Badly hurt," he said quietly, "but he is not in any pain."

"Oh, thank God!" said the old woman, clasping her hands. "Thank God for that! Thank—"

She broke off suddenly as the sinister meaning of the assurance dawned upon her and she saw the awful confirmation of her fears in the other's averted face. She caught her breath, and turning to her slower-witted husband, laid her trembling old hand upon his. There was a long silence.

"He was caught in the machinery," said the visitor at length, in a low voice.

"Caught in the machinery," repeated Mr. White, in a dazed fashion, "yes."

He sat staring blankly out at the window, and taking his wife's hand between his own, pressed it as he had been wont to do in their old courting days nearly forty years before.

"He was the only one left us," he said, turning gently to the visitor. "It is hard."

The other coughed, and rising, walked slowly to the window. "The firm wished me to convey their sincere sympathy with you in your great loss," he said, without looking round. "I beg that you will understand I am only their servant and merely obeying orders."

There was no reply; the old woman's face was white, her eyes staring, and her breath inaudible; on the husband's face was a look such as his friend the sergeant might have carried into his first action.

"I was to say that Maw and Meggins disclaim all responsibility," continued the other. "They admit no liability at all, but in consideration of your son's services they wish to present you with a certain sum as compensation."

Mr. White dropped his wife's hand, and rising to his feet, gazed with a look of horror at his visitor. His dry lips shaped the words, "How much?"

"Two hundred pounds," was the answer.

Unconscious of his wife's shriek, the old man smiled faintly, put out his hands like a sightless man, and dropped, a senseless heap, to the floor.

In the huge new cemetery, some two miles distant, the old people buried their dead, and came back to a house steeped in shadow and silence. It was all over so quickly that at first they could hardly realize it, and remained in a state of expectation as though of something else to happen—something else which was to lighten this load, too heavy for old hearts to bear. But the days passed, and expectation gave place to resignation—the hopeless resignation of the old, sometimes miscalled apathy. Sometimes they hardly exchanged a word, for now they had nothing to talk about, and their days were long to weariness.

It was about a week after that that the old man, waking suddenly in the night, stretched out his hand and found himself alone. The room was in darkness, and the sound of subdued weeping came from the window. He raised himself in bed and listened.

"Come back," he said tenderly. "You will be cold."

"It is colder for my son," said the old woman, and wept afresh.

The sound of her sobs died away on his ears. The bed was warm, and his eyes heavy with sleep. He dozed fitfully, and then slept until a sudden wild cry from his wife awoke him with a start.

"The monkey's paw!" she cried wildly. "The monkey's paw!"

He started up in alarm. "Where? Where is it? What's the matter?"

She came stumbling across the room toward him. "I want it," she said quietly. "You've not destroyed it?"

"It's in the parlor, on the bracket," he replied, marveling. "Why?"

She cried and laughed together, and bending over, kissed his cheek.

"I only just thought of it," she said hysterically. "Why didn't I think of it before? Why didn't you think of it?"

"Think of what?" he questioned.

"The other two wishes," she replied rapidly. "We've only had one."

"Was not that enough?" he demanded fiercely.

"No," she cried triumphantly; "we'll have one more.  Go down and get it quickly, and wish our boy alive again."

The man sat up in bed and flung the bedclothes from his quaking limbs.  "Good God, you are mad!"  he cried, aghast.

"Get it," she panted; "get it quickly, and wish—Oh, my boy, my boy!"

Her husband struck a match and lit the candle.  "Get back to bed," he said unsteadily.  "You don't know what you are saying."

"We had the first wish granted," said the old woman feverishly; "why not the second?"

"A coincidence," stammered the old man.

"Go and get it and wish," cried the old woman, and dragged him toward the door.

He went down in the darkness, and felt his way to the parlor, and then to the mantelpiece.  The talisman was in its place, and a horrible fear that the unspoken wish might bring his mutilated son before him ere he could escape from the room seized upon him, and he caught his breath as he found that he had lost the direction of the door.  His brow cold with sweat, he felt his way round the table, and groped along the wall until he found himself in the small passage with the unwholesome thing in his hand.

Even his wife's face seemed changed as he entered the room.  It was white and expectant, and to his fears seemed to have an unusual look upon it.  He was afraid of her.

"Wish!"  she cried, in a strong voice.

"It is foolish and wicked," he faltered.

"Wish!"  repeated his wife.

He raised his hand.  "I wish my son alive again."

The talisman fell to the floor, and he regarded it shudderingly.  Then he sank trembling into a chair as the old woman, with burning eyes, walked to the window and raised the blind.

He sat until he was chilled with the cold, glancing occasionally at the figure of the old woman peering through the window.  The candle end, which had burnt below the rim of the china candlestick, was throwing pulsating shadows on the ceiling and walls, until, with a flicker larger than the rest, it expired.  The old man, with an unspeakable sense of relief at the failure of the talisman, crept back to his bed, and a minute or two afterward the old woman came silently and apathetically beside him.

Neither spoke, but both lay silently listening to the ticking of the clock.  A stair creaked, and a squeaky mouse scurried noisily through the wall.  The darkness was oppressive, and after lying for some time screwing up his courage, the husband took the box of matches, and striking one, went downstairs for a candle.

At the foot of the stairs the match went out, and he paused to strike another, and at the same moment a knock, so quiet and stealthy as to be scarcely audible, sounded on the front door.

The matches fell from his hand. He stood motionless, his breath suspended until the knock was repeated. Then he turned and fled swiftly back to his room, and closed the door behind him. A third knock sounded through the house.

"What's that?" cried the old woman, starting up.

"A rat," said the old man, in shaking tones—"a rat. It passed me on the stairs."

His wife sat up in bed, listening. A loud knock resounded through the house.

"It's Herbert!" she screamed. "It's Herbert!"

She ran to the door, but her husband was before her, and catching her by the arm, held her tightly.

"What are you going to do?" he whispered hoarsely.

"It's my boy; it's Herbert!" she cried, struggling mechanically. "I forgot it was two miles away. What are you holding me for? Let go. I must open the door."

"For God's sake don't let it in," cried the old man, trembling.

"You're afraid of your own son," she cried, struggling. "Let me go. I'm coming, Herbert; I'm coming."

There was another knock, and another. The old woman with a sudden wrench broke free and ran from the room. Her husband followed to the landing, and called after her appealingly as she hurried downstairs. He heard the chain rattle back and the bottom bolt drawn slowly and stiffly from the socket. Then the old woman's voice, strained and panting.

"The bolt," she cried loudly. "Come down. I can't reach it."

But her husband was on his hands and knees groping wildly on the floor in search of the paw. If he could only find it before the thing outside got in. A perfect fusillade of knocks reverberated through the house, and he heard the scraping of a chair as his wife put it down in the passage against the door. He heard the creaking of the bolt as it came slowly back, and at the same moment, he found the monkey's paw, and frantically breathed his third and last wish.

The knocking ceased suddenly, although the echoes of it were still in the house. He heard the chair drawn back and the door opened. A cold wind rushed up the staircase, and a long loud wail of disappointment and misery from his wife gave him courage to run down to her side, and then to the gate beyond. The street lamp flickering opposite shone on a quiet and deserted road.

# FOR DISCUSSION: The Monkey's Paw

1. This story opens in a pleasant and leisurely fashion. Why do you suppose the author wrote his opening in this way instead of beginning immediately with the monkey's paw itself?
2. By dropping hints throughout his story, an author prepares the reader for what will happen at the conclusion of the story. This technique is called foreshadowing. For example, the sergeant major, in response to a question, says, "The first man had his three wishes, yes. I don't know what the first two were, but the third was for death." Explain how this remark foreshadows the conclusion of the story.
3. What was the husband's third wish? Would you have made it under the circumstances?

# INTRODUCTION: The Facts in the Case of M. Valdemar

No anthology of supernatural literature would be complete without the inclusion of a story by that American master of the macabre and unusual short story, Edgar Allan Poe. You are probably already familiar with his stories *The Black Cat* and *The Tell-Tale Heart*. The following story, in which science and the supernatural blend to produce remarkable and horrible results, may be new to you.

# The Facts in the Case of M. Valdemar

### Edgar Allan Poe

Of course I shall not pretend to consider it any matter for wonder, that the extraordinary case of M. Valdemar has excited discussion. It would have been a miracle had it not—especially under the circumstances. Through the desire of all parties concerned, to keep the affair from the public, at least for the present, or until we had further opportunities for investigation—through our endeavors to effect this—a garbled or exaggerated account made its way into society, and became the source of many unpleasant misrepresentations, and, very naturally, of a great deal of disbelief.

It is now rendered necessary that I give the *facts*—as far as I comprehended them myself. They are, succinctly, these:

My attention, for the last three years, had been repeatedly drawn to the subject of Mesmerism; and, about nine months ago, it occurred to me, quite suddenly, that in the series of experiments made hitherto, there had been a very remarkable and most unaccountable omission—no person had as yet been mesmerized *in articulo mortis*. It remained to be seen, first, whether, in such condition, there existed in the patient any susceptibility to the magnetic influence; secondly, whether, if any existed, it was impaired or increased by the condition; thirdly, to what extent, or for how long a period, the encroachments of Death might be arrested by the process. There were other points to be ascertained, but these most excited my curiosity—the last in especial, from the immensely important character of its consequences.

In looking around me for some subject by whose means I might test these particulars, I was brought to think of my friend, M. Ernest Valdemar, the well-known compiler of the "Bibliotheca Forensica," and author (under the *nom de plume* of Issachar Marx) of the Polish versions of "Wallenstein" and "Gargantua." M. Valdemar, who had resided principally at Harlaem, N. Y., since the year 1839, is (or was) particularly noticeable for the extreme spareness of his person—his lower limbs much resembling those of John Randolph; and, also, for the whiteness of his whiskers, in violent contrast to the blackness of his hair—the latter, in consequence, being very generally mistaken for a wig. His temperament was markedly nervous, and rendered him a good subject for mesmeric experiment. On two or three occasions I had put him to sleep with little difficulty, but was disappointed in other results which his peculiar constitution had naturally led me to anticipate. His will was at no period positively, or thoroughly, under my control, and in regard to *clairvoyance*, I could accomplish with him nothing to be relied upon. I always attributed my failure at these points to the disordered state of his health. For some months previous to my becoming acquainted with him, his physicians had declared him in a confirmed phthisis. It was his custom, indeed, to speak calmly of his approaching dissolution, as of a matter neither to be avoided nor regretted.

When the ideas to which I have alluded first occurred to me, it was of course very natural that I should think of M. Valdemar. I knew the steady philosophy of the man too well to apprehend any scruples from *him;* and he had no relatives in America who would be likely to interfere. I spoke to him frankly upon the subject; and, to my surprise, his interest seemed vividly excited. I say to my surprise; for although he had always yielded his person freely to my experiments, he had never before given me any tokens of sympathy with what I did. His disease was of that character which would admit of exact calculation in respect to the epoch of its termination in death; and it was finally arranged between us that he would send for me about twenty-four hours before the period announced by his physicians as that of his decrease.

It is now rather more than seven months since I received, from M. Valdemar himself, the subjoined note:

MY DEAR P——,

You may as well come *now.* D—— and F—— are agreed that I cannot hold out beyond tomorrow midnight; and I think they have 'hit the time very nearly.

VALDEMAR

I received this note within half an hour after it was written, and in fifteen minutes more I was in the dying man's chamber. I had not seen him for ten days, and was appalled by the fearful alteration which the brief interval had wrought in him. His face wore a leaden hue; the eyes were utterly lusterless; and the emaciation was so extreme that the skin had been broken through by the cheekbones. His expectoration was excessive. The pulse was barely perceptible. He retained, nevertheless, in a very remarkable manner, both his mental power and a certain degree of physical strength. He spoke with distinctness—took some palliative medicines without aid—and, when I entered the room, was occupied in penciling memoranda in a pocketbook. He was propped up in the bed by pillows. Doctors D—— and F—— were in attendance.

After pressing Valdemar's hand, I took these gentlemen aside, and obtained from them a minute account of the patient's condition. The left lung had been for eighteen months in a semi-osseous or cartilaginous state, and was, of course, entirely useless for all purposes of vitality. The right, in its upper portion, was also partially, if not thoroughly, ossified, while the lower region was merely a mass of purulent tubercles, running one into another. Several extensive perforations existed; and, at one point, permanent adhesion to the ribs had taken place. These appearances in the right lobe were of comparatively recent date. The ossification had proceeded with very unusual rapidity; no sign of it had been discovered a month before, and the adhesion had only been observed during the three previous days. Independently of the phthisis, the patient was suspected of aneurism of the aorta; but on this point the osseous symptoms rendered an exact diagnosis impossible. It was the opinion of both physicians that M. Valdemar would die about midnight on the morrow (Sunday). It was then seven o'clock on Saturday evening.

On quitting the invalid's bedside to hold conversation with myself, Doctors D—— and F—— had bidden him a final farewell. It had not been their intention to return; but, at my request, they agreed to look in upon the patient about ten the next night.

When they had gone, I spoke freely with M. Valdemar on the subject of his approaching dissolution, as well as, more particularly, of the experiment proposed. He still professed himself quite willing and even anxious to have it made and urged me to commence it at once. A male and a female nurse were in attendance; but I did not feel myself altogether at liberty to engage in a task of this character with no more reliable witnesses than these people, in case of sudden accident, might prove. I therefore postponed operations until about eight the next night, when the arrival of a medical student with whom I had some acquaintance (Mr. Theodore L——l), relieved me from farther embarrassment. It had been my design, originally, to wait for the physicians; but I was induced to proceed, first, by the urgent entreaties of M. Valdemar, and secondly, by my conviction that I had not a moment to lose, as he was evidently sinking fast.

Mr. L——l was so kind as to accede to my desire that he would take notes of all that occurred; and it is from his memoranda that what I now have to relate is, for the most part, either condensed or copied *verbatim*.

It wanted about five minutes of eight when, taking the patient's hand, I begged him to state, as distinctly as he could, to Mr. L——l, whether he (M. Valdemar) was entirely willing that I should make the experiment of mesmerizing him in this then condition.

He replied feebly, yet quite audibly, "Yes, I wish to be mesmerized"— adding immediately afterwards, "I fear you have deferred it too long."

While he spoke thus, I commenced the passes which I had already found most effectual in subduing him. He was evidently influenced with the first lateral stroke of my hand across his forehead; but although I exerted all my powers, no farther perceptible effect was induced until some minutes after ten o'clock, when Doctors D—— and F—— called, according to appointment. I explained to them, in a few words, what I designed, and as they opposed no objection, saying that the patient was already in the death agony, I proceeded without hesitation—exchanging, however, the lateral passes for downward ones, and directing my gaze entirely into the right eye of the sufferer.

By this time his pulse was imperceptible and his breathing was stertorous, and at intervals of half a minute.

This condition was nearly unaltered for a quarter of an hour. At the expiration of this period, however, a natural although a very deep sigh escaped the bosom of the dying man, and the stertorous breathing ceased —that is to say, its stertorousness was no longer apparent; the intervals were undiminished. The patient's extremities were of an icy coldness.

At five minutes before eleven I perceived unequivocal signs of the mesmeric influence. The glassy roll of the eye was changed for that expression of uneasy *inward* examination which is never seen except in cases of sleep-waking, and which it is quite impossible to mistake. With a few rapid lateral passes I made his lids quiver, as in incipient sleep, and with a few more I closed them altogether. I was not satisfied, however, with this, but continued the manipulations vigorously, and with the fullest exertion of the will, until I had completely stiffened the limbs of the slumberer, after placing them in a seemingly easy position. The legs were at full length; the arms were nearly so, and reposed on the bed at a moderate distance from the loins. The head was very slightly elevated.

When I had accomplished this, it was fully midnight, and I requested the gentlemen present to examine M. Valdemar's condition. After a few experiments, they admitted him to be in an unusually perfect state of mesmeric trance. The curiosity of both the physicians was greatly excited. Dr. D—— resolved at once to remain with the patient all night, while Dr. F—— took leave with a promise to return at daybreak. Mr. L——l and the nurses remained.

We left M. Valdemar entirely undisturbed until about three o'clock in the morning, when I approached him and found him in precisely the same condition as when Dr. F—— went away—that is to say, he lay in the same position; the pulse was imperceptible; the breathing was gentle (scarcely noticeable, unless through the application of a mirror to the lips); the eyes were closed naturally; and the limbs were as rigid and as cold as marble. Still, the general appearance was certainly not that of death.

As I approached M. Valdemar I made a kind of half effort to influence his right arm into pursuit of my own, as I passed the latter gently to and fro above his person. In such experiments with this patient I had never perfectly succeeded before, and assuredly I had little thought of succeeding now; but to my astonishment, his arm very readily, although feebly, followed every direction I assigned it with mine. I determined to hazard a few words of conversation.

"M. Valdemar," I said, "are you asleep?" He made no answer, but I perceived a tremor about the lips, and was thus induced to repeat the question, again and again. At its third repetition, his whole frame was agitated by a very slight shivering; the eyelids unclosed themselves so far as to display a white line of the bell; the lips moved sluggishly, and from between them, in a barely audible whisper, issued the words:

"Yes;—asleep now. Do not wake me!—let me die so!"

I here felt the limbs and found them as rigid as ever. The right arm, as before, obeyed the direction of my hand. I questioned the sleep-waker again:

"Do you still feel pain in the breast, M. Valdemar?"

The answer now was immediate, but even less audible than before:

"No pain—I am dying."

I did not think it advisable to disturb him farther just then, and nothing more was said or done until the arrival of Dr. F——, who came a little before sunrise, and expressed unbounded astonishment at finding the patient still alive. After feeling the pulse and applying a mirror to the lips, he requested me to speak to the sleep-waker again. I did so, saying:

"M. Valdemar, do you still sleep?"

As before, some minutes elapsed ere a reply was made; and during the interval the dying man seemed to be collecting his energies to speak. At my fourth repetition of the question, he said very faintly, almost inaudibly:

"Yes; still asleep—dying."

It was now the opinion, or rather the wish, of the physicians, that M. Valdemar should be suffered to remain undisturbed in his present apparently tranquil condition, until death should supervene—and this, it was generally agreed, must now take place within a few minutes. I concluded, however, to speak to him once more, and merely repeated my previous question.

While I spoke, there came a marked change over the countenance of the sleep-waker. The eyes rolled themselves slowly open, the pupils disappearing upwardly; the skin generally assumed a cadaverous hue, resembling not so much parchment as white paper; and the circular hectic spots which, hitherto, had been strongly defined in the center of each cheek, *went out* at once. I use this expression, because the suddenness of their departure put me in mind of nothing so much as the extinguishment of a candle by a puff of the breath. The upper lip, at the same time, writhed itself away from the teeth, which it had previously covered completely; while the lower jaw fell with an audible jerk, leaving the mouth widely extended, and disclosing in full view the swollen and blackened tongue. I presume that no member of the party then present had been unaccustomed to deathbed horrors; but so hideous beyond conception was the appearance of M. Valdemar at this moment, that there was a general shrinking back from the region of the bed.

I now feel that I have reached a point of this narrative at which every reader will be startled into positive disbelief. It is my business, however, simply to proceed.

There was no longer the faintest sign of vitality in M. Valdemar; and concluding him to be dead, we were consigning him to the charge of the nurses, when a strong vibratory motion was observable in the tongue. This continued for perhaps a minute. At the expiration of this period, there issued from the distended and motionless jaws a voice—such as it would be madness in me to attempt describing. There are, indeed, two or three epithets which might be considered as applicable to it in part; I might say, for example, that the sound was harsh, and broken and hollow; but the hideous whole is indescribable, for the simple reason that no similar sounds have ever jarred upon the ear of humanity. There were two particulars, nevertheless, which I thought then, and still think, might fairly be stated as characteristic of the intonation—as well adapted to convey some idea of its unearthly peculiarity. In the first place, the voice seemed to reach our ears—at least mine—from a vast distance, or from some deep cavern within the earth. In the second place, it impressed me (I fear, indeed, that it will be impossible to make myself comprehended) as gelatinous or glutinous matters impress the sense of touch.

I have spoken both of "sound" and of "voice." I mean to say that the sound was one of distinct—of even wonderfully, thrillingly distinct—syllabification. M. Valdemar *spoke*—obviously in reply to the question I had propounded to him a few minutes before. I had asked him, it will be remembered, if he still slept. He now said:

"Yes;—no;—I *have been* sleeping—and now—now—*I am dead.*"

No person present even affected to deny, or attempted to repress, the unutterable, shuddering horror which these few words, thus uttered, were so well calculated to convey. Mr. L——l (the student) swooned. The nurses immediately left the chamber, and could not be induced to return. My own impressions I would not pretend to render intelligible to the reader. For nearly an hour, we busied ourselves, silently—without the utterance of a word—in endeavors to revive Mr. L——l. When he came to himself, we addressed ourselves again to an investigation of M. Valdemar's condition.

It remained in all respects as I have last described it, with the exception that the mirror no longer afforded evidence of respiration. An attempt to draw blood from the arm failed. I should mention, too, that this limb was no farther subject to my will. I endeavored in vain to make it follow the direction of my hand. The only real indication, indeed, of the mesmeric influence, was now found in the vibratory movement of the tongue, whenever I addressed M. Valdemar a question. He seemed to be making an effort to reply, but had no longer sufficient volition. To queries put to him by any other person than myself he seemed utterly insensible—although I endeavored to place each member of the company in mesmeric *rapport* with him. I believe that I have now related all that is necessary to an understanding of the sleep-waker's state at this epoch. Other nurses were procured; and at ten o'clock I left the house in company with the two physicians and Mr. L——l.

In the afternoon we all called again to see the patient. His condition remained precisely the same. We had now some discussion as to the propriety and feasibility of awakening him; but we had little difficulty in agreeing that no good purpose would be served by so doing. It was evident that, so far, death (or what is usually termed death) had been arrested by the mesmeric process. It seemed clear to us all that to awaken M. Valdemar would be merely to insure his instant, or at least his speedy dissolution.

From this period until the close of last week—*an interval of nearly seven months*—we continued to make daily calls at M. Valdemar's house, accompanied, now and then, by medical and other friends. All this time the sleep-waker remained *exactly* as I have last described him. The nurses' attentions were continual.

It was on Friday last that we finally resolved to make the experiment of awakening, or attempting to awaken him; and it is the (perhaps) unfortunate result of this latter experiment which has given rise to so much discussion in private circles—to so much of what I cannot help thinking unwarranted popular feeling.

For the purpose of relieving M. Valdemar from the mesmeric trance, I made use of the customary passes. These, for a time, were unsuccessful. The first indication of revival was afforded by a partial descent of the iris. It was observed, as especially remarkable, that this lowering of the pupil was accompanied by the profuse out-flowing of a yellowish ichor (from beneath the lids) of a pungent and highly offensive odor.

It was now suggested that I should attempt to influence the patient's arm, as heretofore. I made the attempt and failed. Dr. F—— then intimated a desire to have me put a question. I did so, as follows:

"M. Valdemar, can you explain to us what are your feelings or wishes now?"

There was an instant return of the hectic circles on the cheeks; the tongue quivered, or rather rolled violently in the mouth (although the jaws and lips remained rigid as before); and at length the same hideous voice which I have already described, broke forth:

"For God's sake—quick!—quick!—put me to sleep—or, quick!—waken me!—quick!—*I say to you that I am dead!*"

I was thoroughly unnerved, and for an instant remained undecided what to do. At first I made an endeavor to recompose the patient; but, failing in this through total abeyance of the will, I retraced my steps and as earnestly struggled to awaken him. In this attempt I soon saw that I should be successful—or at least I soon fancied that my success would be complete—and I am sure that all in the room were prepared to see the patient awaken.

For what really occurred, however, it is quite impossible that any human being could have been prepared.

As I rapidly made the mesmeric passes, amid ejaculations of "dead! dead!" absolutely *bursting* from the tongue and not from the lips of the sufferer, his whole frame at once—within the space of a single minute, or even less, shrunk—crumbled—absolutely *rotted* away beneath my hands. Upon the bed, before that whole company, there lay a nearly liquid mass of loathsome—of detestable putridity.

## FOR DISCUSSION: The Facts in the Case of M. Valdemar

1. From the very opening paragraph, Poe piques the reader's interest in the case of M. Valdemar. Analyze the first paragraph and explain how he succeeds in arousing interest.
2. The story is told in a straightforward, matter-of-fact way. Do you think such a style enhances or detracts from the horror of the final scene?
3. Poe does not name many of the characters in his story. Instead, he refers to them as, for example, "Doctors D—— and F——" and Mr. L——l. What effect is he seeking to achieve by omitting these character's names? The device is no longer used in contemporary literature. Why do you suppose modern writers no longer employ it?

## INTRODUCTION: The Dark Door

The story of Lowena Young Owl presented here is a story of spells, sorcery, witchcraft, religion, and certain other supernatural elements. It is a story of suffering and revenge. The setting is a modern one. But the ancient evils released by Lowena Young Owl are as old as time itself and suggest that, although the elder gods may sleep, they do not die.

# The Dark Door
## Leo P. Kelley

When the waiter brought the main course and set it down in front of us, Professor Windrow began rubbing his hands together in eager anticipation over his broiled brook trout. Just then, Lowena entered the restaurant.

I put down the glass of wine I'd been lifting to my lips and frowned. The Professor glanced at me with a puzzled expression on his thin face.

Heads were turning toward Lowena. Whispers like small winds wafted her name about the room from table to table. Eyes, mine included, stared at her in a mixture of awe and uneasiness.

"What is it, Carl?" Professor Windrow asked me. "Are you so easily unnerved by the sight of a ravishing woman?"

I shook my head and managed a weak smile. "She is lovely, isn't she? But no, it isn't that."

"Her lurid past then?"

I drained my glass. "Yes. Let's say that's it." I watched her move across the dining room, a young man at her side, the waiter leading them both to a secluded corner and a choice table on which a sign that said "Reserved" rested beside a single red rose in a crystal vase.

Lowena Derry, I thought. No, more properly, Lowena Young Owl. Derry had been her recently deceased husband's name. But Lowena's Indian name had been Young Owl.

I watched her move through the room as an animal moves through a part of the forest that it senses is hostile to its kind. Quickly. Nervously. Her white dress was bound by a slim girdle of scarlet that swept up in an inverted V to end between her breasts, ripe buds on the young sapling of her body. She wore white slippers and carried a simple white evening bag. Her hair was a jet waterfall that fell to touch the icy whiteness of her shoulders. Her equally black eyes beneath their heavy lashes were ebony fires blazing in the pale cauldron of her face, which was unmarred by any makeup.

Professor Windrow, I noticed, as I looked away to avoid being seen by Lowena, had forgotten his trout. He was staring at Lowena with the longing that age sometimes betrays for days gone and loves lost.

"She's coming over here," he breathed, already rising in his invariably polite fashion.

"Good evening," he said as Lowena arrived to stand beside our table. I looked up. "Hello, Lowena," I said.

She offered me a slim hand on which no rings glittered. "Carl." She paused and the rather handsome young man beside her cleared his throat. "It's been months. You really must call me soon. You shouldn't forget old friends so easily."

"I've been busy. How have you been, Lowena?"

A shadow seemed to dim the sun of her smile momentarily. "Tomorrow?" she asked in that gentle shy way of hers that endeared her to nearly everyone—even to women who tried to hate her for being so very beautiful. "Promise me that you'll phone tomorrow."

"I'm leaving town tomorrow," I told her.

"Well, perhaps another time then. It was good seeing you again, Carl." She turned to the young man whom she had not bothered to introduce to us and they made their way to where a waiter was holding a chair in readiness for her.

"Liar," Professor Windrow said to me. "Why did you tell her that? You're not leaving town tomorrow."

"Why? I don't know. No that's not true. I do know. I lied because I'm afraid of Lowena."

Professor Windrow closed his mouth on the piece of trout he had expertly speared with his fork and almost choked. After he had swallowed with some difficulty, he said, "You're afraid of Lowena Derry?"

"I'm afraid of Lowena Young Owl," I told the man who had been my mentor, confidant and father substitute throughout my years in college after my own father had died of an unexpected angina attack.

"Why?" he asked, in his characteristically direct fashion.

I couldn't refuse to tell him, not any longer. Actually, I badly wanted to tell someone—someone who might not believe me but who would, at least, listen sympathetically and not be likely to recommend a sanitarium. "I was there the night Charles Derry—died," I said.

The rather austere Professor of Marketing Management disappeared and Ross Windrow, sympathetic friend, appeared in his place with curiosity and concern showing on his face as he gazed across the table at me. "You were there? You actually saw what really happened?"

I nodded. The papers had called Chuck's death "murder by person or persons unknown." It had caused a sensation when it happened. Lowena had been cleared completely. There was absolutely no evidence to prove that she had been in any way involved with her husband's death. But I knew better.

"Why didn't you tell the police what you saw at the time?" the Professor asked.

I glanced across to where Lowena was sitting with her new young man. "I've already explained that. Because I was afraid. Besides, I'm certain that no one would have believed me. I've never spoken to anyone of what happened that night and I suspect I never will again. But if I can count on your treating what I have to say in confidence—"

The professor looked chagrined.

"I'm sorry," I said.

"I'm waiting," he said. "It will do you good to get it off your chest—whatever it is."

After he had summoned our waiter and ordered espresso I began to tell him; starting at what was, for me and Charles Derry and Lowena Young Owl, the beginning of what would, within a year, prove to be Charles Derry's terrifying end.

As I talked, I began to feel a sense of relief. It was a feeling akin to the catharsis so familiar to the ancient Greek dramatists, which was fitting since my tale—my experience—held within it the twin seeds of pity and terror that were the bases of all truly tragic drama.

Chuck Derry and I, I explained to Professor Windrow, had spent the previous summer bumming around the country in my old Buick. Our mission: to tape the folk songs and folk music of America's heartland. Chuck was a graduate student in music and I was a senior in the School of Business Administration. When Chuck suggested the jaunt, I jumped at the chance, knowing full well that it would be my last free summer before I'd find myself stuck feet first into some monolithic corporation from which I'd probably never be able to extricate myself.

By the time we reached New Orleans, I had become aware that Chuck had a problem. His problem was, in one word, alcohol. I hadn't seen much of Chuck during the school year—just a party here, a concert there —so I hadn't been aware of what was beginning to happen to him. More times during our summer together than I care to count, he had left me and gone off into the night from which he would emerge the next day red-eyed and weary as if he'd been battling unseen demons. Which, in a way, was true, I guess.

He used to tell me about hearing music in his head. Wild music, he called it. Orgiastic music. He wanted to drown it out because, he told me, it was ruining his capacity to concentrate on his composing which had always produced incredibly sensitive and vaguely sensuous music. And then he'd laugh and tell me I really shouldn't pay any attention to him because surely I knew that all artists were more than a little bit mad. It was a prerequisite, he insisted, for any artist of more than average caliber.

Chuck may not have been mad but he certainly was an oddly angry man that summer. I remembered one night in a bar in the French Quarter when he picked a fight with two merchant seamen for no reason that I could discover. I tried to get him out of the place before it was too late, only to discover that it was already too late. Chairs flew and bottles broke and, when it was over, Chuck and I fled, leaving behind two badly injured men who had been beaten senseless by my friend, whom I had begun to think of as—well, *driven*.

We headed west and I began to hint that our journey should be terminated. I was, frankly, becoming decidedly uneasy as Chuck continued his disappearing act night after night as well as his arguments with waitresses in roadside diners and with gas station attendants—anyone unlucky enough to be present when the fury was loose within him.

In August, we arrived at an Indian reservation, a pathetic vista of parched land and crumbling shacks, which Chuck jokingly referred to as modern America's version of Dante's Inferno. He wanted to stop to see if the Indians could provide him with any material worth recording.

"All I have to do is spread a little wampum around," he joked, "and the singers will start gargling with Alka Seltzer and the musicians will eagerly oil their drum hides."

So we scouted around the reservation, but we found only blank-eyed children, old people too tired to answer Chuck's questions and one or two dispirited young men who looked as if they had never heard of war paint.

It was a hopeless task. A few of the people did sing us a few bawdy songs that they thought might have Indian origins but which were clearly the products of more modern bars and bordellos. It was sad—a bitter experience. But Chuck was unwilling to give up.

And then we saw Lowena.

She was standing beside a water pump in the yard of a house where a few scrawny chickens scratched and clucked disconsolately. She wore a faded print dress and battered shoes. But her face was the face of a sun that no cloud could ever really dim. Even then, even in those dreary surroundings and those awful clothes, she looked regal and somehow above it all.

Chuck nudged me and muttered something obscene and, before I could answer, began moving toward her. I meekly followed him as I had been doing all those weeks.

"Good morning," I heard him say to Lowena. "My name is Chuck Derry and I'm a composer. You know—a musician. I've been trying to find out if your people have any music that I could record. It's for a research project I'm working on at college."

Lowena turned her lively black eyes on him and for a moment I saw something flicker across her face. I'd seen the same expression in other women's eyes because Chuck was a handsome guy. He was all well-placed beef on a graceful but sturdy frame. His hair was thick and long but not that long and he could look absolutely cherubic if he chose. At that moment, he so chose. Lowena was visibly impressed.

"The Indians have forgotten the old ways," she said in a voice that must have been a delight to a musician of Chuck's sensibilities. "Their old gods are dead and their altars fallen to dust."

Chuck glanced at me and raised his eyebrows meaningfully. "You're not one—an Indian, I mean?" he inquired in his most polite manner.

"I am an Indian. My name is Lowena Young Owl."

"Listen," Chuck said, "are you sure there isn't anyone around here who remembers the old war chants or the burial songs or——"

"Have they invited you to the Church?" Lowena asked.

"The Church? What Church?"

"They have a vulgar name for it," she replied cryptically. "In their new Church, they use peyote to open the door to—to otherness."

Chuck was obviously fascinated as much by Lowena's manner of speaking as by her very special kind of dark beauty. I interrupted long enough to introduce myself but Lowena wasn't really interested in me. It was Chuck who had captured her attention as I'd seen him do so many times before with so many other women. He was silently sending out his call of the wild and Lowena's antenna had picked it up. That much was perfectly clear to me.

He asked her some more questions and at last she directed us to an old man we found sitting inside the house behind us. At first, I assumed it was her grandfather but I learned later that he was no relation of Lowena's. He was old and bent, his face a bronze filigree of deep wrinkles. His thin white hair was bound at the nape of his neck by a leather band and he wore the shirt and leggings that I'd seen in a hundred cowboy pictures.

"You come from the Bureau?" were his first suspicious words to us as we entered the house.

Lowena spoke to him in a language neither Chuck nor I could understand and his eyes narrowed.

"You want to go through The Door?" he inquired.

Chuck looked at me and I started to shake my head when he said, "Yes. Yes, we do." He explained about his interest in possibly recording the ceremony and there was some discussion between him and the old man about whether or not that would be considered quite proper. It promptly became proper when Chuck handed the old man twenty dollars.

We spent the night in the man's shack since the next ceremony, he had told us, would not take place until the following evening. I slept little. Chuck slept less. I heard him get up and go outside and a little later I heard the rustle of some soft garment and I knew that Lowena had passed through the room and gone out after him. I heard their voices whispering for a time and then I heard nothing.

The next night, the old man led us to the neighboring house where the ceremony was to be held.

"Where's Lowena?" I whispered to Chuck.

He shook his head. "She's tabu or something in the Church. The old man says she is bad medicine. He told me that the spirits of the Church are not her spirits. He talks a lot of silly gibberish. These people are still pretty much primitives."

"I heard you researching one of those primitives last night."

"Lowena's shy—at first," Chuck said, undismayed by my sly remark. "But beautiful. Oh, wow, is she ever! And she wants to leave the reservation," he concluded meaningfully.

"Now wait a minute!" I protested, knowing Chuck.

"We have room in the car. It might be fun. We can unload her later in Albuquerque or somewhere."

"No," I argued. "Why, she doesn't look a day over seventeen. That kind of trouble, I don't need."

We arrived then at the door of the house and Chuck went inside at once without further comment. I sighed and followed him. The old man showed us where to sit and we took our places among the silent group of people sitting about on the floor. Some time later, they passed the peyote buttons. Chuck chewed his but I dropped mine in my pocket. A little later, I went outside as the hallucinations began to blossom in the minds of the worshippers, Chuck among them, and moans and mutterings filtered out into the night after me.

I stood smoking outside the house for ten minutes or so before becoming aware that someone was standing nearby. I turned and confronted Lowena, a shadow within the darker shadows. I hadn't heard her approach nor had I seen any sign of her arrival.

"Hi," I said.

"Chuck likes me," she said. "You don't."

"That's not true. I mean sure he likes you. Chuck likes lots of pretty girls. I've got nothing against you. Oh, hell, I mean——"

She looked up at the full moon which flooded her lovely face with light. "I must leave the reservation," she said.

"Why?"

She looked at me with a curious expression on her face. "They have not told you what I am called?"

"No."

"The Dark Door."

"I'm afraid I don't understand."

"In there," she said, tossing her head to indicate the Church behind us. "In there, they seek to let the old ones through the door so that they might listen to their counsel. They hope that one day the old ones in their wisdom will lead them into a new land and a better life. But they are wrong. The old ones no longer listen to us because we have betrayed them. They have turned their faces from us and they will no longer hear our laments. I was their priestess once. But the people refused to listen to the ones who came when I called. They said that the ones who came were not the old ones but the evil ones. It does not matter to me now. It is, after all, only a matter of chemistry, isn't it? Chemistry is their new religion now but a laboratory is its proper shrine. Still—what happens, happens."

"True," I said, understanding next to nothing of what she said.

"Oh, Carl, I have to leave here!"

I saw that she was crying. She was not making a sound, but she was crying nevertheless. Her tears made moon-white rivers on her cheeks. I could think of nothing to say. The sight of a woman's tears is something I have never been able to bear. It was then, I think, that the bargain among the three of us was sealed although I did not know it at the time.

"They will have to kill me one day because they want to lock forever my dark door. They fear it. And when people fear something, they destroy it."

"But your family can—"

She shook her head. "I have no family. My mother was taken from the reservation years ago when I was just a child. She was a seeress and she taught me much about making strong medicine. But the BIA—"

"The BIA?"

"The Bureau of Indian Affairs. They said she was sick—schizophrenic. She died in a strait jacket on the way to the hospital. No one knew why. I think she simply chose to die and did. My father went away after that. He just walked off the reservation one day and never came back. I have no one. I need someone."

The someone she needed, it developed, was Chuck Derry. The next day, the three of us left the reservation. Lowena sat in the front seat of the car next to Chuck. Before we left, he told me he thought he was in love with her. He wanted to know if I had ever seen a more beautiful girl. I told him I had not.

Once we arrived back at college, Chuck and I went our separate ways. I didn't see him again until two months later when he phoned to invite me to the impromptu party he and Lowena were giving following their civil marriage ceremony.

"You married her?" I exclaimed over the phone, surprised and yet not totally.

"You make it sound like a crime," he declared, laughing. "Come on over and help us celebrate."

I went to the apartment which Chuck had rented off-campus and tried to share in the general gaiety but found it impossible to do so. I felt like I had lost Lowena although my common sense told me I had never possessed her. I admitted to myself at last that I had wanted her but had not had the courage or the nerve to do anything about the wanting. I cursed myself for a meek fool who would never inherit either Lowena or the earth. But there was another reason for my distress— Chuck. To be precise, it was Chuck's behavior toward Lowena. He treated her as a prize he might have won at some carnival, I soon noticed. He *displayed* her. She was his ornament. His Golden Fleece, his Grail.

As the evening wore on and became somewhat rowdy, I sensed Lowena's anguish. She seemed to wilt, to shrink within herself. When Chuck seized her arm to drag her across the room to meet some late arrival, I could feel her embarrassment. I thought of hunters who displayed their trophies on their walls for admiring eyes—stuffed proofs of their virility. Chuck was using Lowena in that way. And I knew that she knew it. There remained little trace of the tenderness he had shown toward her during our long trip back across the country the summer before. Now he treated Lowena as a mere instrument on which he would compose a score to suit only himself.

I decided to leave early but, before I had reached the door, Lowena saw me slipping into my coat and came over to me.

"Carl," she said, "it was good of you to come."

"I hope you'll both be very happy, Lowena," I said, meaning it sincerely.

"Happy." Her repetition of the word was flat and toneless. "Chuck seems happy, doesn't he?"

I looked across the room to where Chuck reeled, one arm slung over the shoulder of an obliging blonde in a miniskirt.

"Will you come to see us often?" Lowena asked and I heard, not a simple question, but a faintly desperate plea.

"Of course," I replied and leaned over to kiss her cheek.

But I didn't go to see them again. Call it jealousy or whatever you will. I didn't go because I couldn't. I saw Lowena on campus occasionally waiting for Chuck or just strolling in the leafy quiet which she said soothed her. I wondered why she needed soothing.

It was at a New Year's Eve party given by mutual friends that I began to realize how badly wrong things were going for Lowena. As I came up to her, she called my name and threw her arms around me. Her clasp was tight and, I thought, tense. When she looked up at me, I couldn't disguise my sense of shock.

She gave me a wry smile and touched her bruised left eye. "I bumped into an open kitchen cabinet the other night. Clumsy of me."

I pretended to accept her explanation but before the night ended, I knew the name of the "cabinet" she had bumped into. Chuck Derry. I knew because of what happened as the clock struck midnight. A man seized Lowena and gave her a friendly kiss. As he released her, Chuck suddenly appeared beside them.

"*Slut!*" he shouted, and the word stopped the world for a moment as it hung heavy in the suddenly still air of the room. He seized her and spun her around and raised his hand and brought it down in a swift motion against her face. The sound of his slap reverberated in the air.

For a moment, Lowena stood frozen in front of him while the man who had kissed her tried to explain to Chuck who refused to listen to him. I was about to look away in shame when I saw the fury flash in Lowena's eyes. It was gone in an instant. She ran into the bedroom and slammed the door behind her. Slowly, like an aging elephant, the party tried to struggle back to life and failed dismally.

The next time I saw Lowena was at her own apartment. She called me one day in April and invited me to dinner. I tried to make excuses but she would not listen to them. I at last consented to come.

When I arrived, Chuck was not at home. Lowena met me at the door and took me by the hand to lead me into the apartment.

"You'll have a martini," she said, remembering. "On the rocks and with a twist."

"Thank you," I said as she handed me the drink a moment later. "How are you, Lowena?"

"Pregnant," she answered to my surprise.

I studied her face and found no joy in it. Her face was a mask of determination. I noticed the bruise on her arm. "Congratulations. Chuck must be pleased."

"No, he isn't. He says it's too soon. He blames me. Carl, something is happening to Chuck. Something very bad."

"I know. I saw it begin last summer. But I suppose the real beginning was long ago. He—he hurts you, doesn't he?"

She nodded. "But there is much worse than that. He has made me hate him because he insists that I must destroy the child."

Chuck arrived then and our conversation took an abrupt turn into safer channels. The dinner Lowena had prepared was excellent but Chuck could not have appreciated it, considering the way he drank before, throughout and after the meal. By the time Lowena served the coffee—Chuck refused it and poured himself another whiskey—he was like an animal.

"I'm not even sure it's my kid!" he exploded at one point.

"Chuck!" Lowena cried out in shock. "You know I never—"

"Shut up!" he muttered into his glass.

"Chuck," I said nervously. "Come on, man!"

"That slut is capable of anything," he muttered. "I should have left her back there on that dung heap of a reservation. She could spend her time weaving baskets for the tourists instead of manufacturing kids we don't need and can't afford."

Lowena stiffened and got up to leave the room.

Chuck leaped to his feet and grabbed her arm, twisting it behind her. "You're staying!" he bellowed.

She cried out, more of a gasp than a scream.

"Let her go!" I yelled, jumping to my feet. As I did, my wallet fell to the floor. I had been showing them pictures of a girl I had met and with whom I was rapidly falling in love.

Chuck angrily shoved Lowena away from him with an expression of utter disgust and she fell heavily to the floor.

I went to her and helped her to her feet. Chuck swung me around and his fist smashed into my face. I reeled backward, tasting blood from a loosened tooth. Before I could recover my balance, Lowena was beside me and leading me to the door.

"I'm so sorry, Carl," she moaned. "You'd better go. When he's like this, he's dangerous."

"I can't leave you here alone with him. I——"

"Go," she said firmly. "I can handle him."

I found myself out in the hall. Lowena kissed my cheek and told me not to worry. She would be in touch soon, she said. She was sorry about the way things had turned out. But I was not to worry about her.

I made my way down the steps and out of the building and began to walk toward the bus stop. I must have taken a wrong turn because I found myself in an unfamiliar area some time later. I retraced my steps and eventually found the bus stop. Only then did I remember that I had left my wallet in the apartment. I could have gotten it from Lowena in the morning but I decided to go back for it. It would give me a legitimate excuse to return and see if she was all right.

248

When I reached the building, I climbed the stairs as I had done earlier and soon found myself in front of their apartment. I rang the bell and waited. When no one answered, I rang again. Finally, I tried the door. It was unlocked. I went in and found the room in darkness. I couldn't remember where the light switch was and spent some time fumbling about in the darkness trying to locate it, calling Lowena's name softly as I did so. I didn't want to frighten her.

She didn't answer.

I groped my way through the room which was only vaguely lighted by the street light outside. I finally found my wallet on the floor where it had fallen and was down on my hands and knees feeling about for the pictures I had taken from it when I heard the first of the awful sounds.

A faint, faraway chittering as of rats in an abandoned building.

"Lowena?" I whispered in the darkness. "Chuck, is that you?"

And then I saw them both as Lowena appeared beside the window and drew the sheer curtains to admit more light. "Lowena," I whispered, "don't be frightened. It's me. Carl."

Her eyes were closed and she seemed not to have heard me. I glanced at Chuck who lay sprawled in a drunken stupor on the sofa. Lowena was raising her arms toward the ceiling and tilting her head back so that her sightless eyes were also raised to it. Sounds came from between her slightly parted lips—words I couldn't recognize. I moved toward her cautiously, feeling the chill that was either in the room or in my own mind.

Before I reached her, she began to fade. Her body seemed to undulate and then, glowing, it became translucent. I stopped and stared in alarm, unable to believe what I was seeing. A trick of the light, I told myself.

The chittering grew louder. It was coming from Lowena's direction. I took a step toward her and stopped as I realized I could see through her body! But what I saw was not the wall behind her. It was— *somewhere!* Mists swirled there. Blue mists and mauve. Hideous, half-seen figures I could not identify loped through those mists, moving toward me from the place beyond Lowena!

The chittering was, I realized, the voices of the creatures moving in the mist.

And then, suddenly, the first of them entered the room through the translucence that was Lowena. With them came a ghastly odor, a charred odor, that was both disgusting and overpowering. I gagged.

Some of them were furred. Some, feathered. None of them stood more than a foot high. They glided into the room on slick bellies or fluttered with soft fat sounds on leathery wings. They flexed dripping talons and bared yellow teeth and mewled and cried out in thin chitinous shrieks as they moved across the floor to where Chuck lay snoring.

I backed away in horror. The things saw me then and began scurrying to cut off my escape! They took up positions between me and the door leading from the apartment, groping toward me with grotesquely twisted limbs.

A word shot suddenly from between Lowena's lips, a word I had never heard before and hope never to hear again. The things halted at her command.

She spoke again in guttural, consonantal words, redirecting the creatures toward her intended victim.

Chuck screamed once as the creatures crawled over him. A furred one fluttered about his mouth and his cries became gurgles and then low groans as he thrashed about in his struggle with the things Lowena had summoned through the dark door of herself. They pierced his body. They clawed and bit and chewed in an orgy of destruction.

It lasted only seconds.

Afterwards, Chuck lay still, lifeless.

Lowena called out to the creatures from her trance state and they obeyed her commands. I watched as they trooped back through the translucent door that she had become and moved swiftly off into the swirling mists that embraced them as if in welcome and disappeared from sight.

Lowena's body no longer glowed with that ghastly translucence. It firmed, resuming the familiar shape I knew so well. Her head lowered, her lips closed, and she fell to the floor and lay there unconscious.

I ran from the room and down the stairs and out of the building. I can't clearly remember how I got home that night. I do recall that I didn't sleep. I was afraid that I might dream.

Professor Windrow let out a breath he had evidently been holding for some time. "What were those things you saw?" he asked me.

"I don't know," I answered. "But I do know that the people on the reservation were right in calling Lowena the dark door through which unspeakable things can come if she calls them. That night she called them. *They* were the 'person or persons unknown' who killed Chuck Derry."

Professor Windrow glanced covertly across the dining room at Lowena who was holding the hand of her young man and smiling happily at him. "I can readily understand now why you said you were afraid of her," he commented thoughtfully. "But I must say that her escort seems quite contented with his lot."

"I hope he will be kind to her and to the little girl she bore last month," I said softly. "I can't bear to think of what might happen to him if he should treat her cruelly—as Chuck did. She is not the defenseless woman she seems to be."

# FOR DISCUSSION: The Dark Door

1. Which of the three main characters do you like best? Why? Which least? Why?
2. Do you consider Lowena Young Owl a victim or a villain?
3. The use of peyote in inducing "religious" visions is common in parts of America. Do you think it is a valid pathway to follow in the search for the supernatural? Explain.
4. Do you think Chuck's fate is warranted? Explain.
5. What would you say is the dominant characteristic of the narrator of this story?

# Things –
# The Bizarre
# on the
# Human Horizon

# CHAPTER FIVE

Many objects and events that can properly be classified as supernatural nevertheless do not fit into any convenient category. They cannot be called ghost stories, although they may be rather ghostly. They do not feature witches, werewolves, or vampires in their casts of characters. They do not concern themselves with spells or sorcery, gods or devils.

In this chapter, we have gathered together several eminent examples of these difficult-to-classify supernatural stories. They deal primarily with "things." For example, among the seemingly ordinary items you will find in these stories are a rocking horse and a chair. But be warned. The rocking horse and chair are in no way ordinary or even natural.

As you study the stories in this chapter, you will quickly recognize that the range of the supernatural in literature is vast. Although ghosts and witches are probably two of the first things that come to our minds when we think of the supernatural, the authors represented here indicate through their superb variations on supernatural themes that this genre of literature is almost literally boundless.

They show us the range of man's imagination as it speculates on the myriad forms in which the supernatural may—at least in literature—manifest itself. While telling their stories, these authors offer us liberal portions of humor, horror, compassion, fear, terror, and joy—all the feelings that we experience in our daily lives—and while reading our supernatural literature.

Each of these stories offers you an opportunity to examine the art and craft of storytelling in general and supernatural storytelling in particular. Here you will find artists-craftsmen at work. Their literary tools are words. Their techniques are suspense-building, character development, plotting, and narrative power. Their stories result from the skillful use of their tools and the perfection of their techniques.

And I looked, and, behold a whirlwind came out of the north, a great cloud, and a fire infolding itself, and a brightness *was* about it, and out of the midst thereof as the colour of amber, out of the midst of the fire.

Also out of the midst thereof *came* the likeness of four living creatures. And this *was* their appearance; they had the likeness of a man.

And everyone had four faces, and everyone had four wings.

And their feet *were* straight feet; and the sole of their feet *was* like the sole of a calf's foot:   and they sparkled like the colour of burnished brass.

And *they had* the hands of a man under their wings on their four sides, and they four had their faces and their wings.

Their wings *were* joined one to another; they turned not when they went; they went every one straight forward.

As for the likeness of their faces, they four had the face of a man, and the face of a lion, on the right side:   and they four had the face of an ox on the left side; they four also had the face of an eagle.

Ezekiel, Chapter 1, Verses 4–10

## INTRODUCTION: The Lonesome Place

All of us have at one time or another been afraid of the dark or of a particularly scary place—a dark cellar, a gloomy graveyard, a forest, a deserted house. Of course, we knew that such places were not haunted by the things we imagined we could almost, but not quite, see lurking in the shadows. August W. Derleth, in the next story, obviously knows differently.

# The Lonesome Place
## August W. Derleth

You who sit in your houses of nights, you who sit in the theaters, you who are gay at dances and parties—all you who are enclosed by four walls—you have no conception of what goes on outside in the dark. In the lonesome places. And there are so many of them, all over—in the country, in the small towns, in the cities. If you were out in the evenings, in the night, you would know about them, you would pass them and wonder, perhaps, and if you were a small boy you might be frightened ... frightened the way Johnny Newell and I were frightened, the way thousands of small boys from one end of the country to the other are being frightened when they have to go out alone at night, past lonesome places, dark and lightness, somber and haunted. ...

I want you to understand that if it had not been for the lonesome place at the grain elevator, the place with the big old trees and the sheds up close to the sidewalk, and the piles of lumber—if it had not been for that place Johnny Newell and I would never have been guilty of murder. I say it even if there is nothing the law can do about it. They cannot touch us, but it is true, and I know, and Johnny knows, but we never talk about it, we never say anything; it is just something we keep here, behind our eyes, deep in our thoughts where it is a fact which is lost among thousands of others, but no less there, something we know beyond cavil.

It goes back a long way. But as times goes, perhaps it is not long. We were young, we were little boys in a small town. Johnny lived three houses away and across the street from me, and both of us lived in the block west of the grain elevator. We were never afraid to go past the lonesome place together. But we were not often together. Sometimes one of us had to go that way alone, sometimes the other. I went that way most of the time—there was no other, except to go far around, because that was the straight way downtown, and I had to walk there, when my father was too tired to go.

In the evenings it would happen like this. My mother would discover that she had no sugar or salt or bologna, and she would say, "Steve, you go downtown and get it. Your father's too tired."

I would say, "I don't wanna."

She would say, "You go."

I would say, "I can go in the morning before school."

She would say, "You go now. I don't want to hear another word out of you. Here's the money."

And I would have to go.

Going down was never quite so bad, because most of the time there was still some afterglow in the west, and a kind of pale light lay there, a luminousness, like part of the day lingering there, and all around town you could hear the kids hollering in the last hour they had to play, and you felt somehow not alone, you could go down into that dark place under the trees and you would never think of being lonesome. But when you came back—that was different. When you came back the afterglow was gone; if the stars were out, you could never see them for the trees; and though the street lights were on—the old-fashioned lights arched over the crossroads—not a ray of them penetrated the lonesome place near to the elevator. There it was, half a block long, black as black could be, dark as the deepest night, with the shadows of the trees making it a solid place of darkness, with the faint glow of light where a street light pooled at the end of the street, far away it seemed, and that other glow behind, where the other corner light lay.

And when you came that way you walked slower and slower. Behind you lay the brightly lit stores; all along the way there had been houses, with lights in the windows and music playing and voices of people sitting to talk on their porches—but up there, ahead of you, there was the lonesome place, with no house nearby, and up beyond it the tall, dark grain elevator, gaunt and forbidding, the lonesome place of trees and sheds and lumber, in which anything might be lurking, anything at all, the lonesome place where you were sure that something haunted the darkness waiting for the moment and the hour and the night when you came through to burst forth from its secret place and leap upon you, tearing you and rending you and doing unmentionable things before it had done for you.

That was the lonesome place. By day it was oak and maple trees over a hundred years old, low enough so that you could almost touch the big spreading limbs; it was sheds and lumber piles which were seldom disturbed; it was a sidewalk and long grass, never mowed or kept down until late fall, when somebody burned it off; it was a shady place in the hot summer days where some cool air always lingered. You were never afraid of it by day, but by night it was a different place; for then it was lonesome, away from sight or sound, a place of darkness and strangeness, a place of terror for little boys haunted by a thousand fears.

And every night, coming home from town, it happened like this. I would walk slower and slower, the closer I got to the lonesome place. I would think of every way around it. I would keep hoping somebody would come along, so that I could walk with him, Mr. Newell, maybe, or old Mrs. Potter, who lived farther up the street, or Reverend Bislor, who lived at the end of the block beyond the grain elevator. But nobody ever came. At this hour it was too soon after supper for them to go out, or, already out, too soon for them to return. So I walked slower and slower, until I got to the edge of the lonesome place—and then I ran as fast as I could, sometimes with my eyes closed.

Oh, I knew what was there, all right. I knew there was something in that dark, lonesome place. Perhaps it was the bogey-man. Sometimes my grandmother spoke of him, of how he waited in dark places for bad boys and girls. Perhaps it was an ogre. I knew about ogres in the books of fairy tales. Perhaps it was something else, something worse. I ran. I ran hard. Every blade of grass, every leaf, every twig that touched me was *its* hand reaching for me. The sound of my footsteps slapping the sidewalk was *its* steps pursuing. The hard breathing which was my own became *its* breathing in its frenetic struggle to reach me, to rend and tear me, to imbue my soul with terror.

I would burst out of that place like a flurry of wind, fly past the gaunt elevator, and not pause until I was safe in the yellow glow of the familiar street light. And then, in a few steps, I was home.

And Mother would say, "For the Lord's sake, have you been running on a hot night like this?"

I would say, "I hurried."

"You didn't have to hurry that much. I don't need it till breakfast time."

And I would say, "I could-a got it in the morning. I could-a run down before breakfast. Next time, that's what I'm gonna do."

Nobody would pay any attention.

Some nights Johnny had to go downtown, too. Things then weren't the way they are today, when every woman makes a ritual of afternoon shopping and seldom forgets anything; in those days, they didn't go downtown so often, and when they did, they had such lists they usually forgot something. And after Johnny and I had been through the lonesome place on the same night, we compared notes next day.

"Did you see anything?" he would ask.

"No, but I heard it," I would say.

"I felt it," he would whisper tensely. "It's got big, flat clawed feet. You know what's the ugliest feet around?"

"Sure, one of those stinking yellow softshell turtles."

"It's got feet like that. Oh, ugly, and soft, and sharp claws! I saw one out of the corner of my eye," he would say.

"Did you see its face?" I would ask.

"It ain't got no face. Cross my heart an' hope to die, there ain't no face. That's worse'n if there was one."

Oh, it was a horrible beast—not an animal, not a man—that lurked in the lonesome place and came forth predatorily at night, waiting there for us to pass. It grew like this, out of our mutual experiences. We discovered that it had scales, and a great long tail, like a dragon. It breathed from somewhere, hot as fire, but it had no face and no mouth in it, just a horrible opening in its throat. It was as big as an elephant, but it did not look like anything so friendly. It belonged there in the lonesome place; it would never go away; that was its home, and it had to wait for its food to come to it—the unwary boys and girls who had to pass through the lonesome place at night.

How I tried to keep from going near the lonesome place after dark!

"Why can't Mady go?" I would ask.

"Mady's too little," Mother would answer.

"I'm not so big."

"Oh, shush! You're a big boy now. You're going to be seven years old. Just think of it."

"I don't think seven is old," I would say. I didn't, either. Seven wasn't nearly old enough to stand up against what was in the lonesome place.

"Your Sears-Roebuck pants are long ones," she would say.

"I don't care about any old Sears-Roebuck pants. I don't wanna go."

"I want you to go. You never get up early enough in the morning."

"But I will. I promise I will. I promise, Ma!" I would cry out.

"Tomorrow morning it will be a different story. No, you go."

That was the way it went every time. I had to go. And Mady was the only one who guessed. "Fraidycat," she would whisper. Even she never really knew. She never had to go through the lonesome place after dark. They kept her at home. She never knew how something could lie up in those old trees, lie right along those old limbs across the sidewalk and drop down without a sound, clawing and tearing, something without a face, with ugly clawed feet like a softshell turtle's, with scales and a tail like a dragon, something as big as a house, all black, like the darkness in that place.

But Johnny and I knew.

"It almost got me last night," he would say, his voice low, looking anxiously out of the woodshed where we sat as if *it* might hear us.

"Gee, I'm glad it didn't," I would say. "What was it like?"

"Big and black. Awful black. I looked around when I was running, and all of a sudden there wasn't any light way back at the other end. Then I knew it was coming. I ran like everything to get out of there. It was almost on me when I got away. Look there!"

And he would show me a rip in his shirt where a claw had come down.

"And you?" he would ask excitedly, big-eyed. "What about you?"

"It was back behind the lumber piles when I came through," I said. "I could just feel it waiting. I was running, but it got right up—you look, there's a pile of lumber tipped over there."

And we would walk down into the lonesome place in midday and look. Sure enough, there would be a pile of lumber tipped over, and we would look to where something had been lying down, the grass all pressed down. Sometimes we would find a handkerchief and wonder whether *it* had caught somebody; then we would go home and wait to hear if anyone was missing, speculating apprehensively all the way home whether *it* had got Mady or Christine or Helen, or any one of the girls in our class or Sunday School, or whether maybe *it* had got Miss Doyle, the young primary grades teacher who had to walk that way sometimes after supper. But no one was ever reported missing, and the mystery grew. Maybe *it* had got some stranger who happened to be passing by and didn't know about the thing that lived there in the lonesome place. We were sure *it* had got somebody. It scared us, bad, and after something like this I hated all the more to go downtown after supper, even for candy or ice cream.

"Some night I won't come back, you'll see," I would say.

"Oh, don't be silly," my mother would say.

"You'll see. You'll see. It'll get me next, you'll see."

"What'll get you?" she would ask offhandedly.

"Whatever it is out there in the dark," I would say.

"There's nothing out there but the dark," she would say.

"What about the bogey-man?" I would protest.

"They caught him," she would say. "A long time ago. He's locked up for good."

But Johnny and I knew better. His parents didn't know, either. The minute he started to complain, his dad reached for a hickory switch they kept behind the door. He had to go out fast and never mind what was in the lonesome place.

What do grown-up people know about the things boys are afraid of? Oh, hickory switches and such like, they know that. But what about what goes on in their minds when they have to come home alone at night through the lonesome places? What do they know about lonesome places where no light from the street corner ever comes? What do they know about a place and time when a boy is very small and very alone, and the night is as big as the town, and the darkness is the whole world? When grown-ups are big, old people who cannot understand anything, no matter how plain? A boy looks up and out, but he can't look very far when the trees bend down over and press close, when the sheds rear up along one side and the trees on the other, when the darkness lies like a cloud along the sidewalk and the arc-lights are far, far away. No wonder then that things grow in the darkness of lonesome places that way *it* grew in that dark place near the grain elevator. No wonder a boy runs like the wind until his heartbeats sound like a drum and push up to suffocate him.

"You're white as a sheet," Mother would say sometimes. "You've been running again."

"Yes," I would say. "I've been running." But I never said why; I knew they wouldn't believe me; I knew nothing I could say would convince them about the thing that lived back there, down the block, down past the grain elevator in that dark, lonesome place.

"You don't have to run," my father would say. "Take it easy."

"I ran," I would say. But I wanted the worst way to say I had to run and to tell them why I had to; but I knew they wouldn't believe me any more than Johnny's parents believed him when he told them, as he did once.

He got a licking with a strap and had to go to bed.

I never got licked. I never told them.

But now it must be told, now it must be set down.

For a long time we forgot about the lonesome place. We grew older and we grew bigger. We went on through school into high school, and somehow we forgot about the thing in the lonesome place. That place never changed. The trees grew older. Sometimes the lumber piles were bigger or smaller. Once the sheds were painted—red, like blood. Seeing them that way the first time, I remembered. Then I forgot again. We took to playing baseball and basketball and football. We began to swim in the river and to date the girls. We never talked about the thing in the lonesome place any more, and when we went through there at night it was like something forgotten that lurked back in a corner of the mind. We thought of something we ought to remember, but never could quite remember; that was the way it seemed—like a memory locked away, far away in childhood. We never ran through that place, and sometimes it was even a good place to walk through with a girl, because she always snuggled up close and said how spooky it was there under the overhanging trees. But even then we never lingered there, not exactly lingered; we didn't run through there, but we walked without faltering or loitering, no matter how pretty a girl she was.

The years went past, and we never thought about the lonesome place again.

We never thought how there would be other little boys going through it at night, running with fast-beating hearts, breathless with terror, anxious for the safety of the arc-light beyond the margin of the shadow which confined the dweller in that place, the light-fearing creature that haunted the dark, like so many terrors dwelling in similar lonesome places in the cities and small towns and countrysides all over the world, waiting to frighten little boys and girls, waiting to invade them with horror and unshakable fear—waiting for something more. . . .

Three nights ago little Bobby Jeffers was killed in the lonesome place. He was all mauled and torn and partly crushed, as if something big had fallen on him. Johnny, who was on the Village Board, went to look at the place, and after he had been there, he telephoned me to go, too, before other people walked there.

I went down and saw the marks, too. It was just as the coroner said, only not an "animal of some kind," as he put it. Something with a dragging tail, with scales, with great clawed feet— and I knew it had no face.

I knew, too, that Johnny and I were guilty. We had murdered Bobby Jeffers because the thing that killed him was the thing Johnny and I had created out of our childhood fears and left in that lonesome place to wait for some scared little boy at some minute in some hour during some dark night, a little boy who, like fat Bobby Jeffers, couldn't run as fast as Johnny and I could run.

And the worst is not that there is nothing to do, but that the lonesome place is being changed. The village is cutting down some of the trees now, removing the sheds, and putting up a street light in the middle of that place; it will not be dark and lonesome any longer, and the thing that lives there will have to go somewhere else, where people are unsuspecting, to some other lonesome place in some other small town or city or countryside, where it will wait as it did here, for some frightened little boy or girl to come along, waiting in the dark and the lonesomeness . . .

## FOR DISCUSSION: The Lonesome Place

1. What is the origin of the conflict in this story between the narrator as a child and his parents? How does this relate to the story's ending?
2. What is your reaction to the narrator's belief that there was a "thing" in the lonesome place which was created out of childhood fears? Is there another explanation possible for the death of Bobby Jeffers?
3. Most people can remember being uneasy in dark, lonesome places when they were children. How does this memory affect the reader as he follows the action of this story?

# INTRODUCTION: What Was It?

The idea of invisibility has intrigued mankind for a long time. Here we are served a helping of horror that has to do with an invisible "thing" that attacks the people in the story. The tale reminds us that the unseen can be even more terrifying than the most frightful things we can actually see.

# What Was It?

## Fitz-James O'Brien

It is, I confess, with considerable diffidence that I approach the strange narrative which I am about to relate. The events which I purpose detailing are of so extraordinary a character that I am quite prepared to meet with an unusual amount of incredulity and scorn. I accept all such beforehand. I have, I trust, the literary courage to face unbelief. I have, after mature consideration, resolved to narrate, in as simple and straightforward a manner as I can compass, some facts that passed under my observation, in the month of July last, and which, in the annals of the mysteries of physical science, are wholly unparalleled.

I live at No. — Twenty-sixth Street, in New York. The house is in some respects a curious one. It has enjoyed for the last two years the reputation of being haunted. It is a large and stately residence, surrounded by what was once a garden, but which is now only a green enclosure used for bleaching clothes. The dry basin of what has been a fountain, and a few fruit trees ragged and unpruned, indicate that this spot in past days was a pleasant, shady retreat, filled with fruits and flowers and the sweet murmur of waters.

The house is very spacious. A hall of noble size leads to a large spiral staircase winding through its center, while the various apartments are of imposing dimensions. It was built some fifteen or twenty years since by Mr. A——, the well-known New York merchant, who five years ago threw the commercial world into convulsions by a stupendous bank fraud. Mr. A——, as everyone knows, escaped to Europe, and died not long after, of a broken heart. Almost immediately after the news of his decease reached this country and was verified, the report spread in Twenty-sixth Street that No. — was haunted. Legal measures had dispossessed the widow of its former owner, and it was inhabited merely by a caretaker and his wife, placed there by the house agent into whose hands it had passed for purposes of renting or sale. These people declared that they were troubled with unnatural noises. Doors were opened without any visible agency. The remnants of furniture scattered through the various rooms were, during the night, piled one upon the other by unknown hands. Invisible feet passed up and down the stairs in broad daylight, accompanied by the rustle of unseen silk dresses, and the gliding of viewless hands along the massive balusters. The caretaker and his wife declared they would live there no longer. The house agent laughed, dismissed them, and put others in their place. The noises and supernatural manifestations continued. The neighborhood caught up the story, and the house remained untenanted for three years. Several persons negotiated for it; but, somehow, always before the bargain was closed they heard the unpleasant rumors and declined to treat any further.

It was in this state of things that my landlady, who at that time kept a boardinghouse in Bleecker Street, and who wished to move further up town, conceived the bold idea of renting No. — Twenty-sixth Street. Happening to have in her house rather a plucky and philosophical set of boarders, she laid her scheme before us, stating candidly everything she had heard respecting the ghostly qualities of the establishment to which she wished to remove us. With the exception of two timid persons—a sea-captain and a returned Californian, who immediately gave notice that they would leave—all of Mrs. Moffat's guests declared that they would accompany her in her chivalric incursion into the abode of spirits.

Our removal was effected in the month of May, and we were charmed with our new residence. The portion of Twenty-sixth Street where our house is situated, between Seventh and Eighth Avenues, is one of the pleasantest localities in New York. The gardens back of the houses, running down nearly to the Hudson, form, in the summer time, a perfect avenue of verdure. The air is pure and invigorating, sweeping, as it does, straight across the river from the Weehawken heights, and even the ragged garden which surrounded the house, although displaying on washing days rather too much clothesline, still gave us a piece of greensward to look at, and a cool retreat in the summer evenings, where we smoked our cigars in the dusk, and watched the fireflies flashing their dark lanterns in the long grass.

Of course we had no sooner established ourselves at No. — than we began to expect the ghosts. We absolutely awaited their advent with eagerness. Our dinner conversation was supernatural. One of the boarders, who had purchased Mrs. Crowe's "Night Side of Nature" for his own private delectation, was regarded as a public enemy by the entire household for not having bought twenty copies. The man led a life of supreme wretchedness while he was reading this volume. A system of espionage was established, of which he was the victim. If he incautiously laid the book down for an instant and left the room, it was immediately seized and read aloud in secret places to a select few. I found myself a person of immense importance, it having leaked out that I was tolerably well versed in the history of supernaturalism, and had once written a story the foundation of which was a ghost. If a table or a wainscot panel happened to warp when we were assembled in the large drawing room, there was an instant silence, and every one was prepared for an immediate clanking of chains and a spectral form.

After a month of psychological excitement, it was with the utmost dissatisfaction that we were forced to acknowledge that nothing in the remotest degree approaching the supernatural had manifested itself. Once the black butler asseverated that his candle had been blown out by some invisible agency while he was undressing himself for the night; but as I had more than once discovered this gentleman in a condition when one candle must have appeared to him like two, I thought it possible that, by going a step further in his potations, he might have reversed this phenomenon, and seen no candle at all where he ought to have beheld one.

Things were in this state when an incident took place so awful and inexplicable in its character that my reason fairly reels at the bare memory of the occurrence. It was the tenth of July. After dinner was over I repaired, with my friend Dr. Hammond, to the garden to smoke my evening pipe. Independent of certain mental sympathies which existed between the Doctor and myself, we were linked together by a vice. We both smoked opium. We knew each other's secret, and respected it. We enjoyed together that wonderful expansion of thought, that marvelous intensifying of the perceptive faculties, that boundless feeling of existence when we seem to have points of contact with the whole universe—in short, that unimaginable spiritual bliss, which I would not surrender for a throne, and which I hope you, reader, will never, never taste.

Those hours of opium happiness which the Doctor and I spent together in secret were regulated with a scientific accuracy. We did not blindly smoke the drug of paradise, and leave our dreams to chance. While smoking, we carefully steered our conversation through the brightest and calmest channels of thought. We talked of the East, and endeavored to recall the magical panorama of its glowing scenery. We criticized the most sensuous poets—those who painted life ruddy with health, brimming with passion, happy in the possession of youth and strength and beauty. If we talked of Shakespeare's "Tempest," we lingered over Ariel, and avoided Caliban. Like the Guebers, we turned our faces to the east, and saw only the sunny side of the world.

This skilful coloring of our train of thought produced in our subsequent visions a corresponding tone. The splendors of Arabian fairyland dyed our dreams. We paced that narrow strip of grass with the tread and port of kings. The song of the *rana arborea*, while he clung to the bark of the ragged plum tree, sounded like the strains of divine musicians. Houses, walls, and streets melted like rain clouds, and vistas of unimaginable glory stretched away before us. It was a rapturous companionship. We enjoyed the vast delight more perfectly because, even in our most ecstatic moments, we were conscious of each other's presence. Our pleasures, while individual, were still twin, vibrating and moving in musical accord.

On the evening in question, the tenth of July, the Doctor and myself drifted into an unusually metaphysical mood. We lit our large meerschaums, filled with fine Turkish tobacco, in the core of which burned a little black nut of opium, that, like the nut in the fairy tale, held within its narrow limits wonders beyond the reach of kings; we paced to and fro, conversing. A strange perversity dominated the currents of our thought. They would *not* flow through the sunlit channels into which we strove to divert them. For some unaccountable reason, they constantly diverged into dark and lonesome beds, where a continual gloom brooded. It was in vain that, after our old fashion, we flung ourselves on the shores of the East, and talked of its gay bazaars, of the splendors of the time of Haroun, of harems and golden palaces. Black afreets continually arose from the depths of our talk, and expanded, like the one the fisherman released from the copper vessel, until they blotted everything bright from our vision. Insensibly, we yielded to the occult force that swayed us, and indulged in gloomy speculation. We had talked some time upon the proneness of the human mind to mysticism, and the almost universal love of the terrible, when Hammond suddenly said to me, "What do you consider to be the greatest element of terror?"

The question puzzled me. That many things were terrible, I knew. Stumbling over a corpse in the dark; beholding as I once did, a woman floating down a deep and rapid river, with wildly lifted arms, and awful, upturned face, uttering, as she drifted, shrieks that rent one's heart, while we, the spectators, stood frozen at a window which overhung the river at a height of sixty feet, unable to make the slightest effort to save her, but dumbly watching her last supreme agony and her disappearance. A shattered wreck, with no life visible, encountered floating listlessly on the ocean, is a terrible object, for it suggests a huge terror, the proportions of which are veiled. But it now struck me, for the first time, that there must be one great and ruling embodiment of fear—a King of Terrors, to which all others must succumb. What might it be? To what train of circumstances would it owe its existence?

"I confess, Hammond," I replied to my friend, "I never considered the subject before. That there must be one Something more terrible than any other thing, I feel. I cannot attempt, however, even the most vague definition."

"I am somewhat like you, Harry," he answered. "I feel my capacity to experience a terror greater than anything yet conceived by the human mind—something combining in fearful and unnatural amalgamation hitherto supposed incompatible elements. The calling of the voices in Brockden Brown's novel of *Wieland* is awful; so is the picture of the Dweller of the Threshold, in Bulwer's *Zanoni;* but," he added, shaking his head gloomily, "there is something more horrible still than these."

"Look here, Hammond," I rejoined, "let us drop this kind of talk, for heaven's sake! We shall suffer for it, depend on it."

"I don't know what's the matter with me tonight," he replied, "but my brain is running upon all sorts of weird and awful thoughts. I feel as if I could write a story like Hoffman, tonight, if I were only master of a literary style."

"Well, if we are going to be Hoffmanesque in our talk, I'm off to bed. Opium and nightmares should never be brought together. How sultry it is! Goodnight, Hammond."

"Goodnight, Harry. Pleasant dreams to you."

"To you, gloomy wretch, afreets, ghouls, and enchanters."

We parted, and each sought his respective chamber. I undressed quickly and got into bed, taking with me, according to my usual custom, a book, over which I generally read myself to sleep. I opened the volume as soon as I had laid my head upon the pillow, and instantly flung it to the other side of the room. It was Goudon's "History of Monsters," a curious French work, which I had lately imported from Paris, but which, in the state of mind I had then reached, was anything but an agreeable companion. I resolved to go to sleep at once; so, turning down my gas until nothing but a little blue point of light glimmered on the top of the tube, I composed myself to rest.

The room was in total darkness. The atom of gas that still remained alight did not illuminate a distance of three inches round the burner. I desperately drew my arm across my eyes, as if to shut out even the darkness, and tried to think of nothing. It was in vain. The confounded themes touched on by Hammond in the garden kept obtruding themselves on my brain. I battled against them. I erected ramparts of would-be blankness of intellect to keep them out. They still crowded upon me. While I was lying still as a corpse, hoping that by a perfect physical inaction I should hasten mental repose, an awful incident occurred. A Something dropped, as it seemed, from the ceiling, plumb upon my chest, and the next instant I felt two bony hands encircling my throat, endeavoring to choke me.

I am no coward, and am possessed of considerable physical strength. The suddenness of the attack, instead of stunning me, strung every nerve to its highest tension. My body acted from instinct, before my brain had time to realize the terrors of my position. In an instant I wound two muscular arms around the creature, and squeezed it, with all the strength of despair, against my chest. In a few seconds the bony hands that had fastened on my throat loosened their hold, and I was free to breathe once more. Then commenced a struggle of awful intensity. Immersed in the most profound darkness, totally ignorant of the nature of the Thing by which I was so suddenly attacked, finding my grasp slipping every moment, by reason, it seemed to me, of the entire nakedness of my assailant, bitten with sharp teeth in the shoulder, neck, and chest, having every moment to protect my throat against a pair of sinewy, agile hands, which my utmost efforts could not confine—these were a combination of circumstances to combat which required all the strength, skill, and courage that I possessed.

At last, after a silent, deadly, exhausting struggle, I got my assailant under by a series of incredible efforts of strength. Once pinned, with my knee on what I made out to be its chest, I knew that I was victor. I rested for a moment to breathe. I heard the creature beneath me panting in the darkness, and felt the violent throbbing of a heart. It was apparently as exhausted as I was; that was one comfort. At this moment I remembered that I usually placed under my pillow, before going to bed, a large yellow silk pocket handkerchief. I felt for it instantly; it was there. In a few seconds more I had, after a fashion, pinioned the creature's arms.

I now felt tolerably secure. There was nothing more to be done but to turn on the gas, and, having first seen what my midnight assailant was like, arouse the household. I will confess to being actuated by a certain pride in not giving the alarm before; I wished to make the capture alone and unaided.

Never losing my hold for an instant, I slipped from the bed to the floor, dragging my captive with me. I had but a few steps to make to reach the gas burner; these I made with the greatest caution, holding the creature in a grip like a vise. As last I got within arm's length of the tiny speck of blue light which told me where the gas burner lay. Quick as lightning I released my grasp with one hand and let on the full flood of light. Then I turned to look at my captive.

I cannot even attempt to give any definition of my sensations the instant after I turned on the gas. I suppose I must have shrieked with terror, for in less than a minute afterward my room was crowded with the inmates of the house. I shudder now as I think of that awful moment. *I saw nothing!* Yes; I had one arm firmly clasped round a breathing, panting, corporeal shape, my other hand gripped with all its strength a throat as warm, and apparently fleshly, as my own; and yet, with this living substance in my grasp, with its body pressed against my own, and all in the bright glare of a large jet of gas, I absolutely beheld nothing! Not even an outline—a vapor!

I do not, even at this hour, realize the situation in which I found myself. I cannot recall the astounding incident thoroughly. Imagination in vain tries to compass the awful paradox.

It breathed. I felt its warm breath upon my cheek. It struggled fiercely. It had hands. They clutched me. Its skin was smooth, like my own. There it lay, pressed close up against me, solid as stone—and yet utterly invisible!

I wonder that I did not faint or go mad on the instant. Some wonderful instinct must have sustained me; for, absolutely, in place of loosening my hold on the terrible Enigma, I seemed to gain an additional strength in my moment of horror, and tightened my grasp with such wonderful force that I felt the creature shivering with agony.

Just then Hammond entered my room at the head of the household. As soon as he beheld my face—which, I suppose, must have been an awful sight to look at—he hastened forward, crying, "Great heaven, Harry! what has happened?"

"Hammond! Hammond!" I cried, "come here. O, this is awful! I have been attacked in bed by something or other, which I have hold of; but I can't see it—I can't see it!"

Hammond, doubtless struck by the unfeigned horror expressed in my countenance, made one or two steps forward with an anxious yet puzzled expression. A very audible titter burst from the remainder of my visitors. This suppressed laughter made me furious. To laugh at a human being in my position! It was the worst species of cruelty. *Now,* I can understand why the appearance of a man struggling violently, as it would seem, with an airy nothing, and calling for assistance against a vision, should have appeared ludicrous. *Then,* so great was my rage against the mocking crowd that had I the power I would have stricken them dead where they stood.

"Hammond! Hammond!" I cried again, despairingly, "for God's sake come to me. I can hold the—the Thing but a short while longer. It is overpowering me. Help me! Help me!"

"Harry," whispered Hammond, approaching me, "you have been smoking too much opium."

"I swear to you, Hammond, that this is no vision," I answered, in the same low tone. "Don't you see how it shakes my whole frame with its struggles? If you don't believe me, convince yourself. Feel it—touch it."

Hammond advanced and laid his hand in the spot I indicated. A wild cry of horror burst from him. He had felt it!

In a moment he had discovered somewhere in my room a long piece of cord, and was the next instant winding it and knotting it about the body of the unseen being that I clasped in my arms.

"Harry," he said, in a hoarse, agitated voice, for, though he preserved his presence of mind, he was deeply moved, "Harry, it's all safe now. You may let go, old fellow, if you're tired. The Thing can't move."

I was utterly exhausted, and I gladly loosed my hold.

Hammond stood holding the ends of the cord that bound the Invisible, twisted round his hand, while before him, self-supporting as it were, he beheld a rope laced and interlaced, and stretching tightly around a vacant space. I never saw a man look so thoroughly stricken with awe. Nevertheless his face expressed all the courage and determination which I knew him to possess. His lips, although white, were set firmly, and one could perceive at a glance that, although stricken with fear, he was not daunted.

The confusion that ensued among the guests of the house who were witnesses of this extraordinary scene between Hammond and myself— who beheld the pantomime of binding this struggling Something—who beheld me almost sinking from physical exhaustion when my task of jailer was over—the confusion and terror that took possession of the bystanders, when they saw all this, was beyond description. The weaker ones fled from the apartment. The few who remained clustered near the door and could not be induced to approach Hammond and his Charge. Still incredulity broke out through their terror. They had not the courage to satisfy themselves, and yet they doubted. It was in vain that I begged of some of the men to come near and convince themselves by touch of the existence in that room of a living being which was invisible. They were incredulous, but did not dare to undeceive themselves. How could a solid, living, breathing body be invisible, they asked. My reply was this. I gave a sign to Hammond, and both of us—conquering our fearful repugnance to touch the invisible creature—lifted it from the ground, manacled as it was, and took it to my bed. Its weight was about that of a boy of fourteen.

"Now, my friends," I said, as Hammond and myself held the creature suspended over the bed, "I can give you self-evident proof that here is a solid, ponderable body, which, nevertheless, you cannot see. Be good enough to watch the surface of the bed attentively."

I was astonished at my own courage in treating this strange event so ca... ..../; but I had recovered from my first terror, and felt a sort of scientific pride in the affair, which dominated every other feeling.

The eyes of the bystanders were immediately fixed on my bed. At a given signal Hammond and I let the creature fall. There was the dull sound of a heavy body alighting on a soft mass. The timbers of the bed creaked. A deep impression marked itself distinctly on the pillow, and on the bed itself. The crowd who witnessed this gave a low cry, and rushed from the room. Hammond and I were left alone with our Mystery.

We remained silent for some time, listening to the low, irregular breathing of the creature on the bed, and watching the rustle of the bedclothes as it impotently struggled to free itself from confinement. Then Hammond spoke.

"Harry, this is awful."

"Ay, awful."

"But not unaccountable."

"Not unaccountable! What do you mean? Such a thing has never occurred since the birth of the world. I know not what to think, Hammond. God grant that I am not mad, and that this is not an insane fantasy!"

"Let us reason a little, Harry. Here is a solid body which we touch, but which we cannot see. The fact is so unusual that it strikes us with terror. Is there no parallel, though, for such a phenomenon? Take a piece of pure glass. It is tangible and transparent. A certain chemical coarseness is all that prevents its being so entirely transparent as to be totally invisible. It is not *theoretically impossible*, mind you, to make a glass which shall not reflect a single ray of light—a glass so pure and homogeneous in its atoms that the rays from the sun will pass through it as they do through the air, refracted but not reflected. We do not see the air, and yet we feel it."

"That's all very well, Hammond, but these are inanimate substances. Glass does not breathe, air does not breathe. *This* thing has a heart that palpitates—a will that moves it—lungs that play and inspire and respire."

"You forget the phenomena of which we have so often heard of late," answered the Doctor, gravely. "At the meetings called 'spirit circles,' invisible hands have been thrust into the hands of those persons round the table—warm, fleshly hands that seemed to pulsate with mortal life."

"What? Do you think, then, that this thing is—"

"I don't know what it is," was the solemn reply; "but please the gods I will, with your assistance, thoroughly investigate it."

We watched together, smoking many pipes, all night long, by the bedside of the unearthly being that tossed and panted until it was apparently wearied out. Then we learned by the low, regular breathing that it slept.

270

The next morning the house was all astir. The boarders congregated on the landing outside my room, and Hammond and myself were lions. We had to answer a thousand questions as to the state of our extraordinary prisoner, for as yet not one person in the house except ourselves could be induced to set foot in the apartment.

The creature was awake. This was evidenced by the convulsive manner in which the bedclothes were moved in its efforts to escape. There was something truly terrible in beholding, as it were, those secondhand indications of the terrible writhings and agonized struggles for liberty which themselves were invisible.

Hammond and myself had racked our brains during the long night to discover some means by which we might realize the shape and general appearance of the Enigma. As well as we could make out by passing our hands over the creature's form, its outlines and lineaments were human. There was a mouth; a round, smooth head without hair; a nose, which, however, was little elevated above the cheeks; and its hands and feet felt like those of a boy. At first we thought of placing the being on a smooth surface and tracing its outline with chalk, as shoemakers trace the outline of the foot. This plan was given up as being of no value. Such an outline would give not the slightest idea of its conformation.

A happy thought struck me. We would take a cast of it in plaster of Paris. This would give us the solid figure, and satisfy all our wishes. But how to do it? The movements of the creature would disturb the setting of the plastic covering, and distort the mould. Another thought. Why not give it chloroform? It had respiratory organs—that was evident by its breathing. Once reduced to a state of insensibility, we could do with it what we would. Doctor X—— was sent for; and after the worthy physician had recovered from the first shock of amazement, he proceeded to administer the chloroform. In three minutes afterward we were enabled to remove the fetters from the creature's body, and a modeler was busily engaged in covering the invisible form with the moist clay. In five minutes more we had a mould, and before evening a rough facsimile of the Mystery. It was shaped like a man—distorted, uncouth, and horrible, but still a man. It was small, not over four feet and some inches in height, and its limbs revealed a muscular development that was unparalleled. Its face surpassed in hideousness anything I had ever seen. Gustave Doré, or Callot, or Tony Johannot never conceived anything so horrible. There is a face in one of the latter's illustrations to *Un Voyage où il vous plaira,* which somewhat approaches the countenance of this creature, but does not equal it. It was the physiognomy of what I should fancy a ghoul might be. It looked as if it was capable of feeding on human flesh.

Having satisfied our curiosity, and bound everyone in the house to secrecy, it became a question what was to be done with our Enigma? It was impossible that we should keep such a horror in our house; it was equally impossible that such an awful being should be let loose upon the world. I confess that I would have gladly voted for the creature's destruction. But who would shoulder the responsibility? Who would undertake the execution of this horrible semblance of a human being? Day after day this question was deliberated gravely. The boarders all left the house. Mrs. Moffat was in despair, and threatened Hammond and myself with all sorts of legal penalties if we did not remove the Horror. Our answer was, "We will go if you like, but we decline taking this creature with us. Remove it yourself if you please. It appeared in your house. On you the responsibility rests." To this there was, of course, no answer. Mrs. Moffat could not obtain for love or money a person who would even approach the Mystery.

The most singular part of the affair was that we were entirely ignorant of what the creature habitually fed on. Everything in the way of nutriment that we could think of was placed before it, but was never touched. It was awful to stand by, day after day, and see the clothes toss, and hear the hard breathing, and know that it was starving.

Ten, twelve days, a fortnight passed, and it still lived. The pulsations of the heart, however, were daily growing fainter, and had now nearly ceased. It was evident that the creature was dying for want of sustenance. While this terrible life struggle was going on, I felt miserable. I could not sleep. Horrible as the creature was, it was pitiful to think of the pangs it was suffering.

At last it died. Hammond and I found it cold and stiff one morning in the bed. The heart had ceased to beat, the lungs to inspire. We hastened to bury it in the garden. It was a strange funeral, the dropping of that viewless corpse into the damp hole. The cast of its form I gave to Doctor X——, who keeps it in his museum in Tenth Street.

As I am on the eve of a long journey from which I may not return, I have drawn up this narrative of an event the most singular that has ever come to my knowledge.

## FOR DISCUSSION: What Was It?

1. Is it possible that the author of this story deliberately introduced the use of drugs to make the reader wonder if the events described actually occurred other than in a drug-induced hallucination?
2. Does the author at any point in his story suggest that the thing is worthy of pity? What is your dominant feeling toward the thing?

## INTRODUCTION: The Rocking-Horse Winner

One of the reasons many readers enjoy stories of the supernatural is because of the many variations that are possible on supernatural themes. They welcome the diverse manifestations of the supernatural which arise in the fertile imaginations of such writers as the renowned D. H. Lawrence. The following story is an excellent example of an original view of the supernatural in the everyday lives of quite ordinary people in England.

# The Rocking-Horse Winner
## D. H. Lawrence

There was a woman who was beautiful, who started with all the advantages, yet she had no luck. She married for love, and the love turned to dust. She had bonny children, yet she felt they had been thrust upon her, and she could not love them. They looked at her coldly, as if they were finding fault with her. And hurriedly she felt she must cover up some fault in herself. Yet what it was that she must cover up she never knew. Nevertheless, when her children were present, she always felt the center of her heart go hard. This troubled her, and in her manner she was all the more gentle and anxious for her children, as if she loved them very much. Only she herself knew that at the center of her heart was a hard little place that could not feel love, no, not for anybody. Everybody else said of her: "She is such a good mother. She adores her children." Only she herself, and her children themselves, knew it was not so. They read it in each other's eyes.

There were a boy and two little girls. They lived in a pleasant house, with a garden, and they had discreet servants, and felt themselves superior to anyone in the neighborhood.

Although they lived in style, they felt always an anxiety in the house. There was never enough money. The mother had a small income, and the father had a small income, but not nearly enough for the social position which they had to keep up. The father went into town to some office. But though he had good prospects, these prospects never materialized. There was always the grinding sense of the shortage of money, though the style was always kept up.

At last the mother said, "I will see if *I* can't make something." But she did not know where to begin. She racked her brains, and tried this thing and the other, but could not find anything successful. The failure made deep lines come into her face. Her children were growing up, they would have to go to school. There must be more money. The father, who was always very handsome and expensive in his tastes, seemed as if he never *would* be able to do anything worth doing. And the mother, who had a great belief in herself, did not succeed any better, and her tastes were just as expensive.

And so the house came to be haunted by the unspoken phrase: *There must be more money! There must be more money!* The children could hear it all the time, though nobody said it aloud. They heard it at Christmas, when the expensive and splendid toys filled the nursery. Behind the shining modern rocking horse, behind the smart doll's house, a voice would start whispering: "There *must* be more money! There *must* be more money!" And the children would stop playing, to listen for a moment. They would look into each other's eyes, to see if they had all heard. And each one saw in the eyes of the other two that they too had heard. "There *must* be more money! There *must* be more money!"

It came whispering from the springs of the still-swaying rocking horse, and even the horse, bending his wooden, champing head, heard it. The big doll, sitting so pink and smirking in her new pram, could hear it quite plainly and seemed to be smirking all the more self-consciously because of it. The foolish puppy, too, that took the place of the teddy bear, he was looking so extraordinarily foolish for no other reason but that he heard the secret whisper all over the house: "There *must* be more money."

Yet nobody ever said it aloud. The whisper was everywhere, and therefore no one spoke it. Just as no one ever says: "We are breathing!" in spite of the fact that breath is coming and going all the time.

"Mother!" said the boy Paul one day, "why don't we keep a car of our own? Why do we always use Uncle's, or else a taxi?"

"Because we're the poor members of the family," said the mother.

"But why *are* we, Mother?"

"Well—I suppose," she said slowly and bitterly, "it's because your father has no luck."

The boy was silent for some time.

"Is luck money, Mother?" he asked, rather timidly.

"No, Paul! Not quite. It's what causes you to have money."

"Oh!" said Paul vaguely. "I thought when Uncle Oscar said *filthy lucker,* it meant money."

"*Filthy lucre* does mean money," said the mother. "But it's lucre, not luck."

"Oh!" said the boy. "Then what *is* luck, Mother?"

"It's what causes you to have money. If you're lucky you have money.

That's why it's better to be born lucky than rich. If you're rich, you may lose your money. But if you're lucky, you will always get more money."

"Oh! Will you! And is Father not lucky?"

"Very unlucky, I should say," she said bitterly.

The boy watched her with unsure eyes.

"Why?" he asked.

"I don't know. Nobody ever knows why one person is lucky and another unlucky."

"Don't they? Nobody at all? Does *nobody* know?"

"Perhaps God! But He never tells."

"He ought to, then. And aren't you lucky, either, Mother?"

"I can't be, if I married an unlucky husband."

"But by yourself, aren't you?"

"I used to think I was, before I married. Now I think I am very unlucky indeed."

"Why?"

"Well—never mind! Perhaps I'm not really," she said.

The child looked at her, to see if she meant it. But he saw, by the lines of her mouth, that she was only trying to hide something from him.

"Well, anyhow," he said stoutly, "I'm a lucky person."

"Why?" said his mother, with a sudden laugh.

He stared at her. He didn't even know why he had said it.

"God told me," he asserted, brazening it out.

"I hope He did, dear!" she said, again with a laugh but rather bitter.

"He did, Mother!"

"Excellent!" said the mother, using one of her husband's exclamations.

The boy saw she did not believe him; or rather, that she paid no attention to his assertion. This angered him somewhat and made him want to compel her attention.

He went off by himself, vaguely, in a childish way, seeking for the clue to "luck." Absorbed, taking no heed of other people, he went about with a sort of stealth, seeking inwardly for luck. He wanted luck, he wanted it, he wanted it. When the two girls were playing dolls, in the nursery, he would sit on his big rocking horse, charging madly into space, with a frenzy that made the little girls peer at him uneasily. Wildly the horse careered, the waving dark hair of the boy tossed, his eyes had a strange glare in them. The little girls dared not speak to him.

When he had ridden to the end of his mad little journey, he climbed down and stood in front of his rocking horse, staring fixedly into its lowered face. Its red mouth was slightly open, its big eye was wide and glassy bright.

"Now!" he would silently command the snorting steed. "Now take me to where there is luck! Now take me!"

And he would slash the horse on the neck with the little whip he had asked Uncle Oscar for. He *knew* the horse could take him to where there was luck, if only he forced it. So he would mount again and start on his furious ride, hoping at last to get there. He knew he could get there.

"You'll break your horse, Paul!" said the nurse.

"He's always riding like that! I wish he'd leave off!" said his elder sister Joan.

But he only glared down on them in silence. Nurse gave him up. She could make nothing of him. Anyhow he was growing beyond her.

One day his mother and his uncle Oscar came in when he was on one of his furious rides. He did not speak to them.

"Hallo! you young jockey! Riding a winner?" said his uncle.

"Aren't you growing too big for a rocking horse? You're not a very little boy any longer, you know," said his mother.

But Paul only gave a blue glare from his big, rather close-set eyes. He would speak to nobody when he was in full tilt. His mother watched him with an anxious expression on her face.

At last he suddenly stopped forcing his horse into the mechanical gallop, and slid down.

"Well, I got there!" he announced fiercely, his blue eyes still flaring and his sturdy long legs straddling apart.

"Where did you get to?" asked his mother.

"Where I wanted to go to," he flared back at her.

"That's right, son!" said Uncle Oscar. "Don't you stop till you get there. What's the horse's name?"

"He doesn't have a name," said the boy.

"Gets on without all right?" asked the uncle.

"Well, he has different names. He was called Sansovino last week."

"Sansovino, eh? Won the Ascot. How did you know his name?"

"He always talks about horse races with Bassett," said Joan.

The uncle was delighted to find that his small nephew was posted with all the racing news. Bassett, the young gardener who had been wounded in the left foot in the war and had got his present job through Oscar Cresswell, whose batman he had been, was a perfect blade of the "turf." He lived in the racing events, and the small boy lived with him.

Oscar Cresswell got it all from Bassett.

"Master Paul comes and asks me, so I can't do more than tell him, sir," said Bassett, his face terribly serious, as if he were speaking of religious matters.

"And does he ever put anything on a horse he fancies?"

"Well—I don't want to give him away—he's a young sport, a fine sport, sir. Would you mind asking him himself? He sort of takes a pleasure in it, and perhaps he'd feel I was giving him away, sir, if you don't mind."

Bassett was serious as a church.

The uncle went back to his nephew and took him off for a ride in the car.

"Say, Paul, old man, do you ever put anything on a horse?" the uncle asked.

The boy watched the handsome man closely.

"Why, do you think I oughtn't to?" he parried.

"Not a bit of it! I thought perhaps you might give me a tip for the Lincoln."

The car sped on into the country, going down to Uncle Oscar's place in Hampshire.

"Honor bright?" said the nephew.

"Honor bright, son!" said the uncle.

"Well, then, Daffodil."

"Daffodil! I doubt it, sonny. What about Mirza?"

"I only know the winner," said the boy. "That's Daffodil!"

"Daffodil, eh?"

There was a pause. Daffodil was an obscure horse comparatively.

"Uncle!"

"Yes, son?"

"You won't let it go any further, will you? I promised Bassett."

"Bassett be damned, old man! What's he got to do with it?"

"We're partners! We've been partners from the first! Uncle, he lent me my first five shillings, which I lost. I promised him, honor bright, it was only between me and him: Only you gave me that ten-shilling note I started winning with, so I thought you were lucky. You won't let it go any further, will you?"

The boy gazed at his uncle from those big, hot blue eyes, set rather close together. The uncle stirred and laughed uneasily.

"Right you are, son! I'll keep your tip private. Daffodil, eh! How much are you putting on him?"

"All except twenty pounds," said the boy. "I keep that in reserve."

The uncle thought it a good joke.

"You keep twenty pounds in reserve, do you, you young romancer? What are you betting, then?"

"I'm betting three hundred," said the boy gravely. "But it's between you and me, Uncle Oscar! Honor bright?"

The uncle burst into a roar of laughter.

"It's between you and me all right, you young Nat Gould," he said, laughing. "But where's your three hundred?"

"Bassett keeps it for me. We're partners."

"You are, are you! And what is Bassett putting on Daffodil?"

"He won't go quite as high as I do, I expect. Perhaps he'll go a hundred and fifty."

"What, pennies?" laughed the uncle.

"Pounds," said the child, with a surprised look at his uncle. "Bassett keeps a bigger reserve than I do."

Between wonder and amusement, Uncle Oscar was silent. He pursued the matter no further, but he determined to take his nephew with him to the Lincoln races.

"Now, son," he said, "I'm putting twenty on Mirza, and I'll put five for you on any horse you fancy. What's your pick?"

"Daffodil, Uncle!"

"No, not the fiver on Daffodil!"

"I should if it was my own fiver," said the child.

"Good! Good! Right you are! A fiver for me and a fiver for you on Daffodil."

The child had never been to a race-meeting before, and his eyes were blue fire. He pursed his mouth tight and watched. A Frenchman just in front had put his money on Lancelot. Wild with excitement, he flailed his arms up and down, yelling *Lancelot! Lancelot!* in his French accent.

Daffodil came in first, Lancelot second, Mirza third. The child, flushed and with eyes blazing, was curiously serene. His uncle brought him five five-pound notes: four to one.

"What am I to do with these?" he cried, waving them before the boy's eyes.

"I suppose we'll talk to Bassett," said the boy. "I expect I have fifteen hundred now: and twenty in reserve: and this twenty."

His uncle studied him for some moments.

"Look here, son!" he said. "You're not serious about Bassett and that fifteen hundred, are you?"

"Yes, I am. But it's between you and me, Uncle! Honor bright!"

"Honor bright all right, son! But I must talk to Bassett."

"If you'd like to be a partner, Uncle, with Bassett and me, we could all be partners. Only you'd have to promise, honor bright, Uncle, not to let it go beyond us three. Bassett and I are lucky, and you must be lucky, because it was your ten shillings I started winning with. . . ."

Uncle Oscar took both Bassett and Paul into Richmond Park for an afternoon, and there they talked.

"It's like this, you see, sir," Bassett said. "Master Paul would get me talking about racing events, spinning yarns, you know, sir. And he was always keen on knowing if I'd made or if I'd lost. It's about a year since, now, that I put five shillings on Blush of Dawn for him: And we lost. Then the luck turned, with that ten shillings he had from you: that we put on Singhalese. And since that time, it's been pretty steady, all things considering. What do you say, Master Paul?"

"We're all right when we're *sure*," said Paul. "It's when we're not quite sure that we go down."

"Oh, but we're careful then," said Bassett.

"But when are you *sure?*" smiled Uncle Oscar.

"It's Master Paul, sir," said Bassett, in a secret, religious voice. "It's as if he had it from heaven. Like Daffodil now, for the Lincoln. That was as sure as eggs."

"Did you put anything on Daffodil?" asked Oscar Cresswell.

"Yes, sir. I made my bit."

"And my nephew?"

Bassett was obstinately silent, looking at Paul.

"I made twelve hundred, didn't I, Bassett? I told Uncle I was putting three hundred on Daffodil."

"That's right," said Bassett, nodding.

"But where's the money?" asked the uncle

"I keep it safe locked up, sir. Master Paul, he can have it any minute he likes to ask for it."

"What, fifteen hundred pounds?"

"And twenty! And *forty*, that is, with the twenty he made on the course."

"It's amazing!" said the uncle.

"If Master Paul offers you to be partners, sir, I would, if I were you: if you'll excuse me," said Bassett.

Oscar Cresswell thought about it.

"I'll see the money," he said.

They drove home again, and sure enough, Bassett came round to the garden house with fifteen hundred pounds in notes. The twenty pounds reserve was left with Joe Glee, in the Turf Commission deposit.

"You see, it's all right, Uncle, when I'm *sure!* Then we go strong, for all we're worth. Don't we, Bassett?"

"We do that, Master Paul."

"And when are you sure?" said the uncle, laughing.

"Oh, well, sometimes I'm *absolutely* sure, like about Daffodil," said the boy; "and sometimes I have an idea; and sometimes I haven't even an idea, have I, Bassett? Then we're careful, because we mostly go down."

"You do, do you! And when you're sure, like about Daffodil, what makes you sure, sonny?"

"Oh, well, I don't know," said the boy uneasily. "I'm sure, you know, Uncle; that's all."

"It's as if he had it from heaven, sir," Bassett reiterated.

"I should say so!" said the uncle.

But he became a partner. And when the Leger was coming on, Paul was "sure" about Lively Spark, which was a quite inconsiderable horse. The boy insisted on putting a thousand on the horse, Bassett went for five hundred, and Oscar Cresswell two hundred. Lively Spark came in first, and the betting had been ten to one against him. Paul had made ten thousand.

"You see," he said, "I was absolutely sure of him."

Even Oscar Cresswell had cleared two thousand.

"Look here, son," he said, "this sort of thing makes me nervous."

"It needn't, Uncle! Perhaps I shan't be sure again for a long time."

"But what are you going to do with your money?" asked the uncle.

"Of course," said the boy, "I started it for Mother. She said she had no luck, because Father is unlucky, so I thought if *I* was lucky, it might stop whispering."

"What might stop whispering?"

"Our house! I *hate* our house for whispering."

"What does it whisper?"

"Why—why"—the boy fidgeted—"why, I don't know! But it's always short of money, you know, Uncle."

"I know it, son, I know it."

"You know people send Mother writs, don't you, Uncle?"

"I'm afraid I do," said the uncle.

"And then the house whispers like people laughing at you behind your back. It's awful, that is! I thought if I was lucky—"

"You might stop it," added the uncle.

The boy watched him with big blue eyes, that had an uncanny cold fire in them, and he said never a word.

"Well then!" said the uncle. "What are we doing?"

"I shouldn't like Mother to know I was lucky," said the boy.

"Why not, son?"

"She'd stop me."

"I don't think she would."

"Oh!"—and the boy writhed in an odd way—"I *don't* want her to know, Uncle."

"All right, son! We'll manage it without her knowing."

They managed it very easily. Paul, at the other's suggestion, handed over five thousand pounds to his uncle, who deposited it with the family lawyer, who was then to inform Paul's mother that a relative had put five thousand pounds into his hands, which sum was to be paid out a thousand pounds at a time, on the mother's birthday, for the next five years.

"So she'll have a birthday present of a thousand pounds for five successive years," said Uncle Oscar. "I hope it won't make it all the harder for her later."

Paul's mother had her birthday in November. The house had been "whispering" worse than ever lately, and even in spite of his luck, Paul could not bear up against it. He was very anxious to see the effect of the birthday letter, telling his mother about the thousand pounds.

When there were no visitors, Paul now took his meals with his parents, as he was beyond the nursery control. His mother went into town nearly every day. She had discovered that she had an odd knack of sketching furs and dress materials, so she worked secretly in the studio of a friend who was the chief "artist" for the leading drapers. She drew the figures of ladies in furs and ladies in silk and sequins for the newspaper advertisements. This young woman artist earned several thousand pounds a year, but Paul's mother only made several hundreds, and she was again dissatisfied. She so wanted to be first in something, and she did not succeed, even in making sketches for drapery advertisements.

She was down to breakfast on the morning of her birthday. Paul watched her face as she read her letters. He knew the lawyer's letter. As his mother read it, her face hardened and became more expressionless. Then a cold, determined look came on her mouth. She hid the letter under the pile of others and said not a word about it.

"Didn't you have anything nice in the post for your birthday, Mother?" said Paul.

"Quite moderately nice," she said, her voice cold and absent.

She went away to town without saying more.

But in the afternoon Uncle Oscar appeared. He said Paul's mother had had a long interview with the lawyer, asking if the whole five thousand could not be advanced at once, as she was in debt.

"What do you think, Uncle?" said the boy.

"I leave it to you, son."

"Oh, let her have it, then! We can get some more with the other," said the boy.

"A bird in the hand is worth two in the bush, laddie!" said Uncle Oscar.

"But I'm sure to *know* for the Grand National; or the Lincolnshire; or else the Derby. I'm sure to know for *one* of them," said Paul.

So Uncle Oscar signed the agreement, and Paul's mother touched the whole five thousand. Then something very curious happened. The voices in the house suddenly went mad, like a chorus of frogs on a spring evening. There were certain new furnishings, and Paul had a tutor. He was *really* going to Eton, his father's school, in the following autumn. There were flowers in the winter, and a blossoming of the luxury Paul's mother had been used to. And yet the voices in the house, behind the

sprays of mimosa and almond blossom, and from under the piles of irides-
cent cushions, simply trilled and screamed in a sort of ecstasy: "There
*must* be more money! Oh-h-h! There *must* be more money! Oh, now,
now-w! now-w-w—there *must* be more money—more than ever! More
than ever!"

It frightened Paul terribly. He studied away at his Latin and Greek
with his tutors. But his intense hours were spent with Bassett. The
Grand National had gone by: He had not "known," and had lost a hundred pounds. Summer was at hand. He was in agony for the Lincoln.
But even for the Lincoln he didn't "know," and he lost fifty pounds. He
became wild-eyed and strange, as if something were going to explode in
him.

"Let it alone, son! Don't you bother about it!" urged Uncle Oscar.
But it was as if the boy couldn't really hear what his uncle was saying.

"I've got to know for the Derby! I've *got* to know for the Derby!" the
child reiterated, his big blue eyes blazing with a sort of madness.

His mother noticed how overwrought he was.

"You'd better go to the seaside. Wouldn't you like to go now to the
seaside, instead of waiting? I think you'd better," she said, looking down
at him anxiously, her heart curiously heavy because of him.

But the child lifted his uncanny blue eyes.

"I couldn't possibly go before the Derby, Mother!" he said. "I
couldn't possibly!"

"Why not?" she said, her voice becoming heavy when she was opposed. "Why not? You can still go from the seaside to see the Derby
with your uncle Oscar, if that's what you wish. No need for you to wait
here. Besides, I think you care too much about these races. It's a bad
sign. My family has been a gambling family, and you won't know till
you grow up how much damage it has done. But it has done damage. I
shall have to send Bassett away and ask Uncle Oscar not to talk racing to
you, unless you promise to be reasonable about it: Go away to the seaside and forget it. You're all nerves!"

"I'll do what you like, Mother, so long as you don't send me away till
after the Derby," the boy said.

"Send you away from where? Just from this house?"

"Yes," he said, gazing at her.

"Why, you curious child, what makes you care about this house so
much, suddenly? I never knew you loved it!"

He gazed at her without speaking. He had a secret within a secret,
something he had not divulged, even to Bassett or to his uncle Oscar.

But his mother, after standing undecided and a little bit sullen for
some moments, said:

"Very well, then! Don't go to the seaside till after the Derby, if you don't wish it. But promise me you won't let your nerves go to pieces! Promise you won't think so much about horse racing and *events*, as you call them!"

"Oh no!" said the boy casually. "I won't think much about them, Mother. You needn't worry. I wouldn't worry, Mother, if I were you."

"If you were me and I were you," said his mother, "I wonder what we *should* do!"

"But you know you needn't worry, Mother, don't you?" the boy repeated.

"I should be awfully glad to know it," she said wearily.

"Oh, well, you *can*, you know. I mean you *ought* to know you needn't worry!" he insisted.

"Ought I? Then I'll see about it," she said.

Paul's secret of secrets was his wooden horse, that which had no name. Since he was emancipated from a nurse and a nursery governess, he had had his rocking horse removed to his own bedroom at the top of the house.

"Surely you're too big for a rocking horse!" his mother had remonstrated.

"Well, you see, Mother, till I can have a *real* horse, I like to have *some* sort of animal about," had been his quaint answer.

"Do you feel he keeps you company?" she laughed.

"Oh yes! He's very good, he always keeps me company, when I'm there," said Paul.

So the horse, rather shabby, stood in an arrested prance in the boy's bedroom.

The Derby was drawing near, and the boy grew more and more tense. He hardly heard what was spoken to him, he was very frail, and his eyes were really uncanny. His mother had sudden strange seizures of uneasiness about him. Sometimes, for half an hour, she would feel a sudden anxiety about him that was almost anguish. She wanted to rush to him at once and know he was safe.

Two nights before the Derby, she was at a big party in town, when one of her rushes of anxiety about her boy, her first-born, gripped her heart till she could hardly speak. She fought with the feeling, might and main, for she believed in common sense. But it was too strong. She had to leave the dance and go downstairs to telephone to the country. The children's nursery governess was terribly surprised and startled at being rung up in the night.

"Are the children all right, Miss Wilmot?"

"Oh yes, they are quite all right."

"Master Paul? Is he all right?"

"He went to bed as right as a trivet. Shall I run up and look at him?"

"No!" said Paul's mother reluctantly. "No! Don't trouble. It's all right. Don't sit up. We shall be home fairly soon." She did not want her son's privacy intruded upon.

"Very good," said the governess.

It was about one o'clock when Paul's mother and father drove up to their house. All was still. Paul's mother went to her room and slipped off her white fur cloak. She had told her maid not to wait up for her. She heard her husband downstairs, mixing a whisky and soda.

And then, because of the strange anxiety at her heart, she stole upstairs to her son's room. Noiselessly she went along the upper corridor. Was there a faint noise? What was it?

She stood, with arrested muscles, outside his door, listening. There was a strange, heavy, and yet not loud noise. Her heart stood still. It was a soundless noise, yet rushing and powerful. Something huge, in violent, hushed motion. What was it? What in God's Name was it? She ought to know. She felt that she *knew* the noise. She knew what it was.

Yet she could not place it. She couldn't say what it was. And on and on it went, like a madness.

Softly, frozen with anxiety and fear, she turned the door handle.

The room was dark. Yet in the space near the window, she heard and saw something plunging to and fro. She gazed in fear and amazement.

Then suddenly she switched on the light and saw her son, in his green pajamas, madly surging on his rocking horse. The blaze of light suddenly lit him up, as he urged the wooden horse, and lit her up, as she stood, blond, in her dress of pale green and crystal, in the doorway.

"Paul!" she cried. "Whatever are you doing?"

"It's Malabar!" he screamed, in a powerful, strange voice. "It's Malabar!"

His eyes blazed at her for one strange and senseless second, as he ceased urging his wooden horse. Then he fell with a crash to the ground, and she, all her tormented motherhood flooding upon her, rushed to gather him up.

But he was unconscious, and unconscious he remained, with some brain fever. He talked and tossed, and his mother sat stonily by his side.

"Malabar! It's Malabar! Bassett, Bassett, I *know*: It's Malabar!"

So the child cried, trying to get up and urge the rocking horse that gave him his inspiration.

"What does he mean by Malabar?" asked the heart-frozen mother.

"I don't know," said the father stonily.

"What does he mean by Malabar?" she asked her brother Oscar.

"It's one of the horses running for the Derby," was the answer.

And, in spite of himself, Oscar Cresswell spoke to Bassett, and himself put a thousand on Malabar: at fourteen to one.

The third day of the illness was critical: They were watching for a change. The boy, with his rather long, curly hair, was tossing ceaselessly on the pillow. He neither slept nor regained consciousness, and his eyes were like blue stones. His mother sat, feeling her heart had gone, turned actually into a stone.

In the evening, Oscar Cresswell did not come, but Bassett sent a message, saying could he come up for one moment, just one moment? Paul's mother was very angry at the intrusion, but on second thoughts she agreed. The boy was the same. Perhaps Bassett might bring him to consciousness.

The gardener, a shortish fellow with a little brown mustache and sharp little brown eyes, tiptoed into the room, touched his imaginary cap to Paul's mother, and stole to the bedside, staring with glittering, smallish eyes at the tossing, dying child.

"Master Paul!" he whispered. "Master Paul! Malabar came in first all right, a clean win. I did as you told me. You've made over seventy thousand pounds, you have; you've got over eighty thousand. Malabar came in all right, Master Paul."

"Malabar! Malabar. Did I say Malabar, Mother? Did I say Malabar? Do you think I'm lucky, Mother? I knew Malabar, didn't I? Over eighty thousand pounds! I call that lucky, don't you, Mother? Over eighty thousand pounds! I knew, didn't I know I knew? Malabar came in all right. If I ride my horse till I'm sure, then I tell you, Bassett, you can go as high as you like. Did you go for all you were worth, Bassett?"

"I went a thousand on it, Master Paul."

"I never told you, Mother, that if I can ride my horse, and *get there*, then I'm absolutely sure—oh, absolutely! Mother, did I ever tell you? I *am* lucky!"

"No, you never did," said the mother.

But the boy died in the night.

And even as he lay dead, his mother heard her brother's voice saying to her: "My God, Hester, you're eighty-odd thousand to the good, and a poor devil of a son to the bad. But, poor devil, poor devil, he's best gone out of a life where he rides his rocking horse to find a winner."

# FOR DISCUSSION: The Rocking-Horse Winner

1. Do you think the author means to be literal when he speaks of the house whispering of the need for more money? If not, what do you think is the function of this theme in the story?
2. Adults frequently believe that children are less than perceptive about adult motives and remarks. The author in this story shows that such an assumption is false. How does he do so? Give examples.
3. What is the primary force motivating Paul?
4. There are evidences of scepticism on the part of certain characters concerning Paul's supernatural ability. Identify them.
5. Paul talks about "getting there." Why does the author never clearly define where "there" is?

# INTRODUCTION: The Bagman's Story

Charles Dickens created some of the most memorable characters in literature. His men, women, and children live and breathe. In this story, a rare Dickensian excursion into the domain of the supernatural, his talent for characterization does not fail him. Not only is the bagman interesting (a bagman was a traveling salesman); but so is the chair, which is very definitely a major character in the story.

# The Bagman's Story
## Charles Dickens

One winter's evening, about five o'clock, just as it began to grow dusk, a man in a gig might have been seen urging his tired horse along the road which leads across Marlborough Downs, in the direction of Bristol. I say he might have been seen, and I have no doubt he would have been, if anybody but a blind man happened to pass that way; but the weather was so bad, and the night so cold and wet, that nothing was out but the water, and so the traveler jogged along in the middle of the road, lonesome and dreary enough. If any bagman of that day could have caught sight of the little neck-or-nothing sort of gig, with a clay-colored body and red wheels, and the vixenish, ill-tempered, fast-going bay mare, that looked like a cross between a butcher's horse and a two-penny post-office pony, he would have known at once that this traveler could have been no other than Tom Smart, of the great house of Bilson and Slum, Cateaton Street, City. However, as there was no bagman to look on, nobody knew anything at all about the matter; and so Tom Smart and his clay-colored gig with the red wheels, and the vixenish mare with the fast pace, went on together, keeping the secret among them: And nobody was a bit the wiser.

There are many pleasanter places even in this dreary world than Marlborough Downs when it blows hard; and if you throw in besides, a gloomy winter's evening, a miry and sloppy road, and a pelting fall of heavy rain, and try the effect, by way of experiment, in your own proper person, you will experience the full force of this observation.

The wind blew—not up the road or down it, though that's bad enough, but sheer across it, sending the rain slanting down like the lines they used to rule in the copybooks at school, to make the boys slope well. For a moment it would die away, and the traveler would begin to delude himself into the belief that, exhausted with its previous fury, it had quietly lain itself down to rest, when, whoo! he would hear it growling and whistling in the distance, and on it would come, rushing over the hilltops and sweeping along the plain, gathering sound and strength as it drew nearer, until it dashed with a heavy gust against horse and man, driving the sharp rain into their ears, and its cold damp breath into their very bones; and past them it would scour, far, far away, with a stunning roar, as if in ridicule of their weakness, and triumphant in the consciousness of its own strength and power.

The bay mare splashed away, through the mud and water, with drooping ears; now and then tossing her head as if to express her disgust at this very ungentlemanly behavior of the elements, but keeping a good pace notwithstanding, until a gust of wind, more furious than any that had yet assailed them, caused her to stop suddenly and plant her four feet firmly against the ground, to prevent her being blown over.  It's a special mercy that she did this, for if she *had* been blown over, the vixenish mare was so light, and the gig was so light, and Tom Smart such a lightweight into the bargain, that they must infallibly have all gone rolling over and over together, until they reached the confines of earth, or until the wind fell; and in either case the probability is that neither the vixenish mare, nor the clay-colored gig with the red wheels, nor Tom Smart, would ever have been fit for service again.

"Well, damn my straps and whiskers," says Tom Smart (Tom sometimes had an unpleasant knack of swearing), "Damn my straps and whiskers," says Tom, "if this ain't pleasant, blow me!"

You'll very likely ask me why, as Tom Smart had been pretty well blown already, he expressed this wish to be submitted to the same process again.  I can't say—all I know is that Tom Smart said so—or at least he always told my uncle he said so, and it's just the same thing.

"Blow me," says Tom Smart; and the mare neighed as if she were precisely of the same opinion.

"Cheer up, old girl," said Tom, patting the bay mare on the neck with the end of his whip.  "It won't do pushing on, such a night as this; the first house we come to we'll put up at, so the faster you go, the sooner it's over.  Soho, old girl—gently—gently."

Whether the vixenish mare was sufficiently well acquainted with the tones of Tom's voice to comprehend his meaning, or whether she found it colder standing still than moving on, of course I can't say.  But I can say that Tom had no sooner finished speaking, than she pricked up her ears and started forward at a speed which made the clay-colored gig rattle till you would have supposed every one of the red spokes was going to fly out on the turf of Marlborough Downs; and even Tom, whip as he was, couldn't stop or check her pace, until she drew up, of her own accord, before a roadside inn on the right-hand side of the way, about half a quarter of a mile from the end of the Downs.

Tom cast a hasty glance at the upper part of the house as he threw the reins in the hostler and stuck the whip in the box. It was a strange old place, built of a kind of shingle, inlaid, as it were, with crossbeams, with gabled-topped windows projecting completely over the pathway, and a low door with a dark porch, and a couple of steep steps leading down into the house, instead of the modern fashion of half a dozen shallow ones leading up to it. It was a comfortable-looking place though, for there was a strong cheerful light in the bar window, which shed a bright ray across the road and even lighted up the hedge on the other side; and there was a red flickering light in the opposite window, one moment but faintly discernible, and the next gleaming strongly through the drawn curtains, which intimated that a rousing fire was blazing within. Marking these little evidences with the eye of an experienced traveler, Tom dismounted with as much agility as his half-frozen limbs would permit, and entered the house.

In less than five minutes' time, Tom was ensconced in the room opposite the bar—the very room where he had imagined the fire blazing—before a substantial matter-of-fact roaring fire, composed of something short of a bushel of coals, and wood enough to make half a dozen decent gooseberry bushes, piled halfway up the chimney, and roaring and crackling with a sound that of itself would have warmed the heart of any reasonable man. This was comfortable, but this was not all, for a smartly dressed girl, with a bright eye and a neat ankle, was laying a very clean white cloth on the table; and as Tom sat with his slippered feet on the fender and his back to the open door, he saw a charming prospect of the bar reflected in the glass over the chimney piece, with delightful rows of green bottles and gold labels, together with jars of pickles and preserves, and cheeses and boiled hams, and rounds of beef, arranged on shelves in the most tempting and delicious array. Well, this was comfortable too; but even this was not all—for in the bar, seated at tea at the nicest possible little table, drawn close up before the brightest possible little fire, was a buxom widow of somewhere about eight-and-forty or thereabouts, with a face as comfortable as the bar, who was evidently the landlady of the house, and the supreme ruler over all these agreeable possessions. There was only one drawback to the beauty of the whole picture, and that was a tall man—a very tall man—in a brown coat and bright basket buttons, and black whiskers, and wavy black hair, who was seated at tea with the widow, and who it required no great penetration to discover was in a fair way of persuading her to be a widow no longer, but to confer upon him the privilege of sitting down in that bar, for and during the whole remainder of the term of his natural life.

Tom Smart was by no means of an irritable or envious disposition, but somehow or other the tall man with the brown coat and the bright basket buttons did rouse what little gall he had in his composition and did make him feel extremely indignant: the more especially as he could now and then observe, from his seat before the glass, certain little affectionate familiarities passing between the tall man and the widow, which sufficiently denoted that the tall man was as high in favor as he was in size. Tom was fond of hot punch—I may venture to say he was *very* fond of hot punch—and after he had seen the vixenish mare well fed and well littered down, and had eaten every bit of the nice little hot dinner which the widow tossed up for him with her own hands, he just ordered a tumbler of it, by way of experiment. Now, if there was one thing in the whole range of domestic art which the widow could manufacture better than another, it was this identical article; and the first tumbler was adapted to Tom Smart's taste with such peculiar nicety that he ordered a second with the least possible delay. Hot punch is a pleasant thing, gentlemen—an extremely pleasant thing under any circumstances—but in that snug old parlor, before the roaring fire, with the wind blowing outside till every timber in the old house creaked again, Tom Smart found it perfectly delightful. He ordered another tumbler, and then another—I am not quite certain whether he didn't order another after that—but the more he drank of the hot punch, the more he thought of the tall man.

"Confound his impudence!" said Tom to himself. "What business has he in that snug bar? Such an ugly villain, too!" said Tom. "If the widow had any taste, she might surely pick up some better fellow than that." Here Tom's eye wandered from the glass on the chimney piece to the glass on the table; and as he felt himself becoming gradually sentimental, he emptied the fourth tumbler of punch and ordered a fifth.

Tom Smart, gentlemen, had always been very much attached to the public line. It had long been his ambition to stand in a bar of his own, in a green coat, knee-cords, and tops. He had a great notion of taking the chair at convivial dinners, and he had often thought how well he could preside in a room of his own in the talking way, and what a capital example he could set to his customers in the drinking department. All these things passed rapidly through Tom's mind as he sat drinking the hot punch by the roaring fire, and he felt very justly and properly indignant that the tall man should be in a fair way of keeping such an excellent house, while he, Tom Smart, was as far off from it as ever. So, after deliberating over the two last tumblers whether he hadn't a perfect right to pick a quarrel with the tall man for having contrived to get into the good graces of the buxom widow, Tom Smart at last arrived at the satisfactory conclusion that he was a very ill-used and persecuted individual, and had better go to bed.

Up a wide and ancient staircase the smart girl preceded Tom, shading the chamber candle with her hand, to protect it from the currents of air which in such a rambling old place might have found plenty of room to disport themselves in, without blowing the candle out, but which did blow it out nevertheless; thus affording Tom's enemies an opportunity of asserting that it was he, and not the wind, who extinguished the candle, and that while he pretended to be blowing it alight again, he was in fact kissing the girl. But this as it may, another light was obtained, and Tom was conducted through a maze of rooms, and a labyrinth of passages, to the apartment which had been prepared for his reception, where the girl bade him good night and left him alone.

It was a large room with big closets, and a bed which might have served for a whole boarding school, to say nothing of a couple of oaken presses that would have held the baggage of a small army; but what struck Tom's fancy most was a strange, grim-looking high-backed chair, carved in the most fantastic manner, with a flowered damask cushion, and the round knobs at the bottom of the legs carefully tied up in red cloth, as if it had got the gout in its toes. Of any other queer chair, Tom would only have thought it *was* a queer chair and there would have been an end of the matter; but there was something about this particular chair, and yet he couldn't tell what it was, so odd and so unlike any other piece of furniture he had ever seen, that it seemed to fascinate him. He sat down before the fire and stared at the old chair for half an hour—Deuce take the chair, it was such a strange old thing, he couldn't take his eyes off it.

"Well," said Tom, slowly undressing himself and staring at the old chair all the while, which stood with a mysterious aspect by the bedside, "I never saw such a rum concern as that in my days. Very odd," said Tom, who had got rather sage with the hot punch. "Very odd." Tom shook his head with an air of profound wisdom and looked at the chair again. He couldn't make anything of it though, so he got into bed, covered himself up warm, and fell asleep.

In about half an hour, Tom woke up, with a start, from a confused dream of tall men and tumblers of punch; and the first object that presented itself to his waking imagination was the queer chair.

"I won't look at it any more," said Tom to himself, and he squeezed his eyelids together and tried to persuade himself he was going to sleep again. No use; nothing but queer chairs danced before his eyes, kicking up their legs, jumping over each other's backs, and playing all kinds of antics.

"I may as well see one real chair, as two or three complete sets of false ones," said Tom, bringing out his head from under the bedclothes. There it was, plainly discernible by the light of the fire, looking as provoking as ever.

Tom gazed at the chair; and suddenly as he looked at it, a most extraordinary change seemed to come over it. The carving of the back gradually assumed the lineaments and expression of a shriveled human face; the damask cushion became an antique, flapped waistcoat; the round knobs grew into a couple of feet, encased in red cloth slippers; and the old chair looked like a very ugly old man, of the previous century, with his arms akimbo. Tom sat up in bed and rubbed his eyes to dispel the illusion. No. The chair was an ugly old gentleman; and what was more, he was winking at Tom Smart.

Tom was naturally a headlong, careless sort of dog, and he had had five tumblers of hot punch into the bargain; so, although he was a little startled at first, he began to grow rather indignant when he saw the old gentleman winking and leering at him with such an impudent air. At length he resolved that he wouldn't stand it; and as the old face still kept winking away as fast as ever, Tom said, in a very angry tone:

"What the devil are you winking at me for?"

"Because I like it, Tom Smart," said the chair; or the old gentleman, whichever you like to call him. He stopped winking though, when Tom spoke, and began grinning like a superannuated monkey.

"How do you know my name, old nutcracker face!" inquired Tom Smart, rather staggered—though he pretended to carry it off so well.

"Come, come, Tom," said the old gentleman, "that's not the way to address solid Spanish mahogany. Dam'me, you couldn't treat me with less respect if I was veneered." When the old gentleman said this, he looked so fierce that Tom began to grow frightened.

"I didn't mean to treat you with any disrespect, sir," said Tom; in a much humbler tone than he had spoken in at first.

"Well, well," said the old fellow, "perhaps not—perhaps not. Tom—"

"Sir—"

"I know everything about you, Tom; everything. You're very poor, Tom."

"I certainly am," said Tom Smart. "But how came you to know that?"

"Never mind that," said the old gentleman; "you're much too fond of punch, Tom."

Tom Smart was just on the point of protesting that he hadn't tasted a drop since his last birthday, but when his eye encountered that of the old gentleman, he looked so knowing that Tom blushed and was silent.

"Tom," said the old gentleman, "the widow's a fine woman—remarkably fine woman—eh, Tom?" Here the old fellow screwed up his eyes, cocked up one of his wasted little legs, and looked altogether so unpleasantly amorous, that Tom was quite disgusted with the levity of his behavior—at his time of life, too!

"I am her guardian, Tom," said the old gentleman.

"Are you?" inquired Tom Smart.

"I knew her mother, Tom," said the old fellow; "and her grandmother. She was very fond of me—made me this waistcoat, Tom."

"Did she?" said Tom Smart.

"And these shoes," said the old fellow, lifting up one of the red cloth mufflers; "but don't mention it, Tom. I shouldn't like to have it known that she was so much attached to me. It might occasion some unpleasantness in the family." When the old rascal said this, he looked so extremely impertinent, that, as Tom Smart afterward declared, he could have sat upon him without remorse.

"I have been a great favorite among the women in my time, Tom," said the profligate old debauchee; "hundreds of fine women have sat in my lap for hours together. What do you think of that, you dog, eh!" The old gentleman was proceeding to recount some other exploits of his youth, when he was seized with such a violent fit of creaking that he was unable to proceed.

"Just serves you right, old boy," thought Tom Smart; but he didn't say anything.

"Ah!" said the old fellow. "I am a good deal troubled with this now. I am getting old, Tom, and have lost nearly all my rails. I have had an operation performed, too—a small piece let into my back—and I found it a severe trial, Tom."

"I dare say you did, sir," said Tom Smart.

"However," said the old gentleman, "that's not the point. Tom! I want you to marry the widow."

"Me, sir!" said Tom.

"You," said the old gentleman.

"Bless your reverend locks," said Tom—(he had a few scattered horsehairs left)—"bless your reverend locks, she wouldn't have me." And Tom sighed involuntarily, as he thought of the bar.

"Wouldn't she?" said the old gentleman firmly.

"No, no," said Tom; "there's somebody else in the wind. A tall man—a confoundedly tall man—with black whiskers."

"Tom," said the old gentleman; "she will never have him."

"Won't she?" said Tom. "If you stood in the bar, old gentleman, you'd tell another story."

"Pooh, pooh," said the old gentleman. "I know all about that."

"About what?" said Tom.

"The kissing behind the door, and all that sort of thing, Tom," said the old gentleman. And here he gave another impudent look, which made

Tom very wroth, because, as you all know, gentlemen, to hear an old fellow, who ought to know better, talking about these things, is very unpleasant—nothing more so.

"I know all about that, Tom," said the old gentleman. "I have seen it done very often in my time, Tom, between more people than I should like to mention to you; but it never came to anything after all."

"You must have seen some queer things," said Tom, with an inquisitive look.

"You may say that, Tom," replied the old fellow, with a very complicated wink. "I am the last of my family, Tom," said the old gentleman, with a melancholy sigh.

"Was it a large one?" inquired Tom Smart.

"There were twelve of us, Tom," said the old gentleman; "fine, straight-backed, handsome fellows as you'd wish to see. None of your modern abortions—all with arms, and with a degree of polish, though I say it that should not, which would have done your heart good to behold."

"And what's become of the others, sir?" asked Tom Smart.

The old gentleman applied his elbow to his eye as he replied, "Gone, Tom, gone. We had hard service, Tom, and they hadn't all my constitution. They got rheumatic about the legs and arms, and went into kitchens and other hospitals; and one of 'em, with long service and hard usage, positively lost his senses—he got so crazy that he was obliged to be burned. Shocking thing that, Tom."

"Dreadful!" said Tom Smart.

The old fellow paused for a few minutes, apparently struggling with his feelings of emotion, and then said:

"However, Tom, I am wandering from the point. This tall man, Tom, is a rascally adventurer. The moment he married the widow, he would sell off all the furniture and run away. What would be the consequence? She would be deserted and reduced to ruin, and I should catch my death of cold in some broker's shop."

"Yes, but—"

"Don't interrupt me," said the old gentleman. "Of you, Tom, I entertain a very different opinion; for I well know that if you once settled yourself in a public house, you would never leave it as long as there was anything to drink within its walls."

"I am very much obliged to you for your good opinion, sir," said Tom Smart.

"Therefore," resumed the old gentleman, in a dictatorial tone; "you shall have her, and he shall not."

"What is to prevent it?" said Tom Smart eagerly.

"This disclosure," replied the old gentleman; "he is already married."

"How can I prove it?" said Tom, starting half out of bed.

The old gentleman untucked his arm from his side, and having pointed to one of the oaken presses, immediately replaced it in its old position.

"He little thinks," said the old gentleman, "that in the right-hand pocket of a pair of trousers in that press, he has left a letter, entreating him to return to his disconsolate wife, with six—mark me, Tom—six babes, and all of them small ones."

As the old gentleman solemnly uttered these words, his features grew less and less distinct and his figure more shadowy. A film came over Tom Smart's eyes. The old man seemed gradually blending into the chair, the damask waistcoat to resolve into a cushion, the red slippers to shrink into little red cloth bags. The light faded gently away, and Tom Smart fell back on his pillow and dropped asleep.

Morning aroused Tom from the lethargic slumber into which he had fallen on the disappearance of the old man. He sat up in bed and for some minutes vainly endeavored to recall the events of the preceding night. Suddenly they rushed upon him. He looked at the chair; it was a fantastic and grim-looking piece of furniture, certainly, but it must have been a remarkably ingenious and lively imagination that could have discovered any resemblance between it and an old man.

"How are you, old boy?" said Tom. He was bolder in the daylight—most men are.

The chair remained motionless and spoke not a word.

"Miserable morning," said Tom. No. The chair would not be drawn into conversation.

"Which press did you point to?—you can tell me that," said Tom. Devil a word, gentlemen, the chair would say.

"It's not much trouble to open it, anyhow," said Tom, getting out of bed very deliberately. He walked up to one of the presses. The key was in the lock; he turned it and opened the door. There *was* a pair of trousers there. He put his hand into the pocket and drew forth the identical letter the old gentleman had described!

"Queer sort of thing, this," said Tom Smart; looking first at the chair and then at the press, and then at the letter, and then at the chair again. "Very queer," said Tom. But, as there was nothing in either to lessen the queerness, he thought he might as well dress himself and settle the tall man's business at once—just to put him out of his misery.

Tom surveyed the rooms he passed through, on his way downstairs, with the scrutinizing eye of a landlord; thinking it not impossible that before long, they and their contents would be his property. The tall man was standing in the snug little bar, with his hands behind him, quite at home. He grinned vacantly at Tom. A casual observer might have supposed he did it only to show his white teeth; but Tom Smart thought that a consciousness of triumph was passing through the place where the tall man's mind would have been, if he had had any. Tom laughed in his face; and summoned the landlady.

"Good morning, ma'am," said Tom Smart, closing the door of the little parlor as the widow entered.

"Good morning, sir," said the widow. "What will you take for breakfast, sir?"

Tom was thinking how he should open the case, so he made no answer.

"There's a very nice ham," said the widow, "and a beautiful cold larded fowl. Shall I send 'em in, sir?"

These words roused Tom from his reflections. His admiration of the widow increased as she spoke. Thoughtful creature! Comfortable provider!

"Who is that gentleman in the bar, ma'am?" inquired Tom.

"His name is Jinkins, sir," said the widow, slightly blushing.

"He's a tall man," said Tom.

"He is a very fine man, sir," replied the widow, "and a very nice gentleman."

"Ah!" said Tom.

"Is there anything more you want, sir?" inquired the widow, rather puzzled by Tom's manner.

"Why, yes," said Tom. "My dear ma'am, will you have the kindness to sit down for one moment?"

The widow looked much amazed, but she sat down, and Tom sat down too, close beside her. I don't know how it happened, gentlemen—indeed my uncle used to tell me that Tom Smart said *he* didn't know how it happened either—but somehow or other the palm of Tom's hand fell upon the back of the widow's hand and remained there while he spoke.

"My dear ma'am," said Tom Smart—he had always a great notion of committing the amiable—"my dear ma'am, you deserve a very excellent husband—you do indeed."

"Lor, sir!" said the widow—as well she might: Tom's mode of commencing the conversation being rather unusual, not to say startling; the fact of his never having set eyes upon her before the previous night, being taken into consideration. "Lor, sir!"

"I scorn to flatter, my dear ma'am," said Tom Smart. "You deserve a very admirable husband, and whoever he is, he'll be a very lucky man." As Tom said this his eye involuntarily wandered from the widow's face, to the comforts around him.

The widow looked more puzzled than ever and made an effort to rise. Tom gently pressed her hand, as if to detain her, and she kept her seat. Widows, gentlemen, are not usually timorous, as my uncle used to say.

"I am sure I am very much obliged to you, sir, for your good opinion," said the buxom landlady, half laughing; "and if ever I marry again—"

"*If,*" said Tom Smart, looking very shrewdly out of the right-hand corner of his left eye. "*If—*"

"Well," said the widow, laughing outright this time. "*When* I do, I hope I shall have as good a husband as you describe."

"Jinkins to wit," said Tom.

"Lor, sir!" exclaimed the widow.

"Oh, don't tell me," said Tom, "I know him."

"I am sure nobody who knows him, knows anything bad of him," said the widow, bridling up at the mysterious air with which Tom had spoken.

"Hem!" said Tom Smart.

The widow began to think it was high time to cry, so she took out her handkerchief and inquired whether Tom wished to insult her; whether he thought it like a gentleman to take away the character of another gentleman behind his back; why, if he had got anything to say, he didn't say it to the man, like a man, instead of terrifying a poor weak woman in that way; and so forth.

"I'll say it to him fast enough," said Tom, "only I want you to hear it first."

"What is it?" inquired the widow, looking intently in Tom's countenance.

"I'll astonish you," said Tom, putting his hand in his pocket.

"If it is that he wants money," said the widow, "I know that already, and you needn't trouble yourself."

"Pooh, nonsense, that's nothing," said Tom Smart. "*I* want money. 'Taint that."

"Oh, dear, what can it be?" exclaimed the poor widow.

"Don't be frightened," said Tom Smart. He slowly drew forth the letter and unfolded it. "You won't scream?" said Tom doubtfully.

"No, no," replied the widow; "let me see it."

"You won't go fainting away, or any of that nonsense?" said Tom.

"No, no," returned the widow hastily.

"And don't run out and blow him up," said Tom, "because I'll do all that for you; you had better not exert yourself."

"Well, well," said the widow, "let me see it."

"I will," replied Tom Smart; and, with these words, he placed the letter in the widow's hand.

Gentlemen, I have heard my uncle say, that Tom Smart said, the widow's lamentations when she heard the disclosure would have pierced a heart of stone. Tom was certainly very tender-hearted, but they pierced his to the very core. The widow rocked herself to and fro and wrung her hands.

"Oh, the deception and villainy of man!" said the widow.

"Frightful, my dear ma'am; but compose yourself," said Tom Smart.

"Oh, I can't compose myself," shrieked the widow. "I shall never find anyone else I can love so much!"

"Oh yes you will, my dear soul," said Tom Smart, letting fall a shower of the largest-sized tears, in pity for the widow's misfortunes. Tom Smart, in the energy of his compassion, had put his arm round the widow's waist; and the widow, in a passion of grief, had clasped Tom's hand. She looked up in Tom's face and smiled through her tears. Tom looked down in hers, and smiled through his.

I never could find out, gentlemen, whether Tom did or did not kiss the widow at that particular moment. He used to tell my uncle he didn't, but I have my doubts about it. Between ourselves, gentlemen, I rather think he did.

At all events, Tom kicked the very tall man out at the front door half an hour after and married the widow a month after. And he used to drive about the country, with the clay-colored gig with red wheels, and the vixenish mare with the fast pace, till he gave up business many years afterward and went to France with his wife; and then the old house was pulled down.

## FOR DISCUSSION: The Bagman's Story

1. Tom Smart is an enterprising man. Give examples from the story of this personal characteristic which he possesses.
2. Would you say there are any similarities between Tom and the old gentleman?
3. What role does humor play in the story? Is it a major element?
4. Who is the real hero of this story, in your opinion? Is it Tom or the old gentleman?

## INTRODUCTION: Doctor Heidegger's Experiment

We have all heard of Ponce de Leon's search for the fabled Fountain of Youth and the bright promise such a fountain holds for those who would quench their thirst from it. In the story that follows, we meet the venerable Doctor Heidegger who offers four of his friends water from the famous Fountain. We watch with him as his friends' thirsts are quenched—momentarily, and we witness the fulfillment of the Fountain's promise. We, like Doctor Heidegger, may learn something about human nature as the events recorded in this story unfold before us.

# Dr. Heidegger's Experiment
## Nathaniel Hawthorne

That very singular man, old Dr. Heidegger, once invited four venerable friends to meet him in his study. There were three white-bearded gentlemen, Mr. Medbourne, Colonel Killigrew, and Mr. Gascoigne, and a withered gentlewoman, whose name was the Widow Wycherly. They were all melancholy old creatures, who had been unfortunate in life, and whose greatest misfortune it was that they were not long ago in their graves. Mr. Medbourne, in the vigor of his age, had been a properous merchant, but had lost his all by a frantic speculation, and was now little better than a mendicant. Colonel Killigrew had wasted his best years, and his health and substance, in the pursuit of sinful pleasures, which had given birth to a brood of pains, such as the gout, and divers other torments of soul and body. Mr. Gascoigne was a ruined politician, a man of evil fame, or at least had been so till time had buried him from the knowledge of the present generation, and made him obscure instead of infamous. As for the Widow Wycherly, tradition tells us that she was a great beauty in her day; but, for a long while past, she had lived in deep seclusion, on account of certain scandalous stories which had prejudiced the gentry of the town against her. It is a circumstance worth mentioning that each of these three old gentlemen, Mr. Medbourne, Colonel Killigrew, and Mr. Gascoigne, were early lovers of the Widow Wycherly, and had once been on the point of cutting each other's throats for her sake. And, before proceeding further, I will merely hint that Dr. Heidegger and all his four guests were sometimes thought to be a little beside themselves,—as is not unfrequently the case with old people, when worried either by present troubles or woeful recollections.

"My dear old friends," said Dr. Heidegger, motioning them to be seated, "I am desirous of your assistance in one of those little experiments with which I amuse myself here in my study."

If all stories were true, Dr. Heidegger's study must have been a very curious place. It was a dim, old-fashioned chamber, festooned with cob-webs, and besprinkled with antique dust. Around the walls stood several oaken bookcases, the lower shelves of which were filled with rows of gigantic folios and black-letter quartos, and the upper with little parchment-covered duodecimos. Over the central bookcase was a bronze bust of Hippocrates,[1] with which, according to some authorities, Dr. Heidegger was accustomed to hold consultations in all difficult cases of his practice. In the obscurest corner of the room stood a tall and narrow oaken closet, with its door ajar, within which doubtfully appeared a skeleton. Between two of the bookcases hung a looking-glass, presenting its high and dusty plate within a tarnished gilt frame. Among many wonderful stories related of this mirror, it was fabled that the spirits of all the doctor's deceased patients dwelt within its verge, and would stare him in the face whenever he looked thitherward. The opposite side of the chamber was ornamented with the full-length portrait of a young lady, arrayed in the faded magnificence of silk, satin, and brocade, and with a visage as faded as her dress. Above half a century ago, Dr. Heidegger had been on the point of marriage with this young lady; but, being affected with some slight disorder, she had swallowed one of her lover's prescriptions, and died on the bridal evening. The greatest curiosity of the study remains to be mentioned; it was a ponderous folio volume, bound in black leather, with massive silver clasps. There were no letters on the back, and nobody could tell the title of the book. But it was well known to be a book of magic; and once, when a chambermaid had lifted it, merely to brush away the dust, the skeleton had rattled in its closet, the picture of the young lady had stepped one foot upon the floor, and several ghastly faces had peeped forth from the mirror; while the brazen head of Hippocrates frowned, and said,—"Forbear!"

Such was Dr. Heidegger's study. On the summer afternoon of our tale a small round table, as black as ebony, stood in the centre of the room, sustaining a cut-glass vase of beautiful form and elaborate work-manship. The sunshine came through the window, between the heavy festoons of two faded damask curtains, and fell directly across this vase;

---

1. Hippocrates\hĭ ⁀pŏk·ra·tēz\ (approx. 460–377 B.C.), Greek physician known as "Father of Medicine" and credited with devising code known today as Hippocratic oath which is administered to men about to enter the medical profession.

so that a mild splendor was reflected from it on the ashen visages of the five old people who sat around. Four champagne glasses were also on the table.

"My dear old friends," repeated Dr. Heidegger, "may I reckon on your aid in performing an exceedingly curious experiment?"

Now Dr. Heidegger was a very strange old gentleman, whose eccentricity had become the nucleus for a thousand fantastic stories. Some of these fables, to my shame be it spoken, might possibly be traced back to my own veracious self; and if any passages of the present tale should startle the reader's faith, I must be content to bear the stigma of a fiction monger.

When the doctor's four guests heard him talk of his proposed experiment, they anticipated nothing more wonderful than the murder of a mouse in an air pump, or the examination of a cobweb by the microscope, or some similar nonsense, with which he was constantly in the habit of pestering his intimates. But without waiting for a reply, Dr. Heidegger hobbled across the chamber, and returned with the same ponderous folio, bound in black leather, which common report affirmed to be a book of magic. Undoing the silver clasps, he opened the volume, and took from among its black-letter pages a rose, or what was once a rose, though now the green leaves and crimson petals had assumed one brownish hue, and the ancient flower seemed ready to crumble to dust in the doctor's hands.

"This rose," said Dr. Heidegger, with a sigh, "this same withered and crumbling flower, blossomed five and fifty years ago. It was given me by Sylvia Ward, whose portrait hangs yonder; and I meant to wear it in my bosom at our wedding. Five and fifty years it has been treasured between the leaves of this old volume. Now, would you deem it possible that this rose of half a century would ever bloom again?"

"Nonsense!" said the Widow Wycherly, with a peevish toss of her head. "You might as well ask whether an old woman's wrinkled face could ever bloom again."

"See!" answered Dr. Heidegger.

He uncovered the vase, and threw the faded rose into the water which it contained. At first, it lay lightly on the surface of the fluid, appearing to imbibe none of its moisture. Soon, however, a singular change began to be visible. The crushed and dried petals stirred, and assumed a deeping tinge of crimson, as if the flower were reviving from a deathlike slumber; the slender stalk and twigs of foliage became green; and there was the rose of half a century, looking as fresh as when Sylvia Ward had first given it to her lover. It was scarcely full blown; for some of its delicate red leaves curled modestly around its moist bosom, within which two or three dewdrops were sparkling.

"That is certainly a very pretty deception," said the doctor's friends;

carelessly, however, for they had witnessed greater miracles at a conjurer's show; "pray how was it effected?"

"Did you never hear of the 'Fountain of Youth,'" asked Dr. Heidegger, "which Ponce de Leon, the Spanish adventurer, went in search of two or three centuries ago?"

"But did Ponce de Leon ever find it?" said the Widow Wycherly.

"No," answered Dr. Heidegger, "for he never sought it in the right place. The famous Fountain of Youth, if I am rightly informed, is situated in the southern part of the Floridian peninsula, not far from Lake Macaco. Its source is overshadowed by several gigantic magnolias, which, though numberless centuries old, have been kept as fresh as violets by the virtues of this wonderful water. An acquaintance of mine, knowing my curiosity in such matters, has sent me what you see in the vase."

"Ahem!" said Colonel Killigrew, who believed not a word of the doctor's story; "and what may be the effect of this fluid on the human frame?"

"You shall judge for yourself, my dear colonel," replied Dr. Heidegger; "and all of you, my respected friends, are welcome to so much of this admirable fluid as may restore to you the bloom of youth. For my own part, having had much trouble in growing old, I am in no hurry to grow young again. With your permission, therefore, I will merely watch the progress of the experiment."

While he spoke, Dr. Heidegger had been filling the four champagne glasses with the water of the Fountain of Youth. It was apparently impregnated with an effervescent gas, for little bubbles were continually ascending from the depths of the glasses, and bursting in silvery spray at the surface. As the liquor diffused a pleasant perfume, the old people doubted not that it possessed cordial and comfortable properties; and though utter sceptics as to its rejuvenescent power, they were inclined to swallow it at once. But Dr. Heidegger besought them to stay a moment.

"Before you drink, my respectable old friends," said he, "it would be well that, with the experience of a lifetime to direct you, you should draw up a few general rules for your guidance, in passing a second time through the perils of youth. Think what a sin and shame it would be, if, with your peculiar advantages, you should not become patterns of virtue and wisdom of all the young people of the age!"

The doctor's four venerable friends made him no answer, except by a feeble and tremulous laugh; so very ridiculous was the idea that, knowing how closely repentance treads behind the steps of error, they should ever go astray again.

"Drink, then," said the doctor, bowing: "I rejoice that I have so well selected the subjects of my experiment."

With palsied hands, they raised the glasses to their lips. The liquor, if it really possessed such virtues as Dr. Heidegger imputed to it, could not have been bestowed on four human beings who needed it more woefully. They looked as if they had never known what youth or pleasure was, but had been the offspring of Nature's dotage, and always the gray, decrepit, sapless, miserable creatures, who now sat stooping round the doctor's table, without life enough in their souls or bodies to be animated even by the prospect of growing young again. They drank off the water, and replaced their glasses on the table.

Assuredly there was an almost immediate improvement in the aspect of the party, not unlike what might have been produced by a glass of generous wine, together with a sudden glow of cheerful sunshine brightening over all their visages at once. There was a healthful suffusion on their cheeks, instead of the ashen hue that had made them look so corpselike. They gazed at one another, and fancied that some magic power had really begun to smooth away the deep and sad inscriptions which Father Time had been so long engraving on their brows. The Widow Wycherly adjusted her cap, for she felt almost like a woman again.

"Give us more of this wondrous water!" cried they, eagerly. "We are younger—but we are still too old! Quick—give us more!"

"Patience, patience!" quoth Dr. Heidegger, who sat watching the experiment with philosophic coolness. "You have been a long time growing old. Surely, you might be content to grow young in half an hour! But the water is at your service."

Again he filled their glasses with the liquor of youth, enough of which still remained in the vase to turn half the old people in the city to the age of their own grandchildren. While the bubbles were yet sparkling on the brim, the doctor's four guests snatched their glasses from the table, and swallowed the contents at a single gulp. Was it delusion? even while the draught was passing down their throats, it seemed to have wrought a change on their whole systems. Their eyes grew clear and bright; a dark shade deepened among their silvery locks, they sat around the table, three gentlemen of middle age, and a woman, hardly beyond her buxom prime.

"My dear widow, you are charming!" cried Colonel Killigrew, whose eyes had been fixed upon her face, while the shadows of age were flitting from it like darkness from the crimson daybreak.

The fair widow knew, of old, that Colonel Killigrew's compliments were not always measured by sober truth; so she started up and ran to the mirror, still dreading that the ugly visage of an old woman would meet her gaze. Meanwhile, the three gentlemen behaved in such a manner as proved that the water of the Fountain of Youth possessed some intoxicating qualities; unless, indeed, their exhilaration of spirits were merely a lightsome dizziness caused by the sudden removal of the weight of years. Mr. Gascoigne's mind seemed to run on political topics, but whether relating to the past, present, or future, could not easily be determined, since the same ideas and phrases have been in vogue these fifty years. Now he rattled forth full-throated sentences about patriotism, national glory, and the people's right; now he muttered some perilous stuff or other, in a sly and doubtful whisper, so cautiously that even his own conscience could scarcely catch the secret; and now, again, he spoke in measured accents, and a deeply deferential tone, as if a royal ear were listening to his well-turned periods. Colonel Killigrew all this time had been trolling forth a jolly bottle song, and ringing his glass in symphony with the chorus, while his eyes wandered toward the buxom figure of the Widow Wycherly. On the other side of the table, Mr. Medbourne was involved in a calculation of dollars and cents, with which was strangely intermingled a project for supplying the East Indies with ice, by harnessing a team of whales to the polar icebergs.

As for the Widow Wycherly, she stood before the mirror curtsying and simpering to her own image, and greeting it as the friend whom she loved better than all the world beside. She thrust her face close to the glass, to see whether some long-remembered wrinkle of crow's foot had indeed vanished. She examined whether the snow had so entirely melted from her hair that the venerable cap could be safely thrown aside. At last, turning briskly away, she came with a sort of dancing step to the table.

"My dear old doctor," cried she, "pray favor me with another glass!"

"Certainly, my dear madam, certainly!" replied the complaisant doctor; "see! I have already filled the glasses."

There, in fact, stood the four glasses, brimful of this wonderful water, the delicate spray of which, as it effervesced from the surface, resembled the tremulous glitter of diamonds. It was now so nearly sunset that the chamber had grown duskier than ever; but a mild and moonlike splendor gleamed from within the vase, and rested alike on the four guests and on the doctor's venerable figure. He sat in a high-backed, elaborately-carved, oaken arm-chair, with a gray dignity of aspect that might have well befitted that very Father Time, whose power had never been disputed, save by this fortunate company. Even while quaffing the third draught of the Fountain of Youth, they were almost awed by the expression of his mysterious visage.

But, the next moment, the exhilarating gush of young life shot through their veins. They were now in the happy prime of youth. Age, with its miserable train of cares and sorrows and diseases, was remembered only as the trouble of a dream, from which they had joyously awoke. The fresh gloss of the soul, so early lost, and without which the world's successive scenes had been but a gallery of faded pictures, again threw its enchantment over all their prospects. They felt like new-created beings in a new-created universe.

"We are young! We are young!" they cried exultingly.

Youth, like the extremity of age, had effaced the strongly-marked characteristics of middle life, and mutually assimilated them all. They were a group of merry youngsters, almost maddened with the exuberant frolicsomeness of their years. The most singular effect of their gayety was an impulse to mock the infirmity and decreptitude of which they had so lately been the victims. They laughed loudly at their old-fashioned attire, the wide-skirted coats and flapped waistcoats of the young men, and the ancient cap and gown of the blooming girl. One limped across the floor like a gouty grandfather; one set a pair of spectacles astride of his nose, and pretended to pore over the black-letter pages of the book of magic; a third seated himself in an arm-chair, and strove to imitate the venerable dignity of Dr. Heidegger. Then all shouted mirthfully, and leaped about the room. The Widow Wycherly—if so fresh a damsel could be called a widow—tripped up to the doctor's chair, with a mischievous merriment in her rosy face.

"Doctor, you dear old soul," cried she, "get up and dance with me!" And then the four young people laughed louder than ever, to think what a queer figure the poor old doctor would cut.

"Pray excuse me," answered the doctor quietly. "I am old and rheumatic, and my dancing days were over long ago. But either of these gay young gentlemen will be glad of so pretty a partner."

"Dance with me, Clara!" cried Colonel Killigrew.

"No, no, I will be her partner!" shouted Mr. Gascoigne.

"She promised me her hand, fifty years ago!" exclaimed Mr. Medbourne.

They all gathered round her. One caught both her hands in his passionate grasp—another threw his arm about her waist—the third buried his hand among the glossy curls that clustered beneath the widow's cap. Blushing, panting, struggling, chiding, laughing, her warm breath fanning each of their faces by turns, she strove to disengage herself, yet still remained in their triple embrace. Never was there a livelier picture of youthful rivalship, with bewitching beauty for the prize. Yet, by a strange deception, owing to the duskiness of the chamber, and the antique dresses which they still wore, the tall mirror is said to have reflected the figures of the three old, gray, withered grandsires, ridiculously contending for the skinny ugliness of a shrivelled grandam.

But they were young: their burning passions proved them so. Inflamed to madness by the coquetry of the girl-widow, who neither granted nor quite withheld her favors, the three rivals began to interchange threatening glances. Still keeping hold of the fair prize, they grappled fiercely at one another's throats. As they struggled to and fro, the table was overturned, and the vase dashed into a thousand fragments. The precious Water of Youth flowed in a bright stream across the floor, moistening the wings of a butterfly, which, grown old in the decline of summer, had alighted there to die. The insect fluttered lightly through the chamber, and settled on the snowy head of Dr. Heidegger.

"Come, come, gentlemen!—come, Madam Wycherly," exclaimed the doctor, "I really must protest against this riot."

They stood still and shivered; for it seemed as if gray Time were calling them back from their sunny youth, far down into the chill and darksome vale of years. They looked at old Dr. Heidegger, who sat in his carved arm-chair, holding the rose of half a century, which he had rescued from among the fragments of the shattered vase. At the motion of his hand, the four rioters resumed their seats; the more readily, because their violent exertions had wearied them, youthful though they were.

"My poor Sylvia's rose!" ejaculated Dr. Heidegger, holding it in the light of the sunset clouds; "it appears to be fading again."

And so it was. Even while the party were looking at it, the flower continued to shrivel up, till it became as dry and fragile as when the doctor had first thrown it into the vase. He shook off the few drops of moisture which clung to its petals.

"I love it as well thus as in its dewy freshness," observed he, pressing the withered rose to his withered lips. While he spoke, the butterfly fluttered down from the doctor's snowy head, and fell upon the floor.

His guests shivered again. A strange chillness, whether of the body or spirit they could not tell, was creeping gradually over them all. They gazed at one another, and fancied that each fleeting moment snatched away a charm, and left a deepening furrow where none had been before. Was it an illusion? Had the changes of a lifetime been crowded into so brief a space, and were they now four aged people, sitting with their old friend, Dr. Heidegger?

"Are we grown old again, so soon?" cried they, dolefully.

In truth they had. The Water of Youth possessed merely a virtue more transient than that of wine. The delirium which it created had effervesced away. Yes! they were old again. With a shuddering impulse, that showed her a woman still, the widow clasped her skinny hands before her face, and wished that the coffin lid were over it, since it could be no longer beautiful.

"Yes, friends, ye are old again," said Dr. Heidegger, "and lo! the Water of Youth is all lavished on the ground. Well—I bemoan it not; for if the fountain gushed at my very doorstep, I would not stoop to bathe my lips in it—no, though its delirium were for years instead of moments. Such is the lesson ye have taught me!"

But the doctor's four friends had taught no such lesson to themselves. They resolved forthwith to make a pilgrimage to Florida, and quaff at morning, noon, and night, from the Fountain of Youth.

## FOR DISCUSSION: Doctor Heidegger's Experiment

1. Define the nature of Doctor Heidegger's experiment. What was its purpose? What did Doctor Heidegger seek to learn from it? What did he conclude as a result of it?
2. Characters in a story frequently differ sharply from one another. Because they do, each casts light on the thinking and behavior of the others. With this fact in mind, discuss Doctor Heidegger's attitude toward the supernatural water as compared with that of the Widow Wycherly.
3. Doctor Heidegger first experiments with the withered rose. Suppose he had used, for example, an aged dog instead of the rose. Would the author's purpose still have been served?
4. When the water spills on the floor, it briefly rejuvenates a dying butterfly. Can this element of the narrative be said to have a function in terms of the story's theme?

H. P. Lovecraft was one of the most successful American tellers of macabre and supernatural stories. He has few peers in creating eerie atmospheric effects, a weird sense of the mysterious and a pervading sense of grim horror. The story below is a classic of its kind in which the "thing" who tells the story arouses in the reader fear and loathing and, surprisingly, pity.

# The Outsider
## H. P. Lovecraft

Unhappy is he to whom the memories of childhood bring only fear and sadness. Wretched is he who looks back upon lone hours in vast and dismal chambers with brown hangings and maddening rows of antique books or upon awed watches in twilight groves of grotesque, gigantic, and vine-encumbered trees that silently wave twisted branches far aloft. Such a lot the gods gave to me—to me, the dazed, the disappointed; the barren, the broken. And yet I am strangely content and cling desperately to those sere memories, when my mind momentarily threatens to reach beyond to *the other*.

I know not where I was born, save that the castle was infinitely old and infinitely horrible, full of dark passages and having high ceilings where the eye could find only cobwebs and shadows. The stones in the crumbling corridors seemed always hideously damp, and there was an accursed smell everywhere, as of the piled-up corpses of dead generations. It was never light, so that I used sometimes to light candles and gaze steadily at them for relief, nor was there any sun outdoors, since the terrible trees grew high above the topmost accessible tower. There was one black tower which reached above the trees into the unknown outer sky, but that was partly ruined and could not be ascended save by a well-nigh impossible climb up the sheer wall, stone by stone.

I must have lived years in this place, but I can not measure the time. Beings must have cared for my needs, yet I can not recall any person except myself, or anything alive but the noiseless rats and bats and spiders. I think that whoever nursed me must have been shockingly aged, since my first conception of a living person was that of something mockingly like myself, yet distorted, shriveled and decaying like the castle. To me there was nothing grotesque in the bones and skeletons that strewed some of the stone crypts deep down among the foundations. I fantastically associated these things with everyday events, and thought them more natural than the colored pictures of living beings which I found in many of the moldy books. From such books I learned all that I know. No teacher urged or guided me, and I do not recall hearing any human voice in all those years—not even my own; for although I had read of speech, I had never thought to try to speak aloud. My aspect was a matter equally unthought of, for there were no mirrors in the castle, and I merely regarded myself by instinct as akin to the youthful figures I saw drawn and painted in the books. I felt conscious of youth because I remembered so little.

Outside, across the putrid moat and under the dark mute trees, I would often lie and dream for hours about what I read in the books; and would longingly picture myself amidst gay crowds in the sunny world beyond the endless forest. Once I tried to escape from the forest, but as I went farther from the castle the shade grew denser and the air more filled with brooding fear; so that I ran frantically back lest I lose my way in a labyrinth of nighted silence.

So through endless twilights I dreamed and waited, though I knew not what I waited for. Then in the shadowy solitude my longing for light grew so frantic that I could rest no more, and I lifted entreating hands to the single black ruined tower that reached above the forest into the unknown outer sky. And at last I resolved to scale that tower, fall though I might; since it were better to glimpse the sky and perish, than to live without ever beholding day.

In the dank twilight I climbed the worn and aged stone stairs till I reached the level where they ceased, and thereafter clung perilously to small footholds leading upward. Ghastly and terrible was that dead, stairless cylinder of rock; black, ruined, and deserted, and sinister with startled bats whose wings made no noise. But more ghastly and terrible still was the slowness of my progress; for climb as I might, the darkness overhead grew no thinner, and a new chill as of haunted and venerable mold assailed me. I shivered as I wondered why I did not reach the light, and would have looked down had I dared. I fancied that night had come suddenly upon me, and vainly groped with one free hand for a window embrasure, that I might peer out and above, and try to judge the height I had attained.

All at once, after an infinity of awesome, sightless crawling up that concave and desperate precipice, I felt my head touch a solid thing, and knew I must have gained the roof, or at least some kind of floor. In the darkness I raised my free hand and tested the barrier, finding it stone and immovable. Then came a deadly circuit of the tower, clinging to whatever holds the slimy wall could give; till finally my testing hand found the barrier yielding, and I turned upward again, pushing the slab or door with my head as I used both hands in my fearful ascent. There was no light revealed above, and as my hands went higher I knew that my climb was for the nonce ended; since the slab was the trapdoor of an aperture leading to a level stone surface of greater circumference than the lower tower, no doubt the floor of some lofty and capacious observation chamber. I crawled through carefully, and tried to prevent the heavy slab from falling back into place, but failed in the latter attempt. As I lay exhausted on the stone floor I heard the eery echoes of its fall, but hoped when necessary to pry it up again.

Believing I was now at a prodigious height, far above the accursed branches of the wood, I dragged myself up from the floor and fumbled about for windows, that I might look for the first time upon the sky, and the moon and stars of which I had read. But on every hand I was disappointed; since all that I found were vast shelves of marble, bearing odious oblong boxes of disturbing size. More and more I reflected, and wondered what hoary secrets might abide in this high apartment so many eons cut off from the castle below. Then unexpectedly my hands came upon a doorway, where hung a portal of stone, rough with strange chiseling. Trying it, I found it locked; but with a supreme burst of strength I overcame all obstacles and dragged it open inward. As I did so there came to me the purest ecstasy I have ever known; for shining tranquilly through an ornate grating of iron, and down a short stone passageway of steps that ascended from the newly found doorway, was the radiant full moon, which I had never before seen save in dreams and in vague visions I dared not call memories.

Fancying now that I had attained the very pinnacle of the castle, I commenced to rush up the few steps beyond the door; but the sudden veiling of the moon by a cloud caused me to stumble, and I felt my way more slowly in the dark. It was still very dark when I reached the grating—which I tried carefully and found unlocked, but which I did not open for fear of falling from the amazing height to which I had climbed. Then the moon came out.

Most demoniacal of all shocks is that of the abysmally unexpected and grotesquely unbelievable. Nothing I had before undergone could compare in terror with what I now saw; with the bizarre marvels that sight implied. The sight itself was as simple as it was stupefying, for it was merely this: instead of a dizzying prospect of treetops seen from a lofty eminence, there stretched around me on the level through the grating nothing less than *the solid ground* decked and diversified by marble slabs and columns, and overshadowed by an ancient stone church, whose ruined spire gleamed spectrally in the moonlight.

Half unconscious, I opened the grating and staggered out upon the white gravel path that stretched away in two directions. My mind, stunned and chaotic as it was, still held the frantic craving for light; and not even the fantastic wonder which had happened could stay my course. I neither knew nor cared whether my experience was insanity, dreaming, or magic; but was determined to gaze on brilliance and gaiety at any cost. I knew not who I was or what I was, or what my surroundings might be; though as I continued to stumble along I became conscious of a kind of fearsome latent memory that made my progress not wholly fortuitous. I passed under an arch out of that region of slabs and columns, and wandered through the open country; sometimes following the visible road, but sometimes leaving it curiously to tread across meadows where only occasional ruins bespoke the ancient presence of a forgotten road. Once I swam across a swift river where crumbling, mossy masonry told of a bridge long vanished.

Over two hours must have passed before I reached what seemed to be my goal, a venerable ivied castle in a thickly wooded park, maddeningly familiar, yet full of perplexing strangeness to me. I saw that the moat was filled in, and that some of the well-known towers were demolished; whilst new wings existed to confuse the beholder. But what I observed with chief interest and delight were the open windows—gorgeously ablaze with light and sending forth sound of the gayest revelry. Advancing to one of these I looked in and saw an oddly dressed company, indeed; making merry, and speaking brightly to one another. I had never, seemingly, heard human speech before and could guess only vaguely what was said. Some of the faces seemed to hold expressions that brought up incredibly remote recollections, others were utterly alien.

I now stepped through the low window into the brilliantly lighted room, stepping as I did so from my single bright moment of hope to my blackest convulsion of despair and realization. The nightmare was quick to come, for as I entered, there occurred immediately one of the most terrifying demonstrations I had ever conceived. Scarcely had I crossed the sill when there descended upon the whole company a sudden and unheralded fear of hideous intensity, distorting every face and evoking the most horrible screams from nearly every throat. Flight was universal, and in the clamor and panic several fell in a swoon and were dragged away by their madly fleeing companions. Many covered their eyes with their hands, and plunged blindly and awkwardly in their race to escape, overturning furniture and stumbling against the walls before they managed to reach one of the many doors.

The cries were shocking; and as I stood in the brilliant apartment alone and dazed, listening to their vanishing echoes, I trembled at the thought of what might be lurking near me unseen. At a casual inspection the room seemed deserted, but when I moved toward one of the alcoves I thought I detected a presence there—a hint of motion beyond the golden-arched doorway leading to another and somewhat similar room. As I approached the arch I began to perceive the presence more clearly; and then, with the first and last sound I ever uttered—a ghastly ululation that revolted me almost as poignantly as its noxious cause—I beheld in full, frightful vividness the inconceivable, indescribable, and unmentionable monstrosity which had by its simple appearance changed a merry company to a herd of delirious fugitives.

I can not even hint what it was like, for it was a compound of all that is unclean, uncanny, unwelcome, abnormal, and detestable. It was the ghoulish shade of decay, antiquity, and desolation; the putrid, dripping eidolon of unwholesome revelation, the awful baring of that which the merciful earth should always hide. God knows it was not of this world —or no longer of this world—yet to my horror I saw in its eaten-away and bone-revealing outlines a leering, abhorrent travesty on the human shape; and in its moldly, disintegrating apparel an unspeakable quality that chilled me even more.

I was almost paralyzed, but not too much so to make a feeble effort toward flight; a backward stumble which failed to break the spell in which the nameless, voiceless monster held me. My eyes bewitched by the glassy orbs which stared loathsomely into them refused to close, though they were mercifully blurred, and showed the terrible object but indistinctly after the first shock. I tried to raise my hand to shut out the sight, yet so stunned were my nerves that my arm could not fully obey my will. The attempt, however, was enough to disturb my balance; so that I had to stagger forward several steps to avoid falling. As I did so I became suddenly and agonizingly aware of the *nearness* of the carrion thing, whose hideous hollow breathing I half fancied I could hear. Nearly mad, I found myself yet able to throw out a hand to ward off the fetid apparition which pressed so close; when in one cataclysmic second of cosmic nightmarishness and hellish accident *my fingers touched the rotting outstretched paw of the monster beneath the golden arch.*

I did not shriek, but all the fiendish ghouls that ride the nightwind shrieked for me as in that same second they crashed down upon my mind a single and fleeting avalanche of soul-annihilating memory. I knew in that second all that had been; I remembered beyond the frightful castle and the trees; and recognized the altered edifice in which I now stood; I recognized, most terrible of all, the unholy abomination that stood leering before me as I withdrew my sullied fingers from its own.

But in the cosmos there is balm as well as bitterness, and that balm is nepenthe. In the supreme horror of that second I forgot what had horrified me, and the burst of black memory vanished in a chaos of echoing images.  In a dream I fled from that haunted and accursed pile, and ran swiftly and silently in the moonlight.  When I returned to the church-yard place of marble and went down the steps I found the stone trap-door immovable; but I was not sorry, for I had hated the antique castle and the trees.  Now I ride with the mocking and friendly ghouls on the night wind, and play by day amongst the catacombs of Nephren-Ka in the sealed and unknown valley of Hadoth by the Nile.  I know that light is not for me, save that of the moon over the rock tombs of Neb, nor any gaiety save the unnamed feasts of Nitokris beneath the Great Pyramid; yet in my new wildness and freedom I almost welcome the bitterness of alienage.

For although nepenthe has calmed me, I know always that I am an outsider; stranger in this century and among those who are still men. This I have known ever since I stretched out my fingers to the abomina-tion within that great gilded frame; stretched out my fingers and touched *a cold and unyielding surface of polished glass.*

## FOR DISCUSSION: The Outsider

1.  Although this story contains no dialogue, which usually helps to make characters seem real to the reader, the protagonist nevertheless seems very real.  How does Lovecraft make him so?  Give specific exam-ples of the technique used.
2.  The atmosphere of this story is especially eerie.  Which details at the beginning of the story help create the atmosphere?  How does the author reinforce it as the story progresses?
3.  The author succeeds in holding off the revelation of the identity of the "monster beneath the golden arch" until the last dramatic mo-ment.  How does he manage this?
4.  What function or functions do references to "the catacombs of Nephren-Ka," the "sealed and unknown valley of Hadoth by the Nile," and the "rock tombs of Neb" have in the story?